WHAT DOES GREEN MEAN?

THE HISTORY, PEOPLE, AND IDEAS OF THE GREEN PARTY IN CANADA AND ABROAD

JAMES GS MARSHALL

Suite 300 - 990 Fort St
Victoria, BC, V8V 3K2
Canada

www.friesenpress.com

Copyright © 2019 by James GS Marshall
First Edition — 2019

All rights reserved.

No part of this publication may be reproduced in any form, or by any means, electronic or mechanical, including photocopying, recording, or any information browsing, storage, or retrieval system, without permission in writing from FriesenPress.

ISBN
978-1-5255-5285-4 (Hardcover)
978-1-5255-5286-1 (Paperback)
978-1-5255-5287-8 (eBook)

1. POLITICAL SCIENCE, POLITICAL PROCESS, POLITICAL PARTIES

Distributed to the trade by The Ingram Book Company

Cover artwork by Shaun Hayes-Holgate
https://www.hazetoonz.ca/

From left to right:

Front row: **Peter Bevan-Baker** (Leader of the PEI Greens, MLA since 2015), **David Coon** (Leader of the New Brunswick Greens, MLA since 2014), **Andrew Weaver** (Leader of the BC Greens, MLA since 2013), **Elizabeth May** (Leader of the Green Party of Canada, MP since 2011), **Mike Schreiner** (Leader of the Ontario Greens, MPP since 2018), **Isabella Lövin** (Deputy Prime Minister of Sweden since 2016, Spokesperson for Swedish Greens, former MEP), **Wangari Maathai** (2004 Nobel Peace Prize Winner, founder of the Green Belt Movement and the Green Party of Kenya, former Assistant Minister for Environment and Natural Resources in Kenya), **Joschka Fischer** (Vice Chancellor and Foreign Minister of Germany 1998-2005)

Second row: **Adam Olsen** (MLA in British Columbia since 2017), **Sonia Furstenau** (MLA in British Columbia since 2017), **Kevin Arseneau** (MLA in New Brunswick since 2018), **Megan Mitton** (MLA in New Brunswick since 2018), **Hannah Bell** (MLA in PEI since 2017), **Caroline Lucas** (MP in United Kingdom since 2010, former leader of the Green Party of England and Wales), **Alexander Van Der Bellen** (President of Austria since 2017, Spokesperson for Austrian Greens 1997-2008), **Winfried Kretschmann** (Minister-President of Baden-Württemberg since 2011, President of the German Bundesrat 2012-2013)

Third Row: **Michele Beaton** (MLA in PEI since 2019), **Lynne Lynd** (MLA in PEI since 2019), **Karla Bernard** (MLA in PEI since 2019), **Steve Howard** (MLA in PEI since 2019), **Jesse Klaver** (Leader of GroenLinks since 2015, Member of the Dutch House of Representatives since 2010), **Pekka Haavisto** (Minister of Foreign Affairs for Finland, former Minister of the Environment), **John Gormley** (Former Minister for the Environment for Ireland, former leader of the Irish Greens), **Kazumi Inamura** (Mayor of Amagasaki since 2010, member of Greens Japan)

Fourth Row: **Pete Fry** (City Councilor in Vancouver since 2018), **Mike Weibe** (City Councilor in Vancouver since 2018), **Ole Hammarlund** (MLA in PEI since 2019), **Trish Altass** (MLA in PEI since 2019), **Martin Bursík** (Deputy Prime Minister and Minister of Environment of Czech Republic 2007-2009, Chairman of Czech Green Party 2005-2009), **Isabelle Durant** (Deputy Prime Minister of Belgium 1999-2003, Deputy Secretary General of UNCTAD since 2017), **Raimonds Vējonis** (President of Latvia since 2015, former Minister of Defense and Minister of Environment), **James Shaw** (Minister for Climate Change of New Zealand, co-leader of New Zealand Green Party),

Back row: **Adriane Carr** (City Councilor in Vancouver since 2011), **Bob Brown** (Senator in Australia 1996-2012, former leader of Australian Greens 2005-2012)

TABLE OF CONTENTS

PREFACE VII
ACKNOWLEDGEMENTS XI
OUTLINE XIII

1. **THE FIRST GREEN PARTIES**   1
   a. Green Island in the South 7
   b. Ecological Philosophers 23
2. **WHO ARE THE GREENS?**   35
   a. The Idea of Ecologism 43
   b. Who Gets to Be Called Green? 59
3. **THE GREEN BEGINNINGS IN EUROPE**   77
   a. The 1970s 85
   b. The 1980s 93
   c. The 1990s 101
4. **THE EARLY GREENS IN CANADA**   109
   a. The First Green Party in North America 111
   b. The First Elections for Canada's Greens 123
5. **PROFESSIONALIZING CANADA'S GREEN PARTIES**   133
   a. Near Breakthroughs in Early Elections 145
   b. Greens in Canada's Remaining Provinces 155
6. **ELIZABETH, ANDREW, DAVID, PETER, AND MIKE**   189
   a. Elizabeth May 189
   b. Breaking into Provincial Politics 199
   c. Building a Caucus 213
   d. Queens Park, and Another Minority 223
7. **THE GREEN GOVERNMENTS OF GERMANY**   233
   a. The First Attempts at Green Coalition-Building 242
   b. Joschka Fischer: The Revolutionary 249
   c. The Red-Green Coalition 259

- 8. **THE CONSERVATIVE GREENS** — **271**
    - a. The Conservative Greens 273
    - b. Winfried Kretschmann: The Statesman 274
    - c. Greens as Government Leaders 283
- 9. **GREEN GOVERNANCE CHALLENGES AND MISTAKES** — **295**
    - a. The Irish Greens 301
    - b. The Swedish Greens 317
- 10. **OUR CANADIAN GREEN PARLIAMENTARIANS** — **329**
    - a. The First Green in Parliament 332
    - b. A Minority Government in British Columbia 343
    - c. Governments in the Maritimes 359

FINAL THOUGHTS **371**

PREFACE

In 1988, I participated in my first election, campaigning in support of the Green Party of Canada in the 34th Canadian Federal Election. I wasn't particularly aware of my own involvement, but I'm told that having an adorable five-month-old on hand led to a lot of doors not being shut on my father, who was running to represent the British Columbian district of Port Moody–Coquitlam, a suburban district outside of Vancouver. This was the second election that the Green Party had contested, and my father was the proud recipient of 368 votes out of a total of 53,983. He had just over half of a percent of the votes in the riding, defeating only the candidate from the Libertarian Party. Compared to the national average for the Green Party, he had done quite well; however, the Greens ended the election with one-third-of-one-percent of the vote, just shy of the total received by the Rhinoceros Party, a parody political party that, amongst other things, called for a repeal of the Law of Gravity and whose leader was an actual rhinoceros from the Toronto Zoo (named Cornelius the First).

Twenty-nine years later, in 2017, I once again was participating in an election with the Green Party, except this time it was the provincial Green Party of British Columbia and I was standing as a candidate myself in the riding of Vancouver–West End. My father was helping me out this time, having been talked into taking on the unenviable job of Campaign Finance Officer (although with a budget one-thirtieth of that of the other parties, it wasn't quite so arduous a task).

In this election, the provincial Greens fared significantly better, receiving the best results of a Green party in Canadian history and one of the best results of any Green party worldwide. After everything was counted, the Green Party of British Columbia secured the support of just over one-sixth of British Columbians (16.84 percent). That was the highest percentage that a North American Green Party had received to date, and the highest percentage that had been achieved worldwide in a Canadian-style electoral system. Despite being the choice of one-sixth of British Columbians, the Greens only managed to elect three individuals out of eighty-seven seats. This is due to the nature of BC (and Canada's) electoral system, often referred to as "first past the post," which elects just one person per geographic district. This type of system has long been a major challenge for Green parties, who typically have broad support across the entire country or province, instead of massive support in any specific geographic area. The election of these three Members of the Legislative Assembly was, in fact, the first time that multiple Greens had ever been elected in North America in anything above a municipal level.

Although three individuals elected to a legislature of eighty-seven people might seem like a pretty small deal, the impact of these three Greens was huge in the aftermath of the election. The other two major political parties contesting for British Columbia's votes, the BC Liberal Party and the BC New Democratic Party (BCNDP), had wound up virtually tied in the vote result. With barely 1,500 votes separating them, the BC Liberals had gained forty-three seats and the BC NDP forty-one, both short of the forty-four needed to secure the barest of majorities. This put the three Greens in a position that many in the media dubbed "the Kingmakers." Whichever of the two large parties wanted to form government would need the support of the Greens in order to do so (unless they wanted to work with each other, which they clearly did not). Yet another first: for the first time in North America, a Green Party would have the chance to participate in government, at least in some small way.

Although this election set numerous records in North America and involved so many "firsts," it was hardly the first success for Green parties worldwide. In fact, Green parties in Europe have been electing members to their legislatures for thirty years and have participated in over a dozen governments already. This is because much of Europe uses a different system of conducting elections, one in which a party's seats are allocated according to their support countrywide. Interestingly, Green parties in Europe have had much greater success with much less support than their BC counterparts due to this difference in the way individuals are elected. At the time of writing this book, the German Bundestag contained sixty-three members of parliament from Die Grünen (the German Green Party) after securing only about 8 percent of the vote in their last election, a lower vote-share than that of the British Columbian Greens.

As of 2019, Green parties have been elected at the national level in dozens of countries worldwide, and have participated in national government in twenty-one countries, as well as many more at state and municipal levels. They have done so in coalitions with parties on the left, on the right, and as part of broad coalitions spanning the political spectrum. A Green party has never won a parliamentary majority on its own, but Greens have led multiparty coalition governments as they do in the German state of Baden-Württemberg at the time of writing.

But what makes a party a "Green" party, and what gave rise to politically active individuals' perceived need to create a new movement set apart from the traditional party archetypes of the Conservative, the Liberal, the Labour, the Socialist, the Progressive, and the Nationalist? Political pundits like to divide all political thought into the "left" and the "right" and to place all political movements somewhere on this spectrum. This is especially prevalent in states that have a dominant two-party system, such as the United States of America. In Canada, perhaps due to our proximity to the USA and the massive amount of cultural export from our neighbours to the south, we also tend to divide our politics into two sides. But many Greens don't like to accept this duopoly of possible opinion. A common phrase Greens often use worldwide is that they are "neither left, nor right, but forward." Yes, this is a bit cheesy, but it's how many Greens feel we are best described.

In 1987, at the Third Congress of European Greens, Swedish Nobel Laureate Hannes Alfvén suggested the idea that each century would spawn an ideology that would go on to define the next. In the eighteenth century, Liberalism bloomed and went on to dominate the nineteenth, which gave birth to the idea of Socialism, which spread through the world in the twentieth. Alfven optimistically (from the Green point of view) suggested that maybe Green political thought would go on to be the definitive political ideology of the twenty-first century. Surely the twenty-first century is going to face challenges that no century before it has had to deal with.

If we continue on our current path, then the changes in the world's environment brought on by human activity will lead to an upset in our civilizational order greater than any that have come before. The Industrial Revolution, the Enlightenment, the Colonial Era: all of these great realignments of the global order led to the creation and dissolution of multiple forms of political thought. It would be silly to assume that our generation's crises won't lead to new politics and philosophies to address the enormous issues we face. Whether those philosophies will be Green ones is unknown, but it's the prediction and desire of Green politicians and supporters worldwide that they will.

A Note on the 2019 Election in Prince Edward Island

As I was writing this book, my goal was to have it published in time for the 2019 Canadian federal election. As the election closed in, I tried to hold off submitting the final copy for as long as possible, in the hope that I could include the results of the election in Prince Edward Island, in which the Greens were polling very well.

On April 23rd of 2019, island voters in Canada's smallest province awarded the Green Party of Prince Edward Island eight seats in PEI's legislature, out of a possible twenty-seven, based on the Greens achieving 30% of the vote in the province. This was the best result for a Green Party in Canadian history. The Progressive Conservatives won twelve seats, two shy of a majority. The defeated Liberal incumbents won six seats.

On April 24th I submitted the final copy of this book for publishing.

Therefore I will not be able to be able to cover the aftermath of the election in PEI, in which the Progressive Conservatives are expected to form a minority government. I hope to be able to revisit the island's politics in a future version of this book.

ACKNOWLEDGEMENTS

First of all, I want to thank my family, who raised me and instilled the values in me that made me want to write a book like this in the first place. My wonderful parents, Bill Marshall and Kate Smith, provided countless intellectual, material, and emotional support in making this book happen. My aunts, Marilyn Smith and Patricia Williams, likewise have provided me with boundless encouragement for my entire life. And thank you to Masheed Salehomoum, my partner who put up with me spending my evenings and weekends writing a book rather than hanging out with her.

I also need to thank my friends, some of whom contributed editing and reviewing, and others who just supported me and built me up when I needed positive encouragement, or even just listened to me ramble about political issues. Special thanks to Shaun Hayes-Holgate for drawing me an amazing book cover.

Many people within the Canadian Green volunteer corps and party staff have been wonderful over the years as I fleshed out the ideas and history in this book. Special thanks to the BC Greens team, including Liz Lilly, Cam Butt, Stefan Jonsson, Jillian Oliver, Evan Pivnick, Ryan Clayton, Taylor Hartrick, Jonina Campbell, and the many others that I've met through my activity there. Thanks to the Vancouver Greens organizers and elected officials, including Pete Fry, Michael Wiebe, David Wong, Stuart Mackinnon, Anthony Hughes, John Whistler, Jacquie Miller, Tracy Dundass, and countless others.

I conducted many, many interviews while writing this book. I want to thank Andrew Weaver, Sonia Furstenau, Adam Olsen, David Coon, Peter Bevan-Baker, Hannah Bell, Adriane Carr, Frank de Jong, Jonathan Dickie, Stuart Parker, Sharon Labchuk, Nick Wright, Jean Ouimet, Trevor Hancock, Judy Fainstein, Paul George, Andrew Scorer, Steve Kisby, Bob Brown, Mike Ward, Jakop Dalunde, and Erïch Jacoby-Hawkins for being willing to talk with me. Thank you to Jan Marczona and Arne Jungjohann for making me feel welcome when I traveled to Germany to do research on the German Greens.

Writing an acknowledgements page is intimidating, because I think that every person that I've met an interacted with in my life has affected my thinking and values in some way. There are people that I could thank here that don't even know I exist, but who have written or spoken publicly and greatly influenced my development as a person. This book was made possible by every person that I've spent time with, playing board games or music or just sitting down for a beer. Any time I've spent living and enjoying life with friends has re-energized me and allowed me to spend my free time thinking and writing. Every person who's mentioned, even in passing, that they appreciate the work I've put in has given me the confidence to keep working. If I started naming everyone, I don't know when I'd be able to stop.

No thanks go to my cat, who constantly stood in front of my computer screen while I tried to write.

OUTLINE

This book was written over a period starting in the summer of 2017 and ending just before its publication in late 2019, just prior to the Canadian federal election of that year. As such, parts of it will likely soon be made out-of-date. The book is a mixture of Green history from past decades as well as modern analysis of the Canadian and international Green movement. I hope to have the opportunity to revise it in the future as circumstances change and evolve.

The goal of the book is to outline the history of the global Green political movement, and the ideology that it is created from. The focus is particularly on the view of Green politics from a Canadian perspective. At the time I wrote this book, the Canadian Green party has been experiencing a period of growth as Green politicians are finally elected at various levels around the country. Now that Green politicians are much more visible in the public sphere, it's leading many people to take notice and to try to understand what goals and ideologies drive these individuals.

It's with that questioning spirit in mind that I wrote this book. I hope that the takeaway for the reader will be a better understanding of the society that Green politicians and supporters are trying to build, and of the steps that Greens are suggesting that would transition us to that society.

The book is divided broadly into two parts, with a total of ten chapters between them. Each chapter is then subdivided into a couple sections, to provide more bite-sized reading opportunities. The first half of the book is intended to cover the earlier history of Green political ideas, where they came from, and how the movement was built. The second half of the book covers what happens when those ideas are actually put into practice as Greens are elected into positions of responsibility.

As you're reading this book, feel free to skip a section if you're not finding it interesting or relevant to the questions that you're curious about. The book jumps around between being hyper-focused on Canadian politics and covering the experiences of international Green parties. If you're only interested in our local Canadian history, then I hope you'll enjoy just reading the Canadian-focused chapters. If you'd prefer to focus on the broader insights from international party's experiences, then that's fine too.

Chapter One of the book covers the first attempts to form a political party based on ecological principles back in the 1970s. It's an introduction to the ideas that would become Green ideology, before there was a name or consensus on these ideas.

Chapter Two builds off of the first chapter, and dives into the historical and ideological ideas that were introduced there. It's probably the driest and densest chapter, as it discusses economics, philosophy, and other heavy ideas. If it's too intimidating or dry, don't hesitate to skip it for now and return to it later.

Chapter Three covers the real explosion of the Green Party movement in Europe. Europe is where these ideas really came together and were fleshed out before they were exported out to the rest of the world.

Chapter Four is the first section to outline the history of Green politics in Canada. It specifically focused on the very beginning of the various Canadian Green parties (both federal and provincial).

Chapter Five continues the history that was presented in the previous chapter. It covers the middle period of the Canadian Greens, when they transitioned from being very small and niche parties to instead running professional, competitive campaigns.

Chapter Six (the start of the second part of the book) covers the period when the Canadian Greens started actually succeeding. It covers the personal biographies of the federal and provincial Green politicians that had been elected at the time of this book's writing.

Chapter Seven transitions to an international focus. The chapter covers the political situation of Germany, where Green politics has arguably been most successful. In particular, it covers the period in the late '90s to early 2000s when the local Green party served as part of the country's government.

Chapter Eight continues the coverage of Germany, but this time looking specifically at the Greens in one of Germany's states in which the party leads the government, rather than being only a junior partner as they were on the federal scale. It also discusses the idea of Green Conservatism, which is a much rarer perspective in the Canadian context.

Chapter Nine covers the experience of the Green parties of Ireland and Sweden. Both of these parties served in their country's national government and had an exceptionally difficult time during their terms. We can look at their stories as precautionary tales of things that Green parties should be prepared for when they first take the responsibility of governing.

WHAT DOES GREEN MEAN?

Chapter Ten is the final chapter, and it covers the experience of the elected Greens in Canada since they've taken their seats in their respective legislatures. It covers the achievements and challenges that they've experienced, and outlines what a small group of non-mainstream politicians have been able to do with the small amount of power that they've managed to gain.

I hope that someone who finishes reading this entire book can look at Canada's Green parties with the same understanding of "what it means to be Green" that Green politicians and campaigners have about themselves.

Most of all, I hope it'll help people understand that, contrary to the popular assertion, the Greens are far, far more than a "single-issue party."

CHAPTER 1

THE FIRST GREEN PARTIES

"It's 3:23 in the morning
and I'm awake
because my great great grandchildren
won't let me sleep.
my great great grandchildren
ask me in my dreams
what did you do while the Planet was plundered?
what did you do when the Earth was unravelling?
surely you did something
when the seasons started failing?
as the mammals, reptiles, and birds were all dying?
did you fill the streets with protest
when democracy was stolen?
what did you do
once
you
knew?"

(Drew Dellinger, 2011)

THE FIRST GREEN PARTIES

During the 2017 provincial election in British Columbia, we identified a group of core issues on which we wanted to focus our campaign. Those core issues varied between the dense urban electoral districts in Vancouver and Victoria, the suburban districts that surrounded the big cities, and the more rural or mixed districts that defined the interior and north of the province. I was the candidate for a part of Vancouver known as the West End, the northern half of Vancouver's downtown peninsula that contained multitudes of older historic mid-rises, newer super towers, and the city's world-famous Stanley Park.

Downtown Vancouver's most pressing issue was extremely clear: housing affordability. Vancouver is one of the world's most expensive cities to live in and the Liberal/Conservative government of BC for the past sixteen years was being accused of not just failing to fix the problem, but wilfully encouraging it in order to keep the real estate market booming. The second biggest issue that we heard on the ground, and thus decided to focus on, was education. The government of BC had just lost a supreme court case fifteen years in the making in which the British Columbia Teachers' Federation (BCTF) accused the government of acting illegally during a 2002 labour dispute. Since then, the education system in the province was seen by many as being brutally underfunded. The leader of the BC Green Party wanted to make our core issue that of education funding. Before entering politics, he came from a career as a scientist and university professor who considered education to be the greatest investment that a society could make in itself.

Readers who aren't particularly familiar with the Green Party might think it strange that neither of these two core campaign issues are the usual ones that people associate with a Green party—namely, the environment. Sure enough, during the campaign, I very often had people asking me, "Why are you talking so much about housing and education? I thought you guys were the Green Party. Don't you care about environmental issues?"

I'd planned my answer, and we'd talked about it in party meetings during the campaign: "Yes, we are the Green Party. People already know our stance on environmental issues. It's the *only* thing many people know about us. We want them to understand that we're a lot more than that. Our policies and plans for the province go far beyond a single-issue. You already know that we're the strongest party on environmental issues, so it's not something we need to be talking about unless asked."

This is the great challenge when Canadian Greens talk to voters who aren't deeply tuned in to the political philosophy of the Green movement. It's especially difficult in areas where Greens haven't yet had a major electoral breakthrough and are seen as a fringe party. Many people still see Greens as a single-issue party, a group of environmental hippies who care about only one thing and shouldn't be trusted with government because they don't have any interest or knowledge about the many other parts of running a province or country. It can get even worse. Several times I had people on the street mistake the Green Party for being a marijuana advocacy party. I had one young man ask me if the Greens had a favourite dispensary that we liked to go to after a hard day of campaigning.

For Greens in other countries, the idea of a broader Green political philosophy is much better understood. Green philosophy goes much deeper than just advocating for fewer pipelines and more solar panels. The core idea of the Green philosophy is that we should champion sustainability over growth-at-any-cost. Although this might be most obvious in environmental contexts, it applies all over the spectrum of human experience. Greens want sustainability in employment, in economics, in housing, in quality of life, in everything. But many Greens did come to the realization that they held this philosophy due to seeing how poorly we manage the planet's environment.

It is generally agreed that two parties were the first of the world's Greens. These two parties formed within two months of each other and as far as anyone has been able to glean had no initial connection or knowledge of each other. The circumstances that led to the formation of these two rather different political entities parallel the public perception and deeper values of Green parties today. The United Tasmania Group, formed in the southern Australian island state of Tasmania for their statewide elections, was birthed from a purely conservationist campaign. Meanwhile the Values Party of New Zealand was the first party to demonstrate what would later become the core of the Green movement's greater political philosophies of well-being and quality of life over consumerism and materialism.

"We are all born bonded to nature; that's why we put depictions of flowers and forests, rather than bulldozers or log piles, on our walls."

(Bob Brown, Australian Senator and former Leader of the Green Party of Australia)

GREEN ISLAND IN THE SOUTH

In the northeastern corner of British Columbia, close to the borders of Alberta and the territory of the Yukon and as far as you can get in BC from the population centres of Vancouver and Victoria where the BC legislature meets, runs the Peace River. Historically, the Peace River has had great significance for both First Nations peoples and later for the pioneers and colonists involved in the fur trade. The lands of the Peace River valley are still home to many third- and fourth-generation farming families who inherited their land from these first colonists. The river is also a wilderness haven for tourists, providing opportunities for sightseeing, canoeing, fishing, birdwatching, swimming, and camping.

The river has two hydroelectric dams on it already: the WAC Bennett and Peace Canyon dams. In 2010, the BC Liberal provincial government of British Columbia announced that it would be building a third dam on the river and gave it the placeholder name of the Site C Dam (Site C being the third potential site on the river for a dam, sites A and B having already been constructed). The dam was in planning for several years, and Premier Christy Clark was quoted as saying that she'd like the dam to be at "the point of no return" by May of 2017, incidentally when there was going to be a provincial election.

By the 2017 election, construction of the dam was indeed well underway although many were arguing that it was by no means past the point of no return. As you may have predicted, opposition to the construction of the dam was fierce and passionate, and was a defining election issue for many British Columbians. Advocates for the dam said that it was needed to provide for the growing energy needs of British Columbia, and that it would be a wonderful source of clean, emissions-free energy. Opponents claimed that the energy produced by the hydroelectric dam was not in fact needed, but was instead meant to be provided to the hydraulic fracking industry that the BC Liberals were trying to build in BC's north, as well as to the immensely dirty Alberta tar sands. The construction of the dam would also involve the widening of eighty-three kilometers of the river by up to three times its current width, flooding acres upon acres of not just beautiful valley land, but also arable farmland and important First Nations' historical sites.

Large energy projects like the Site C dam are often election issues in British Columbia and Canada, and the pressure is on parties to take stances on whether they support or oppose them. In May 2017, the BC Liberals and the BC Green Party were both very clear: the Liberals planned to go ahead with the project as they were of course the ones who introduced it, while the Greens would order it immediately halted. The third major party in British Columbia, the BC New Democratic Party (BC NDP) attempted as best as it could to not take a position, just saying that it would put the project "to review."

In the Beginning

Forty-five years before BC's 2017 election, a similar story was unfolding on the opposite side of the world. The Australian state of Tasmania is an island just south of the southeast corner of the main Australian landmass. Although it is as beautiful and vibrant a place as any in the country, it is remote and obscure enough that it has a history of being forgotten on maps produced by outside organizations and even the Australian government. When Australia itself held the Olympic Games in 2000, some of the literature that they produced featured a map of Australia with the southern island missing. Outside of Australia, most people's only knowledge of Tasmania would be as the home of the long extinct Tasmanian tiger, one of the best examples of an animal that we've lost forever due to human activity.

Buried in the mountains and forests of the Tasmanian wilderness, Lake Pedder is the namesake of the surrounding national park. The first European to reach the lake, John Wedge, wrote of his encounter with the lake,

> On the 11th of March we reached two beautiful lakes, which were named Lake Pedder and Lake Maria, lying in the heart of the most romantic scenery and being surrounded by lofty mountains. (1835, https://lakepedder.org)

CHAPTER 1 – THE FIRST GREEN PARTIES

In his 1983 book "The Mountains of Paradise: The Wilderness of South-West Tasmania", Les Southwell wrote a more detailed description of the lake and surrounding area:

> It will be appreciated that the formation of Lake Pedder was a rare chance occurrence, it being the only such glacial-outwash lake in Australia. And its special attraction was difficult to attribute to any single feature, for it formed an interwoven complex of many elements: the lake itself, the lagoon system and the Serpentine; the dark forests, the buttongrass plains and mountain streams that surrounded the lake; and the wild, magnificent setting. It had the air of a mysterious valley ringed with sombre, imposing mountains—remote, secluded and peaceful.
>
> To stand on the beach on a clear summer's night was an unforgettable experience. The firm white sands underfoot, the broad sweep of the beach swinging away in a wide arc towards the distant Serpentine and the Crumbledown. A ragged line of mountains circled the horizon. Overhead the great vault of the southern sky, a luminous darkness pierced with a myriad of starpoints gathered up in homely patterns.
>
> Here the air has a purity and a transparence unknown to urban dwellers. There was a stillness of tiny sounds: the soft lap of the crystal waters, the distant cry of a night bird. (Southwell, 1983)

The lake and its national park reside deep in the sparsely populated southwest of the island and was popular with wilderness enthusiasts, bushwalkers, birdwatchers, and other outdoorsy types. The national park had been established in 1955 and gave the entire area a protected status. The vast majority of Tasmania's population lives on the eastern coast in and around the capital city of Hobart, and Lake Pedder was about as far into the wilderness as you could get for most of the island's population.

Tasmania gets more rainfall on average than the rest of Australia, a country known for being mostly dry desert, and as early as 1914 Tasmania's Hydro Electric Commission (HEC) had made a policy priority of encouraging large power-consuming industries in the state. This policy was championed by the long-time Premier of Tasmania, Eric Reece, whose unwavering support had even earned him the nickname of "Electric Eric." The HEC, meanwhile, was headed by Sir Allan Knight, who by 1971 had been the HEC's commissioner for over twenty-five years. The two men were powerhouses in Tasmanian politics. Unusually, the HEC had been given much more independence than government commissions usually receive. Some citizens accused the government of just being a rubber stamp for whatever scheme the HEC wanted to undertake.

By the 1950s, Tasmania had embarked on a program of massive hydroelectric construction, spending a huge portion of the government's budget on hydro schemes. This expansion of the hydroelectric industry at the expense of other developments meant that the state fell behind the rest of Australia on many other modernization fronts, such as the construction of railways and ports.

Water and Power

This massive hydro focus was nonetheless left unopposed until 1967, when a watchdog organization of hikers, birdwatchers, and other wilderness fans discovered that the government's hydro expansion plan involved the flooding of Lake Pedder and the surrounding national park. Activists in the public decided to act. The effort went through the usual channels that we now expect a public opposition campaign to follow. A petition was circulated and quickly amassed ten thousand signatures, the most that any petition to the Tasmanian state government had ever gathered. A "Lake Pedder Action Committee" (LPAC) was established that lobbied the government against the park flooding. One of the committee members organized a meeting in which a member of Tasmanian Parliament attended and surprisingly agreed to submit a proposal to put the project to a referendum. He introduced the motion in the legislature a few days later, but it was soundly rejected by his colleagues.

The government's unwillingness to entertain any opposition to the plan was steadfast. When a second petition, this time with over a quarter of a million signatures from all across Australia, was presented to the Tasmanian parliament, the Attorney General refused to accept it. He stated that it was "in conflict with government policy," somehow missing that that was the entire point. In addition, several members of the Premier's government described the conservationists as "crackpots." "Electric" Eric Reece, the Premier of Tasmania from 1958–1969, and from 1972–1975, was quoted as saying:

> There was a National Park out there, but I can't remember exactly where it was . . . at least, it wasn't of substantial significance in the scheme of things. The thing that was significant was that we had to double the output of power in this state in ten years in order [to] supply the demands of industry and the community. And this was the scheme that looked as though it could do a greater part of [the] job for us.

The government of Tasmania was not used to the public opposing their decision-making process, or demanding public consultation on matters as big and important as energy policy. Even the attitude of the general public towards the Lake Pedder activists was fairly negative. It was said at the time in political literature that "Tasmanians had become accustomed to a life in a benevolent technocracy" (Walker, 1986, page 18). It was true that the government of the state was not known for being an open and transparent entity that looked to its citizens for guidance.

The activists weren't able to find any friendly allies in the official opposition party either. Eric Reece, introduced above, was not actually the Premier at the time of the LPAC's founding. Instead, he sat as leader of the opposition, having been defeated just recently in the 1969 election. The governing Liberal Party of Premier Angus Bethune had only been in power for two years and had come to power after decades of uninterrupted dominance by the Labour Party. The hydro-industrialization schemes had therefore been launched and championed by the Labour Party and then picked up happily by the Liberal Party when they took over. Neither party had any interest in challenging the long-standing, established wisdom of the HEC and its plans for Tasmania's hydropower expansion.

US President John F. Kennedy is quoted as saying, "Those who make peaceful revolution impossible will make violent revolution inevitable." When it comes to public activism campaigns, when groups have tried and failed to protest through the "proper" channels, they will often begin protesting in more and more radical ways. We need only to look at the Dakota Access Pipeline protests in 2016, in which a coalition of Native Americans and allies established a camp at the pipeline's construction location and refused to move despite enduring over three hundred injuries and nearly five hundred arrests when the government decided to crack down on them.

Thankfully, the protests around Lake Pedder never turned violent. This may be due to an event that had no connection to the Lake Pedder protests but gave the protesters an unexpected new opportunity to achieve their goals.

Although the Liberal party had a majority in the Tasmanian Legislature and thus was able to form government, they had a majority by only the slimmest possible margins. The 1969 election had left the two parties with exactly equal numbers of seats, with the legislature's remaining seat being occupied by Kevin Lyons who had been elected as the sole representative of his own "Centre Party." After the exact tie between the Liberals and Labour put the two parties at an impasse, Lyons agreed to join with the Liberal party to enable them to form the government.

A Door Opens

In 1972, Lyons unexpectedly resigned his seat in the legislature, losing the Liberals their bare majority, and triggering a surprise election. His resignation had nothing to do with the Lake Pedder protests, but was instead rumoured to be due to accusations of bribery by powerful figures in the tobacco and gambling industries. Regardless of his reasons for leaving the legislature, the sudden election in the midst of their protest campaign gave the Lake Pedder conservationists an amazing opportunity.

The way Tasmania conducts its elections is different than ours in Canada. In Canada we divide the country into 338 individual districts. In each of these districts, the single candidate who gets the most votes is elected. Tasmania, on the other hand, has only five districts. Each district elects seven representatives, and so a candidate has to achieve one-seventh of the votes in their region to be elected. This method of electing its members means that it's much easier for an independent candidate or smaller party to be elected to the legislature. Canada's system, known as first-past-the-post, gives all of the power to whichever party is biggest. Tasmania's system, known as proportional representation, spreads the power around based on the support that each party or candidate obtains.

Kevin Lyons himself was a perfect example of an independent being elected under their system, and being able to influence the government on behalf of his voters. The Lake Pedder activists saw this, and saw their opportunity. What followed was the first time in world history that a political party would be formed and contest an election primarily to advocate for an environmental cause.

At an LPAC meeting on March 23rd, 1972, it was resolved that:

> In order that there is a maximum usage of a unique political opportunity to save Lake Pedder, now an issue of global and national concern, and to implement a national well-researched conservation plan for the State of Tasmania, there be formed a Single Independent Coalition of primarily conservation-minded candidates and their supporters. (The United Tasmania Group, Pamela Walker, page 11)

The founders of the new political party included Dr. Richard Jones, the chair of the LPAC, who would become the leader of the new party; Brenda Hean, a piano teacher; Brian Proudlock, an engineer; and many others.

The First Environmental Political Party

The membership of the LPAC thus formed their own political party. The United Tasmania Group (UTG) was registered in order to contest an election that would be held only one month hence. With so little time before the voting day, and the election itself already underway, the UTG wasn't able to constitute itself into a full-fledged party until several years after the election. However, the UTG was operating as the political wing of the LPAC and functioned as an organized entity, not just a loose conglomeration of independents. They were able to field twelve candidates across four of the five Tasmanian electoral districts.

With only four weeks to campaign and build enough of a profile to see themselves elected, the UTG had a great challenge on their hands. They were a party specifically formed around what they saw as the most important election issue of their time, but it was a cause that the dominant Liberal and Labour parties specifically went out of their way to claim was *not* an election issue. The established parties were fighting to maintain their traditional way of managing the state, which was from the top down and without the interference of the governed people.

During the campaign, the UTG ran into the problem that every candidate for a Green party today knows extremely well: that of voters not wanting to cast their vote for what they see as a single-issue party, regardless of how important that issue might be. But although the UTG was formed around the issue of Lake Pedder, their actual political theory went far beyond that. The LPAC had spent massive amounts of time and effort attempting to persuade their government to listen to them and to compromise with them, only to be met with outright hostility and attempts to silence their activism.

In an early UTG newsletter, Dr. Richard Jones, the chairperson of both the LPAC and the UTG, wrote, "Our struggle to preserve Lake Pedder pushed us into the political arena. Our values were so threatened that we were forced to seek political power." This summarizes what was the true goal of the UTG, whether the membership were fully aware of it or not, and what would become a monumentally important party of later Green political thought.

The UTG was fighting to awaken the people to the dangers of a state dominated by closed government, by secrecy of decision-making, by hostility to public consultation, and by an overwhelming focus on industrialization at any cost as the primary goal of the government and economy. 1972 was the same year that the Club of Rome published the seminal book *"The Limits to Growth,"* the same year that the Ecologist published *"A Blueprint for Survival,"* and only a year before E. F. Schumacher published *Small Is Beautiful*. These books and studies were awakening something in the population. There was a growing number of environmental groups arising in these years because "more and more people turned to count the mounting costs of unbridled economic growth and sought to reassert non-material values." The UTG was just the first group to bring this new emerging political and economic theory to the public as an actual election platform.

The New Ethic

In order to show the voters that they meant to be taken seriously and that they stood for more than just the single issue of saving an individual lake, the UTG published a short manifesto that they titled *"The New Ethic."* This manifesto espoused the same values and ideas that would later be labelled as "environmentalism" or "ecologism," but at the time had no established label. It read as follows:

> We citizens of Tasmania and members of the United Tasmania Group,
> United in a global movement for survival;
>
> Concerned for the dignity of humanity and the value of cultural heritage while rejecting any view of humans which gives them the right to exploit all of nature;
>
> Moved by the need for a new ethic which unites humans with nature to prevent the collapse of life support systems of the earth;
>
> Rejecting all exclusive ideological and pragmatic views of society as partial and divisive;
>
> Condemning the misuse of power for individual or group prominence based on aggression against humanity or nature;
>
> Shunning the acquisition and display of individual wealth as an expression of greed for status or power;
>
> While acknowledging that Tasmania is uniquely favoured with natural resources, climate form and beauty;
>
> Undertake to live our private and communal lives in such a way that we maintain Tasmania's form and beauty for our own enjoyment and for the enjoyment of our children through unlimited future generations;
>
> Undertake to create aesthetic harmony between our human structures and the natural landscape where our individual and communal needs demand modification to the natural environment;
>
> Undertake to regulate our individual and communal needs for resources, both living and non-living, while preventing the wholesale extraction of our non-replenishable resources for the satisfaction of the desire for profit;

CHAPTER 1 – THE FIRST GREEN PARTIES

Undertake to husband and cherish Tasmania's living resources so that we do minimum damage to the web of life of which we are part while preventing the extinction or serious depletion of any form of life by our individual, group or communal actions;

And we shall:

Create new institutions so that all who wish may participate in making laws and decisions at all levels concerning the social, cultural, political, and economic life of the community;

Provide institutions for the peaceful and unimpeded evolution of the community and for the maintenance of justice and equal opportunity for all people;

Change our society and our culture to prevent a tyranny of rationality, at the expense of values, by which we may lose the unique adaptability of our species for meeting cultural and environmental change;

Prevent alienation of people in their social and work roles and functions while, making scientific, technical and vocational knowledge and practice free and open to all;

Create a new community in which men and women shall be valued for their Personal skills, for the material and non-material worth of these skills to groups and the whole community, for their service to the community, and for their noncompetitive achievement in. all aspects of life;

Live as equal members of our society to maintain a community governed by rational non-sectional law;

Preserve specific areas of private and group life where private thought, speech and action is of group importance and does not interfere unreasonably, with others;

And vest our individual and communal rights in a parliament of representatives chosen by all to enforce our law for as long as that power is not used unfairly to advantage or disadvantage any individual or group in the community.

(UTG Manifesto 1972, the "New Ethic")

Over the ensuing years the UTG fought to convince Tasmanians that they were a legitimate political entity with a coherent political philosophy. This led them to develop a large and comprehensive election platform. In 1976 the *Examiner*, Tasmania's newspaper, actually conceded that "Dr. Jones' little party has produced more teasing relevant ideas for Tasmanians than all the other party policy writers put together."

The Uphill Battle

This is a challenge that Green parties face even in the modern era. During the provincial election for which I was a candidate, the BC Green Party put out an extensive document outlining our ideas and policy goals. I naively assumed that it would be read by anyone in the media commenting publicly on the election. It was later admitted to me by one of British Columbia's legislative reporters that he was the only one to have read the platform, and was often asked by his colleagues for insight on the Greens because the rest couldn't be bothered to read it. Most of those in the media writing op-ed columns on the Greens hadn't even read our platform.

The UTG experienced a massive growth of support during the 1972 election, but unfortunately that growth was not quite enough to get them to their goal of electing a representative. "Electric" Eric Reece and his Labour Party achieved a parliamentary majority, but when all the votes were counted the UTG had achieved 4 percent of the state's overall vote. They'd gotten nearly 7 percent in the districts of Denison and Franklin, where the party was strongest and where they concentrated their effort. They'd come just short of electing someone in these two districts. They achieved this despite having only formed a month before the day of the election and operating on an extreme shoestring budget. They achieved this despite the cooperative efforts of both major parties in insisting that the values of the UTG were not election issues.

They also achieved this despite the Hydro-Electric Commission utilizing public funds to directly intervene and campaign against them.

The HEC was a government industrial commission, meaning that it was funded by taxpayers. A repeating trend in political campaigns is the attempts by the incumbent government party to use public money to campaign on their own behalf. We dealt with it in the 2017 British Columbia election, but not nearly to the extent that the UTG had to suffer it in 1972. The HEC ran public advertisements urging voters that they would endure significant increases in charges for electricity if there were any changes to the Lake Pedder flooding scheme, directly targeting the United Tasmania Group. The ads were paid for with public money. After the election was over the UTG called for a Royal Commission into the HEC's improper, maybe illegal, role in the election campaign.

CHAPTER 1 – THE FIRST GREEN PARTIES

Denied a Voice

The government once again refused to consider anything that might delay the plan to flood the lake. It led to a minor crisis for the government when Mervyn Everett, the Attorney General, resigned from Cabinet when the rest of his caucus would not allow a court challenge to the Lake Pedder plan. The Tasmanian Bar Association, along with a considerable portion of the public, condemned the move and the denial of access to the courts by citizens. As a response, the government passed a "Doubts Removal Bill" in which they essentially voted to validate themselves in continuing with the dam project.

Although the UTG wasn't successful in electing anyone for the sudden 1972 election, they would go on to be an enduring force in Tasmanian and Australian history and politics. The UTG contested the next state election in 1976 and again didn't elect anyone. But their success story was coming soon.

Lake Pedder is now sadly gone. Where there once was a small and beautiful shallow lake with sandy shores now stands Australia's largest freshwater body of water, a 240-square-kilometer man-made impoundment and diversion reservoir. Those 240 square kilometers used to be the surrounding wilderness, and the surface and beaches of the original lake now sit forty meters below the water. Several species such as the Lake Pedder earthworm and the Pedder galaxias are now considered to be extinct as a result of the dam's construction.

But the efforts to save Tasmanian wilderness were not ended by the loss. The movements started by the LPAC activists and UTG politicians set the stage for another showdown between 1978 and 1983. This time the government of Tasmania was up against both disgruntled citizens and also the federal Australian government as well as and the country's supreme court. The Franklin Dam Controversy is an amazing story that is covered far more extensively in other books, but the lead up to it is a repeat of the story that we just covered. In 1978, the HEC once again proposed building a new dam, and the Lake Pedder protest movement reassembled itself to fight the same fight once again. This time they were *far* more successful.

Try, Try Again

The campaign to stop the Franklin Dam generated over 30,000 letters of support in several weeks, and in 1980 an estimated ten thousand people marched in the streets of the Tasmanian capital of Hobart, the largest rally in the history of the state. The government this time decided to allow for a referendum on the issue; however, the referendum had only two options: either the original plan to build the new dam, or a slightly modified plan that the government had declared was a "compromise." The referendum allowed no option to oppose the dam project entirely.

The result of the referendum was that 47 percent had voted for the original dam proposal, 8 percent had voted for the compromise, and the remaining 45 percent had informally written "no dams" on their ballot or otherwise spoiled their ballot. The opposition and controversy led the government to fall apart. The governing Labour party fractured due to differences in support among its members either in favour of or against the dam. A new election was called, and since the Labour party was in such disarray, the staunchly pro-dam Liberal party was elected with a new majority.

The new Premier, Robin Gray, adamant that he had been elected on a platform of pro-dam construction, immediately ordered the original plan to go ahead and for construction to be started. Opinion in the rest of Australia was very critical of the dam plan, so Premier Gray threatened the Australian federal government that if they attempted to interfere in any way, Tasmania would secede from the Commonwealth and declare itself as its own independent country.

The crackdown only galvanized the protesters, who now regularly numbered in the thousands at anti-dam events. In 1982, Bob Brown, a former UTG candidate, organized a blockade of the dam's construction. Thousands participated, and at its peak the blockade was growing by at least fifty people per day. Police went on to arrest 1,217 people for being present, and nearly five hundred were actually imprisoned for participating, including Bob Brown as well as famed British botanist and broadcaster David Bellamy and Australian author John Marsden. The opposition and protests now had international attention.

Less than half a year after the blockade, Australia had a federal election and the Labor party of Bob Hawke won with a decisive majority. New Prime Minister Hawke had promised to stop the dam from being constructed, as the dam proposal was unpopular among voters on the Australian mainland. Hawke's government passed the new World Heritage Properties Conservation Act. This declared the Franklin River as a World Heritage Site and put a stop to the Tasmanian government's construction along the river. Premier Robin Grey of Tasmania ordered the construction crews to simply ignore the federal government's order and to continue the construction. He claimed that the federal government had no powers under the constitution to pass such legislation.

The case went to the Australian Supreme Court and became known as "Commonwealth v Tasmania." In a landmark decision, the court ruled in favour of the federal government due to the fact that the federal government had signed the international *UNESCO Convention Concerning the Protection of the World Cultural and Natural Heritage* treaty. This meant that the government was able to pass legislation in order to comply with international treaties and protect the UNESCO world heritage site that the dam would destroy. The high court ruling ended the dam's construction and no attempt has been made to revive it.

Bob Brown, meanwhile, was released from prison, and on the day of his release became the member of Tasmania's parliament for the House of Assembly seat of Denison. Norm Sanders, the previous holder of that seat, had resigned from it while Bob was imprisoned. In the Tasmanian election system voters are able to rank the candidates on their ballot, marking their first, second, third choices, and so forth. In Canada, when a member of parliament resigns, it triggers a by-election to select a new member. In Tasmania, when a member of parliament resigns, the seat instead is given to the second choice of the voters who elected the resigning member. Bob Brown had unsuccessfully run in the 1982 election and had been the second choice of the voters who had elected Norm Sanders, so when he resigned Brown was offered the job. The top protestor for the dam project was now in the parliament staring down the government that had been determined to make the dam happen.

A Green Seat at the Table

Bob Brown became the first member of the UTG to be elected, although the party itself had fizzled by that time. Bob had listed himself on the ballot in 1982 as an "Independent Green." In 1986, he was joined by another independent colleague, Gerry Bates, and then in 1989 another three, bringing the total of elected Greens up to five. The five independent Greens then officially formed the Green Party of Tasmania, seen as the successor to the United Tasmania Group.

In the 1989 election, and then again in 1996, neither the Labour Party nor the Liberals were able to elect a majority of members. On both occasions the large parties opted to form a minority government with the support of the Greens rather than choose to work with each other. This was a bit ironic, considering that they probably had far more in common with each other than they did with the Greens. But it finally gave the Greens the seat at the table that their predecessors had been seeking in 1972.

After the 1996 election, the two big parties, frustrated at the fact that they were no longer able to command large majorities due to the popularity of a third party, conspired and passed legislation to reduce the number of seats in the parliament overall. Labour MP David Llewellyn confirmed in a 2011 radio interview that the goal had been to make it harder for the Greens to elect members by reducing the number of seats and making the threshold for election higher. It worked, and in 1998 the Greens were reduced to a single elected member, despite receiving nearly the same percentage of the vote as in the previous election.

Despite the attempts by the "Laborials," as the UTG was originally fond of calling the two big parties, the Tasmanian Green Party has continuously had representation in the Tasmanian Parliament. To date, they still are the only third party to make any sort of dent on the dominance of the Labour and Liberal parties. Members of the Tasmanian Greens also went on to found the federal Green Party of Australia, which has achieved similar success. At the time of this book's writing, the Australian Greens are represented in the Australian House of Representatives, the Australian Senate, and the parliaments of six of the eight Australian states.

They may have failed in their first attempt to stop the flooding of Lake Pedder, but the United Tasmania Group had a lasting impact. They brought down a government, forced the issue of protecting Tasmania's wilderness to go to the Australian Supreme Court and won, and finally got themselves elected and treated as a core element of Australian politics.

"People don't need enormous cars; they need admiration and respect. They don't need a constant stream of new clothes; they need to feel that others consider them to be attractive, and they need excitement and variety and beauty. People don't need electronic entertainment; they need something interesting to occupy their minds and emotions. And so forth. Trying to fill real but nonmaterial needs—for identity, community, self-esteem, challenge, love, joy—with material things is to set up an unquenchable appetite for false solutions to never-satisfied longings. A society that allows itself to admit and articulate its nonmaterial human needs, and to find nonmaterial ways to satisfy them, would require much lower material and energy throughputs and would provide much higher levels of human fulfillment."

(Donella H. Meadows, The Limits to Growth: The 30-Year Update)

ECOLOGICAL PHILOSOPHERS

Not far to the east of Tasmania lies another archipelago, known to its original Maori inhabitants as Aotearoa. In English we call it New Zealand. When most people think of New Zealand, the first thing that comes to mind are its landscapes, made famous as the setting for Middle Earth in the *Lord of the Rings* movies. For such a small country, New Zealand has an amazing variety of biomes, including deciduous forests, savannah grasslands, barren shrublands, mountain ranges, and tundra. Many people living outside of New Zealand and looking at how the country is presented in the media and tourism advertising would assume that environmental stewardship was very important to New Zealanders. So it doesn't surprise many people to learn that the southern nation was where one of the world's first Green parties was born.

However, back in the 1950s and 1960s, New Zealand wasn't famous for its environmental record. It was governed for most of that time by a traditional conservative party, known as the National Party. The story of New Zealand's contribution to Green history begins very similar to Tasmania's: in the 1960s, the National Party government of New Zealand introduced plans to build a power station on Lake Manapouri, which would involve raising the level of the lake by up to thirty meters and joining it with the adjacent Lake Te Anau. By 1970, almost 10 percent of the country's population had signed a "Save Manapouri Lake" petition, but the National Party government still planned on going ahead with the construction.

This is where the stories diverge, because unlike in Tasmania, the future of Lake Manapouri *was* an election issue in the 1972 federal election. The Labour Party, the opposition party in New Zealand's two-party legislature, endorsed the movement to save the lake and made it an election promise. The environmental campaigners had the Labour Party on their side, and thus had no need to form a political party to achieve a specific conservation goal as was occurring in Tasmania at the exact same time. New Zealand was in much better democratic shape than Tasmania and had politicians willing to listen to the campaigners. Even some individual elected politicians within the National Party were supportive of the campaign.

Ecologism

Nevertheless, only two months after the United Tasmania Group formed, a new political movement in New Zealand was also coalescing. There's no evidence that the two parties knew anything about each other when they first formed, although it wasn't long afterward that they became aware of each other and began sharing ideas and literature. The Values Party of New Zealand, formed to contest the 1972 election, are not immediately recognizable as a "Green party" to someone whose only idea of Green parties was that they advocated for the environment. Instead, it was a party that displayed what would later be recognized as the overall political philosophy of the Green movement: the philosophy often called Ecologism.

The 1960s and 1970s are well known as being the decades where anti-systemic thought flourished. These were the decades of "flower power," of anti-Vietnam war peaceniks, of Woodstock, of nuclear bomb testing and Greenpeace, of women's liberation movements, of the Stonewall riots that sparked the gay liberation movement, of civil rights protests in America, of student and worker strikes and the Situationists in France, the Aldermaston marches against nuclear weapons in Britain, and many more events. All of these ideas and more were swirling around the consciousness of New Zealand, having been brought there by the increasing connectedness of the world's information networks. As well, young New Zealanders were travelling and living abroad more than they ever had in the past and bringing back ideas with them when they returned. In the '60s and '70s, it was becoming more and more common and acceptable to critique the way that the world fundamentally worked, and why we decided to make it work that way.

Protest and advocacy organizations were being set up in New Zealand at a rapid pace in these decades. The country's first women's liberation groups began operating in 1970, and New Zealand's gay liberation movement formally began in 1972. Anti-war sentiment was high, and a demonstration in Christchurch against a US plan to operate a nuclear submarine navigation system in the country drew a record protest of over four thousand people in 1968. Apartheid in South Africa, along with the two countries' shared love of the sport of rugby, led to a New Zealand anti-apartheid organization called Halt All Racist Tours that called for a sporting boycott of South Africa in order to force it to stop the racist separation of white and black players into separate teams. Emboldened by oppressed groups in America organizing themselves, the indigenous Maori people of New Zealand were asserting their own rights with language and land campaigns.

Let's Brainstorm

When imagining the birth and growth of new political movements, it's easy to picture a group of young students holed up in a coffee shop or bookstore basement and throwing around radical new ideas. It's a mental picture often associated with Marxism, but it's equally valid for any of the many philosophies that have been born out of university campus brainstorms. On May 30th, 1972, one of these meetings was called by a twenty-four-year-old journalism and political science student named Tony Brunt. He wanted to present a new political idea that he'd been working on turning into a coherent philosophy. The meeting was to be held at the Student Union Hall at Victoria University, and attracted about sixty attendees.

One of the most notable aspects of Green philosophy that sets it apart from other political and economic philosophies is its core focus on "quality of life" as the most important goal. Green philosophy thinks that the most successful nation is the one with the happiest, most content people. Not the richest country, not the most powerful country, not the most productive country, but instead the country that has the best feeling of "well-being."

There are nearly two hundred countries that have membership in the United Nations. Almost all of them share a common metric for determining the success of their nation: the gross domestic product (GDP). The GDP is a measurement, in dollars or other currency, of the market value of all goods and services produced in a particular amount of time within that country. The GDP is the primary way that the world tracks which countries are doing better than others, and thus which countries are seen as the leaders. Various groups of nations such as the G7 (Group of Seven) and the G20 (Group of Twenty) gather together to make decisions about world affairs and they're listened to by the other countries that strive to be as wealthy as they are.

There is only one nation that claims to not concern itself with GDP. In 1979, the King of the small Himalayan country of Bhutan said during an interview, "We do not believe in Gross National Product. Gross National Happiness is more appropriate." The government of Bhutan does indeed attempt to gather data on the overall happiness of its populace to gauge its success. Some critics describe the idea of Gross National Happiness as government propaganda to distract from its human rights issues, but it's still a fascinating idea.

In the first meeting of the Values Party of New Zealand, where Tony Brunt outlined his ideas for a new political movement, it was immediately obvious that the focus was on quality of life rather than on economic productivity. Brunt argued that the system needed to

> stop over-emphasizing economic growth, technological advance, the importance of consumer goods in our lives, increasing productivity, competition between people, individualism, and increasing profits. (Dann, 1999, page 257)

This idea of *not* putting "growth" on a pedestal as the sacred goal of civilization is what sets Green political thought apart. The most capitalist right-wing party and the most socialist left-wing party will both claim that their philosophies are the ones that will most quickly and effectively lead to economic growth. This is because both agree that "growth" is the goal of an economy. You will rarely see a Green politician claiming that their approach will lead to growth, since part of the core philosophy is that growth is not something to be worshipped and attained at any cost. Growth can be encouraged in areas where we're absolutely sure that it will lead to a better quality of life, but should never be a goal for its own sake. And it should always be understood that we live inside a system that has limits on growth, and that ignoring those limits will only lead us (or our descendants) into destruction. After all, we can't have infinite growth on a finite planet.

Tony Brunt, at the first meeting of what was soon to be called the Values Party of New Zealand, outlined his ideas for how a society should organize itself and what he saw as the most immediate concerns for New Zealand. Ideas included bulldozing the country's new maximum-security prison and rethinking the entire law and order policy, reducing display advertising that feeds into the worship of growth and materialism, restricting the usage of cars in cities, beautifying cities with more greenery and indigenous art, increasing youth participation in parliament, increasing foreign aid, and severing ties with countries performing nuclear weapons tests in the Pacific Ocean. Very little of this initial speech was actually dedicated to the environment, but it was still an important part of the equation. Brunt, in 1972, said:

> Fighting pollution and preserving nature are key planks in the Values Party platform and I don't think the Government is taking strong enough action in this area, but reducing pollution is only a small part of the attempt to increase the quality of life. (Dann, 1999, page 263)

Brunt's speech and ideas proved popular, and the burgeoning movement quickly attracted like-minded people. Brunt had announced that he intended to stand for election in his home electoral district of Island Bay, and others began to contact him offering both their support and their willingness to run as candidates in New Zealand's other districts. Norman Smith, an early organizer, contacted the New Zealand Broadcasting Corporation (the state broadcasting authority) and informed them that the new party would require advertising time since they would be fielding twenty-five candidates. The Broadcasting Corporation at the time thought this was a hilarious joke. By the time the election writ dropped, the Values Party had confirmed candidates in forty-two districts, out of a possible eighty-seven.

A Green Blueprint

The party also produced a manifesto, entitled *"Blueprint for New Zealand: An Alternative Future."* This was very likely named after the influential *"Blueprint for Survival,"* a recent and pivotal edition of *The Ecologist* which argued for a radically restructured society in order to prevent "the breakdown of society and the irreversible disruption of the life-support systems on this planet." The first printing of the manifesto sold out within the week and the new party found itself ordering reprint after reprint.

The group found itself getting attention in the media as well. First, a group of professional filmmakers volunteered to donate their time and effort to produce a television ad. Then an important local current affairs programme, *"Gallery,"* produced a twelve-minute party profile that aired on primetime network television. Brunt even received a personal message from native New Zealander Sir Edmund Hillary. Hillary and his climbing partner Tenzing Norgay were the first two people to reach the summit of Mount Everest, which made him a national hero. In the message Hillary remarked, "I do agree with many of your contentions. As to whether there is the interest and will in New Zealand to carry out such programs, time alone will tell."

The party was also contacted by representatives from the women's liberation movement, Homosexual Law Reform Society, Wellington Tenants Protection Society, United Nations Association, the Abortion Law Reform Association of New Zealand, and more. Many of the contacts wanted information on the party's stance on civil rights and liberties issues, since the policies that the party was proposing—full decriminalization of homosexuality and a more liberal abortion policy—were not in any of the other party platforms.

The Values Party was a very youth-dominated movement. In fact, the average age of its candidates for the 1972 election was twenty-nine. Most of them had no political experience whatsoever. This was on display in the way that the party advertised itself in the election campaign which some described as "street theatre." Their attention-grabbing strategies included going to an auto show and prostrating themselves in front of the expensive display cars to satirize devotion to materialism as well as having supporters dressed as coins and dollar bills chasing each other down main streets. Candidates launched their campaigns with rock shows, and Tony Brunt himself regularly drew massive crowds anywhere he went to speak.

Because it was new and youth dominated, the party was able to innovate in its usage of media. Its techniques were novel in getting the attention of voters who didn't feel connected to the traditional political parties. In 1978, the party chair Dave Woodhams reflected, "Political action is theatre on the grand scale. With the right script, the right setting and the right issue, a creative group of people can command the attention of the media, and bring to life an issue that would be dead if handled by the usual press statement routine." (Dann, 1999, page 280)

When the election day arrived in November of 1972, the Values Party had signed up candidates in nearly half of the electoral districts in the country. Unfortunately, like their neighbours the United Tasmania Group, their surge in popularity didn't result in actually electing anyone. Unlike in Tasmania where the electoral system made it more possible to elect independents or members from small parties, in New Zealand it did not. New Zealand in 1972 used the same method of electing representatives that Canada, the US, and the UK currently use. This meant that the 1972 election, like most elections before it, returned only members for the dominant two parties.

But the success that the Values Party did have was important, and historic. The party's candidates got a combined twenty-seven thousand votes across the country. Each of New Zealand's eighty-seven electoral districts contained about fifteen thousand voters. The party had enough voters to completely fill two electoral districts, if only they'd all happened to live in the same place. But they didn't. They were spread throughout the country, which meant that the small number of votes that Values Party candidates got in each district amounted to nothing.

Blocked by the System

This is the great difficulty that Green parties, or most new parties, have to face when they run in an election under a "first-past-the-post" system. The best way to elect someone in a first-past-the-post election is to dominate a single, very limited geographic area. This usually means that any new party that breaks through is hyper-focused on a specific regional issue, and irrelevant to the rest of the country. The Values Party wasn't trying to be a regional issues party. It was trying to reach educated, young, and progressive voters across all of New Zealand.

In Canada we have a party called the Bloc Quebecois, which only runs candidates in Quebec and advocates for Quebec sovereignty and the strengthening of French culture and Quebec issues. In the 2008 Canadian federal election, 10 percent of Canadians cast their vote for Bloc Quebecois candidates. The Bloc was only running candidates in the seventy-five Quebec districts, and didn't participate in the other 233 across the rest of Canada. They managed to win in forty-nine of the limited districts in which they ran candidates.

Meanwhile, in the same election, 18 percent of Canadians voted for candidates from the New Democratic Party (NDP); nearly twice the number of voters supported the NDP than had

CHAPTER 1 – THE FIRST GREEN PARTIES

supported the Bloc. However, the NDP was running candidates in all 308 districts, and only won in thirty-seven of them. With nearly double the number of voters across the nation, the NDP had elected far fewer members than the regionally focused Bloc Quebecois.

In that election the Green Party of Canada elected no one, despite their candidates receiving the votes of nearly 7 percent of Canadian voters. They had broad support but couldn't win any individual district. The Values Party had the same problem as the Canadian Greens: it had widespread popularity across the nation, but not enough in any particular region to be the dominant choice of the local voters.

The march forward of the Values Party would continue despite their unsuccessful first attempt at achieving electoral success. The party contested the next election in 1975 and tripled its vote share after running candidates in every district, but again failed to elect anyone. They also contested elections in 1978, 1981, 1984, and 1987 with a similar lack of success. The party did have some victories at the local level, electing members to the councils of cities around New Zealand. Tony Brunt himself served as a City Councillor in Wellington from 1974-1980, and Helen Smith, the first person elected on the Values ticket, remained a Councillor in Porirua (a Wellington suburb) from 1973 until 2001.

By the end of the 1980s, the Values Party was declining in support and interest. They were discouraged by their lack of success and their inability to crack through the ceiling imposed by the country's electoral system. But in 1990, there was a resurgence of support when the remnants of The Values Party merged with a number of other environmental groups to form the Green Party of Aotearoa New Zealand. In the subsequent election, their vote share climbed to nearly 7 percent.

The following year, the new Green Party joined with four other minor political parties (the Democrats, Liberals, Mana Motuhake, and NewLabour) into an electoral coalition named the Alliance. Their goal was to band together in order to break through the first-past-the-post electoral barrier by avoiding the splitting of the "anti-establishment vote" between their various parties. Their plan worked, and the new Alliance party achieved over 18 percent of the vote in the 1993 election. Even with this much higher level of support they only managed to elect two members. But it was the first time they'd cracked through first-past-the-post.

Alongside this election, New Zealanders were being asked a very important question. Back in 1985, the Labour Party government had started investigating whether New Zealand should switch away from the first-past-the-post system and adopt a proportional representation system like the one used in Tasmania and most of the rest of the world. This might seem noble, but they were looking into it for selfish reasons. In both 1978 and 1981, the Labour Party had actually gotten *fewer* seats than the National Party even though *more* New Zealanders across the country had voted for Labour Party candidates. This bizarre result is relatively common under first-past-the-post. It has happened in Canada on multiple occasions, and is currently the case in the province of New Brunswick.

During the 1993 election, New Zealand held a referendum on if they should switch electoral systems. It was included alongside the election ballot for every voter to mark their preference. A majority of voters agreed that they would like to change to the new system.

Finally, Political Success

The 1996 election was the first in the country's history in which voters could be confident that their vote wouldn't go to waste. Somewhat surprisingly, the Green Party decided to remain part of the Alliance. The relationship was still good, and they didn't want to ruin their chances by breaking away too soon. Among the thirteen Members of Parliament elected by the Alliance in 1996 were three Greens, including co-leaders Jeanette Fitzsimons and Rod Donald who had both been former members of the Values Party. The successor to the Values Party had finally made it into Parliament.

For the 1999 election, the Green Party split off from the Alliance to stand as its own party and increased its caucus to seven members. The party's number of elected representatives has fluctuated between six and fourteen in the elections since then.

The Greens are currently the fourth largest party in the New Zealand legislature, behind the National and Labour parties and the New Zealand First Party. After the 2017 election, the Greens agreed to support a Labour Party and New Zealand First coalition government in something called a "confidence-and-supply agreement." This is the same type of agreement that the Green Party of British Columbia entered into after the 2017 provincial election in BC. The agreement signed by the BC Green Party and the BC New Democratic Party was even modelled after the agreement produced by the New Zealand Greens.

It took several decades, and even a change in the country's electoral system, for the Values Party to get any traction. But they did finally get there, and no one would dispute that the Green Party of New Zealand is now a core element of New Zealand politics.

Retrospectives on Their Parties' Histories

In researching the history of these two parties, I spoke with Bob Brown, the Australian Senator and Green leader who led the opposition to the Franklin Dam, and Mike Ward, a New Zealand artist who helped found the Values Party, as well as serving as its final leader before it became the Green Party of New Zealand. Mike was later elected with the Green Party of New Zealand and served as a member of parliament between 2002 and 2005.

These days, Bob is retired from being a professional politician and instead works for his own non-profit, the Bob Brown Foundation. With his foundation, he advocates for the same

CHAPTER 1 – THE FIRST GREEN PARTIES

environmental issues that he's spent his life working on. He's still not above getting himself arrested either. In 2016, he was arrested after refusing to leave the Lapoinya Forest in his home of Tasmania, where he was protesting logging. He's also been writing his own books and memoirs about his long life of political and advocacy work. I'd highly recommend his book *Optimism: Reflections on a Life of Action*, which is a number of small vignettes throughout his life, including many from his time in the United Tasmania Group. It also includes the letter that he sent to his parents from his jail cell after his arrest. The top of the letter states that it is being sent from "Her Majesty's Prison," and Bob cheerfully begins the letter with:

> Please disregard the above address as it is only temporary. But I wouldn't mind staying longer: the food is extra good (chops and vegetables for tea tonight, corn silverside etc. for lunch). So is the company—there are 48 in the yard where my cell is, all arrested on the river and fine people from all walks of life. (2015, page 54)

He also explains how the young policeman who arrested him was so nervous that he nearly fell in the river, and Bob had to grab his hand to prevent him from toppling in.

Bob is the exact sort of character that you'd expect to come from a party that began over an environmental conservation campaign, and Mike Ward is likewise the exact person you'd expect to come from a counterculture party formed around the ideas of post-materialism and anti-industrialism. Mike is an artist through-and-through, and while asking him about his history in Green politics he focused on his attempts to get people to put value into the non-material aspects of our world. Mike wants humanity to find more worth in art, music, and creativity than it does in wealth and productivity.

Mike is an optimist and a revolutionary. I asked him about his political philosophy and what he felt needed to be done to get our society on track. Even forty-five years after the Values Party's founding, in 2017, his answer reflected their original goals: "We need to be collaborative, urgent, optimistic, and creative."

In discussing what sets Greens apart, Mike focused on the common desire among Greens to have collaborative politics, find common ground, and come together to produce the best ideas rather than just attempting to tear down anyone who comes from a different party. He stressed the urgency of climate change and of how fast we're depleting the world's resources. And his belief is that we need to maintain our optimism that change *can* still happen and that humans are creative and inventive enough to fix our problems.

Mike wants to fundamentally realign what people find important in their lives. Bob does as well. Greens see our world as being focused solely on material possessions, on economic growth at all costs, and on the accumulation of wealth. The major philosophical concept that draws all Greens together is this opposition to the worship of the industrial way of life.

Bob even goes so far as to suggest that the worship of growth and materialism is the real dominant religion in the world. In his book, he writes:

> Materialism worships the god Growth and, as with most cults, thrives on fear. The high priests of Materialism warn that nothing so dreadful awaits us as the anti-Growth of an economic downturn, bringing with it the punishment of unemployment, poverty and social upheaval . . .
>
> Materialism accepts and happily incorporates earlier religions - as long as they reject frightful ideas like wealth being sinful, and stories like the one of Jesus upturning the businessmen's tables outside the Temple in Jerusalem. Growth incorporates the old gods by rewriting their scriptures. The Golden Rule is out…
>
> It is worshipped by, and cossets most ardently, the wealthiest people. They are the chosen ones. And, paralleling earlier belief systems, the high priests of Materialism excoriate those with the least wealth for their obvious personal failure to uphold Growth . . .
>
> Just as earthquakes, typhoons and massacres presented a problem for those promoting the earlier almighty god of love, so belief in the supreme saving grace of Growth requires faith over logic. The core problem of faith over fact is Earth itself. It is a Growth-stopper simply because it is finite. (2015, page 57)

CHAPTER 2

WHO ARE THE GREENS?

"Only economists still put the cart before the horse by claiming that the growing turmoil of mankind can be eliminated if prices are right. The truth is that only if our values are right will prices also be so."

(Nicholas Georgescu-Roegen, one of the fathers of the field of ecological economics)

WHO ARE THE GREENS?

One of the most important things that a political party can do in order to win elections is to know who its voters are. Political parties devote huge amounts of money towards creating a profile of their supporters and commission numerous studies and reports to try to determine who these people are and how to reach them. If a party knows the type of people who are likely to vote for them, then they can target those demographics with outreach, advertisements, and get-out-the-vote campaigns.

Green parties, of course, have done this research for themselves, as well. In my home of Canada where we divide the country up into distinct geographic electoral districts, knowing who our voters are means knowing where we should focus our resources. The Green Party of Canada simply doesn't have enough money to run a fully funded campaign in each one of Canada's 338 individual electoral districts. The party must choose in which parts of the country to invest its limited party funds. Green leader Elizabeth May moved from one side of the country to the other in order to run in a district that had specifically been identified as "winnable," and the research paid off when she was elected as Canada's first Green member of parliament.

So we have a fairly good idea of who Green voters actually are. We know what segments of the population they belong to, what unites them, which factors have an effect on a Green supporter, and which factors have no effect whatsoever. In the scholarly work *Green Parties in Europe,* author Emilie van Haute presents a profile of Green voters in Europe. The study sampled nearly twenty thousand voters from fifteen European nations to find what Greens in different countries have in common.

The study examined four sets of variables.

First, it looked at socio-demographic characteristics, meaning age, gender, education, religiousness, and occupation.

Second, it looked at the political preferences of the respondents. The researchers asked how people feel about government intervention in economics and inequality and how much the government should interfere in progressive cultural issues such a same-sex marriage. They asked about the importance of environmental issues, whether respondents prefer a government that's more libertarian or more authoritarian, and how they feel about immigration.

Third, it studied people's social and political activism. It determined how active they were in casual social groups as well as in organized social or political groups. It studied how active they were in organizations such as unions and protest groups.

Finally, it studied the respondents' trust towards politics and government institutions, their satisfaction on the current state of politics, and their general interest in political issues.

The study found several factors that are highly predictive of a person being a Green voter. It also found numerous factors that have no predictive effect at all. It gives us a general profile about who an average Green voter likely is, although it should be obvious that this is only an average. Like any political movement, Green voters are still quite diverse.

The Profile of a Green Supporter

The socio-economic factors are some of the clearest for identifying Green voters. The study confirmed what most Green parties already know: that their voters tend to be younger, higher educated, and urban. They're probably less religious than the average person, and more likely to be women. Green voters are more likely to be found in urban districts with a highly educated population. Green political organizations tend to have more women and more young, educated people than other political organizations. The study didn't find much when it looked at respondents' occupations. Self-employed individuals are slightly more likely to vote Green than average, and the unemployed less likely. Other occupation factors were unclear, with no significant discoveries.

The second factor, the issue-based indicators, are even more clear. Voters that care about environmental issues are more likely to vote for a Green party, although this should be obvious. Green voters are also more culturally liberal and progressive, and more pro-immigration. When the researchers looked at the scale of libertarianism versus authoritarianism, they found that Greens were more libertarian. This libertarian streak among Greens, paired with their cultural progressivism, is a key distinguisher between Greens and other parties. Labour and socialist parties tend to be culturally progressive, but are usually more authoritarian. Meanwhile, conservative parties tend to be more libertarian, but are less culturally progressive. Greens form a third option: culturally progressive, but anti-authoritarian. Greens take great pride in describing themselves as grassroots, favour decision-making from the bottom up, and promote devolving power down to the local level as much as possible.

The data from the third variable (the respondents' degree of activism and interest in politics) surprised the researchers. Most of the responses showed little correlation, or even went against the hypotheses of the pollsters. They did correctly predict that Green voters are more likely to be engaged in "unconventional forms of participation" such as signing petitions, wearing campaign badges and stickers, publicly protesting and demonstrating, and engaging in boycotts. Green voters are also less likely to engage in traditional political participation such as becoming a party member, joining a union, or working actively on a political campaign. What surprised the scientists was that Green voters are *less* likely to be interested in politics in general. The scientists suggest that this shows that Green voters are not as interested in general conventional politics but instead mobilize around specific "niche" issues that they care about.

Lastly, on the issues of trust and satisfaction with governments, the study showed little connection with the Green vote. The researchers interpreted this as showing that Green parties have lost some of their status as the party for "protest voting," although readers should remember that this study was done on voters in Europe, not Canada. It's far easier to elect Green party members under the electoral systems used in Europe than under our Canadian system, so many European Green parties are no longer seen as "protest parties."

This combined data gives us the picture of an average *European* Green voter. They're probably young, probably educated, living in an urban area, and more likely to be a woman. They're probably not actively engaged in politics or a political organization, but feel strongly about several specific issues and are more willing to protest, boycott, sign petitions, and visibly support groups advocating for these issues. They're socially progressive, but could be considered somewhat left-libertarian, favouring decision-making distributed to lower levels rather than top-down from an authoritarian government.

Canadian Green Supporters

The profile covered above was done on Green voters across Europe, but it's likely that the profile of a Canadian Green supporter is relatively similar. Unfortunately, we haven't had a study of the Canadian Green parties that was as deep as the ones conducted in Europe. We do, however, have a study conducted in 2005 by Simon Fraser University Professor Cara Camcastle. Cara's study was of the Green Party of Canada's official members, as well as supporters that had provided the party with their contact information over the years. It didn't include regular voters who've voted for Green candidates but aren't formally associated with the party.

She found a few interesting bits of data. Green Party of Canada members were considerably more likely to have a university degree and more likely to have finished high school when compared to any other Canadian political party. When compared to the general population, Green members were much more likely to work in science or artistic fields, and much less likely to be in retail, sales, and trades work. The distribution between those that were self-employed, privately employed, or working in the public sector was fairly even, and was similar to the breakdown for the Liberal Party of Canada. This contrasted with the NDP, which attracted a lot of public sector employees, and the Canadian Alliance and Progressive Conservative parties, which attracted a lot of self-employed members.

She also asked the members several questions about their beliefs and priorities. Three quarters of respondents wanted more power to be devolved to cities and municipalities, rather than to be held by the provinces and the federal government. This is a position usually associated with the political right wing, and to Conservative parties. Likewise, when asked about how much role they wanted business and government to have in the economy, Green members answered similarly to members of the Canadian Liberal Party. When asked about their priorities for government spending, the members answered environmental issues first, then education, and then healthcare.

One of Cara's biggest takeaways from the survey was that she placed the Green Party of Canada's members somewhere in the centre of Canada's political spectrum. They weren't just a fractured wing of the NDP that was more concerned with the environment, as they are often portrayed. Instead, the Greens seemed to align in values with each of Canada's other political parties in different ways, making them difficult to categorize using our traditional political spectrum. But the biggest difference was that 96 percent of members that responded to her survey could be identified as post-materialists, or at least partially post-materialists. This means that they placed more value on ideas such as self-expression, quality of life, equality, and autonomy rather than materialist economic concerns.

In my time in politics, I can think of a lot of Green party supporters and members who meet this description. But I can also think of a lot who don't. Studies like these don't tell us exactly who Greens are. They just tell who they're more likely to be. In the real world, the Green coalition is broad and diverse and can't be pigeonholed into any one class or demographic. But these studies do tell Greens who they're currently managing to reach and who is most receptive to their message. It also shows them who they need to try harder to reach, and who they're failing to communicate with.

Finding a way to pitch your message to the whole diversity of humanity is challenging. There are parts of the population that Greens have clearly managed to reach, but there are far more people who don't understand what Greens want and what they're trying to do.

"The politics of the Industrial Age, left, right, and centre, is like a three-lane motorway, with different vehicles in different lanes, but all heading in the same direction. Greens feel that it is the very direction that is wrong, rather than the choice of any one lane in preference to the others. It is our perception that the motorway of industrialism inevitably leads to the abyss—hence our decision to get off it, and seek an entirely different direction."

(Sir Jonathon Porritt, 1984)

THE IDEA OF ECOLOGISM

Green political thought is an established field in political theory, and has been studied and written about and bound into large, expensive political textbooks and collections of essays. Andrew Dobson is one of the political writers who has tried to define Green politics and has had a long career as a professor of politics, political theory, and environmental politics at Keele University in England. His book, *Green Political Thought*, outlines in detail the ideology of Ecologism.

Ecologism is one of the names that political theorists give to the ideology of Green parties and Green thinkers. Andrew Dobson is also adamant that environmentalism and Ecologism are very different ideas. In his words:

> Environmentalism argues for a managerial approach to environmental problems, secure in the belief that they can be solved without fundamental changes in present values of patterns of production and consumption . . .
>
> Ecologism holds that a sustainable and fulfilling existence presupposes radical changes in our relationship with the non-human natural world, and in our mode of social and political life. (2007, page 2-3)

This places Ecologism as a distinct political ideology in the same way that Liberalism, Conservatism, Socialism, or Communism are distinct ideologies. Not all people who would consider themselves environmentalists would also consider themselves Ecologists. There can be environmentalist conservatives, and environmentalist socialists, but it becomes more difficult to merge Ecologism itself with the other major global political ideologies. This is why it's frustrating for many Greens when the media and the public insist on placing Greens somewhere along the left-right political spectrum. For those people who are truly Ecologists and not just environmentalists, the similarities between conservative and socialist parties are *greater* than their difference. In other words, Ecologists see these traditional parties as having more in common with *each other* than they do with the Greens.

Jonathon Porritt, the British Ecologist and Green philosopher, says the following about the dominant conservative and socialist ideologies:

Both are dedicated to industrial growth, to the expansion of the means of production, to a materialist ethic as the best means of meeting people's needs, and to unimpeded technological development. Both rely on increasing centralisation and large-scale bureaucratic control and coordination. From a viewpoint of narrow scientific rationalism, both insist that the planet is there to be conquered, that big is self-evidently beautiful, and that what cannot be measured is of no importance. (Finlayson, 2003, page 382)

Popular media and political commentators like using the spectrum of left-wing and right-wing politics and try to place every party somewhere between these two poles. Nándor Tánczos, who was elected as an MP with the Green Party of New Zealand, prefers to imagine a political triangle rather than a two-sided political spectrum. Nándor was a strange sight in the parliament of New Zealand when he was first elected in 1999. He's a dreadlocked Rastafarian skateboarder, with university degrees in psychology, sociology, permaculture, and sustainable land management. He's not the type of person that you'd find anywhere along the traditional political spectrum.

> A left / right continuum is simply incapable of representing Green politics. Our most defining issues don't figure on it at all and neither are the solutions to them a simple application of any one ideology, whether ecosocialism or green capitalism. Both the left and the right have valuable contributions to make to this discussion, but more important for the Greens is the opportunity to articulate uniquely Green solutions as the third point in a left / right / green triangle. (Nándor Tánczos, personal blog, 2017)

The classic struggle between the political right and the political left is about how best to achieve high productivity, not about whether the production of "stuff" itself is a value to be championed. For Ecologists, the biggest issue isn't whether the collective or the individual owns the means of production; rather, it's if production itself should be encouraged in our society.

CHAPTER 2 – WHO ARE THE GREENS?

Ecologism vs. Liberalism, Conservatism, Socialism

It is possible, however, to contrast Ecologism with other major ideologies, and to find places where there's agreement and space to work together. Andrew Dobson devotes a chapter of "Green Political Thought" to some very in-depth comparisons of Ecologism with conservatism, classical liberalism, and socialism. His writings show how Ecologism can draw in people who previously connected to different ideologies, and how their previous ideological stances draw them to different parts of Green political philosophy.

Liberalism champions the ideas of personal freedom, limited government, strong civil liberties, free markets, and private property. This makes it difficult to square with Ecologism. Liberalism values individualism, the pursuit of private gain, and market freedoms, which contrast with Ecologism and its calls for personal responsibility, collective good, and economic intervention and restrictions to achieve the betterment of all. Those Liberals who try to blend their ideology with Ecologism often adopt the compromise of social Liberalism and economic Ecologism. They value ecological issues but want to find "market solutions" to solve them while still preserving their values of economic and individual freedom. They try to find the most Liberal and "hands-off" methods of achieving these goals. These ideas and solutions are argued in such works as "Green Liberalism" by Dutch Professor Marcel Wissenburg and "The Intelligent Person's Guide to Liberalism" by Conrad Russell, a Liberal Democrat member of Britain's House of Lords.

Green political thought and Conservatism can find common ground as well, although this tends to surprise many Canadians. This is mostly because Conservatism in the Western world has been steadily moving away from what philosophers consider to be "classical" Conservatism by its original definition. Conservatives in Canada and America have largely embraced Neoliberalism in addition to their conservative roots. If we remove the ideology of Neoliberalism from the equation and look at original Conservative values, it becomes easier to find some common ground with Green philosophy.

Classical Conservatism is based around values of tradition, hierarchy, authority, and human imperfection. There are a couple of areas in which Green and Conservative thinking can align, one of which being the fallibility of humans and the need for humans to recognize their own limitations. Conservatives are often skeptical of what they call "large-scale social experiments," and similarly, Greens tend to favour a precautionary approach to new technological and social ideas that we may not fully understand. John Gray, a British political philosopher who seeks to unite Conservatism and Ecologism, says:

> Many of the central conceptions of traditional conservatism have a natural congruence with Green concerns: the... idea of the social contract, not as an agreement among anonymous ephemeral individuals, but as a compact between the

generations of the living, the dead, and those yet unborn; Tory skepticism about progress, and awareness of its ironies and illusions; conservative resistance to untried novelty and large-scale social experiments; and, perhaps most especially, the traditional conservative tenet that individual flourishing can occur only in the context of forms of common life. (Dobson, 2007, page 160)

The words "conservatism" and "conservation" have the same roots. Likewise, there should be ways for Conservatives and Greens to find common ground. Conservatives care deeply about conserving traditional ways of life, and this is something they share with Greens. They just often disagree on which parts of our society and world we should be conserving and which parts we should be letting go of and embracing progress.

Fiscal Conservatism concerns itself with the balancing of budgets as one of government's main responsibilities. A common justification is that if we're spending more money than we currently have, then we're forcing future generations to repay that money. Conservatives see that as irresponsible and unfair to our descendants. Greens tend to agree, but take it further. They also see the world as having an "ecological budget." By consuming more resources now than the Earth is able to replenish, we're stealing the prosperity of future generations. We're taking more than our fair share in the present, and leaving the repercussions to our grandchildren.

Bringing conservatives into ecological thinking remains difficult, as in the current world most Green parties tend to draw their support from those previously engaged in more left-wing thinking. This leads to Green Conservatives sometimes feeling out of place and not listened to in modern Green parties. Climate-change denial has also taken hold in the conservative movements of many countries, which makes them natural opponents of Ecological thinking.

Eco-socialism is the attempt to combine Ecologism and Socialism. It is probably the most common attempt to merge Green thinking with another major political ideology. However, many difficulties and differences still appear between the two ideologies. In fact, many Green activists and campaigners have experienced anger and frustration directed at them from Socialists. The friction mostly comes from the belief among Socialists that the goals of Ecologists will come about as a result of the goals of Socialists. Eco-socialists believe that once the capitalist system is dismantled and the power restored to the common people, Green goals of environmental sustainability will naturally occur as people are freed from the greed that capitalism perpetuates.

Greens tend to be skeptical of this claim. They stress the similarities between capitalist and socialist countries, in that both believe that maximizing production is the best way to address the needs of their populations. To many Ecologists, Socialism isn't the cure for capitalist-greed. It's just another way to achieve the same desires. Greens also see socialists as being so laser-focused on equalization between the rich and the poor that ecological issues will always be relegated to a backseat position. By the time the class system is abolished and Socialists are ready to address ecological issues, it may be too late.

Regardless of the differences between Green ideologies and other ideologies around the world, one of the main tenets of Green philosophy has been the need for diverse people with diverse ideas to work together for the common good. Realistically, Green parties know that they're unlikely to be suddenly given a majority government and the ability to enact their policies without opposition. Even if they were, they'd likely be concerned for their own integrity, since Greens commonly believe that power inevitably corrupts those that have it. Therefore, they've embraced collective decision-making and compromise as a way to advance their ideas. Throughout the history of Green parties serving in governments, they have worked alongside Socialists in so-called red–green governments, Conservatives in blue–green governments, and in broad rainbow-coalitions with multiple parties including Liberals, Conservatives, Socialists, and more.

Ecological Economics and the Steady-State Economy

The idea of a "steady-state economy" could fill an entire book, and it has in fact filled many. If you're interested in delving into all the myriad of ways that our world would change in an economy that is committed to *not* growing, then I'd recommend "Prosperity without Growth" by Tim Jackson as the closest thing that the sustainability movement has to a gospel, or "Enough Is Enough" by Rob Dietz and Dan O'Neill as a more practical and accessible guide to what effect these ideas would have on our lives and how we would go about enacting them. British economist Kate Raworth has also been trying to find ways to simply and clearly explain post-growth ideas to a mass audience, and in 2017 she published "Doughnut Economics: Seven Ways to Think Like a 21st Century Economist."

The simple summary is that our world currently has more people living on it than it can handle, given our rate of consumption of resources. Our current economic system is based around the idea that our economy will keep growing each year, and in fact *requires* our economy to continuously grow to prevent the entire system from failing. This economic system is unsustainable because our planet is not growing any bigger, and more resources are not magically appearing for us to remove from the planet and to turn into goods. The opposite is true, and we know it. The steady-state economy idea calls for a new economic model that *isn't* based around pursuing growth. This seems to many to be a pretty radical idea. It would require massive overhauls of how our societal and economic systems are designed to work. But if we don't undertake these changes, our economy is eventually going to fail catastrophically when we reach a point where the planet just doesn't have enough space or resources for us to continue growing.

In "Enough Is Enough", Dietz and O'Neill refer to some calculations about how many humans the Earth could sustain, based on how many resources these people consume. They quote the Worldwatch Institute, whose calculations suggest that the planet could sustain 13.6 billion people if they were all living at the same rate of consumption as low-income individuals in what's usually called the "third world," but only 1.4 billion people living at the level of consumption of the average American. The actual population of humans on Earth is currently over seven billion, and the United Nations has predicted that it will rise as high as twelve billion by the year 2100. Obviously, this presents a problem.

This doesn't mean that those of us not living in rural poverty need to divest ourselves of all belongings and technology and "return to the caves," as opponents of a sustainable economy often accuse us of wanting. Quite the opposite. Advocates for the steady-state economy worry that we'll all be stuck living in caves once we burn through the Earth's stock of resources without a plan on how to live without them. If we want to maintain our comfort and way of life, it means that we need to change the way we structure our economy very soon so that it doesn't rely on constantly growing, because if we don't then we will inevitably destroy our own way of life. In other words: if we want things to stay the same, then things are going to have to change.

GDP Myths and Tricks

I mentioned in the first chapter how the world currently judges the success of countries based on their GDP (gross domestic product), and on how much growth there is in the GDP each year. At first glance, the GDP seems like a reasonable way to score countries against each other, since surely the country that is generating more income for its citizens will be better off, right? However, the more you look at how GDP works and what it actually measures, the more you see how inadequate it is as a method for judging the actual well-being of people.

For instance, in 2017, the country in mainland Africa with the highest per capita GDP (the total GDP, divided by the total population) was the tiny nation of Equatorial Guinea. Equatorial Guinea is very easy to miss on a map, as it's sandwiched in between Gabon and Cameroon in the west of the continent, very close to the equator. The country itself is about the size of Montenegro in Europe, or the American state of Massachusetts. It has a population of just over a million people, three-quarters of whom are living on less than a dollar a day. Equatorial Guinea is known as one of the most unequal countries in the world, and its regime is often cited alongside other more obviously corrupt governments like those in North Korea or Somalia. Even though Equatorial Guinea's GDP is the highest in Africa, nearly all of that money is concentrated in the hands of an extremely small group of fabulously wealthy and powerful individuals, with the vast majority of the population living in abject poverty.

CHAPTER 2 – WHO ARE THE GREENS?

GDP has many problems that make it a terrible way to determine a country's success. As in Equatorial Guinea, GDP doesn't differentiate between whom the money is going to. If more money is being made then GDP goes up, even if that money is all going towards a small group. Many things that make society objectively worse can make GDP increase, as well. If a major oil spill happens and large amounts of money are spent on clean-up efforts, then that spent money increases the GDP. If a family breaks apart and incurs costly legal fees to resolve their disputes, that spent money contributes to GDP. If a burglar breaks my window, and I then pay to have it repaired, GDP goes up.

GDP also encourages us to do things that aren't necessary, all in the name of growth. If I stay home from work to care for my own children, GDP does not go up. However, if I pay someone else to care for my children while I work, GDP increases. It might bring me joy to spend time and effort raising my kids, but if I did so, I wouldn't be able to create an increase in the GDP. It's possible that some of the things that we've stopped doing ourselves in the name of GDP growth are positive things that would help our mental health and well-being.

Likewise, the obsession with GDP and growth means that if I invent a way to do something twice as quickly and efficiently, that doesn't mean that I'm now going to have to work half as much and thus have more time for hobbies and family. Our growth obsession means that the incentive is for me to work the same amount, but to produce twice as much instead. Would it make me happier and more content with my life to produce twice as much? Or would I gain greater happiness from more free time to spend on the things I love? Only one of these options adds to the GDP, and therefore only one is encouraged by our economic system.

Tracking a country's success based on the growth of its economy and GDP doesn't tell us about a lot of the things that we *should* be considering. It doesn't tell us anything about if the people living in that country are getting happier. It doesn't tell us if they're getting healthier, if they're living better lives, if they're spending their time doing activities that they want to be doing, if they feel safe, if they feel fulfilled, or if they feel confident about the future. All it tells us is that more money is being produced. Of course, when people have more money, many aspects of their lives may get better. If you're struggling to feed and provide shelter for your family, then more money is going to make you much happier. But at some point, enough becomes enough, and the pattern of well-being rising with GDP slows down or even stops. If you aren't meeting all your basic needs, then it's important to have more. But if all your basic needs are met, then what is it that you really want more of?

> In the face of the fabulous promises of economic growth, at the beginning of the 21st century we are confronted by an awful fact. Despite high and sustained levels of economic growth in the West over a period of 50 years—growth that has seen average real incomes increase several times over—the mass of people are no more satisfied with their lives now than they were then. (Clive Hamilton, 2003, page 3)

What Do We Need to Measure?

There are other metrics that can be used to chart the well-being of an economy and of a society. One such alternative is the GPI, the genuine progress indicator. The GPI attempts to include the costs associated with economic growth into the calculation of the GDP, so that the number we generate accurately tells us if the well-being of the people is increasing or decreasing. The GPI factors in things like income inequality; unemployment; the costs of water, air, and noise pollution; the loss of wetlands, farmlands, and forests; the costs of CO_2 emissions and ozone depletion; and the costs of crime, family dysfunction, commuting, and loss of leisure time. Obviously, many of these factors are very challenging to quantify and come up with concrete numbers to represent. Critics argue that they're subjective, and that we can't assign a number to them and therefore we can't measure them. No one ever said it would be easy. But as Herman Daly said in "Ecological Economics: Principles and Applications",

> Even if we can never quantify [satisfaction or happiness] . . . as precisely as we currently quantify GNP (gross national product) . . . perhaps it is better to be vaguely right than precisely wrong. (2003, page 234)

Regardless of how we try to measure progress, if the growth that we are measuring is only the growth of the "productivity" of the economy then we are eventually going to hit a wall. The economy takes place inside the environment. When our economy grows too big to fit inside the environment, it will halt. Advocates of the steady-state economy suggest that there is a point where "enough is enough," where any further growth produces more negatives than it does positives. Therefore, any sectors pursuing growth should also be sure that it leads to an increase in the well-being and life satisfaction of people rather than just growth for the sake of growth itself. If that growth will eventually lead to a depletion of resources, then it needs to be re-evaluated. A steady-state economy is one that does *not need* to grow in order to be successful, and it would only pursue growth in sectors that it knows are both sustainable and that truly provide well-being to humanity.

> The economy is a subsystem of the finite biosphere that supports it. When the economy's expansion encroaches too much on the surrounding biosphere, we begin to sacrifice natural capital (animals, plants, minerals and fossil fuels) that is worth more than the manmade capital (roads, factories, appliances) added by "growth." (Herman Daly 2008,)

CHAPTER 2 – WHO ARE THE GREENS?

What Would Steady-State Look Like?

A steady-state economy would look very different in many ways from the economy that we live in now. There are many organizations and published works looking at the specific steps that we'd have to take to reform our system into one that doesn't worship growth. Organizations such as the Center for the Advancement of the Steady State Economy (CASSE) dedicate themselves to answering the questions of what this society would look like, and how it would work. Authors, scientists, and economists such as Herman Daly, Nicholas Georgescu-Roegen, Molly Scott Cato, Tim Jackson, Brian Czech, Bill McKibben, Clive Hamilton, and others have written books for both a general audience and for students of economics and policy.

Banking would look different in a steady-state economy, in that we would no longer allow banks the liberty to create money on their own, or to use tricks of debt and lending to generate and inflate currency.

Manufacturing would look different, in that we would prioritize longevity and hardiness of products and punish "planned obsolescence," which is the practice of making products that are supposed to wear out so that consumers will buy new ones or buy the next model. Repair, re-use, and upgrading of existing products would be the goal, instead of just replacing the product entirely. Planning to extend the life of such products when they are built conserves precious resources but keeps people working to maintain them.

Our population would need to stabilize, rather than continue to constantly grow. This means that our retirement and social aid programs would have to be funded differently, since they currently require a constantly increasing stock of new, young, working-age people to support the elderly and infirm. Businesses would transition towards selling services rather than just products. Material products would of course still exist, but the focus of a business would instead be on what the product provides to the consumer rather than just the existence of the product itself. Businesses would need to find ways to provide that service with as much efficiency in material cost as possible.

Some Ecologists are even calling for controlled *de*growth in certain economic sectors, in order to get us back to a level where our economic activity is sustainable. Modern economists often talk about a *recession* as the worst possible thing that could happen to an economy, and any government that takes actions that result in a recession quickly has the populace calling for their heads. We're told again and again that negative economic growth is apocalyptic, and must be avoided at all costs. But academic institutions like Research & Degrowth and researchers like Giorgos Kallis (who holds a PhD in environmental policy, and master's degrees in economics and environmental engineering) are instead trying to find ways to create purposeful, sustainable, strategic *shrinking* of production and consumption as a policy goal itself. In 2018, they had their Fifth International Degrowth Conference in Sweden, and over six hundred scientists and thinkers gathered together to work through these ideas. If the world ever comes to terms with the fact of infinite growth inside a finite system being impossible to sustain, we may be glad that someone has tried to plan for a solution. As Milton Friedman said,

> Only a crisis—actual or perceived—produces real change. When that crisis occurs, the actions that are taken depend on the ideas that are lying around. That, I believe, is our basic function: to develop alternatives to existing policies, to keep them alive and available until the politically impossible becomes the politically inevitable. (Milton Friedman)

While these ideas are widespread within Green circles, they're still very foreign concepts to most people, as well as most other political parties. But through the work of Greens around the world they're starting to gain some traction. In 2018, I attended the first Post-Growth Conference at the European Union, which was organized and hosted by the European Green Party. In the opening panel of the conference, Philippe Lamberts, the chair of the European Greens, remarked that "it's not helpful to be right on your own." The existence of the conference itself, held at the location of the highest level of European decision-making, was substantial in normalizing the ideas of post-growth. But Philippe was particularly proud that the Greens were joined as hosts at the conference by members of four of the seven other Euro-parties from both the left and the right of the political spectrum. Greens want their ideas to be the "new normal," and although we're not there yet, we can at least see it starting to happen.

Land, as the Basis of Everything

Near my apartment in downtown Vancouver there is an empty lot. It's on Robson Street, which is a primary commercial thoroughfare and one of the busiest and developed streets in the city. The lot is surrounded on all sides by towers and active construction projects, but it just sits there empty, covered in grass and featuring a single lonely tree. At first, I thought it was just a badly maintained park, but it turns out that it's privately owned land. It has sat empty since the mid-1970s and is owned by a small group of people through a registered corporation in Hong Kong. There are plenty of rumours about why it's been left empty for over forty years, but no journalist has yet managed to get in contact with the owner and get a clear explanation.

One thing that's for certain is that the lot is a very successful investment. It's not clear how much the buyers paid for the lot back in the '70s, but it has massively increased in value since then. A journalist looking into the lot in 2015 found that it was assessed at $8.5 million dollars (CAD). A follow-up in 2016 learned that its assessed value had jumped up to $15.7 million in that single year. I'm scared to even go and check how much its considered worth is now.

CHAPTER 2 – WHO ARE THE GREENS?

The existence of this empty lot brings up a core question of land value and the profit that's derived from it. Why did the accepted value of this empty lot of land increase? Who is responsible for the increase in the value of a plot of land? And most importantly, who benefits and profits from that increase?

The absentee owners in Hong Kong are clearly not responsible for the land value increasing. It's possible that they've forgotten they even own this little piece of land on the other side of the planet. No one has built anything on that land, so the responsible party can't be a developer who's invested in improving the land, either. The real reason that the land has increased in value is because of the community surrounding it. The land increased in value because a city grew up around it, and it's a city that millions of people have invested their time and energy and money and souls into building and creating. Vancouver is an incredibly desirable city to live in, and thousands of individual factors all combine and add up to make it that desirable. The clearest party that's responsible for the increase in the small Robson Street plot of land's value is the people of Vancouver and the community they've built around it.

So when that plot of land is finally sold, why will all of the profit derived from that increase in value go to a group of people on the other side of the world who've left it bare and unused for half a century? Why isn't that added value captured by the people who were actually responsible for creating that value?

This economic example brings up another key difference in the philosophy of Green parties, and another factor that sets them apart from the traditional "left" and "right" wings of our narrow political spectrum. It demonstrates the often-forgotten consideration of the value, ownership, and inherent rights of *land* itself.

A Short History of Economics

The modern concept of economics really took off with the publication of Scottish economist Adam Smith's *The Wealth of Nations* in 1776. Smith was followed up by a number of great economic thinkers who struggled to understand the complex ways in which humanity functions economically, and how to wrangle a system in a way that would produce the results that we wanted from it. One of those thinkers was Henry George, an American born in 1839.

Adam Smith had suggested that there were three *factors of production* that drove the economy: *labour*, *capital*, and *land*. Labour is human effort and expertise, or the contribution of an individual working towards a goal. Capital is any man-made product or good that's used in the production of other goods. This can include machinery, tools, buildings, and facilities, as well as liquid money itself. And land is the natural resources of the planet itself that are extracted to be made into goods. Land is also the *location* itself.

A working factory demonstrates all three factors of production: the building and the tools within are the *capital*; the workers in the factory are the *labour*; and the resources used in production as well as the piece of the planet that the factory is sitting on are the *land*. We also have words for profit derived from each of the three factors. Profit derived from *labour* is called *wages*, profit from *capital* is called *interest*, and profit from *land* is called *rent*.

The concepts of labour and capital should be familiar to readers. The political figures and movements associated with them should also be obvious. Our current economic system is known as *capitalism*, and it's based around the societal power being in the hands of those that own capital. Marxism and Communism have a heavy focus on labour. Marxism champions the labourer, and aims to put the societal power into the hands of those individuals that can contribute labour, rather than those that own capital.

The world's mainstream political parties also are obviously connected to these two concepts as well. The left-wing party in many countries is known as the "Labour" party, such as in the United Kingdom, New Zealand, and Australia. Here in Canada, the New Democratic Party is widely considered to be our "Labour Party" despite not having the name. Conservative and Liberal parties are, likewise, generally considered to be more *capitalist*, holding capital as their most important economic consideration. Much of the last hundred years has been defined by the struggle between capitalist and socialist countries and ideologies.

So what happened to the third factor of production? Why have considerations of land seemingly disappeared in our economic calculus? If capitalism is the political theory that capital is the most important factor of production, and Marxism is the political theory that labour is the most important factor, what political theory concerns itself with land in the same way?

Henry George

That was Henry George's thesis. He believed that land, and the ownership of that land, was at the core of our economy. He believed that our societal problems could be solved through managing the ownership of, and value derived, from land. And he wasn't a fringe figure, either. In 1879, he published his theories in a book titled *Progress and Poverty: An Inquiry into the Cause of Industrial Depressions and of Increase of Want with Increase of Wealth: The Remedy*," and it was *massively* successful. In fact, the book sold millions of copies, and in its time it sold more copies than any other book on the planet except the Bible. The book spawned the movement known as Georgism, and is considered by some to have been the biggest factor in setting off the period of time known as the Progressive Era. George also came within a hair of becoming Mayor of New York City in 1886, losing to Abram Hewitt but placing ahead of future President Theodore Roosevelt.

CHAPTER 2 – WHO ARE THE GREENS?

But in the modern day, in the twenty-first century, Henry George is not a household name, nor is the label "Georgist" on equal footing with "Capitalist" or Marxist." Henry George is not even in the top tier of economic thinkers that most people could name. If you ask a random person to name an economic thinker, they'd probably start with someone like Marx, and work their way down through figures like Adam Smith, Milton Friedman, John Maynard Keynes, Friedrich Hayek, John Stuart Mill, and others depending on how deep their economic knowledge went. Despite writing a book that outsold every other economic treatise up to that point, Henry George appears to have been forgotten in our popular timeline of economic thought.

The Georgist theory is that Henry George's ideas were purposefully cut out of the public dialogue by rich landowners who wanted to preserve their wealth. George's ideas were a direct attack on the method that landed aristocracy used to generate their wealth and privilege. It also conflicted with the American value that claimed that a person's success and wealth was solely determined by their hard work and commitment. George had revealed their secret: that success was determined by the land that you owned, exploited, and had likely just inherited. After George published his ideas, the rich landowners of America suppressed the ideas by setting up and funding economics departments in universities, and installing economic thinkers who pushed the idea that land was just another form of capital.

Their efforts were successful, and by the late twentieth century, Henry George and his ideas had mostly been forgotten in the public sphere, and were greatly minimized even in academic economics. In mainstream economics, land had been removed as a factor of production and simply merged into capital. As Fred Harrison writes in the foreword to *The Corruption of Economics* by Mason Gaffney,

> Henry George had to be stopped, because his was the rational, evolutionary path to The Good Society…
>
> Marx was evidently no threat to the class interests of those who controlled society; he could be left alone to wade through his manuscripts in the British Museum, and even allowed to inspire revolution on the outer reaches of eastern Europe. Henry George was another matter; he had to be stopped, and to this day we live with the consequences of that plot to kill his message." ( )

This may sound overly conspiratorial. But as Mason Gaffney writes:

> To most modern readers, probably George seems too minor a figure to have warranted such an extreme reaction. This impression is a measure of the neoclassicals' success: it is what they sought to make of him. ( )

This is where the connection to Green parties comes in. If Labour parties are the ones championing the ideas of Marx and the value of *labour*, and Liberal and Conservative parties remain focused on the ideas of economists like Friedrich Hayek and the value of *capital*, then Green Parties are the closest thing we have to a political ideology that embraces *Georgism* and the value of *land*. Green parties and their members, whether they fully appreciate it or not, are trying to reassert the value of the popularly forgotten third factor of production. Once again we can point out a way in which Greens don't fit nicely on the traditional political spectrum. Greens aren't left (labour) or right (capital). They're in a third direction (land).

Cara Camcastle's survey of the Canadian Green Party's members in 2005 displays this in a clear way. One of the questions she asked the surveyed members was if they believed that nature itself has an intrinsic value and thus is not merely a resource to be used by humankind. 97 percent of Green members and supporters agreed with this statement. You wouldn't find that level of agreement in any other political party.

Everything Comes Back to Land

This is why it perplexes and confuses Greens when they're labelled as a "single-issue" party because of their focus on environmental issues. For a Green, everything comes back to land. Land is at the core of the rest of our political and economic systems. Land and the environment is not just a factor among many that sit on top of society and the economy. Our society and economy exist within the environment, on the land. Land isn't a piece of capital that an individual can own and exploit. Land is the substrate of our society, and therefore we have a responsibility to shepherd and care for it. Thus, the wealth derived from land should be returned to society as a whole instead of directed into the bank accounts of the already wealthy individuals who've used their wealth to control it.

Erich Jacoby-Hawkins is the National Revenue and Ecological Fiscal Reform critic in the Green Party of Canada's Shadow Cabinet. A Shadow Cabinet is a group of experts inside an opposition party whose job it is to "shadow" the government ministers for various topics and to propose their party's alternatives. As his title suggests, Erich is the top Green Party point person on topics of fiscal reform and taxation, and on how a Green government would raise national revenue to pay for government programs. He is an avowed Georgist, regularly travelling around the world for Georgist conferences, and a multi-time candidate for the Green Party in the Barrie, Ontario area. I spoke with him about Georgist ideas and how they fit into Green Party thought.

The core tenet of Georgism is that land value itself is the thing that we should be taxing, because the increasing value of land should be returned to the community rather than to an individual who has used their wealth to purchase ownership of that land. In the case of the empty lot on Robson

CHAPTER 2 – WHO ARE THE GREENS?

Street near my apartment, the increased value of the lot was generated by the community, and therefore the value derived from that lot should be returned to the community. Interestingly, Henry George wasn't concerned with environmental issues. He was looking at ways of alleviating poverty, and of producing fairness in the economy. The environmental connection was simply simpatico.

Both the Green Party of Canada and various provincial Green parties have explicitly embraced Georgism in their platform development processes throughout the years, although the term itself is absent from the platform documents that are published for the public. Moving the basis of the economy from a purely capitalist system to a Georgist system would be similar in scope to moving it to a Marxist system, so most Green platforms have only a few mentions of the first few steps that they'd take in that direction.

One of the more interesting Georgist tax ideas of the Green parties concerns income tax. Income tax is unpopular with *Georgists*. It's a tax on an individual's labour, which is something we should be promoting rather than dissuading by taxing it. In other words, income tax is a tax on someone's *earned income*, the income derived from their own personal effort. Georgists believed that earned income is the absolute last thing that we should be taxing. Instead, Georgists would rather we tax people's *unearned income*, meaning the income obtained by just owning things that increase in value. Georgists believe that the increase in value of something that is privately owned should go to the people who are responsible for that increase in value, not the ones who happen to own it.

In other words, a long-term goal for Georgists, and thus for many Green parties, is to remove or reduce the income tax, and to replace it with tax on the unimproved value of owned land. Erich Jacoby-Hawkins remarked to me that our current federal system in Canada means that the vast majority of an individual's tax money is paid to the federal or provincial governments through income and sales tax (both of which are taxes on labour), with a small minority of it being sent to municipal governments (who mostly raise money through property taxes, which are a combined land and capital tax). The federal and provincial governments then hand money downwards to the local municipalities, often earmarking it for specific uses that meet the government's goals. Erich thinks that this is completely backwards. The cities themselves should be the primary tax-gatherers, done through aggressive taxation of unimproved land values. The cities should then hand that money upwards to the provincial and federal governments, who would have minimal revenue streams of their own due to low (or non-existent) income and sales taxes.

Again, this demonstrates the decentralized and municipal-focused viewpoint of Green party thought. It also demonstrates how deeply different Green economic ideas, and even their system of values, are from the other mainstream political party families.

"In the course of history, there comes a time when humanity is called to shift to a new level of consciousness, to reach a higher moral ground. A time when we have to shed our fear and give hope to each other. That time is now.

We are called to assist the Earth to heal her wounds and in the process heal our own—indeed, to embrace the whole creation in all its diversity, beauty and wonder. This will happen if we see the need to revive our sense of belonging to a larger family of life, with which we have shared our evolutionary process.

You cannot protect the environment unless you empower people, you inform them, and you help them understand that these resources are their own, that they must protect them.

Throughout Africa, women are the primary caretakers, holding significant responsibility for tilling the land and feeding their families. As a result, they are often the first to become aware of environmental damage as resources become scarce and incapable of sustaining their families.

The generation that destroys the environment is not the generation that pays the price. That is the problem."

(Wangari Maathai, 2004 Nobel Peace Prize winner, Founder of the Mazingira Green Party of Kenya and the Green Belt Movement, Member of Kenyan Parliament and Assistant Minister of Environment 2003–2005)

WHO GETS TO BE CALLED GREEN?

In Chapter One I recounted the beginnings of the world's first Green parties. The United Tasmania Group and the Values Party of New Zealand are widely acknowledged as the pioneers of what would eventually become a worldwide movement, a network of parties in nearly every country with shared ideas and goals and values.

However, what exactly qualifies a party as being a "Green" party? Political parties running for office in an individual nation, state, or city naturally focus their efforts and message on what they see as important in their own situation and community. So what is it that unites political parties in places as different as Finland and Zambia, or Colombia and Japan? Who gets to decide who can call themselves a Green party, or who Green supporters from one country can acknowledge as a fellow Green from across the globe?

Most people have never heard the term "political international," but all of our major political parties in Canada belong to one. A political international is a group of political parties from across the globe with shared ideologies. They exist as a way for political parties to share ideas and experiences, and to build the strength of political movements across borders.

The Liberal Party of Canada is a member of Liberal International, which contains such other parties as the Liberal Democrats of the United Kingdom, the Free Democratic Party of Germany, the People's Party for Freedom and Democracy in the Netherlands, and Fianna Fáil in Ireland.

The Canadian New Democratic Party belongs to the *Progressive Alliance*, a large grouping including the Australian Labour Party, the Socialist Party of France, the Social Democratic Party of Germany, the Indian National Congress, the Democratic Party of Italy, and the Democratic Party of the United States.

The Conservative Party of Canada is a member of the International Democratic Union, alongside the Liberal Party of Australia, the Kuomintang of Taiwan, the Conservative Party of the United Kingdom, the Republicans of France, the Christian Democratic Union of Germany, the Liberal Korea Party of South Korea, the Republican Party of the United States, and many others. In fact, at the time of this book's writing in 2018, former Canadian Prime Minister Stephen Harper is the Chair of the International Democrat Union.

Of course, the Green Party of Canada belongs to one of these political internationals as well, called the Global Greens.

In 1979, a group of minor political parties from across Europe organized themselves into a rough group called the Coordination of European Green and Radical Parties (CEGRP) to contest the very first election to the European Parliament. The European Union (EU) was formed at the end of the Second World War, and up until 1979 the governments of the member countries of the EU had appointed the members of the European Parliament. This meant that each country's MEPs (Members of European Parliament) came from that country's governing party, rather than being a representative group of the politics of the nation. In 1979, the EU decided instead to begin having elections to form the parliament. This made it the first international election in history.

I mentioned in the last section that the Greens were joined by several MEPs from other parties when I attended the Post-Growth Conference at the European Union. From the first election in 1979, parties from each of the many countries that make up the EU have banded together into "Euro parties" based on their values and ideas, finding like-minded parties in their neighbouring countries and forming shared election platforms to run on across all of Europe. In this first election, the groups included the Social Democrats, the Christian Democrats, the Conservatives, the Far Left and Communists, the Liberals, and the Nationalists.

Building the Global Greens

The CEGRP had agreed to work together and coordinate between themselves, their only uniting factor at the time being that they were a collection of fringe groups. There were huge differences between the parties that made up the agreement, and they failed to form any sort of pan-European election platform, nor to elect anyone to the parliament. Nonetheless, the groups tried again at the next pan-European election in 1984. This time the Greens split themselves off from the other fringe radical parties and formed the European Green Coordination (EGC). They fared far better

CHAPTER 2 – WHO ARE THE GREENS?

than their first attempt, electing eleven individuals to the parliament from the countries of West Germany, Belgium, Denmark, Italy, and the Netherlands. In 1989, the Greens increased their total to thirty members, adding elected members from France, Spain, and Portugal.

This coordination of European Greens was the first official attempt to unify the Green movements that had been sprouting around the world, which had previously been united only by an informal sharing of information and support. The formation of the EGC, which would later be reformed and renamed as the European Federation of Green Parties, allowed the Green parties of Europe to collectively decide who they would count amongst themselves. It let them decide who would qualify as a "Green Party."

The European Union provided a built-in system for the various Green Parties of Europe to unite and to organize themselves. However, there existed parties all over the world that were demonstrating the same values and ideologies as the European Greens, and no such global parliament existed in which all the Greens worldwide could come together. An opportunity came in 1992 when the United Nations held a conference in Rio de Janeiro, Brazil, entitled the United Nations Conference on Environment and Development (UNCED). The UNCED was attended by 172 governments (including the heads of state of 116) and was intended to address issues such as lead-based gasoline and poisonous waste, alternative sources of energy to replace fossil fuels, moving towards public transit, and the growing overuse of water supplies.

The conference itself was a triumph for environmental organizations who had been pushing their goals and messages on their national governments for decades, and would lead to such agreements as the United Nations Framework Convention on Climate Change, the Kyoto Protocols, and the recent Paris Climate Accords. Greens around the world saw this as the perfect opportunity to come together and have a first official meeting, as well as to draft an official statement of support and shared goals.

In the days before the UNCED, Greens from twenty-eight countries gathered in Rio de Janeiro to convene the first Planetary Meeting of the Greens. The event was hosted by the local Partido Verde do Brasil (Green Party of Brazil), along with the European Green Coordination, the Partido Verde Ecologista de México (Green Party of Mexico), and the Green Party of the United States. The gathering was even opened with a speech by the mayor of Rio de Janeiro, Marcello Alencar. The meeting produced a three-thousand-word statement outlining the shared concerns and values of the many different national parties attending, and opened with a declaration of the need for their own existence:

> Experience teaches us that governments are only moved to take environmental problems seriously when people vote for environmental political parties.

The meeting in 1992 was the first of many for the global Green movement. Another was held in Mexico in 1999, and then in 2001 the first Global Green Congress was held in Canberra, Australia. The 2001 congress set up a number of formal mechanisms for ongoing organization and coordination, as well as drafting an official charter of the Global Greens.

After 2001, the Global Greens would have formal methods for coordinating membership, decision-making between congresses, sharing and communicating between the members, and strengthening and building the movement worldwide. The charter that was drafted in Canberra underwent numerous revisions as well as hundreds of proposed amendments that were debated one by one on the floor of the convention centre. The final document was agreed upon by acclamation of over eight hundred Green activists and politicians from over seventy countries. It outlined six key principles that all Green parties agreed upon, and that they all shared and felt united them:

Ecological Wisdom
Social Justice
Participatory Democracy
Nonviolence
Sustainability
Respect for Diversity

There were, of course, some disagreements between the many delegates and countries, but the six core principles represent the areas in which all the parties and politicians from around the world were in agreement. Bob Brown, who was a sitting Senator in Australia at the time and was instrumental in setting up the congress, speaks about the event with a massive amount of pride. During interviews with Green politicians in the process of my writing this book, I'd often ask them to describe to me how they'd answer the question, "What makes a party a *Green* party?" Bob immediately spoke glowingly of the herculean effort put into drafting the official charter of the Global Greens:

> [The Global Greens Congress] wasn't just to get together and talk about things, it was to get together and decide what it is that makes us Green . . . At that conference *the* prime task, and *the* big outcome was the Global Greens Charter . . . and any party that becomes part of the Global Greens, or is calling itself a Green Party is effectively required to agree to that charter. (2017)

The rest of this chapter will be dedicated to outlining what each of these core values mean, and how it describes Green parties from around the world.

CHAPTER 2 – WHO ARE THE GREENS?

Ecological Wisdom

As you might expect, the first of the six Green principles focuses on the environment. It's the shared passion that brought so many people together in the first place to form parties that would later become Green. It's the principle that is so taken for granted with Green parties that we barely need to campaign on it anymore. If you're an environmentally conscious voter, you know which party is going to be the greatest champion of that value.

> The Global Charter simply states:
>
> We acknowledge that human beings are part of the natural world and we respect the specific values of all forms of life, including non-human species.
>
> We acknowledge the wisdom of the indigenous peoples of the world, as custodians of the land and its resources.
>
> We acknowledge that human society depends on the ecological resources of the planet, and must ensure the integrity of ecosystems and preserve biodiversity and the resilience of life supporting systems.
>
> This requires
> - that we learn to live within the ecological and resource limits of the planet
> - that we protect animal and plant life, and life itself that is sustained by the natural elements: earth, water, air and sun
> - where knowledge is limited, that we take the path of caution, in order to secure the continued abundance of the resources of the planet for present and future generations.

In actual practice, the specific policies and platform pieces that lead to these goals differ between the Green parties around the world. Some parties push certain policies harder than others, and are more or less willing to compromise with larger parties on them. Common goals tend to be an aggressive focus on moving to renewable energy sources, weaning humanity off of our dependence on fossil fuels, maintaining food security by growing local food for more of our diets, agriculture that's designed to enrich rather than destroy local ecosystems, low-carbon forms of transportation of goods and public transport for people, taxation on dirty energy producers to keep the burden of the environmental costs of pollution on the producer instead of the taxpayer, a fair treatment of animals and livestock, and a diversified economy that avoids relying on resource extraction industries.

Social Justice

The second of Green politics' core values is a commitment to equality, justice, and fairness for all. It's a value that has long been an integral part of Green identity, from the early days of the Values Party of New Zealand pushing for decriminalization of homosexuality, to the modern Green commitments to reducing the inequality gap inside individual countries and around the world.

The Charter states:

We assert that the key to social justice is the equitable distribution of social and natural resources, both locally and globally, to meet basic human needs unconditionally, and to ensure that all citizens have full opportunities for personal and social development.

We declare that there is no social justice without environmental justice, and no environmental justice without social justice.

This requires
- a just organization of the world and a stable world economy which will close the widening gap between rich and poor, both within and between countries; balance the flow of resources from South to North; and lift the burden of debt on poor countries which prevents their development
- the eradication of poverty, as an ethical, social, economic, and ecological imperative
- the elimination of illiteracy
- a new vision of citizenship built on equal rights for all individuals regardless of gender, race, age, religion, class, ethnic or national origin, sexual orientation, disability, wealth or health

A stance against inequality and poverty is an obvious and easy one for a global political movement to take, and can be found in the charters and manifestos of many other non-Green parties as well. However, a commitment to equality in all of its forms is a tough sell for a movement that contains diverse members from across the globe.

The commitment to the rights of LGBT individuals in particular was a difficult one to agree on at the 2001 Canberra Congress, due mostly to pushback from the African Green parties. This wasn't due to disagreement on the value from the African Greens members themselves, but rather that many parts of Africa are still extremely homophobic, and any party that includes LGBT rights in its platform opens itself up to hostility from the voters and a refusal to consider them even if these voters agree with the rest of the party's platform. In parts of Africa the promotion of LGBT rights is even illegal, which opened the African parties up to possible clashes with the law. Similarly, most Green parties around the world support access to abortion services for women, although several Green parties from deeply Catholic countries registered their objection to including it as a Global Green commitment, because of political concerns at home.

Participatory Democracy

From the surface, the United Tasmania Group may have looked like it formed solely to protest an environmentally destructive energy project, but a large part of their frustration was due to having a government that refused to take the wishes of the public into account. A receptive and transparent government is an extremely important value for the Greens. The Green approach to democracy and governance is bottom-up, and is based around grassroots participation, individual empowerment, citizen-powered funding of political parties instead of large corporate donors, and fairness in elections.

> The Charter states:
>
> We strive for a democracy in which all citizens have the right to express their views, and are able to directly participate in the environmental, economic, social and political decisions which affect their lives; so that power and responsibility are concentrated in local and regional communities, and devolved only where essential to higher tiers of governance.
>
> This requires
> - individual empowerment through access to all the relevant information required for any decision, and access to education to enable all to participate
> - breaking down inequalities of wealth and power that inhibit participation
> - building grassroots institutions that enable decisions to be made directly at the appropriate level by those affected, based on systems which encourage civic vitality, voluntary action and community responsibility
> - strong support for giving young people a voice through educating, encouraging and assisting youth involvement in every aspect of political life including their participation in all decision-making bodies
> - that all elected representatives are committed to the principles of transparency, truthfulness, and accountability in governance
> - that all electoral systems are transparent and democratic, and that this is enforced by law

- that in all electoral systems, each adult has an equal vote
- that all electoral systems are based on proportional representation, and all elections are publicly funded with strict limits on, and full transparency of, corporate and private donations.
- that all citizens have the right to be a member of the political party of their choice within a multiparty system

Notable in the preceding bullet points is a commitment to all elections taking place under proportional representation. We've covered some of the aspects of the different ways elections are conducted in the previous chapters when we looked at how the Tasmanian and New Zealand Green parties and their predecessors fared under their different systems. We saw how the New Zealand Greens were unable to truly flourish until the country changed electoral systems from the old first-past-the-post to a newer proportional representation system.

Greens deeply believe that you should able to cast your vote for the party or candidate that you most want to represent you. Therefore, any system that distorts the power of that vote is a fundamentally broken system. A non-proportional system fails this test because it encourages voters to "strategically" vote for candidates that *aren't* their first choice, so that their vote isn't "wasted." Greens agree that a democracy is healthiest when the many different opinions and ideologies of its citizens are represented and are not suppressed through a system that isolates power in the hands of two large, impenetrable parties (as inevitably occurs in non-proportional systems).

It also states that power should be devolved to the lowest level when possible. This is the "libertarian" aspect of Green thought that was mentioned above, and it's a value that Greens tend to share with Conservatives. Greens usually believe that the best decisions are made on the local level, and that the government should strive to avoid top-down lawmaking when possible. Of course some decisions still need to be made by national governments, but those governments should at least be trying to empower local communities instead of centralizing power within themselves.

Nonviolence

Many Green parties around the world began out of the nuclear disarmament movement, and took form during the Cold War at a time when mutually assured destruction was seen as a guillotine hanging over everyone's head. Greens are not a strict pacifist movement, but they do believe that the focus should always be on nonviolent means of resolving conflicts.

The Charter states:

We declare our commitment to nonviolence and strive for a culture of peace and cooperation between states, inside societies and between individuals, as the basis of global security.
We believe that security should not rest mainly on military strength but on cooperation, sound economic and social development, environmental safety, and respect for human rights.

This requires
- a comprehensive concept of global security, which gives priority to social, economic, ecological, psychological and cultural aspects of conflict, instead of a concept based primarily on military balances of power
- a global security system capable of the prevention, management and resolution of conflicts
- removing the causes of war by understanding and respecting other cultures, eradicating racism, promoting freedom and democracy, and ending global poverty
- pursuing general and complete disarmament including international agreements to ensure a complete and definitive ban of nuclear, biological and chemical arms, antipersonnel mines and depleted uranium weapons
- strengthening the United Nations (UN) as the global organisation of conflict management and peacekeeping
- pursuing a rigorous code of conduct on arms exports to countries where human rights are being violated.

Per Gahrton, one of the founders of the Swedish Green Party, wrote a book entitled *Green Parties, Green Future*, in which he dedicates a section to understanding the Green position on pacifism. He identifies a series of escalating questions that you can ask someone to determine when they think military force is justified. From the responses to these questions he then tried to tease out an "average" Green position.

Most Green Party platforms maintain a commitment that military intervention is only permissible with a United Nations mandate, and Greens in general feel very positively about the UN and what it should be able to achieve as a place for diplomacy and understanding. Most Greens agree that military force is legitimate in defense during an outright attack against their country by a foreign military, and that militarily occupied peoples have a legitimate right to defend themselves and engage in armed resistance against their occupiers. Most agree that it is permissible for a country to support an armed resistance in another foreign nation if it is a legitimate struggle for liberation, although this is where opinions begin to diverge. Most Greens do *not* consider it permissible to attack an entire nation accused of harbouring individual terrorists, that so-called "preventative" to prevent a nation from attacking other states are not legitimate, and that wars should not be started in the name of "regime change" and to install democracy.

There are, of course, differences between different Green parties around the world, as well as differences between the individuals within those parties, but the general feeling for Greens in terms of military engagement is that it should be the last option after all attempts at diplomacy have failed.

Sustainability

Sustainability is core to the entire Green way of thinking. The simple fact of survival on Earth is that the planet has a limited amount of resources, and a limited "carrying capacity" for life. The Earth is able to replenish some of its resources given enough time, but others are simply non-renewable, and once we use them all up they will be gone. Greens advocate for building a society that can sustain itself indefinitely, and by planning for the long term by conserving our resources so that future generations will not have a lower quality of life than we do.

> The Charter states:

> We recognise the limited scope for the material expansion of human society within the biosphere, and the need to maintain biodiversity through sustainable use of renewable resources and responsible use of non-renewable resources.
> We believe that to achieve sustainability, and in order to provide for the needs of present and future generations within the finite resources of the earth, continuing growth in global consumption, population and material inequity must be halted and reversed. We recognise that sustainability will not be possible as long as poverty persists.

CHAPTER 2 – WHO ARE THE GREENS?

This requires

- ensuring that the rich limit their consumption to allow the poor their fair share of the earth's resources
- redefining the concept of wealth, to focus on quality of life rather than capacity for over-consumption
- creating a world economy which aims to satisfy the needs of all, not the greed of a few; and enables those presently living to meet their own needs, without jeopardising the ability of future generations to meet theirs
- eliminating the causes of population growth by ensuring economic security, and providing access to basic education and health, for all; giving both men and women greater control over their fertility
- redefining the roles and responsibilities of trans-national corporations in order to support the principles of sustainable development
- implementing mechanisms to tax, as well as regulating, speculative financial flows ensuring that market prices of goods and services fully incorporate the environmental costs of their production and consumption
- achieving greater resource and energy efficiency and development and use of environmentally sustainable technologies
- encouraging local self-reliance to the greatest practical extent to create worthwhile, satisfying communities
- recognising the key role of youth culture and encouraging an ethic of sustainability within that culture.

Here is the difficult challenge of attaining a *steady state economy* that we covered above. The Green charter outlines some of the recognitions that we have to make, and the steps that we'll have to take in order to move the world away from a growth-based philosophy.

It's a big change, and no one claims that it will be easy. But Greens view it as the only way possible for humanity to ensure its survival and prosperity. The other option is that we burn through everything we have, and let our grandchildren deal with the aftermath.

Respect for Diversity

The final value in the Charter outlines the inclusive type of world that Greens want to live in. It establishes the Green desire for a world where diverse peoples and cultures can respect each other and work together despite differences.

The Charter states:

We honour cultural, linguistic, ethnic, sexual, religious and spiritual diversity within the context of individual responsibility toward all beings.

We defend the right of all persons, without discrimination, to an environment supportive of their dignity, bodily health, and spiritual well-being

We promote the building of respectful, positive and responsible relationships across lines of division in the spirit of a multi-cultural society.

This requires
- recognition of the rights of indigenous peoples to the basic means of their survival, both economic and cultural, including rights to land and to self determination; and acknowledgment of their contribution to the common heritage of national and global culture
- recognition of the rights of ethnic minorities to develop their culture, religion and language without discrimination, and to full legal, social and cultural participation in the democratic process
- recognition of and respect for sexual minorities
- equality between women and men in all spheres of social, economic, political and cultural life
- significant involvement of youth culture as a valuable contribution to our Green vision, and recognition that young people have distinct needs and modes of expression.

Most Green parties who hail from countries with indigenous minority populations (New Zealand, Australia, Canada) try to be the most outspoken and ardent advocates for their First Nations populations. Most Greens are welcoming of immigration, although there are disagreements over how to integrate new immigrants and cultures, and how much separation there should be between linguistic and cultural groups in a nation.

CHAPTER 2 – WHO ARE THE GREENS?

Global Greens

The English version of the Charter is a short document, only eighteen pages, and contains a number of steps, requirements, and endorsements that any member of the Global Greens is expected to agree with, although during the drafting of the Charter certain Green parties in attendance registered their official disagreement with various statutes.

At the date of the writing of this book the Global Greens contain eighty full members from every continent and region of the world, as well as sixteen associate and candidate members (developing parties that have speaking rights but not voting rights at the Global Congress). There are also a huge number of partner organizations (non-profit, non-governmental organizations) that are able to participate and speak, but not vote, at Congress events. Green parties at the state/province or municipal level can't be accepted as full voting members of the Global Greens, but are instead expected to coordinate through their national level Green parties.

The Global Greens organize themselves into four geographic federations, each with their own President and organizational team. These four federations and their members can be found at the end of this chapter. At the time of this book's writing, eight Global Green member parties are serving as part of the national government of their countries, and many more are in governing positions at the state and municipal level.

GLOBAL GREEN FEDERATIONS AND MEMBERS

EUROPEAN GREEN PARTY (EGP)

Full Members:
1. Albania: Albania Te Gjelberit / Greens of Albania
2. Andora: Andorra Partit Verds d'Andorra
3. Austria: Die Grünen
4. Belgium: Groen
5. Belgium: Ecolo
6. Bulgaria: Zelena Partija Bulgaria / Bulgarian Green Party
7. Bulgaria: Zelenite / The Greens
8. Cyprus: Cyprus Green Party
9. Czech Republic: Strana Zelenych
10. Denmark: Socialistisk Folkeparti
11. Estonia: Eestimaa Rohelised
12. Finland: Vihreät-De Gröna
13. France: Europe Ecologie - Les Verts (EELV)
14. Georgia: Sakartvelo's mtsvaneta partia / Green Party of Georgia
15. Germany: Bündnis '90/Die Grünen
16. Greece: Oicologoi-Prasinoi / Ecologist Greens
17. Hungary: Lehet Más a Politika (LMP)
18. Ireland: Comhaontas Glas
19. Italy: Federazione dei Verdi
20. Latvia: Latvijas Zala Partija (ZLP) / Latvia Green Party
21. Luxembourg: Déi Gréng
22. Malta: Alternattiva Demokratika - The Green Party
23. Moldova: Partidul Verde Ecologist
24. Netherlands: De Groenen
25. Netherlands: Groenlinks
26. Norway: Miljøpartiet De Grønne
27. Poland: Partia Zieloni
28. Portugal: Partido Ecologista - Os Verdes
29. Romania: Partidul Verde
30. Slovenia: Stranka mladih - Zeleni Evrope / SMS-Zeleni

CHAPTER 2 – WHO ARE THE GREENS?

31. Spain - Equo
32. Spain: Iniciativa per Catalunya Verds (ICV)
33. Sweden: Miljöpartiet de gröna
34. Switzerland: Grüne / Les Verts / I Verdi
35. Ukraine: Partija Zelenych Ukrajiny (PZU)
36. United Kingdom: Green Party of England and Wales
37. United Kingdom: Scottish Green Party

Associate Members:

1. Azerbaijan: Azərbaycan Yaşıllar Partiyası / Azerbaijzan Greens
2. Belarus: Bielaruskaja Partyja "Zialonye" / Belarus Greens
3. Russia: Green Russia
4. Russia: Zelenaya Alternativa (GROZA)

Candidate Members:

1. Croatia: Zelena Lista / Croatia Greens / ORaH (Održivi razvoj Hrvatske)
2. Macedonia: Democratic Renewal of Macedonia (DOM)
3. Turkey: Turkey Yesiller / Greens of Turkey

FEDERACIÓN DE PARTIDOS VERDES DE LAS AMERICAS (FPVA)

Full Members:

1. Bolivia: Partido Verde Ecologista
2. Brasil: Partido Verde
3. Canada: Green Party of Canada / Parti Vert du Canada
4. Chile: Partido Ecologista Verde
5. Colombia: Partido Alianza Verde
6. Dominican Republic: The Green Party of the Dominican Republic
7. Mexico: Partido Verde Ecologista de México
8. Peru: Alternativa Verde
9. United States: Green Party US
10. Venezuela: Movimiento Ecológico de Venezuela

Associate Members:

1. Argentina: Partido Verde
2. Costa Rica: Partido Verde Ecologista
3. Guatemala: Movimiento Verde
4. Nicaragua: Alianza Verde Ecologista

ASIA-PACIFIC GREENS FEDERATION (APGF)

Full Members:

1. Australia: Australian Greens
2. India: Uttarakhand Parivartan Party (UKPP)
3. Indonesia: Sarekat Hijau (Indonesian Green Union)
4. Japan: Greens Japan
5. Korea (Republic of): Green Party Korea
6. Lebanon: Green Party of Lebanon
7. Mongolia: Mongolian Green Party
8. Nepal: Nepali Greens
9. New Zealand: Green Party of Aotearoa New Zealand
10. Pakistan: Pakistan Green Party
11. Philippines: Philippine Green Party (Greens PH / Partido Kalikasan)
12. Taiwan: Green Party Taiwan

Associate Members:

1. Fiji: Green Party of Fiji
2. Indonesia: Atjeh Greens
3. Indonesia: Partai Hijau Indonesia (PHI)
4. Palestine: Green Party of Palestine
5. Taiwan: Taiwan Friends of the Global Greens
6. Taiwan: Trees Party Taiwan

AFRICAN GREENS FEDERATION (AGF)

Full Members:

1. Burkina Faso: Rassemblement Des Ecologistes du Burkina Faso
2. Chad: Union des Ecologistes Tchadiens - LES VERTS
3. Democratic Republic of Congo: Parti Ecologiste Congolais - Les Verts (PECO)
4. Egypt: Egyptian Green Party
5. Madagascar: Parti Vert Hasin'I Madagasikara
6. Mali: Parti Ecologiste du Mali
7. Mauritius: Les Verts Fraternels Mauritius
8. Niger: Rassemblement pour un Sahel Vert/Parti Vert du Niger
9. Rwanda: Democratic Green Party of Rwanda
10. Senegal: Convergence des Ecologistes du Sénégal (CES)
11. Sierra Leone: Sierra Leone Green Party
12. Togo: Afrique Togo Ecologie
13. Uganda: Ecological party of Uganda
14. Zambia: Green Party of Zambia

Associate Members:

1. Algeria: Parti Algérien Vert pour le Développement
2. Angola: Partido Nacional Ecológico de Angola
3. Burundi: Burundi Green Movement
4. Central African Republic: Mouvement des Verts de Centrafrique
5. Republic of Congo: Mouvement des Verts Congolais (Brazaville)
6. Gabon: Parti Vert Gabonais/Gabon Green Party
7. Guinea: Parti des Écologistes de Guinée (PVG) / Guinea Green Party
8. Ivory Coast: Rassemblement des Ecologistes du Côte d'Ivoire
9. Kenya: Afrogreens Party of Kenya
10. Kenya: Green Congress of Kenya
11. Morocco: Parti de la Gauche Verte Maroc
12. Mozambique: Ecological Party of Mozambique
13. South Africa: Ecological Movement of South Africa
14. Tunisia: Parti Tunisie Verte
15. Zimbabwe: Zimbabwe United Crusade for Democracy/ UCAD-Green Party

CHAPTER 3

THE GREEN BEGINNINGS IN EUROPE

"We have stood up and said continuing growth in the Western world is unjust, inappropriate and potentially destabilising. Having said that, we understand why governments do it, so there is an onus on us to show there are other stories and to identify the institutional innovations you might need in order to arrive at this other place."

(Tim Jackson, British Ecological Economist and Author)

THE GREEN BEGINNINGS IN EUROPE

Before moving on to dig into the formation of the first European Green parties and the first successful Green parties, we need to stop and cover something that we've addressed a few times so far, but not in full detail. We need to cover the factor that perhaps most impacts the diverse ways that different countries' Green parties develop and grow: the impact of electoral systems.

Many people don't give a lot of thought to the way their elections are run, and what it means to vote for and elect someone. The majority of any country's population probably doesn't fully understand the system being used in its own country, let alone is able to compare and contrast it with the systems used in other countries. I've spoken to people who were surprised to find out that there even *was* a different way to conduct an election, or that it was possible for a country to change from one system to another. However, the environment that political parties are forced to operate in has a massive effect on the kinds of policies they advocate for, the tactics they use, and ultimately whether or not they are successful. A Green party, or any political party for that matter, can only be fully understood by understanding and appreciating the electoral arena in which they are playing.

The world's methods of electing government can be widely divided into two groups: the majoritarian and the proportional. In reality each system exists in a spectrum between these two extremes, and those who study electoral systems will often refer to some systems being "more proportional" than others. There's even a formula (called the Gallagher index) for scoring systems on where they lie along the majoritarian-proportional axis. But the nitty-gritty of individual systems isn't what we need to understand in order to understand how political parties exist within them. The only thing we need to understand is what the different systems encourage and discourage, and therefore how parties and politics change within different systems.

Many people glaze over when someone tries to explain the difference between a majoritarian system and a proportional one. However, there's a very simple way to differentiate between them that even someone with a low interest in politics can appreciate.

What Does Your Vote Accomplish?

Whenever an election is held, we divide the population into geographic "districts." The population is sorted into these districts and each district then votes to elect one or more representatives. In Canada we have 338 districts, and each district elects a single representative. But this is not the case in most other countries.

That's the big difference between a majoritarian or proportional system: how many representatives are elected from each district. A majoritarian system is one in which each district has only a single representative. That single person is expected to represent every person in the district, whether they voted for them or not. This is a challenging task, since those who voted for a candidate who "lost" probably disagree with many things that the "winning" elected representative campaigned on. In effect, by having only a single elected representative, the system gives all of the power to whichever group of voters is the biggest. Anyone who's not part of that group might see their votes as "wasted," or as "losing" votes. It's a system that's built on having winners and losers.

Furthermore, the "winner" of an election using this method might not even have the support of a majority of the district's voters. In a two-way race, one candidate will always have the support of more than half of the voters. But in a three-way race or a four-way race, this isn't always true. This creates situations where most voters wanted someone other than the eventual winner.

On the other hand, a proportional system is one in which there are multiple representatives elected from a single district. Generally, the more representatives each district has, the more proportional the result is to the way people voted. If there are multiple people elected in a single district, then far fewer votes are "wasted" since far more of the votes cast are used to elect someone. A system with multiple representatives is less about picking winners and losers, and more about electing a group of people who are representative of the proportions of voters.

That's the core difference at its simplest form. In a majoritarian system such as first-past-the-post (as it's called in Canada), each voter has only a single representative for their district. In a proportional representation system, each voter has multiple representatives for their district. Beyond that, the specific systems can get more complicated, but it always comes back to that simple difference.

How Does the System Change Politics?

Studying the political and societal differences that occur in countries with different systems is one of my personal favourite fields of political science. And I'm not alone in having an interest in how a country's system changes its political realities. Dutch political scientist Arend Lijphart has investigated the many differences in political norms between majoritarian and proportional systems, in his book *"Patterns of Democracy: Government Forms and Performance in Thirty-Six Countries"*.

Since majoritarian systems are built to have a clear "winner" and a "loser," they encourage parliaments that are aggressive and adversarial. They also usually cause a political system to collapse down to only two parties, each of which exists mostly to oppose the other. Voting for a third party is risky inside a majoritarian system, and those who do are often accused of wasting their vote. A majoritarian system encourages an "us versus them" mentality between the eventual two major political parties, and the party in the minority often considers its main political task to be to destroy and defeat its rival party.

The United States of America is the world's most obvious majoritarian nation, but countries like Canada, Australia, the United Kingdom, France, Singapore, Nigeria, Bangladesh, and others across the world use systems that are primarily majoritarian. In the United States, we witness a political arena that has collapsed down to only two parties that stand any chance of electoral success, while in other countries like Canada there still exist more than two parties with elected representation. In majoritarian countries, a single political party almost always controls government entirely since with a majority of elected representatives, they are able to vote to pass legislation and set budgets without having to involve opposition parties.

A proportional system, on the other hand, encourages a country's parliament to be made up of parties and individuals based on the proportion of support they have throughout the country (or state, or city). In a proportional system, if a political party achieves 5 percent of the overall vote countrywide, it should wind up holding 5 percent of the seats in the parliament. How elections are done in this way isn't important for this book, but the important thing to understand is that it means that a party or candidate doesn't need to have the majority of support in any given geographic area in order to have a place in parliament. In other countries, this makes it easier for Green parties to be elected since their support is usually spread throughout the country rather than clustered in one place.

Parliaments elected under proportional systems almost always contain more than two parties. What this means is that countries that use proportional systems rarely elect one party with a complete majority of power. Instead, once their votes are counted and the seats in parliament occupied, parties need to talk and make agreements with each other until enough members of parliament come together in an alliance in order to form a government. The emphasis is placed on collaboration, cooperation, and consensus building. Parties operating in a proportional electoral arena don't tend to try to destroy each other, since if a government falls and a new election is called, there still likely won't be a single party with a majority. Instead, they'll all be back in parliament trying to create a new alliance, just this time with different sized parties and more people angry at each other over their actions during the election.

Most of Europe operates under proportional systems, as do numerous countries all over the world, such as Argentina, Israel, Zimbabwe, New Zealand, Turkey, and many more.

In the first chapter we introduced two political parties that formed under different systems: the United Tasmania group under Tasmania's proportional system, and the Values Party of New Zealand under New Zealand's (at the time) majoritarian system. The electoral system that a Green party, or any party, evolves within influences the path of its growth. A proportional system makes it far easier for a new party to gain electoral success, whereas a majoritarian system makes it extremely difficult for a party even with broad support to elect anyone at all.

In Europe, we can see the differences between the Green Party UK (from the United Kingdom) and Die Grüne (the German Green party). The former was the first of the European Green parties to contest an election and yet has only a single elected member after over thirty years of existence. Die Grüne has had a solid group of elected representatives since just its second contested election and has been part of a government coalition multiple times. The Green Party UK is forced to operate under a majoritarian system in which a candidate can only be elected if they are the single highest vote-getter in an individual election district, whereas in Germany a political party qualifies for representation as long as it gains at least 5 percent of the overall country's vote.

Since most of Europe utilizes proportional systems, European Greens were the first to really achieve success and influence in elections, and thus became the leaders of the worldwide political movement. Over the rest of this chapter, we'll look at a few of the Green parties of Europe and their development and histories.

CHAPTER 3 – THE GREEN BEGINNINGS IN EUROPE

The First European Greens

Although I wish it were as simple as saying "Green parties will exist and be strong in places where the electoral system allows them to," it can never be distilled down to such an easy explanation. Although the ease of a new party entering a country's legislature plays a big role in how successful a Green party (or any new party) can be after its creation, it plays a smaller role in whether a Green party will form in the first place. Political scientists have looked at what factors Green parties around the world have in common and haven't yet been able to reach an obvious consensus on how the stage needs to be set for a strong Green party to form. There are plenty of factors that can definitely be seen to contribute.

The United Tasmania Group shows how a Green party can form out of a concentrated single-issue environmental movement and the activism and gathering of people that come from such an effort. The Values Party of New Zealand shows how a Green party can form out of a general dissatisfaction with the direction of the mainstream parties and out of a desire for something radically different than what the current politicians and parties are offering. Europe and the rest of the world's Green parties tend to come from one of these two broad origins, although each party has unique circumstances that led to its formation that make it different from its partner parties only a border away.

The existence of the European Union gave European Green parties an easy way to collaborate and share ideas with each other as well as to inspire each other's success. The global information age allowed that collaboration and fellowship to bloom out into the rest of the world, encouraging Green parties to form in places without any of the structural connections that the European parties enjoyed.

"What I have learned over the years is that we must be patient, persevering and committed. When we plant trees, people sometimes say to me: 'I do not want to plant this tree because it will not grow fast enough.'
I must remind them that the trees they cut today, they did not plant. They were planted by their predecessors, so today they must plant the trees that will benefit the communities of tomorrow."

(René Dumont, candidate for President of France in 1974, forefather of the French Green Party)

THE 1970S

Less than a year after the formation of the United Tasmania Group and Values Party of New Zealand, the first of Europe's Green parties was coming together in Britain. The PEOPLE Party (written purposefully in capitals) is considered to have officially formed in 1973 in Coventry, England, at its first conference where it published a document entitled "Manifesto for a Sustainable Society." The idea of the party itself had originated the preceding year with Tony and Leslie Whittaker, a married couple who had been active in city politics with the UK's Conservative Party. Tony had been a city councillor in Kenilworth, a town of around twenty thousand people right in the geographic centre of England. His wife Leslie, a Conservative party activist herself, had bought a copy of *Playboy* (an admittedly odd start to this story) in which there was an interview with American biologist Paul R. Ehrlich about overpopulation.

Paul Ehrlich had published a best-selling book in 1968 entitled "*The Population Bomb*" in which he argued that the rapidly growing world population would lead to mass starvation and other societal upheavals, and controversially argued for government action to limit population growth. Leslie showed the article to her husband, and they brought together a small group of professionals and businesspeople who they thought the ideas would resonate with. They named themselves the "Club of Thirteen" since the group first met on the 13th of October, in 1972. The group began planning for the UK's next election, which was to take place in 1974.

In the February 1974 UK general election, the new party fielded six candidates out of a possible 635 electoral districts, including Leslie herself. Leslie fared the best, gaining just over 1,500 votes, or about 3.9 percent of the votes in her district. The other five candidates ranged from 0.7 percent to 2.8 percent.

As an aside, the February 1974 election itself was an oddity in British politics in that the dominant Labour and Conservative parties ended with extremely close seat totals, with neither of them gaining a full majority. The results were strange even for a majoritarian election, which often results in parliaments wildly different from the way people voted. The two big parties had both garnered about twelve million votes and had each elected about three hundred members of parliament. Meanwhile, the less popular Liberal party had gained six million votes, over half the amount of the big two parties, and yet had only managed to elect fourteen people. In yet another twist, the Labour party had actually received *fewer* votes than the Conservative party, and yet wound up with *more* members elected.

Political parties using majoritarian systems are unused to the idea of collaborating with another party, and sure enough neither large party was able to come to an agreement with the smaller Liberal Party to form an alliance. Instead, the two big parties decided to just throw a new election in the hope that the system would wipe out the Liberal party electorally and hand one of them a full majority. In October of the same year, the UK held a second election, and the PEOPLE Party quickly rallied for the unexpected sudden election and fielded five candidates, including Leslie Whittaker again.

In this case, the PEOPLE Party experienced one of the common struggles that small parties operating in majoritarian systems suffer: people saw that their vote for a small party hadn't accomplished anything and so they returned to one of the bigger parties. They were afraid that by voting for a small party they'd be enabling the party that they liked least to win. The support for the PEOPLE Party was cut in half, with even Leslie only earning 0.8 percent of the vote in her district. The gambit in calling for a new election paid off for the Labour Party. They gained a slim majority of elected members, and thus formed government on their own.

The PEOPLE Party continued to soldier on, and in 1975 voted to change its name to the Ecology Party to gain more recognition as the party of environmental issues and concern. In an interview in 1975, Leslie Whittaker stated that

> voters did not connect PEOPLE with ecology. What I wanted was something that the media could look up in their files so that, when they wanted a spokesman of the issue of ecology, they could find the Ecology Party and pick up the phone. It was as brutal and basic as that. PEOPLE didn't communicate what we had hoped it would communicate.

In the 1979 UK election, the now-named Ecology Party experienced an explosion in support, fielding fifty-three candidates for election, which entitled them to publicly funded radio and television broadcasts. Jonathon Porritt, who would be granted a British Knighthood in 2000 for his environmental work, joined the party during these years and was instrumental in raising the party's public profile. By 1979, the party's membership had grown from five hundred members to over five thousand, and this level of support meant that they were the fourth largest party in UK politics.

Despite this, the party was still competing in an electoral system in which it was exceptionally difficult for any but the two largest parties to succeed. The Ecology Party would continue for many more years simply trying to break into the UK's political system. The party did manage to start electing city councillors, starting with a 1976 win in East Sussex, and those local successes continues. But it took until 2010 for the party to finally elect their first Member of Parliament at the federal level.

The French

In 1974, Green political movements were beginning in another part of Europe as well. France uses an election system different from that of the UK or any of the other countries we've mentioned so far. France elects both a parliament and a single President separately, similar to how elections function in the United States. France's election system is majoritarian, although with a special tweak. If in the initial election (either for President or for any of France's over five hundred National Assembly seats) no candidate gains a majority (over half) of the votes, then a second election is held in which only the top two finishers are on the ballot. This means that the first ballot of French elections is usually a crowded affair with sometimes over a dozen candidates before the crowd is narrowed to only the two most popular.

In 1974, France was having a presidential election, which was contested by no fewer than twelve candidates from every possible flavour of political party. Putting his name forward in this busy field was René Dumont, a professor in Agricultural Sciences, bestselling author, and prominent French environmentalist. Although he would only receive 1.3 percent of the votes in the first round of the presidential election, his candidacy opened the way for environmentalism as a political concept in France. After all, 1.3 percent of the French Presidential vote was still three hundred thousand people. That's a significant number of supporters.

René's candidacy petitioned the French public on the ideas of pacifism, countering aggressive capitalism and advocating environmental responsibility and protection of Earth's resources. In a memorable TV advertisement during the 1974 election, he appeared seated in front of the camera wearing a bright red shirt and holding a glass of water. In a fast-talking and somewhat urgent appeal he stated,

We will soon run out of drinking water, and that is why I drink a glass of precious water in front of you. Before the end of the century, if we continue with such an overflow, it will be gone.

Although René's results weren't nearly enough to be recognized as a real contender for the French presidency, he brought a new wave of attention to environmental issues and the ideas that would become the basis of Green political philosophy. In the next round of French elections in 1978, many Green candidates contested local and federal elections under various party banners such as Ecology 78, Ecology Europe, and Ecology Today. The Green movement remained fractured during the 1970s as different parties contested elections all over France. They wouldn't coalesce into a single French Green identity until later on.

The Austrians

To the east of France, in Austria, a Green movement was beginning out of a unique environmental issue just like in Tasmania. In 1972, a ceremony was held to mark the completion of Austria's first nuclear power reactor, a plant near the small two-thousand-person town of Zwentendorf. Only two weeks after the ceremony, before the plant had even been turned on, a powerful earthquake damaged the foundation of the structure. Parts of it had to be torn down and replaced before the plant could become operational, and it was another four years before the plant was ready for a second groundbreaking ceremony.

An anti-nuclear movement formed in Austria in response to the event, with Austrians understandably worried about what would have happened if the new plant had been running when the earthquake occurred. Nuclear power plants had been in operation for nearly twenty years at this point in other parts of the world, but this was the first plant built in Austria. The country became divided on whether the potential risks of embracing nuclear power were worth the benefits that it would bring.

The government of Austria, at the time led by Bruno Kreisky of the Austrian Socialist Party, was convinced that nuclear power was in Austria's best interest and that the people of Austria agreed with him. He was supported in this by heads of Austrian unions, industry, and the Chamber of Commerce. Wanting to secure a clear direction of support from the Austrian people, he authorized a referendum on the issue of nuclear power in Austria, to be held in November of 1978.

His gamble failed, as a slight majority of 50.47 percent of votes was cast *against* the operation of any and all nuclear power plants in the country. Even though this was a bare majority opposed, Kreisky had wanted a clear mandate to support his position, so this was a brutal defeat. Bowing to the will of the public, the Austrian National Assembly passed a law prohibiting nuclear energy in

Austria. The Zwentendorf Nuclear Power Plant became the only nuclear energy facility in world history to be fully built and completed and then never turned on.

The organizational structures that were built by anti-nuclear activists to campaign against the Zwentendorf plant in 1978 would eventually become the basis for the Austrian Green party, known as Die Grüne Alternative (The Green Alternative) in the early 1980s.

Opposition to nuclear power will become another common thread in the formation of Europe's Green parties, and a common policy throughout many Green parties around the world. As I'm writing this book in 2019, it has become more difficult for Greens to justify opposition to nuclear power, as advancements in technology mean that many of the safety concerns that worried people in the mid-twentieth century are no longer as concerning. There's also a schism between those environmentalists who believe that nuclear energy is too dangerous and those environmentalists who see nuclear energy as a relatively safe and effective way to get humanity off of its dependence on fossil fuels faster as we work our way towards entirely relying on renewables. It's a debate that's worth having, but in the 1970s and 1980s, opposition to nuclear energy was common and accepted among environmentalists, and for good reason.

Indeed, in 1979, it was only one year after the Austrian nuclear referendum that an accident occurred at the Three Mile Island Nuclear Generating Station in Pennsylvania, USA. The accident started as a mechanical failure, and was worsened when human operators didn't initially notice the problem. Although real disaster was averted and the health effects of the accident are generally agreed to be very low, the possibility that things could have gone disastrously wrong triggered protests around the world and gave a great deal of credibility to existing anti-nuclear groups and political movements.

The First to Be Elected

At the tail end of the 1970s, another milestone in Green history was reached when the first Green candidate was elected to a national parliament. In 1975, Daniel Brélaz had joined an environmental advocacy group in the Swiss city of Lausanne, and when Switzerland held its national elections in 1978 he became the first candidate running on an explicitly environmental platform to be elected to its country's highest-level parliament.

The political party landscape in Switzerland has always contained a large number of diverse parties, and during the 1970s the various environmental and ecological groups operating throughout Switzerland hadn't yet formed into a single, central Green party. Daniel Brélaz was standing in the district of Vaud, in the French-speaking west of the country, and in 1978 received 6.4 percent of the local vote. However, unlike in the UK or France, Switzerland uses a proportional system for its elections in which each district sends multiple representatives to the Federal Assembly. Since the canton of Vaud was electing sixteen representatives, Daniel's vote total was enough for him to win one of the spots.

Finally, as was mentioned in the last chapter, 1979 marked the first time that the new Green political parties throughout Europe first attempted to coordinate for an election for the European parliament. CEGRP (Coordination of European Green and Radical Parties) was set up to coordinate various Green and Radical parties, but it failed to form a coherent election platform on which all the groups could campaign. Although the effort was unsuccessful in electing anyone, it prepared the groups for their second attempt in 1984 in which five European countries would succeed in sending twenty Green representatives to help guide the path forward for the European union.

"The profound political changes we need in order to heal our planet will not come about through fragmented problem solving or intellectual analyses that overlook the deepest yearnings and intuitions of the heart . . . As we begin to cultivate a rich inner life and experience our connection with all life, we realize how little of what society tells us we need is actually important for our well-being . . . Green politics must address the spiritual vacuum of industrial society."

(Petra Kelly, founder of the German Green Party)

THE 1980S

The 1970s brought us burgeoning Green political movements in Australia, New Zealand, the United Kingdom, France, Austria, and Switzerland. The 1980s brought us a Green tidal wave. The '80s are generally agreed to be when the idea of Green politics really began to spread and catch on, and it's the time in history when most of the world's more successful Green parties first formed.

The Germans

In the final few months of the 1970s, a political party formed that would go on to be (at the time of writing) the most established and successful of the world's Green parties. On September 30th of 1979, a group of over seven hundred ecologists gathered in the city of Sindelfingen and founded Die Grüne Baden-Württemberg, a local Green party for West Germany's southwest state. Only a few months later on January 13th, 1980, the federal version of Die Grüne was founded in the city of Karlsruhe.

In the previous chapter we covered the six core principles of the Global Greens, and the German Green Party was where four of these concepts were first clearly put into words. At this meeting, Die Grünen proclaimed their Four Pillars of the Green Party as social justice, ecological wisdom, grassroots democracy, and nonviolence. The German Greens were also the party that came up with the word "Green" to describe the movement. In Germany, the political parties are commonly referred to by their official colours, and so the German ecologists thought green would be a great label for themselves due to its connection to nature. Also, the colour hadn't been taken yet by the other parties.

The success of the German Greens came quickly. In the German state of Bremen a group of Greens was elected to the state legislature in 1979, although they were running just as a "Green list" and not as a fully constituted party. The Baden-Württemberg state Greens were the first to be elected as an official party, which they did in early 1980. The Greens at the federal level attempted to enter the Bundestag (the federal West German legislature) in the 1980 federal elections, but despite their successes in several individual states, they were unsuccessful in their first federal election.

The Greens resonated with people as something of an anti-party. There were three dominant parties in German politics, and they had all been in existence since at least the end of World War Two. The conservative Christian Democratic Union and the worker's rights Social Democratic Party both predated the war, and the classical liberal Free Democratic Party had formed in 1948. German elections usually resulted in either the Christian Democrats or the Socialists alternating between winning the most votes, with the Free Democrats winning just enough to be needed by the winning larger party as a coalition partner. Many voters thought that the three big parties had stopped being *Volksparteien* (parties of the people) and had instead becomes *Staatsparteien* (parties of the state), and were eager to see a new political movement that championed issues that the big parties seemed uninterested in.

Germany's proportional system meant that Die Grünen only needed to reach 5 percent of the vote in an election to successfully gain entry to the Bundestag, which they did in the 1983 election. By then they were already represented in seven of Germany's state parliaments, having reached the 5 percent threshold in local state elections. Twenty-eight Greens took their seats in the six-hundred-seat Bundestag in the West German capital of Bonn that year. In 1987, Die Grünen increased that number to forty-four. The first leader of Die Grünen, Petra Kelly, would become one of the most influential figures in Green political history and development, as well as being the first female head of a political party in German history.

In a recently published report, thirty years after the first Greens were elected in the Federal Republic of Germany, authors Andrei Markovits and Joseph Klaver looked back on the day when the Greens first entered the Bundestag to take their seats:

> To be sure, the iconography of the actual entrance into the hallowed halls of the Bundestag on 29 March 1983 still bespoke a clear desire on the part of these twenty-eight new members of parliament to be seen as decidedly anti-establishment. There was Walter Schwenninger with a long hand-woven peasant sweater alongside Dieter Drabiniok and Gert Janssen with their flowing locks and wild beards; Marieluise Beck appeared with a pine tree pockmarked by acid rain slung

over one shoulder; Petra Kelly was also there, carrying a large bouquet of fresh flowers; and then there was Gabriele Potthast sporting a tuxedo-like quintessentially male garment in a clear attempt at gender bending and thus confronting the establishment with its square sense of sexuality and its boring bourgeois habitus and mores, not to mention its evil sexism. (Markovits and Klaver 2012, 7)

Die Grünen was far from the only Green political party to form in the 1980s. 1981 saw the formation of the Miljöpartiet de gröna in Sweden and the Ecology Party of Ireland, as well as a Belgian election in which two new Belgian Green parties (one Flemish-speaking and one French-speaking) both succeeded in electing members. In France, another prominent environmentalist, Brice Lalonde, ran for election as president and received over one million votes. Later in the 1980s, Lalonde would be recognized for his expertise and accomplishments when he was appointed as the Minister of the Environment for France. In 1982, Os Verdes formed in Portugal, and the disparate French Green parties united into a movement called Les Verts. In 1983, De Gronne in Denmark, De Groenen in the Netherlands, Dei Greng in Luxembourg, and the Federation of Green Parties of Switzerland all officially formed. The Green wave was sweeping through the countries of Europe.

Each of the Green Parties has a unique story of its formation, and longer books than this one have been written that go into great detail about each party's early years and the reasons for its formation. Any one of them could make for a fascinating book, filled with idealistic characters and brutal challenges and hardships. As much as I'd love to write a chapter on each one of them, that would balloon this book far past its intended length. But it's still worth just touching on some of the unique circumstances for each of them.

The Belgians

In Belgium, two Green separate parties had formed, which is understandable since Belgian elections are divided into two distinct districts. Belgium is a union of the French-speaking south and the Flemish-speaking north, and each linguistic region elects its representatives separately.

Ecolo, the French-speaking Green party of Belgium, officially formed in 1980 after surprising itself with an unexpectedly strong result in the 1979 European Parliament election as a group of loosely affiliated independents. The Flemish Green movement, called Agalev, evolved from a community group centred around a Jesuit priest named Anders Gaan Leven (thus A-Ga-Lev) who advocated for environmental and social issues. In the 1970s, the group would just endorse environmentally-minded candidates from other parties but eventually began to run as candidates themselves. In 1981, they succeeded in electing a couple of members to Belgium's parliament, and surprised themselves in doing so. In 1982, the elected representatives officially incorporated themselves into a party. In the parliament, they joined forces with their French siblings in Ecolo, although the two remained as separate parties as that's how things are done in Belgium.

1984 was without a doubt the most pivotal and important year in Europe's Green party development thus far. After attempting to gather together Europe's environmentalist movements for the 1979 European Parliament elections and not quite succeeding, the organizers tried again for the elections in 1984. This time they were fantastically successful and elected a strong group of delegates from five countries. The success of the Greens in the European elections sent a message across Europe that Green politics were viable, and that Green political parties forming in Europe could expect to be successful. Die Grüne Alternative in Austria and Federazione dei Verdi of Italy formed shortly after, along with Vihrea Liito in Finland, Miljøpartiet De Grønne in Norway, The Green Party of Bulgaria, GroenLinks in the Netherlands, Eesti Rohelised in Estonia, and Alternattiva Demokratika in Malta later in the decade.

The Dutch

In the Netherlands, the path towards their own Green party took an unfamiliar route, different than most of what we've seen so far. In 1983, a Dutch Green party called De Groenen formed, and contested the 1986 election. The Netherlands is known for having one of the *most* proportional electoral systems in the world, and for having the lowest threshold for election. While countries like Germany set a minimum of having to receive 5 percent of all votes before entering parliament, the Netherlands has a threshold of only 0.7 percent, meaning it is possibly the easiest place in the world for a new political party to get someone elected. However, even with this exceptionally low barrier to entry, the Dutch Green party was unsuccessful in 1986. The reasons for its failure are complicated, but can be generalized as infighting, bad organization, and a platform that was *too* pure in its Green philosophy for Dutch voters to accept.

More interesting than the stillborn De Groenen is the Netherlands' second formed Green party. In 1989, a number of established left-wing parties came together and merged into a single entity, naming themselves GroenLinks, the Green Left. While most Green parties form out of a uniting environmental issue or a radical new philosophy that rejects the left-right spectrum, GroenLinks is relatively unique in that it is an unabashedly left-wing coalition of radical parties that over time embraced Green ideologies and incorporated them into their own, even going so far as to rename themselves as such.

Four parties came together to form GroenLinks: The Communist Party of the Netherlands, the Pacifist Socialist Party, the Political Party of Radicals, and the Evangelical People's Party. Despite the two latter parties having religious roots, neither actually campaigned as particularly religious parties, and both were far more progressive than the churches they had been associated with. The two parties are often considered as early Green parties, suggesting Green solutions to problems before a real coherent Green political philosophy was an accepted idea.

The four parties had been trending towards the nascent Green ideas, and although they all had elected members of parliament at the time of the merger, their support had been decreasing over the previous years. Since they now considered themselves to have more in common than what separated them, the parties joined forces and reinvented themselves. The internal dynamics between the members and ideologies of these four political groups in their early days would make for an interesting book on its own, as each part of the coalition clashed with the others on some issues and yet agreed completely on other ones. However, their strategy paid off and the united GroenLinks doubled their number of seats in the 1989 election. They've gone on to be one of the more successful Green parties in Europe, although always a bit of an odd-man-out due to their avowed and proud left-wing history.

Pan-Europe

Broadening our scope, in the 1989 European Parliament election, the pan-European Green coalition improved its results and elected thirty individuals from seven different European countries. However, the most interesting Green-related result of the 1989 election was what occurred in one of the countries that *didn't* elect any Greens.

Each country in the European Union is allowed to select the electoral system that it wants to use when electing members to the European Parliament. This means that each country elects its delegates in wildly different ways, some proportional and some majoritarian. In 1989, most of the European Union's countries were using the same proportional system that they used for their national elections. Oddly, some countries, such as France, were using proportional systems for these elections even though they used majoritarian systems for their own national elections. The United Kingdom was the only country using a majoritarian system to elect its representatives.

1989 marks the best ever performance for the Green Party of the UK, which changed its name from the Ecology Party in 1985. The Green Party received over two million votes, nearly 15 percent of the total votes across the United Kingdom. One in six voters cast their ballot for the Green Party to represent them. And these one-in-six voters elected no one. The majoritarian system meant that the Greens were entirely shut out, despite their impressive result. Meanwhile, in proportional France, Les Verts received 11 percent of the vote and sent ten Greens to the EU parliament, and in West Germany Die Grünen received 8 percent of the vote and sent eight elected Greens. This must have been extremely frustrating for the Greens in the United Kingdom.

Miljöpartiet de gröna, the Green Party of Sweden, was unsuccessful in its first two elections in 1982 and 1985. Similar to Austria, it had formed out of a nuclear power referendum held in the country. Despite its attempts to push environmentalist and Green political ideas as worth considering, the Swedish electorate during these years were far more focused on other matters. However, in the 1988 election, the environment was the absolute top of people's concerns and the successful Swedish Greens wound up being the first new party in seventy years to break into Sweden's parliament.

There's a reason that support for Green parties in the late 1980s was suddenly so strong. Part of it is just due to the hard work and effort that Greens had been putting into building their organizations and disseminating their message. But a large part was that in 1986 the Chernobyl nuclear power plant in Ukraine suffered a catastrophic accident, the worst nuclear disaster in history.

On April 26 in 1986, a combination of design flaws and human error caused an uncontrolled reaction and subsequent steam explosion at the plant near the Ukrainian town of Pripyat. Unlike the Three Mile Island accident in the '70s, the Chernobyl accident was a genuine disaster that led to the nearby town being evacuated, the plant being entirely shut down and quarantined, and a significant amount of radioactive material being released into the atmosphere.

The use of nuclear power was already controversial in the 1970s and 1980s, and the Chernobyl disaster meant that any election happening in the late '80s was going to have nuclear power as one of the core issues. Since many of Europe's Green parties originated in anti-nuclear movements, they were able to benefit from people's newfound attention to the nuclear controversy.

By the end of the 1980s, Green politicians were present in the national parliaments of West Germany, Belgium, Switzerland, Sweden, Finland, Luxembourg, and the Netherlands. Greens from Italy, Portugal, Spain, and France were also present as members of the Parliament of the European Union.

"Those who are ahead of their time often live out of earshot for years."

(Robert Jungk, Green Party Candidate for President of Austria in 1992, author of Brighter than a Thousand Suns: A Personal History of the Atomic Scientists*)*

THE 1990S

At the beginning of the 1990s, Die Grüne, the German Greens, was the best positioned of the world's Green parties. In the 1987 West German parliamentary election, they had elected forty-four members to the German Bundestag, putting them on equal footing with the much older and more established Free Democratic Party and its forty-eight members. The Greens were also present in a number of the state-level parliaments of West Germany, and in 1985 the Greens in the state of Hesse had actually joined with the Social Democrat Party (SPD) in what would be the first red-green coalition government of many to come. By the mid-90s, most Greens were expecting that they would be invited to be the junior partner in a coalition government at the federal level any day now, forming government alongside either the larger Social Democrat Party or the Christian Democrat Party. But they'd gotten to that point following a near collapse of the party in 1990, and a major overhaul that followed.

Over forty years earlier, at the end of World War Two, Hitler's Nazi Germany had been defeated and partitioned by the victorious Allied forces. The western and eastern halves of Germany were split into two different countries: the Federal Republic of Germany supported by the United States and its European allies, and the German Democratic Republic supported by the Soviet Union. The city of Berlin, of course, was a political enclave entirely surrounded by Soviet Germany, its western and eastern halves bisected by the Berlin Wall. During the nearly fifty years in which the two countries were separate, many wondered if they'd ever reunite into a single nation.

The Surprising Test of German Unification

In the 1980s, the Soviet Union was struggling both politically and economically, and had thus scaled back its intervention in European politics. In 1989, there were revolutions all across the Soviet sphere of influence, and in East Germany the "Peaceful Revolution" had led to the opening of German borders, the fall of the Berlin Wall, and East Germany's first and only free elections in 1990. The East German election of 1990 resulted in the defeat of the formerly dominant Socialist Unity Party of Germany, which had until then governed East Germany effectively as a one-party state. The new, freely elected German government voted 299-80 to join the western Federal Republic of Germany in September of 1990, and the two Germanies were then united into a single state.

An East German Green Party had actually formed in time to compete in the free East German elections, and succeeded in electing eight members in a combined alliance list with another party, the Independent Women's Association. Another alliance of small parties that called itself Alliance '90 had also elected twelve members in this election, and had run on a Green-ish platform. The West German Die Grüne had ready allies in the new eastern provinces.

The problem was that the western Greens weren't even in agreement that unification with East Germany was something that they wanted. While the rest of Germany was preparing for unification, Greens in the west were still arguing about how and if the union would work at all. The Green groups on either side of the now-defunct border also had trouble working together, as they'd been operating in isolation from each other and had very little time to come together and coordinate before a new election for the whole of Germany was called for December of the same year.

While the other major parties like the Christian Democratic Union (CDU) and the Social Democratic Party (SPD) of the west quickly funnelled money and support towards their eastern equivalents, the Greens didn't manage to combine their operations in time for the first unified German election. The Greens were still a new party, and their lack of experience and organization led to the western Greens and the eastern Greens running as separate parties in the December election, with the plan being to formalize a merger afterwards, when there was more time to hash out the details.

This was a critical failure on behalf of the western Greens. The election of 1990 was entirely focused around the issues of German reunification, and since the western Greens still hadn't figured out their positions, they campaigned instead on their usual issues of ecologism and sustainability. The German public wasn't interested, and punished the Greens for it.

When the results of the election were revealed, the west German Greens had only achieved 4.8 percent of the vote in the western states, meaning they had actually missed the 5 percent cut-off for parties to enter the Bundestag. All forty-four of the Greens' members of parliament lost their seats, and the west German Greens were completely wiped out in the federal parliament. Meanwhile, their allies in the east wound up with 6.1 percent in the eastern states and therefore succeeded in electing eight members. Had the two groups managed to unite before the election, their combined totals would have been enough to elect twenty-six members.

Fundis and Realos

This unexpected loss rocked the party. Although they did go ahead with the planned merger between the western and eastern parties, they also began a period of introspection and reforms within the party itself. Any Green party is always made up of two major camps, usually referred to as the *fundis* (fundamentalists) and the *realos* (realists). *Fundis* are those who advocate for radical change, for being an anti-party, for refusing to imitate the structures of major established parties, for protest instead of participation, and for more focus on the grassroots.

Realos are those who want to work within the system to achieve change, who are happy with incremental progress instead of sudden radical leaps, who find value in emulating the structures of major parties, and who want to participate in governments as partners to achieve their goals. After the electoral wipe-out in 1990, the *realos* within Die Grüne jumped on the opportunity to reform the party to work more similarly to their major party rivals, so that they could become competitive again.

Although many *fundis* might argue that these reforms meant that Die Grüne was losing its soul, they certainly worked to get Greens elected. After the 1994 German election, the newly professionalized Greens were back at forty-nine members, which was even more than the traditional third party in German elections, the Free Democratic Party. The Greens were now the third of the five parties in the Bundestag. In 1998, the Greens fared very slightly worse and lost two members, but finally succeeded in the goal that they had thought was just on the horizon back in 1990 before their collapse.

Power-Sharing Breakthroughs

After sixteen years and four elections of dominance, German Chancellor Helmut Kohl of the Christian Democrat Party was defeated. Gerhard Schroder and the Social Democratic Party (SPD) were the winners in the election with the most members elected, but still didn't have enough to form a majority government. The SPD turned to the Greens, still the third largest party in the Bundestag, to form a coalition government. Green Leader Joschka Fischer became the Deputy Chancellor and Minister of Foreign Affairs of Germany. The SPD and Die Grüne formed

Germany's first red–green (named for the official colours of the two parties) federal government, governing a country of eighty-two million people.

Germany wasn't the only place in Europe where Green parties were having breakthroughs. While Germany's proportional electoral system meant that Greens just needed to reach a simple cut-off to make it into parliament, the challenge was much greater in majoritarian France. As covered earlier, France uses a fairly unique two-round system in which a second runoff election is called unless a candidate receives an absolute majority of votes in the first round. In the 1993 legislative elections, French Green candidates received nearly 11 percent of all votes in the first round. While this is a higher percentage than the Greens in Germany achieved at any point in the '90s, only two individual Greens managed to get enough votes to qualify for a second round run-off. In those subsequent run-offs, neither Green candidate was elected. Despite this failure to actually elect anyone, the 11 percent of the vote achieved by the French Greens was the highest yet in French legislative elections.

The "Rally for the Republic" (RPR) party of Jacques Chirac was the big winner of the 1993 French elections. Chirac himself left the French legislature two years later to run successfully for French President, leaving Alain Juppé as the head of the RPR in the legislature. In 1997, President Chirac and Prime Minister Juppé tried to take the French left wing by surprise by calling an early election. Opinion polls showed that the right wing would easily win another majority, so they figured a snap election was a smart move to consolidate power.

Antoine Waechter, the leader of the French Greens in 1993, had been opposed to any sort of electoral alliance with non-Green parties, and the Greens had elected no one despite their strong showing in the total vote percentage. But Waechter had been replaced after the election by Dominique Voynet, one of the two Green politicians who had finished well enough in the first round of the 1993 elections to make it into the second round. In 1997, Dominique agreed to an election alliance with four other parties on the left of the French political spectrum. This decision was unpopular with conservative Greens, and those Greens who agreed with Waechter that ecologists should contest the elections on their own, but the alliance paid off in getting Greens elected.

The results of the 1997 election were a shock to the right wing, who had called the early election in the first place. It was the first time in over a hundred years in which the President of France lost a legislative election that he had called. The "Plural Left" alliance containing the Greens gained a strong majority, which included the election of seven Greens. A coalition government was formed between the five parties of the left, with Lionel Jospin from the Socialist Party as Prime Minister and Dominique Voynet from the Greens as Minister of Planning and Environment. It was a roundabout way for the French Greens to have their breakthrough, but they'd gotten there.

In the mid '90s, Green parties joined the governments of other European countries as well. The 1995 election in Finland resulted in a broad "Rainbow Coalition" between five parties, with Green League MP Pekka Haavisto joining Prime Minister Paavo Lipponen's cabinet as the Minister of the Environment. In Italy, the 1996 election resulted in Prime Minister Romano Prodi inviting Green MP Edo Ronchi to be the Minister of Environment and Protection of Land and Sea. In 1990, Toomas Frey in Estonia, a Green politician, was made Minister of the Environment, as was Marcian Bleahu of the Romanian Greens in 1991, and Radosław Gawlik of the Polish Greens in 1997. In the Belgian elections of 1999, the two Belgian Green parties (Ecolo and Agalev) were invited to join a centre–left coalition, and were each given two ministerial portfolios. Isabel Durant and Olivier Deleuze from Ecolo were given the Ministries of Transport and Energy, respectively; while Magda Aelvoet and Eddy Boutmans from Agalev were given the Ministries of Environment and Development Cooperation.

By the turn of the millennium, Green politicians could be found in national and state legislatures all over Europe, as well as in countless town councils and municipal governments. Greens were serving as junior coalition partners and ministers in several national-level governments, as well as many state-level governments. In the parliament of the European Union, the Greens formed the fourth largest political block, with members elected from twelve European nations. Even in the United Kingdom, a country whose election system had been incredibly hostile to Green participation, Greens were starting to make inroads. For the 1999 European Union election, the United Kingdom had finally decided to abandon first-past-the-post and adopt a proportional system like the rest of Europe, and thus two Greens were elected as delegates from the UK. A referendum in Scotland led to the creation of a Scottish Parliament separate from the parliament of the whole United Kingdom. The newly formed parliament had decided to follow the example of the rest of Europe and use a proportional system for its elections. Robin Harper became the first Green elected to the Scottish Parliament.

Green Parties at the Turn of the Millennium

Political scientists and historians who try to understand the history of social and political movements like to create structures and lenses that they can use to view this history. Finding a common pathway that any new political movement will take allows us to categorize and compare parties and movements as they pass through their history.

Per Gahrton proposed in his book *Green Parties, Green Future* that there are five steps that lead to the establishment of a new political party:

> First, grassroots movements/local protest actions. Second, membership movements, like the Sierra Club, and other pressure groups. Third, lobby groups/professional actions/theatre, Greenpeace, etc. What these first three steps have in common is that they all aim at changing the behaviour of those who hold the power. When environmentalists get fed up with not achieving their goals

through protest and pressure, they may be tempted to try to build the society they wish for, to create their Green Utopia. This is step four, the construction of 'green alternative islands'. The fifth step is the creation of a political party. (2015, page 12)

This is certainly accurate for the Green parties of Europe, Australia, and New Zealand that we've looked at so far. Most parties began with a protest or other attempt to get the attention of the government. When that didn't move fast enough or was ignored entirely, passionate people decided to try to cut out the middleman. If the government wasn't willing to listen to them, they'd become the government.

In terms of the lifecycle of a party itself, Mogens Pedersen, a Danish professor of political science, proposed a pathway for a "party lifespan" that consists of four steps:

1. The threshold of declaration, which corresponds to the parties' origins, when they declare their first participation to elections;
2. The threshold of authorisation, which refers to the meeting of legal regulations or requirements in order to participate in elections;
3. The threshold of representation, that is, the gaining of the first seats in parliament;
4. The threshold of relevance, which corresponds to an impact on government formation and policy output. (Pedersen and van Haute 2016, page 4)

It's easy to see how these steps align with the parties described in this chapter. It can almost be charted on a per decade basis: the 1970s for the declaration of intent; the 1980s for the meeting of requirements and actually running in elections; and the 1990s for the gaining of first seats—give or take a few years in either direction for each party—which means that the new millennium would bring Green parties to the threshold of relevance. Green parties would begin to seriously impact government, to serve as part of it, or even to lead it.

The Canadian Situation

In North America, Green parties are still at the fringes of our political systems. Like the United Kingdom, most of North America still uses majoritarian electoral systems that make it extremely difficult for any new party to break in. In Canada, our elections are usually fought between three very old parties: the Liberal Party, which has existed since the mid-1800s; the Conservative Party, which has undergone a few different incarnations and transformations but also originated in the same time period; and the comparatively young New Democratic Party (NDP) whose roots began in the 1930s.

CHAPTER 3 – THE GREEN BEGINNINGS IN EUROPE

While the New Democratic Party has formed a few governments at the provincial level in Canada, it still has yet to form a federal government, even after over seventy years of existence. In certain Canadian provinces such as Prince Edward Island and New Brunswick, the local provincial-level New Democrats have never even elected more than a single member of parliament at a time. Canadian governments bounce back and forth between the Liberals and Conservatives, with the New Democrats only forming the official opposition (the party with the second highest number of seats) once in their history.

If it's so difficult for an old party such as the New Democrats, which has existed since before most Canadians were born, to break into the Canadian system, then one can imagine how difficult it has been for the Canadian Greens, which have only existed since the early 1980s. But in countries with proportional systems, the Greens have been an established political participant for decades, and by the end of the '90s and the early 2000s were not only well represented in parliaments, but also participating in governments.

It's possible that Canadian Greens will follow a similar trajectory to the New Democratic Party: struggling to make progress at the federal level, but managing to successfully break through at the provincial level. The New Democratic Party won its first majority government in the province of Saskatchewan in 1944, becoming the first "socialist party" to be elected anywhere in North America. At the time it was called the Co-operative Commonwealth Federation, and its leader, Tommy Douglas, would be remembered as one of history's greatest Canadians. His government created North America's first single-payer healthcare system, a system that the rest of Canada would later adopt.

The hope of many Canadian Greens is that we'll be able to do the same. In 1938, in the election just prior to Tommy Douglas and the New Democrats' historic win, the party had garnered just over 18 percent of the vote. In 1944 they shot up in popularity, winning not only a majority of seats but a majority of votes as well, which is a rarity in Canadian politics.

Likewise, in the province of Alberta, the local NDP formed a majority government in 2015, gaining a 30 percent jump in voter support from their previous result of 10 percent in 2011, and unseating the Alberta Progressive Conservative government for the first time in over forty years. In the 2017 election in my home province of British Columbia, the BC Green Party received nearly 17 percent of the vote. And 2019 in Prince Edward Island the Greens formed the official opposition to a minority Progressive Conservative government. At the provincial level Canadians seem willing to give a chance to new parties and new governments, even if they're not willing to do the same at the federal level.

With the idea that we could soon possibly see a Green government in Canada, it's worth looking at how Green-supported or led governments around the world have worked so far. Later on in the second half of this book, we'll look at a couple examples of European and other Greens in government, some successful and some unsuccessful. But before we get to those we'll dive into Canadian history and look at the beginnings of the Greens in Canada.

CHAPTER 4

THE EARLY GREENS IN CANADA

"Any intelligent fool can make things bigger, more complex, and more violent. It takes a touch of genius—and a lot of courage—to move in the opposite direction."

(Ernst F. Schumacher, Small Is Beautiful: Economics as if People Mattered*)*

THE EARLY GREENS IN CANADA

On a Thursday morning at 9:00 a.m. in 2017, I sat down at the kitchen table of Adriane Carr and Paul George. It was the best (and only) time we could find to do an interview, as Adriane was the sole city councillor from the Green Party of Vancouver and thus led an extremely busy life. She mentioned that she had about an hour before she had to run off to another meeting, and that she had at least eight lined up for that day alone. Paul was happy to hang around and chat for longer, as his day was probably going to be spent at the party's office doing some general volunteer administration work.

Thirty-seven years before that morning interview, Paul and Adriane had met while distributing calendars for an environmental fundraising campaign, and two years later they'd founded North America's first Green party.

The First Green Party in North America

In the summer of 1977, Paul George, then a young and passionate environmental activist, and a few friends were camped out on Lyell Island. Lyell Island is part of the Haida Gwaii archipelago, a triangular-shaped group of islands off of British Columbia's northern coast. At the time they were known as the Queen Charlotte Islands, but were returned to their Indigenous name in 2010. Haida Gwaii is the traditional heartland of the Haida Nation, an Indigenous maritime territory that in the age before European colonialism was renowned for its seamanship, trading networks, and artistic craftsmanship. The first Europeans to encounter the island arrived in 1774, but relations between the Haida and the Europeans were never particularly friendly. The Haida even captured and sank a pair of European vessels in the late eighteenth century.

In the 1970s, there were plans by British Columbia's logging industry to start forestry operations in the southern islands, and residents of the islands had been campaigning in opposition to the proposal. Paul, then living in the city of Victoria on nearby Vancouver Island, had become passionate about the archipelago after studying it for a school assignment. He'd been looking for ways to help the conservation campaign from his home in the province's capital. His initial idea had been for a fundraiser coffee table book full of pictures of Haida Gwaii's wilderness, but the idea soon fizzled, and Paul and his friends instead turned to petitioning British Columbia's government directly from their homes in the province's capital.

Working mostly on their own, they set their sights on an upcoming revision of BC's Forestry Act, hoping they could secure an exemption for the southern islands of Haida Gwaii. They went directly to British Columbia's provincial legislature to make an official presentation to the government while it was debating the Forestry Act. They quickly ran into the powerful force of the forestry lobby, as Paul George writes in his memoir book *Big Trees Not Big Stumps*:

> On the way out of the building I couldn't believe my eyes. Pouring out of the front doors of the Legislature were dozens of big forest company executives dressed in suits and half-cut on booze. They were drinking and celebrating. They obviously had been drinking all evening, confidently starting their victory celebration early. (2006, page 12)

Paul and his small group of environmentalists realized that they were not going to be able to budge the government with just a well-spoken argument. They were going to need massive public support behind them if they wanted the government to even give them the time of day. As Paul writes,

> It was my first reality check regarding BC politics. Government was there to facilitate "business as usual"—and that included automatic renewals of Tree Farm Licenses. I don't think those in power even understood what it meant to act on behalf of the greater public good. Moreover, I think they saw First Nations and local environmental groups as simply getting in the way. (2006, page 15)

CHAPTER 4 – THE EARLY GREENS IN CANADA

Seeing a need to generate public support and awareness of the wilderness areas that he was looking to conserve, Paul turned his efforts towards the already established environmental organizations such as Greenpeace and the Sierra Club. He was unsuccessful with the Sierra Club since as an American organization, it wasn't particularly interested in Canadian conservation campaigns. Greenpeace was supportive but admitted that it just didn't have the time or resources to dedicate to yet another campaign. Seeing no other option, Paul and his close friend and campaign partner Richard Krieger opted to simply start their own environmental conservation society. Having never done something like this before, they managed to stumble through registering an official society, which they called the Western Canada Wilderness Committee.

The Western Canada Wilderness Committee (WCWC) was the training ground where those who eventually founded North America's first Green party learned organizational skills, campaign strategies, and made the connections that are needed to form a functioning party. The WCWC's main campaign during its early years was the printing and distribution of a Canadian wilderness calendar with each month featuring a different threatened wilderness area as well as information about groups seeking to protect the particular piece of land. By doing this, the WCWC was able to build connections and contacts with other environmental groups who, in the 1970s and 1980s often felt like they were working in a vacuum. In the modern era with the invention of the internet, we can often forget how difficult it was for groups to gain recognition and awareness without the help of mass media and the information networks we now take for granted.

It was during one of these calendar distribution campaigns that Paul met a young woman named Adriane Carr who at the time was a teacher at Vancouver's Langara College. Paul recalls writing down in his notebook "a really good calendar seller" to describe Adriane after she agreed to take fifty calendars to resell on her own. He also recalls that Adriane was officially member number fifteen on the WCWC's as-of-yet small membership list.

Fast-forward to 1983 and Adriane and Paul, now a couple, had a new strategy for getting the attention of British Columbia's politicians. Paul had realized that elected politicians were often quite happy to accept posters featuring beautiful photography of the province. They liked to decorate the walls of their offices and enjoyed seeing well-produced pictures of their province. In addition, the Legislature had a free picture-framing service for Members of the Assembly, so elected officials tended to take advantage and get any art that they received framed and hung somewhere visible.

The WCWC had several posters printed featuring the wilderness areas they were looking to conserve and then distributed them to as many elected politicians as they could. The hope was that when it came to a vote on protecting a particular wilderness area that the politicians would remember that they had a picture of that area hung on their own wall, and that this would make them more likely to vote to protect it. It would create a personal connection to a far-flung piece of the province that they otherwise wouldn't care about.

Petitioning the Existing Parties

Paul and friends showed up at the annual convention for the governing Social Credit Party with a stack of posters in hand. The Social Credit Party was a bit of a long shot for a group looking for wilderness conservation, as they were British Columbia's right-of-centre, business-friendly, free-market party. Nonetheless, the posters proved popular, with many delegates to the convention happily accepting the free handouts. Paul even managed to hand one to May Richards Bennett, who was the mother of the current Premier and the wife of BC's most famous former Premier (former Premier W. A. C. Bennett and at-the-time Premier Bill Bennett, who were father and son).

There were only two parties represented in BC's legislature at the time. A few weeks after the Social Credit convention the WCWC planned to repeat their poster campaign at the convention for the British Columbia New Democratic Party (BC NDP), BC's major left-of-centre labour and socialist party. The BC NDP was seen as much friendlier ground for environmentalists as they had included environmental protection issues in their platform before.

As BC NDP supporters themselves, Adriane came up with the idea that in addition to handing out posters, they could propose an actual resolution at the convention to include protection for the southern Haida Gwaii wilderness areas. It was a long shot, but it would at least bring it to the attention of the party bigwigs and general members. It was also how the democratic process was supposed to work in grassroots parties: individual members proposing platform ideas for the membership to vote on.

Adriane and Paul arrived at the convention, once again with posters in hand, and while Paul began handing out the posters Adriane went to work trying to see if a last-minute resolution could be added into the schedule. The party had a process for exactly this situation: they dedicated a period of time to last-minute resolutions brought up at the convention. The submissions were ranked and selected by a committee charged with deciding which of the many last-minute resolutions were worth bringing up to the membership.

Adriane and a friend of hers who was a BC NDP delegate tirelessly ran around the convention hall handing out posters and gathering support for her resolution, and by the end of the day Adriane felt that most of the delegates on the floor were actually in support. In the final meeting with the selection committee, she was informed that the resolution would be number seven on the list, which meant that they stood a good chance having it brought up for a vote if the previous resolutions weren't too controversial and didn't take up too much discussion time. Adriane and Paul went home for the evening, happy and looking forward to day two of the convention.

The next morning the couple arrived bright and early, ready to spend the day handing out posters and working towards support for their resolution. The official schedule for day two had been posted and Adriane wandered over to have a look. She scanned the schedule looking for the official notice of their resolution but couldn't find it.

CHAPTER 4 – THE EARLY GREENS IN CANADA

Eventually she spotted it, just about at the bottom of the list. Although she had been told the previous day that it would be scheduled at the number seven spot, the proposal had been moved to number fourteen, just about as far down the list as it could go. Even worse, it was scheduled right after a last-minute proposal on same-sex marriage rights, which was about as controversial as a resolution could be in the early '80s. There was almost no chance that the convention was going to have time for their proposal.

Disillusioned

At the time Adriane and Paul were shocked and couldn't understand what had happened. They had trusted the democratic structures of the party and had gone through all the right processes and jumped through all the hoops that they had been told to jump through. Adriane and Paul told me that at the time they didn't know how entrenched and strong the International Woodworkers of America Union was inside the power structure of the BC NDP. Although they have no concrete proof of its involvement, their suspicion now is that the Woodworkers Union or some other pro-forestry union force inside the party had vetoed the resolution and had it pushed to the back of the line to get it out of the way. Feeling defeated, Paul and Adriane and the other WCWC members left the convention, making a beeline straight for the bar.

On the way to the bar, Adriane grabbed a newspaper off of a rack in the hotel lobby. The story on the politics page was about an organization that the WCWC members knew very little about. On the other side of the world in West Germany, a brand-new political party called Die Grüne (the Greens) had just won nine seats in an election in the German state of Hesse, the first electoral victory for the German Greens.

Over beers, the friends read the article, which outlined some high-level philosophy of what the German Green Party was all about. They liked what they heard. Paul remembers saying, "Well, that's it for me and the BC NDP. We'll just have to start a Green Party here." In the following weeks, Paul and Adriane wrote to the German Greens asking them for any literature they had on the party and its ideas. Die Grüne immediately wrote back and sent a package of information in perfect English (as Germans tend to do), and the small group of Canadians were immediately enamoured with what they read. The platform and ideas matched perfectly with their own philosophies, and the hard work of forming a platform and governing philosophy was already done for them.

On February 4th, 1983, Adriane, Paul, and fourteen others signed the paperwork to found the Green Party of British Columbia, the first official Green political party in North America.

Early Growth across Canada

Although the formation of the BC Greens in 1983 was the first official and fully constituted ecological party to exist in North America, it was by no means the first time anyone had talked about the need for such a party in Canada, nor was it even the first attempt to form one. Since as early as the mid-1970s there had been discussions circulating throughout Canada similar to those that had circled through New Zealand and Australia and the rest of the world in the early years of the ecological movement.

One of the earliest attempts at starting the discussion was by Trevor Hancock, a medical doctor who had moved to Canada from the United Kingdom in the early 1970s. As covered in Chapter 2, the UK's Green political movement started with the PEOPLE Party in 1972, which eventually transformed into the UK's modern-day Green Party. Trevor had been an area organizer for the PEOPLE party in England and had even been a delegate at the party's founding convention just before he left to come to Canada. Upon his arrival in Ontario, he began to look around for a Canadian equivalent, but was disappointed to find none.

In 1977, the Science Council of Canada, a government advisory board on scientific issues, published a report entitled "Canada as a Conserver Society" which went into detail about how Canada could and should retool itself into a society built around conservation and ecological wisdom instead of around consuming resources. It was authored by Ursula Franken, who led a team to create the 103-page report. The report was a critique of Canadian society and made suggestions of steps that it could make, but it didn't go so far as to call for a new political movement for the worldview of the report. Alongside the report, however, the Science Council published the "Notes of the Conserver Society" in which followers of the report's ideas could submit articles to add to the discussion.

It was in these notes that Trevor Hancock published an opinion piece asking, "Where is Canada's Ecological Party?" A few years later, he would contribute to starting that ecological party and would be selected as the first leader of the Green Party of Canada.

There was one other notable attempt before the first successful formation of Canada's Green parties. For the 1980 election, a group of environmental activists organized themselves to run as independents across six of Canada's provinces. One of the primary organizers of the group was Elizabeth May, then a twenty-five-year-old waitress in Cape Breton who later would become leader of the Green Party of Canada and its first elected Member of Parliament. The thirteen candidates ran under the unofficial banner of the "Small Party," referencing the 1973 book *Small Is Beautiful* by economist E. F. Schumacher. Canadian election rules require a minimum number of candidates in order for a party to be officially registered, so the Small Party candidates were never an official party. They all were listed as independents, but they did their best to coordinate between themselves. Elizabeth herself racked up over two thousand dollars in campaign debt and had to try to

CHAPTER 4 – THE EARLY GREENS IN CANADA

earn it back by selling her car and going on a televised game show (the footage of which can still be found online).

Although efforts during the 1970s and for the 1980 election didn't result in a real, organized and official ecological party, the formation of the BC Greens in 1983 gave a kick-start to other groups around Canada.

The Green Party of Canada

One of my personal earliest memories involves going to visit my godparents on Vancouver Island. Betty Nickerson and Seymour Treiger lived in a small home near Yellow Point Lodge just south of the city of Nanaimo, and the only memories I have from this visit are scattered recollections of eating a huge number of blackberries and becoming violently ill as a result.

I mention this non-sequitur anecdote because Betty Nickerson has the distinction of being the Green Party of Canada's very first election candidate, and her husband Seymour Treiger was its second leader.

In May of 1983, there was a provincial election in British Columbia, and Paul and Adriane and the other new BC Greens had wrangled together four candidates (out of a possible fifty-seven districts) to run for election. Adriane herself ran in Vancouver–Point Grey as well as acting as the tiny party's first leader. The party also ran candidates in Surrey, Cariboo, and Nanaimo. As you would expect for a first attempt, it wasn't a very strong result, although just over three thousand people cast their vote for the four Green candidates.

Just a month after that election, the Member of Parliament for the federal district of Mission–Port Moody suddenly resigned from his seat mid-term. This triggered a by-election for voters to select his replacement, the winner of which would go on to join the parliament of Canada. The next Canada-wide election wasn't scheduled until the next year, so this sudden opening caught the new Greens in British Columbia by surprise. They'd had the notion of fielding candidates for the federal election in addition to the provincial election, but they'd thought they had another year to plan and recruit. Pulling a campaign together quickly, the Greens nominated local writer and sociologist Betty Nickerson to be their candidate.

Betty and her husband Seymour had already led extremely successful lives when they got involved with the early Greens. Seymour held a PhD in education from Columbia and was active in the Veterans for Peace movement after he served in World War Two. Betty likewise held a PhD from McGill and had worked in the promotion of arts and cultural programs for Canadian youth. When she ran as the first federal Green candidate, she'd already written several books, and she continued to write many more afterwards. If they had been running in an established party, they might have been considered star candidates.

117

For Betty's by-election, the federal Green Party of Canada didn't legally exist yet. On the actual election ballot, Betty Nickerson is listed as "unaffiliated" and she's also listed as such in federal records from the election. Her distinction as the first Green Party of Canada candidate is unofficial and is based on her campaign being organized by the same people who were in the process of registering the party, and by all of her own communications and campaign material listing her as the candidate for the Green Party of Canada.

The local Greens *had* actually managed to register the Green Party of Canada with Elections Canada a month before the election. The initial registration paperwork was hastily signed by: Paul George; my father, Bill Marshall; my godfather, Seymour Treiger; Ed McDonough; and Ted Mousseau, who was, at least on paper, the first leader of the party. However, becoming an officially listed federal party in Canada requires a certain number of candidates to run, and since the party was running for a single seat in a by-election they hadn't yet had the chance to run enough candidates to qualify.

Betty received 508 votes, just over 1 percent of those cast in the district. In the full Canadian election the next year, the Green Party of Canada fielded sixty candidates, enough for it to be officially registered as a party.

The Ontario Greens, and Doing the Federal Party Right

Although British Columbia has the distinction of being where the first official Green Party was formed, it was followed very soon after by a number of others. I spoke with Andrew Scorer, an Ontarian who remembers hearing about a group in Ontario who were meeting to discuss starting their own Ontarian Green Party. He and others had also been inspired by hearing about the German Greens who were getting a strangely high amount of interest from the Canadian press given that they were a new, small European party on the other side of the globe.

> They got in the news a *lot*. They were our inspiration at the very beginning to actually have a Green party. (Andrew Scorer, from an interview with the author, 2017)

Andrew joined five other aspiring Greens in Ontario, meeting at the 519 Church Street Community Centre. The 519 is a well known and respected charitable organization in Toronto, started in 1975 and known as a safe home for LGBT communities in Toronto. Meeting every Monday night in one of the community centre's rooms, Andrew and the others discussed and planned what both a Green Party of Ontario and a Green Party of Canada would look like. The

CHAPTER 4 – THE EARLY GREENS IN CANADA

person leading the discussion was Dr. Trevor Hancock, who had finally taken it upon himself to do what he had hoped someone else would do years earlier.

Trevor was already deeply involved in public policy development in Ontario. His focus was (and continues to be) on how to design cities that promote public health. At the same time as he was organizing a new political party, he was also personally organizing a major health conference called Beyond Health Care. A few years later, he was involved in the *Ottawa Charter for Health Promotion*, a major international agreement organized by the World Health Organization. He went on to found the international Healthy Cities and Communities movement, as well as the Canadian Association of Physicians for the Environment and the Canadian Coalition for Green Health Care. These days he's a professor at the University of Victoria, as well as being involved in numerous NGOs and boards.

The first group of Greens in Ontario were paying attention to what was being organized in BC. They'd seen the BC Greens run in the provincial election and were in contact with Adriane and the others there who were organizing things. They also wanted to be involved if a federal Green party was being officially set up. In fact, they were a bit annoyed that the Greens in British Columbia had gone ahead and registered the federal party without them.

The first push to properly organize the Green Party of Ontario and the Green Party of Canada happened simultaneously by the same group of Ontarians. Registering a political party in Ontario was actually quite difficult, and required the signatures of ten thousand voters on the initial paperwork. In British Columbia, it was easy: you just had to sign some papers, and it was done. Andrew Scorer organized the effort to get volunteers out and standing on street corners across Ontario to gather the signatures needed while others within the group talked with the BC Greens about how to organize a proper federal party.

The First Convention

The official paperwork for the Green Party of Canada had been hastily filed by a small group in the attempt to get ready for the surprise by-election in British Columbia, but Greens across the rest of Canada wanted to do things correctly before the full federal election the next year. Late in 1983, the Ontario group convened a convention, to be held at Carleton University, where the Green Party of Canada would officially be declared, along with electing a board of directors and laying out some core platform and policy ideas. The schedule and plan for the convention was ambitious: the group hoped to come away from the weekend's event with a solid core of ideas and structures. The word was sent out across Ontario and Canada about the event. The BC Greens were in full support.

The convention turned out to be a disaster. Andrew Scorer had mostly suppressed it from his own memory as he was telling me the story of the early years, but when I brought it up he recoiled, saying,

Ohhh yeah, I'd forgotten about that one . . . Oh yeah . . . that was a mess. It was horrible. I think that pretty well didn't accomplish anything. But we kept going anyway. (Andrew Scorer, from an interview with the author, 2017)

Another early organizer, Steve Kisby, also had some harsh words about this first attempt as mass organizing:

They had this convention before the general election. It was really well attended but it disintegrated. They spent the whole first day fighting about how to make decisions. They had all these policies that they were all going to ratify at this convention, but they couldn't get past the first step, which is supposed to only take about half an hour. It took all day, and they didn't have an agreement at the end of the first day of how they were going to make decisions. Then that night apparently some committees eventually came up with some sort of a compromise between the various factions that were at the meeting. They eventually passed something and then they passed a few other things. They passed a decision-making process and then they passed a rough structure and then the meeting lost form. (Steve Kisby, from an interview with the author, 2017)

The Greens in their earliest days generated a huge amount of interest. But much of that interest came from individuals with new or radical ideas that they'd never managed to find a home for. There was feminism, bio-organics, resource and land use issues, whaling, world peace issues, and so on. Many of the people who jumped on board at the very beginning had tried to introduce their ideas to other more established political parties but hadn't found anyone who was interested in humouring them. When a new political movement began picking up steam, they saw it as an opportunity to get in on the ground floor with their ideas. This meant that at many of these first meetings the discussions were dominated by strong personalities trying to push their very specific issues. This happened at multiple meetings where the core group of organizers had to force a meeting back to order when it was derailed by a particularly passionate attendee.

A few concrete things did come out of these first meetings. Most notably, an official leader was selected by the membership. Although Ted Mousseau had been listed as "party leader" on the official registration documents earlier that year, Trevor Hancock is generally accepted as the first real (elected) leader of the Green Party of Canada, as opposed to one who was just put into the registration paperwork as a placeholder. One of the other things that these new political activists learned was that a federal party in Canada needed to run at least sixty candidates in an election in order to qualify as an official party and thus to be able have its name beside a candidate on the ballot and to do important things like issue tax receipts for political donations. Trevor took the lead in calling around Canada in order to get sixty people who were willing to run in the upcoming election.

The first election for the Greens was less than a year away.

"We stand now where two roads diverge. But unlike the roads in Robert Frost's familiar poem, they are not equally fair. The road we have long been traveling is deceptively easy, a smooth superhighway on which we progress with great speed, but at its end lies disaster. The other fork of the road—the one less traveled by—offers our last, our only chance to reach a destination that assures the preservation of the earth."

(Rachel Carson, Author of Silent Spring)

THE FIRST ELECTIONS FOR CANADA'S GREENS

In 1984, the Green Party of Canada contested its first full election, fielding the required sixty candidates. The party managed to recruit candidates in British Columbia, Alberta, Saskatchewan, Ontario, Quebec, and Prince Edward Island. They were unable to find any candidates to run in Manitoba, the Territories, or the rest of the Maritimes in this first election. The party's candidates got almost twenty-seven thousand votes across the sixty districts they competed in.

This was more than the Libertarian, Social Credit, Communist, and Commonwealth of Canada parties, all of whom fielded a similar number of candidates. It was, however, fewer overall than the Rhinoceros Party of Canada, a parody protest party whose leader was a real rhinoceros from the Toronto zoo, and whose primary campaign slogan was "a promise to keep none of our promises." Which they did.

As another interesting bit of trivia, this was also the last federal election in Canadian history in which one party got a majority of all votes cast.

Brian Mulroney's Progressive Conservative party received a bare majority of support, with 50.03 percent of the votes cast in the election for Progressive Conservative candidates. As covered in chapter 2, in the first-past-the-post electoral system a party can often achieve a majority government with significantly less than a majority of voter support, so this majority of votes was an absolute blowout for the Progressive Conservatives. Mulroney's Conservatives won 211 of the 282 seats in the legislature, leaving a tiny rump of Liberals and New Democrats to form the opposition.

The Provincial Focus

With this first federal election under their belt, the new Greens in Canada continued to organize for their provincial elections. During this time the focus of Green organizers was much more on the side of provincial elections rather than federal ones. The federal Green party was seen as something that should continue to exist, but that no one really wanted to take stewardship of. Organizing on a full-Canadian scale took too much maintenance for the small number of active Green organizers, and they suspected they could have much more success if they focused their energies on the smaller-scale provincial races.

It's also worth noting that many of the issues that Greens are concerned with lay within the responsibility of provincial governments, rather than the Canadian federal government. Canada is a federation, with different powers assigned to the federal parliament and its provincial counterparts. Focusing on provincial elections makes sense for Greens, because it's where many of their most important ideas would need to be implemented.

The Ontario Green Party competed in its first election in 1985, fielding nine candidates (including Andrew Scorer and Trevor Hancock). Green parties also began to organize in other Canadian provinces. Quebec was an early adopter, first contesting the 1985 Quebec provincial election. The other provincial parties took significantly longer to get started. In 1993, the Green Party of Alberta first competed. They were joined by the Green Party of Manitoba and the Green Party of Saskatchewan in 1999. The maritime Green parties didn't form until even later, with Nova Scotia in 2006, Prince Edward Island in 2007, and New Brunswick in 2010. The provincial Green family was most recently expanded by the Yukon Green party in 2011. The only province still missing a local Green Party is Newfoundland and Labrador (the Northwest Territories and Nunavut don't have parties).

For much of the 1980s and 1990s, the Green Party of Canada continued to be a secondary organization that was managed through a partnership of the provincial parties, mostly the Ontario and British Columbia Green parties. After the 1985 federal election, Andrew Scorer travelled to British Columbia to meet with Greens there and to ask them to take over, keeping the Green Party of Canada running while they focused on their upcoming provincial race. Trevor Hancock gave up his title of leader and it passed onto Dr. Seymour Treiger, my godfather and Betty Nickerson's husband. The leadership title (mostly a caretaker role) and responsibility for the federal party then passed back and forth between Ontario and British Columbia for the next few elections.

CHAPTER 4 – THE EARLY GREENS IN CANADA

The Early Challenges of a Radical New Party

Internal democracy in the early days of the Canadian Green parties was a challenge. The greatest difficulty for a new party with radically different ideas is to find the line between electability and purity of ideals. For many of the early Canadian Greens there was a massive frustration with the way things were done in traditional politics. They wanted the new Green parties to operate far removed from those entrenched and accepted structures.

One of the most difficult issues that the Greens struggled with was a desire for strong decentralization, and for creating a party based around grassroots consensus agreements instead of a dictatorial charismatic leader and bare majority votes on a convention floor. For a long time Canadian democracy has been trending towards being focused on a party's leader rather than on the local candidates that we actually elect. In the days before television and radio, you *had* to run a strong local candidate because your local candidate was most people's connection to the party. Over time, as more and more people became connected to mass media, the focus shifted onto a strong charismatic leader where people were able to directly hear from and see the leader on TV. In our modern era, most voters think of a party's leader *as* the party itself. If you casually ask someone who they voted for in the last election they're more likely to say "I voted for Justin Trudeau" or "I voted for Stephen Harper" than they are to personally name the local candidate that they *actually* voted for.

The Greens didn't want to be a party defined by its leader. For this reason they actually went out of their way to not have a leader at all. The official paperwork required by Elections Canada specifies that a political party needs to have a leader, and actually gives some legal power to the leader to determine who can be a candidate for the party. Therefore, the Greens had to pick someone to be the leader on paper, even though their internal organizational structure was based around not having one. For internal matters the Greens elected a number of "spokespeople" to be the points of contact for media enquiries, and who were trusted to work to build the party. The media was confused by this, which probably contributed to the very small amount of media attention that was given to these early Green parties.

Ontario Experiments

While the BC Green Party had begun with the purposeful disorganization that characterized all the early Green parties, the Green Party of Ontario was engaging in an experiment in radical decentralization. I spoke with Frank de Jong about these years for the party. Frank was the first recognized leader of the Green Party of Ontario, but only became leader in 1993, a full ten years and three elections after the party had been founded. The post had been purposefully left vacant until that point.

> It was originally decided to be a super decentralized organization. There was no leader. There was not allowed to be a leader. There was no membership list. It was meant to be chapters. Modelled on the Committee of Correspondence at the beginning of the United States and the New England states. It was a coalition of chapters and it stayed a coalition of chapters for a long time. It flitted along at a very, very low level for the first ten years. (Frank de Jong, from an interview with the author, 2017)

Frank referred to the Committees of Correspondence, a series of shadow governments set up by the thirteen American colonies shortly before the American Revolution. They operated primarily on their own, and only coordinated to share information about what activities each chapter was up to. The Greens in Ontario operated similarly, in that each chapter was largely in charge of its own actions, and the central party only existed as a place for the chapters to share information. Chapters didn't even have to be purely geographical. A particular chapter could just be a group with similar interests that came together.

> The philosophy was that we would be an open coalition of chapters, and that the chapters could be geographical or could be a food co-op or could be a small group of people, or a housing co-op or organic farming group or whatever. We had three or four in Toronto at some point. (Frank de Jong, from an interview with the author, 2017)

The party's purposeful lack of a leader frustrated some members. Frank de Jong remembers that although the media were interested in them on occasion, whatever reporter was trying to talk to them would often give up when faced with how much work it would be to actually understand the group. In regards to coverage by the news media, Frank told me,

> We had no leader. We only had spokespeople. We would have three spokespeople, and I became one of those spokespeople, but we had no leader, which, of course, was really confusing to the media, because if they even wanted to talk to us they'd say,
>> "We would like to talk to your leader."
>> We'd reply, "We don't have a leader."
>> They'd say, "Who the hell do I talk to?"
>> We'd say, "You talk to our spokespeople."
>> We'd just hear, *click* as they hung up the phone.
>> We were just so small that I don't blame them.

CHAPTER 4 – THE EARLY GREENS IN CANADA

It wasn't until 1993 that the party decided that they finally had to normalize and centralize if they ever wanted to be anything beyond a group of social clubs. That year they undertook a number of organization initiatives. They started keeping a members list, they asked members to pay dues so that they'd have some money to work with, and they elected a formal leader. Frank ran against Jim Harris (who would later become leader of the Green Party of Canada) and won, becoming the Ontario party's first leader. There had been, of course, leaders of the party on paper before because the province's paperwork requires it, but Frank was the first who was actually empowered to speak on behalf of the party. The next election for the Green Party of Ontario was in 1995, and it was the first one in which the media actually had a Green leader to interview.

Consensus-Based Decision-Making: The Good and the Bad

The Greens also wanted all of their meetings to be held using consensus-based decision-making. The idea was that simply having a vote on party matters overrules anyone who's voting in the minority, and that this wasn't fair to those people. Instead, they felt that decisions could be made that were supported by everyone as long as the effort was put in to discuss the issue long enough to get everyone in agreement. For many things this worked wonderfully, and it tended to work well with smaller groups. However, it became very easy for one individual to completely derail meetings by refusing to compromise and insisting that they got their way. It took some time and a lot of effort for the Green organizers to figure out a way to deal with people whose mission seemed to be abusing the process.

Anyone who works or volunteers inside political parties has a story or two (or a dozen) about problematic volunteers or activists that strain the patience and energy of the rest of the organization. It doesn't matter if you're a Conservative, a Liberal, a Socialist, or a Green; if you've spent enough time in internal party politics, you have a list of names in your head. If someone even so much as mentions one of these names to you you'll immediately break out into sweats and have to struggle to get your breathing under control. In the 1980s, the Greens attracted an inordinate number of these particular individuals. Early organizer Stuart Parker recalled one particular meeting that went even further off the rails than normal:

> He (the member in question) had his hands up, saying, "I block!"
> (The emcee replied,) "There's no motion on the floor."
> "I'm blocking anyway"
> "On what grounds?"
> "I'm tired, and I don't know what's going on!"

Another bizarre early incident occurred for the new federal Green Party during their first election in 1984. The party had appointed a candidate to run for one of the Ottawa ridings, but suddenly faced an aggressive takeover attempt of the local Green association by an infamous Canadian political figure. John Turmel currently holds the Guinness World Record for most elections contested and lost, with a stunning count of ninety-eight attempts at the time of this book's writing. Turmel, who had already unsuccessfully run in sixteen elections at this time, attempted to capitalize on the organization of a new political party by signing up a large number of his friends and family. He then tried to overwhelm the local group that had been organizing for the election and ran his own separate nomination process parallel that of the Greens.

Green leader Trevor Hancock personally rejected his candidacy and the Greens later voted to expel him from the party membership. As revenge, Turmel instead ran as an independent in the same riding as Trevor. He signed up several members of his family (including his mother) to run as candidates against the Greens in Ottawa, all also as independents.

The media and the public likely had no idea that all this was going on. They were focusing on the big parties, and who was going to form government and become Prime Minister. A bunch of minor parties and independents feuding was far below their attention. The whole ridiculous incident was a huge headache for the Greens, who had no former experience in politics. It also demonstrated to the Greens why it was actually useful to have a leader (even if just on paper) with the power to reject candidates.

Building Connections and Negotiating Truces

In British Columbia, one of the people who's spent the most time over his life managing and trying to build compromise between frustrated, passionate, and disgruntled party members is Steve Kisby. Steve never ran for election himself and has never served as a party leader (figurehead or not), so his name doesn't appear as often in the history of the Canadian Greens as others. However, he possibly has more volunteer hours logged than any other Green across his thirty years with the movement.

Stuart Parker jokingly referred to him as "Data" when discussing party history (after the android character from Star Trek), as Steve was responsible for most of the backend of the party's

CHAPTER 4 – THE EARLY GREENS IN CANADA

organization. Someone has to do the bureaucratic work of filing minutes, drafting proposals, organizing meetings, disseminating newsletters, maintaining membership numbers and databases—basically all of the thankless and unnoticed work that keeps a party running. For much of the British Columbia Greens' early history, that was Steve's job.

During most of the 1980s Steve positioned himself as a truce-maker between different factions of the BC Green Party's membership, keeping them from destroying the party over their frustrations with each other. When I sat down with Steve, he scribbled a graph curve for me of how he saw the interest and membership of the BC Greens from when it first formed in 1983 and in the rest of the decade. The interest immediately spiked to a massive high as soon as it formed, but quickly plummeted until it reached a more steady and sustainable level. Huge numbers of people signed up initially, thinking that the party would be their outlet for the issues that they felt strongly about and that they wanted to share with the world. Over time the more extreme elements drifted away, but their chaotic presence unfortunately also chased away a lot of other less volatile members who just didn't have the energy or interest to deal with them. Paul and Adriane reminisced on the initial wave of signups when they started the party:

> Adriane: Most of the people came from, I would say, grassroots movements. The peace movement, the environment movement, women's rights. Three big ones, I would say. There were people too also from Indigenous rights. Agriculture was big too, lots of people who were organic farmers. The other big group were small cottage industries, small businesses. Independent people. They weren't in political parties. We were attracting people that weren't part of that.
>
> Paul: Well, we were attracting some disgruntled people . . . But we had seventeen hundred members within two months!
>
> Adriane: To begin with I would say it was just a real buzz, a real excitement. It didn't look like it was going to be that fractious. We didn't even think about it that way, it was just exciting. (Paul George and Adriane Carr, from an interview with the author, 2017)

In addition to the radical ideas that just weren't workable and turned people away, the early Greens also wound up adopting a number of ideas and procedures that turned out to be very popular and brought people in. Thinking about some of these, Steve recalls,

> I remember when we were here and we had meetings that we always had made sure that women spoke as much as men and stuff like that. We actually had quota

systems. We had quota systems for executives and we also had a separate speaker's list for males and females and made sure that it alternated so that women were speaking as much as men, because up to that point there was a real problem where women didn't really have a voice in politics.

When I came, I remember seeing Adriane there dealing with some difficulties and I was really impressed by her and others. I had never seen powerful women in charge like that before. I just thought it was great. I was really impressed by that. (Steve Kisby, on the early BC Green party, from an interview with the author, 2017)

Steve's other job during these early years was trying to identify all of the groups out there who were interested in Green politics and to bring them together to organize and cooperate. This was the 1980s, and so there was no internet to connect people, nor did most households (or volunteer organizations) even have computers to organize their data. Steve therefore spent countless hours trying to track down and catalogue contact information for any organization or individual across Canada who might be interested in organizing on the ground. When he found someone he'd start to include them on a newsletter about Green happenings across Canada (whether they wanted it or not). The goal was to let people know that there were others out there who had the same ideas that they did, and not to get discouraged or think that they were alone. Steve talked a lot with me about the work that was put into this:

Saskatchewan had a group in their major city at some point in the early '80s, but it had crashed and no one was interested in doing anything further. I contacted them after they had crashed; if I contacted them before they crashed, I might have been able to keep them alive, but they had died.

In Manitoba, it was a similar thing, where there was a group that formed in the early '80s, inspired by the information coming out of Europe and also inspired by the media coming out of Germany and Ontario. Again, it couldn't sustain itself, it was too small of a group, and it ended up falling apart.

In one province, I can't remember which, we had a gatekeeper problem. Because there was no structure there and this person had the authority of being recognized as the contact for the Green Party candidate in the province, they tended to control all the shots in the province. If you didn't get along with this person, you were on the outs. That was the gatekeeper syndrome.

CHAPTER 4 – THE EARLY GREENS IN CANADA

Building a Public Profile

It's difficult to keep a political party running between elections, especially if the party is a small one with no elected representatives. Another challenge for the early Greens was figuring out how to keep people engaged and excited between election periods. The parties wanted to grow and build to prepare themselves for their next elections, but keeping people interested when that next chance wasn't for four years was difficult. The Greens in BC kept themselves busy by advocating on specific issues that were relevant for them. This also served to bring attention to the party and to bring more people in as volunteers and supporters.

Steve Kisby joined the party after seeing the Greens active during Expo '86 in Vancouver. Expo '86 was officially titled the "1986 World Exposition on Transportation and Communications," and was intended to show off great futuristic ideas of transportation. Vancouver's first large-scale rapid transit system, the SkyTrain, was built as a legacy project for the Expo.

The BC Greens looked at all of this focus on expensive, futuristic transportation projects and decided to try to contrast the Expo with a message about how to make Vancouver a more bicycle-friendly city. At the time, it was against the rules to take bicycles on city buses in Vancouver. The Greens created a pair of life-sized papier-mâché bicycles and began bringing them on buses, since this was allowed with no problem. This got Steve's attention and inspired him to join up with the small party. Currently in Vancouver, all buses are now equipped with a two-bicycle rack on the front of the vehicle. This allows Vancouverites to transport themselves and their bikes to bike trails without relying on cars, and to use bikes for part of their trip and transit for other parts.

Adriane recalls early campaigns undertaken by the BC Greens to get some kids in the city of Gibsons a skateboard park, and to start up a recycling depot. The very first project that they spent any party money on was supporting a protest to get a new park in Vancouver's Downtown Eastside. Adriane and Paul went and asked them how the Greens could help support what they were doing, and the protesters remarked that they really needed an outhouse so that protesters didn't have to keep leaving to find bathrooms. Adriane told me, "The first project that we invested in for the Green Party of BC was to rent a portable john."

During the first ten or so years of the BC Green Party's existence, the members understood and accepted that they weren't actually likely to get anyone elected in Canada's electoral system. Because of that understanding the party spent most of its efforts on projects like those described above, and never really had a push to professionalize their own internal operations. Many people who joined the party because they enjoyed the projects that the Greens were working on quickly became frustrated with the chaos of the party's actual political meetings.

In the early nineties, a group of those new members, led by a student named Stuart Parker (introduced above), found their own solution to the problem.

CHAPTER 5

PROFESSIONALIZING CANADA'S GREEN PARTIES

"I have come to the conclusion that politics are too serious a matter to be left to the politicians."

(Charles de Gaulle)

PROFESSIONALIZING CANADA'S GREEN PARTIES

I joined Stuart Parker in a noisy Chinese food restaurant in Surrey, one of the cities that makes up metro Vancouver, and one of the fastest-growing cities in Canada. Stuart, now in his forties, is a large curly-haired man whose mind travels a million miles a minute. Partway through the interview I remarked to him on how incredibly detailed and specific his account of past events were and Stuart agreed, describing his memory as "his curse." These days he works as a lecturer in political theory, and he's had over twenty years to build a very philosophical and detailed view of party politics and electoral systems, and how they all interact with the many individuals that try to organize themselves within those systems.

In the early nineties, Stuart joined the BC Green Party. He became frustrated by the mess of the party's internal attempts at decision-making, so he decided to form a group inside the bigger Green party called the "Young Greens." Most political parties have a youth wing separate from the main membership of the party, but in the BC Greens' case the youth wing would eventually wind up taking over the party.

Stuart had gotten himself selected as the party's election coordinator and had thrown himself fully into the job, traveling all over BC and working to build regional Green support outside of the Vancouver and Victoria core. In the 1986 provincial election, the BC Greens had run just nine candidates, and received almost no attention from BC's news media. Being covered by the media is possibly the most important part of winning an election. The media essentially gives millions of dollars of free advertising to parties that it chooses to cover, and that's not something that a party could ever make up for on its own.

Stuart, as part of his election coordinator job, had approached media representatives and asked them what the Greens would have to do in order to be treated equally with the other parties, and to receive the same amount of attention and coverage. The media clearly told him that the problem was that they were only running a handful of candidates. Even if a miracle happened and all of their candidates got elected there still wouldn't be enough of them to form a government, and why should the media cover a party that wasn't able to become the province's next government?

Stuart took them at their word and began the hard work of building Green support all across the province. His goal was to run candidates in enough districts to be actually treated as a serious contender. He toured extensively, forming regional Green associations and recruiting eager candidates. When the 1991 election rolled around, the BC Greens fielded forty-two candidates out of a possible seventy-five. Since a majority in the legislature would be thirty-eight elected members (half of the total), these forty-two candidates actually *could* form government if they were to get elected. The other big parties were fielding candidates in every single district, but the Greens could at least now claim that they were actually running to win. This was a big milestone for a party who'd only had candidates in the single digits until that point.

> By the time we went into the '91 election, my work was basically done, except of course the plan was an abject failure. The provincial media had never seriously meant any of those things they said, and in fact, were increasingly hostile to us as we started demanding them. (Stuart Parker, on the 1991 election, from an interview with the author, 2017)

Stuart's plan was completely unsuccessful. The media had already decided that the Greens were not to be taken seriously, and hadn't actually expected the young nineteen year-old election coordinator to call their bluff and recruit a majority's worth of candidates. The Greens were given just as little attention with forty-two candidates as they were given with nine.

This could have deterred Stuart and caused him to give up, but it had the exact opposite effect. From talking with Stuart, I could tell that he was still deeply frustrated and angry at BC's provincial media, and proudly delighted in every time throughout his life and career that he had managed to beat them. When the media in 1991 refused to give the Greens the attention that Stuart felt they deserved, he took it as a challenge.

CHAPTER 5 – PROFESSIONALIZING CANADA'S GREEN PARTIES

In 1993, Stuart and the youth wing effectively took over the party. In his election coordinator job, Stuart had been responsible for signing up a massive number of new young members, and he was very popular with them. Despite failing to get the media to pay attention to the party during the last election, Stuart personally had gotten a large amount of media coverage as a result of a campaign he and the Young Greens had been running to get restaurant giant McDonald's to stop using ozone-destroying foam packaging. They'd actually been successful, and Stuart was probably the most well-known and recognizable Green—at least among the party's members. The new membership was able to replace most of the old guard in their leadership roles, and Stuart was elected party leader. With the support of a newly revitalized membership the party drafted a new constitution, instituted new rules of order, and essentially turned itself into a real, professional political party. The Germans would have called it a victory for the *realo* wing.

When the German Greens were first elected in 1983, they had to rapidly professionalize because they'd succeeded in actually electing people. For the BC Greens there had never been a need to undertake these kinds of changes, since many within the party were happy to basically remain as a social club and advocacy group. Stuart's leadership was the biggest push that the party had had to become a professional organization. Many within the party were thrilled with the new direction. Others were not.

Determined to force the media into taking the party seriously, Stuart continued his non-stop touring of British Columbia. This time he wanted to run a full slate of candidates for the next election in 1996. If the Greens ran an candidate in every single district, then the media would have no excuse not to treat them as seriously as the established parties. He almost succeeded; the party was just four candidates short of a full slate. The party even managed to field more candidates than the new Progressive Democratic Alliance Party, which had been formed by former BC Liberal MLA and Opposition Leader Gordon Wilson after he was ousted from his leadership spot (and thus quit the party).

The BC Political Deck is Shuffled

The 1996 election in British Columbia was a mess. Prior to 1991 there had effectively just been two serious political parties: the BC NDP and the Social Credit Party. They were the only two parties to consistently elect members for the last several decades. The Social Credit Party in particular had dominated the BC political scene for ages. In 1991, there was a massive upset when the governing Social Credit Party completely fell apart, and the BC NDP was elected to government for the first time since the 1970s. The BC Liberal party, which had been contesting elections unsuccessfully for years, went from zero to seventeen elected members, and the Social Credit Party dropped from forty-seven to only seven. In the years between 1991 and 1996, the old Social Credit politicians and the new Liberal politicians scrambled around trying to figure out what this new realignment of BC politics would mean, and how they would fit inside it.

For the 1996 election, there were an unheard of *five* parties running almost full slates of candidates, along with the shell of the Social Credit party which was still hobbling along and trying to function. The governing BC NDP and official opposition BC Liberals both ran full slates. So did the newly formed Reform Party of BC, which had been created by four of the seven elected Social Credit MLAs in an attempt to rebrand the conservative movement in BC and drop the baggage of the old SoCred name. The Progressive Democratic Alliance, mentioned above, had been formed by the ousted leader of the BC Liberals after he had been booted from the job for having an extramarital affair with another one of the Liberal's elected caucus members, Judi Tyabji. Then of course, the BC Green party was also fielding a nearly full slate. The two-party dominance of BC politics had been split into a half-dozen competing movements.

While the BC media had been used to only covering two or three parties, they suddenly had at least six parties possibly worth covering for the 1996 election. And if they wanted to include the two brand new parties, then they knew they'd also have to include the Greens. They'd lost their excuse to avoid doing so. The media attempted to organize a debate involving the leaders of all the parties, but the BC NDP refused to participate in any debate that would involve the Greens. The BC NDP had been carefully cultivating an environmental wing of their party in order to keep a big enough coalition together to compete against the BC Liberals. They desperately didn't want their environmentally focused voters to know about the BC Greens, because they worried that the Greens might appeal to them more than the BC NDP did. It was in the BC NDP's best interest for voters to have no idea that the BC Greens existed.

The First Debate . . . Sort of

Since they couldn't come to an agreement with the big parties, the CBC organized an alternative format instead of a debate: a series of six televised thirty-minute segments where the same small group of voters would sit down with each of the parties' leaders and ask them questions and discuss the issues. Eight regular British Columbians were selected to represent a cross-section of the province's voter base and to interview the party leaders. The voters went into the segment with Stuart not knowing or really understanding what the Green Party was, and repeatedly asking why the Green members didn't just join one of the other parties and advocate for their ideas there. The session opened with a question by one of the voters:

The question is, in my mind and in the mind of many voters, is to why the Green party exists, other than to profile the fact that environmental concerns must be addressed? (Tom Spring, retired high school principal and participant in CBC's 1996 leaders' panel)

CHAPTER 5 – PROFESSIONALIZING CANADA'S GREEN PARTIES

To which Stuart replied,

> Well, I think that's a really important issue, and I think one of the problems is that other parties will address the environment through their environmental policy, but won't address it through their economic policy. Every other party in this election is saying that what we need in order to get our economy working in this province is more growth. We need to consume more resources, we need to produce more products at an increasing rate—at about 4 percent per year increasing. And that's sort of assuming that the circumference of the Earth is increasing. That somehow there will be more trees to cut down next year, and that by 2020 we'll be taking 50 percent more fish out of the sea and cutting down 50 percent more trees. And that's not reality. And so we're advancing an economic platform that has a very different basis than what other parties are advancing. And I think, sure, we could work within other parties and get our parks policy adopted, or get our forest tenure policy adopted, but being able to have our economic policy adopted is something that would be beyond the capacity of the NDP or Liberals to adopt.

Stuart, at the time just twenty-four years old, surprised the voters at the panel and impressed them with his well-thought-out answers and his understanding of complex and very specific government issues. At the end of the segment, Stuart was led offstage and the host of the segment returned to chat with the voters about what they thought about the party and leader. The voters unanimously agreed that they would like to see a Green elected to the legislature, and many agreed that if Stuart himself was running in their district that they would vote for him personally. One of the voters described her understanding at the end of the segment,

> They're not just a single-issue party like a lot of us had the impression they were. But their ideas on health and education are really good in terms of college boards and a lot of prevention instead of dealing with acute illnesses like we've seen with other parties. So if we did have someone like Stuart in the legislature, I think other people would have to be more accountable, or at least the issues would be more high profile. (Balbir Gurm, nursing instructor and participant in CBC's 1996 leaders' panel)

It was the first time that the Greens had been able to express their ideas to British Columbians in a high-profile televised segment. But despite the unanimous endorsement of the panellists that it would benefit the legislature to have at least some Greens present, the BC electorate was not so generous. Once the votes were counted, the Greens achieved just under 2 percent of the overall vote. The Social Credit Party was wiped out entirely, and the brand new Reform and Progressive Democrat parties elected only three members between them (and were wiped out in the next election). The brief experiment in BC politics of having more than two parties was over.

The unusually large number of party options for voters also produced a strange result. First-past-the-post is designed for elections that only have two parties. The higher the number of parties competing in a first-past-the-post election, the more likely it is that the results became confusing and unexpected. In 1996, the BC NDP was elected to a second majority government even though it got about forty thousand *fewer* votes than the BC Liberals. This confusing "wrong-winner" election result happens occasionally in first-past-the-post systems due to the votes being geographically clustered in a way that benefits one party and hands them the government even though they had less overall support than another party. It's why electoral reform advocates get extremely frustrated when they hear the talking point that "first-past-the-post" produces simple results.

Despite finally making a break into televised media, the BC Greens were still badly under-covered as compared to the other political parties. The Greens were frequently just not mentioned by the media when discussing voter options, the leader's schedule wasn't reported alongside the touring schedules of the other party leaders, and when candidates were listed in individual districts in the newspapers the Greens were often just omitted. This last oversight led to Stuart and the Greens filing a formal complaint with the BC media's oversight board. The complaint was actually verified, and after the election the BC media newspapers were forced to write an acknowledgement that they had treated the BC Greens unfairly in their coverage of the election. Both Stuart Parker and Steve Kisby took particular pride in this anecdote, recounting their victory with great satisfaction.

It was still a huge step for the Greens. For the first time they'd ran a campaign with an almost full slate of candidates, they'd at least gotten *some* media coverage, and they were in a stronger place than ever before.

Greens in French Canada

The most successful early performance by a Green party in Canada was actually in the province of Quebec, for the 1989 provincial election. Although the local Green party had formed in the early '80s and contested an election in 1985, it had since mostly fallen apart. The party was officially registered and continued to exist on paper, but barely any of the individuals who were running the party in 1985 were still active.

Jean Ouimet had recently returned from travels in Europe, where he had been inspired by the way that some European countries, particularly Switzerland, ran their politics. He had also recently read *The Limits to Growth*, the highly influential book about how a society focused on growth at any cost was eventually going to run into a wall where demand outpaced the planet's supply of resources. Upon returning to Quebec, Jean looked around for a political movement that was advocating for these ideas and discovered the mostly non-functioning Parti Vert du Quebec (Green Party of Quebec). He joined the party, revitalized it, got himself elected as leader, and then began preparing for the next election in 1989.

Much of Quebec's recent political history has been dominated by the idea of sovereignty. Support for Quebec to secede from Canada and form an independent country really began to grow in the 1960s, and in 1970 the first members from the newly created sovereigntist Parti Québécois were elected to the Quebec Legislature. In 1980, the first unsuccessful Quebec Independence Referendum was conducted, and although the referendum was a failure for those advocating for Quebec independence, the Parti Québécois wound up being elected to government a year later anyway. The party underwent an internal crisis as the members struggled to find their place as the governing party after losing a referendum that they so strongly supported.

The Parti Québécois was defeated and replaced by the Liberal Party of Quebec in 1985. Two years later, Canadian Prime Minister Brian Mulroney gathered the Premiers of all ten provinces for a conference at Meech Lake in Quebec. The purpose of the conference was to draft the Meech Lake Accords, a series of amendments to the Constitution of Canada. The province of Quebec had never formally approved of the Constitution Act (which had passed without Quebec's support) and the amendments drafted at Meech Lake were intended to persuade the government of Quebec to endorse the Constitution by providing for some of Quebec's desires and demands.

The conference reignited the sovereigntist discussions in the French-speaking province. Opponents of the accords, including former Prime Minister Pierre Trudeau, saw it as a giveaway to Quebec that would embolden separatists by giving them too much of what they wanted. The accords needed to be ratified by every provincial legislature within three years of the drafting, which meant that after being adopted at Meech Lake they hovered in limbo between 1987 and 1990.

The 1989 Quebec provincial election was held during these three years, and it was into this environment than Jean Ouimet and his Parti Vert attempted to inject themselves into the discussion. Jean was (and still is) passionate about democratic systems and how they empower or suppress voters to make their voices heard. I spoke with him in a phone interview and he reminded me of BC's Stuart Parker. Both party leaders have a deep philosophical understanding and appreciation for political systems and how they shape the society that uses them.

A Different Sort of Sovereignty

While the political scene in Quebec was deeply engaged in questions about Quebec's sovereignty as a country, Jean wanted to also get people discussing how Quebec (either sovereign or part of Canada) could reform its own democratic institutions to make the government more representative of voters. He wanted democratic reforms to better engage and educate voters so that they could make better decisions with their votes. While the province struggled with the idea of sovereignty from Canada, Jean wanted voters to think about their own personal sovereignty.

Jean's eventual goal was to create the type of society that could avoid the collapse described in "The Limits of Growth." He had spent time trying to understand why society as a whole had gotten to the point that it had. Eventually he decided that the functioning of Canada's political systems, in which a single party without majority support could lock down the entirety of the government, was stifling the ideas and discussions that would get people to understand the threats described in "The Limits of Growth."

He especially admired the system used by Switzerland, in which the government was usually formed of at least four political parties cooperating together and finding common ground. Switzerland's proportional system allowed a large range of parties and ideas to get elected. There was also the expectation of political cooperation that was built into the Swiss system and the Swiss political psyche meant that its legislature was far more collaborative, with far more of an exchange of ideas and educated debate. He saw the system as less prone to narcissistic power-hungry politicians because the system itself was designed to only reward those who were able to work together, not those who tried to rule like dictators.

Off to a Good Start

Jean's ideas and leadership for the Parti Vert du Québec attracted wide support and revitalized the party. The party went from fielding ten candidates in 1985 to fielding forty-six in 1989. Over ten times as many voters cast their votes for the Parti Vert, beating out the result for the Quebec wing of the New Democratic Party, who had even fielded ten more candidates than the Greens. Parti Vert candidates averaged about 5 percent in their districts, although candidate Denis Hubert got nearly 15 percent in his district of Saguenay. It was by far the best result for a Canadian Green candidate thus far. Unfortunately, no Green candidate was elected.

Despite a massive jump in support for the party since the previous election, Jean and his team were still disheartened. Although they had new and interesting ideas and a political climate that should have been ripe for discussion of those ideas, Jean felt that his party had been totally ignored by the Quebec media. In a system in which the Greens were a long shot, the media had no interest

CHAPTER 5 – PROFESSIONALIZING CANADA'S GREEN PARTIES

in covering anybody except the biggest two parties. He also believed that the media and the larger parties didn't want voters to know about the Greens' ideas since they would upset the system that they were used to operating in. The Greens' repeated attempts to interest the political journalists in discussing their ideas hit wall after wall, even after the Greens surged ahead of the established New Democrat party.

After the 1989 election, Jean and many of his team decided that the Parti Vert was not going to work as the vessel for the ideas that they wanted to bring to Quebec. He and a number of his colleagues left the party and joined the Parti Québécois, with the plan of changing the already established and successful party from the inside. Jean became an ecology advisor for Jacques Parizeau, the leader of the Parti Québécois and later the Premier of Quebec. Although he's been working for years within the party and within Quebec politics to advance Green ideas, they still aren't anywhere near the mainstream state that he and other Parti Vert members wanted. In 2005, Jean even ran for the leadership of the Parti Québécois, but was unsuccessful.

With Jean gone the Parti Vert once again returned to the low-functioning state that it had been in when he joined. The party managed to contest the 1994 election, but they were back down to only eleven candidates. The party then disbanded and was officially deregistered.

The Parti Vert du Quebec operated mainly in French, and remained almost completely separate from the organizers of the federal Green Party of Canada in Quebec, who were mostly Anglophones. Although the Parti Vert disbanded, the federal Greens in Quebec continued to be active. They eventually restarted the party once again in 2001, and kept it running this time, although they still haven't managed to crack 5 percent in an election since.

"It is somewhat ironic that Green parties are criticized for being single-issue parties when the ideology - ecologism - from which they draw their inspiration is devoted to showing how it is the connections between various aspects of social, political, and economic life that produce environmental problems."

(Andrew Dobson, Green Political Thought)

NEAR BREAKTHROUGHS IN EARLY ELECTIONS

Back in BC, in the aftermath of the 1996 election, British Columbians were rather disgruntled. More of them had voted for the BC Liberals than for the BC NDP, and yet here they were with another BC NDP majority government. This seemed completely wrong to many voters. Meanwhile, one-fifth of British Columbian voters had voted for neither of those two parties, and had received next to no representation for those votes.

This led to resentment of the BC NDP government, and also led to a push by the BC Liberals to adopt a new electoral system: a proportional representation system like what was used in many other democracies around the world. The BC Liberals promised that, if elected in the next election in 2001, they would enact the change in electoral system for British Columbia. The members of the unsuccessful Reform Party of British Columbia, who had been accused of vote-splitting the support away from the BC Liberals and allowing an NDP government, also campaigned in favour.

For the BC Green Party, much more attention was on them in the years after the 1996 election. Polling of voter preferences put the Greens' support as high as 11 percent, which was a massive boost from the 2 percent that the party received in '96. As dissatisfaction with the BC NDP government grew due to a series of scandals and resignations, many politically active volunteers who had supported the BC NDP also began migrating over to the BC Greens. With the newfound attention on the Greens, many who used to be involved with the party but who had left during the Stuart Parker years began to return as well.

The changeover from Stuart Parker's leadership to Adriane Carr's return was considered remarkably messy even by politics' usual low standards. I was not personally politically active or knowledgeable during this period, and so have no firsthand account of what happened. I attempted through interviews to piece together exactly what occurred, but I got scattered accounts from the people on different sides who are still obviously hurt by the events. Personal attacks were brought out, and lawyers even got involved. Stuart describes it as the worst experience of his life, and the worst that he's ever been treated. It was a contentious struggle between factions that eventually led to a leadership race for who would head the party.

A Return to Its Original Leadership

The result of the 2000 BC Green leadership election saw Stuart Parker replaced by Adriane Carr, who had returned to the party after reducing her involvement during the Parker years. Many of the people close to Stuart resigned from the party, and Stuart himself left the Greens and swore them off. He joined the BC NDP and for the next twenty years he would instead attempt to change the party from within, until 2018 when he quit over the courting of the fracking industry by the new BC NDP government.

With new leadership at the top, the Green Party prepared itself for the 2001 election. Adriane's focus was—as it has always been and continues to be for Canada's Green parties—trying to get equal media attention. She was determined this time to get into an actual, formal leaders' debate, rather than the strange compromise that was held in 1996. Adriane recalls what she thinks was the event that led to the major media finally deciding to invite her to that election's debate:

> We had a press conference, and so when all the media showed up and were asking questions, the media just focused onto me and asked me question after question on every area of policy. It went on forever. And I still remember (the reporter) from *Global TV*, Keith Baldrey, he was just pacing at the back and just looking at me. And I felt . . . I remember feeling at the time like I was in a movie, this person was watching me, all these questions were coming at me. It was so surreal. And of course I knew all the answers because I'd written or at least drafted the whole platform. I'm academically trained, I knew the stuff. And so after all the questions ended we gave them all copies of our Green book, and about two hours later Keith Baldrey called me and said: you're on the debates. You're on the leaders' debates. So I think it was really that professional performance of

the party. They could see that it wouldn't be foolish, in terms of us not having responses to questions they asked. They knew that we'd be able to hold our own. And that's what I guess they had been worried about before. (Adriane, from an interview with the author, 2017).

The governing BC NDP was, once again, not happy about this. They complained to the CBC (Canadian Broadcasting Corporation) that they wouldn't do the debate unless the media also invited the leader of the British Columbia Unity Party, a brand-new party that been founded from a union of five smaller conservative groups, including the previous Reform and Social Credit parties. The BC NDP was worried that giving attention and airtime to the Greens would pull votes away from the BC NDP on its environmental flank, and wanted the BC Liberals to have an equal attack from a party looking to draw away their traditional voters. In the end the media refused to include the Unity Party and told the BC NDP that the Greens were coming whether they liked it or not. The governing party capitulated and 2001 became the first election to include a Green Party leader in its debates.

We can't really know if the Greens really did eat away at the BC NDP's usual voter base, but we do know that it didn't actually matter if they did. The BC Liberals did so well in the election that it wouldn't have mattered if you'd added all the BC NDP and Green votes together. The BC NDP was absolutely crushed in the 2001 election, being reduced from thirty-nine seats to only two. The BC Liberals won seventy-seven out of the possible seventy-nine seats. The formerly governing BC NDP being reduced to only a pair of MLAs meant that they even lost "official party status" in the legislature, which by BC law requires you to have at least four elected members.

The Best Result for the Greens Yet

The Greens, meanwhile, had their highest-yet result with over 12 percent of the vote. Unfortunately, they still elected no one. Still, the Greens came second in a number of districts, beating their BC NDP rivals. Andrew Lewis in the district of Saanich North and the Islands came the closest to being elected, a result that would later be looked at by Elizabeth May's team when determining where to run the Green Party of Canada leader for the best chance of getting her elected. Adriane did very well in her district of Powell River, but she blames the BC NDP for targeting her specifically because they didn't want to see a Green win and thus give the party the legitimacy of having an elected representative.

> They did all these polls in my riding (district) of Powell River Sunshine Coast, and I was at 31 percent, the NDP were at 25 percent, and I was climbing, so then

the NDP decided they didn't want to see me win, so they threw everything at it. Three phone calls to every constituent! They pulled volunteers from Dosanjh's (the leader of the BC NDP) riding to my riding to defeat me, and he was furious. And then he didn't win (his own district). They used a whole bunch of [tactics] and they knocked me back four points 27 percent, and they came up to 27 percent. Oh and then the NDP message was that we came "a distant third" when we were like fifty votes away from second. It was so close, it was unbelievable. (Adriane Carr, on the 2001 election, from an interview with the author)

The Liberals wound up winning Adriane's district, while the BC NDP threw considerable resources into making sure that Adriane didn't place better than third. The BC NDP in fact put a massive amount of effort into fighting the Greens rather than competing against the BC Liberals. They knew that their time was up and that they weren't going to win against the BC Liberals. They at least didn't want to get beaten by the Greens.

Electoral Reform? Maybe Not

After the election, the newly elected BC Liberal party did an abrupt about-face on their promise of electoral reform for British Columbia. In 1996, they had suffered due to the strangeness of our first-past-the-post electoral system, but in 2001 they had massively benefited from it. They received over 57 percent of the province-wide vote, a feat that's almost unheard of in Canadian elections, and with this actual majority of voter support they had almost completely eliminated their rivals. When the system was working against them it was bad, but when it was working for them it was very good. Justin Trudeau used the same argument after he decided to abandon his electoral reform promise from the 2015 election.

The BC Greens during this time took up the mantle of champion for electoral reform. The BC NDP was not particularly interested in reform since they benefited from the unbalanced system in 1996 and they hoped to be able to repeat that performance in the next election. They hoped the pendulum wound swing back in their direction. So the BC Green Party, despite not electing anyone to the legislature, began pushing the BC Liberal government to hold to their promise of reform.

Eventually the pressure both from the Greens and from journalists and British Columbians who remembered their promise got to the BC Liberals, and they agreed. Concurrent with the 2005 election there would be a referendum on whether British Columbia would move to a proportional representation system. However, the BC Liberals sabotaged the referendum from the start. They set an extremely high threshold for whether the referendum would pass, declaring that the reforms would only take effect if over 60 percent of British Columbians voted in favour, rather than a simple majority of 50 percent. They also required that a majority of the seventy-nine electoral districts would have to vote in favour of it. Neither the BC Liberals or BC NDP actually campaigned in favour of the reforms. They both sat back and hoped that it would fail.

The Greens had spent the four years between 2001 and 2005 trying to act as an opposition party to the BC Liberals from outside of the legislature. Since the BC NDP had only elected two members, the Greens were on nearly equal footing with them. Both parties had to try to hold the government to account without the resources usually given to the opposition party in the legislature. Adriane stayed on as leader and the Greens hoped that by 2005 they would be able to replace the BC NDP as the choice of British Columbians who didn't want to see another BC Liberal government.

In the 2005 election, the BC Liberals were re-elected to another term as government, and the BC NDP returned to the legislature as an official party with thirty-three elected members. The BC Greens vote share decreased down to 9 percent. Again, no one was elected from the Greens. The 2001 election had been the big chance for the Greens to replace the BC NDP as the opposition to the BC Liberals' free-market coalition, and they had hoped that they'd get another big chance in 2005. But by then people had forgotten their distaste for the BC NDP and returned them to the post. Knowing that they probably couldn't defeat the Liberals in 2001, the BC NDP had instead focused heavily on making sure that the upstart Green party wouldn't replace them, and the strategy worked. By 2005 things were back to normal: the way the BC NDP wanted it.

Furthermore, in the 2005 referendum on electoral reform, seventy-seven of British Columbia's seventy-nine districts voted in favour of moving British Columbia to a proportional representation system. Nearly 58 percent of voters also voted in favour. But because this number was 2 percent short of the 60 percent goal that the BC Liberals had set, they declared that it was a failure and that British Columbians did not want a new system. The old system would stay.

The 2005 election was a big disappointment for the BC Greens, who had hoped that their momentum would keep going, and had hoped that their work as an extra-parliamentary opposition to the BC Liberals would be noticed. Adriane retired from her leadership position after the election and went on to join her friend Elizabeth May to become the deputy leader for the federal Greens. She was succeeded as BC Green leader by Dr. Jane Sterk, a psychologist and city councillor from Esquimalt.

Organizing in Ontario and in the Federal Arena

In Ontario, the Greens also continued to expand and improve. The provincial election in 2003 was the first in which the party was able to break above 1 percent of the vote. Like in BC, they had put in the effort to finally run a full slate of candidates (they were only one short, after someone who had planned to run dropped out at the very last minute) and their final vote total was just under 3 percent. This seemingly small result was still a huge boost for the party and represented a quadrupling of their results from the last election.

Until the election of the first Ontario Green MPP (Member of Provincial Parliament) party leader Mike Schreiner in 2018, the election of 2007 was the closest that the Ontario Greens came to a breakthrough. Once again running a full slate of candidates, the Greens finished with 8 percent overall. This number was just about half the number of votes as the provincial NDP, who elected ten members to parliament. This was, and still is, their strongest result in terms of overall support, but it was spread out so evenly across the province that no single Green was elected. Green candidate Shane Jolley placed second in the central Ontario district of Bruce–Grey–Owen Sound, earning an impressive 33 percent of the vote in his attempt to unseat the Progressive Conservative incumbent. At the time this was the best performance of any Green candidate anywhere in Canada. The Greens also managed to knock the NDP into fourth place in a few of the province's other districts.

The Greens' popularity in this election is mostly attributed to their proposal to end government funding for Ontario's Catholic schools, and to move Ontario to a single public school system. The election was dominated by the issue of funding religious private schools after the Progressive Conservative leader had proposed extending funding to all of Ontario's faith-based schools. At the time, the Catholic school system was fully funded by taxpayers in the same way as non-religious schools, but schools for other faiths such as Judaism, Islam, or Evangelical Christianity received no public funding. The Conservative proposal turned out to be deeply unpopular, and most voters aligned with the Liberals and NDP, both of whom were opposed to extending the funding to other religions but continued to back the funding of Catholic schools. The Greens' proposal to end religious school funding entirely appealed to a significant number of voters who were willing to move their votes over to Green Party candidates.

Long-time leader Frank de Jong retired as leader of the party after the election, although he stayed with the Ontario Greens for one more run at office in 2011 as a regular candidate before moving to the Yukon and eventually becoming leader of the Yukon Green Party. Frank had wanted to stay as the party leader in Ontario, but after being at the head for four elections he understood that it might be good for the party if he stepped aside and let a fresh face take over. Mike Schreiner, a Toronto-based food delivery entrepreneur who had joined the party in 2005, was acclaimed as the next leader of the party.

In 2011, the party dropped significantly from its high point in 2007, its vote total cut in half. By 2014 they'd begun climbing back up, ending with just under 5 percent, and stayed about the same in the 2018 election when they finally succeeded in electing a single member to parliament.

CHAPTER 5 – PROFESSIONALIZING CANADA'S GREEN PARTIES

The Federal Greens Pick up the Pace

The federal Green Party professionalized during the early 2000s, as well. Although in the beginning the federal party had functioned as an extension of the British Columbia and Ontario parties it eventually developed enough support and organization outside of the two provinces that it began to be run independently. Eventually the federal party broke off from its provincial counterparts, and now operates as an independent organization with no formal structural ties to any of the provincial Green parties. The federal and provincial parties continue to coordinate in ways that are legally allowed but don't share funds or information, since they now exist as separate official entities.

Up until the mid-2000s, the federal party had gone through a number of leaders, usually with relatively short terms. Then in 2004, Jim Harris was elected as leader. Jim was a long-time Green candidate and volunteer. He'd first run with the Ontario Greens in 1990, and he'd been a steady and capable organizer for the provincial party. He'd even run for the provincial party leadership, but had been beaten by Frank de Jong.

Before getting involved with the Greens, Jim had been active in Canada's Progressive Conservative Party, but after reading a book about the rise of the German Greens had realized that his political home was elsewhere. Still, he came from a more conservative background than many of the other Greens that were involved in the party at the time. He was passionate about business issues and was deeply involved in the corporate sector. Before becoming leader of the party, he was already a professional speaker and had authored several books on topics of business innovation.

Jim was a bit of an unconventional choice for leader of the party. His history with the Progressive Conservatives rankled some of the Green members who had migrated to the party from the opposite end of the political spectrum. But Jim's background gave him the tools to do something that the party had never managed to do before: organize and professionalize itself on a national scale.

The federal Greens had never run a full slate of candidates by the time Jim became leader. In the most recent election (in 2000), they had run candidates in barely a third of the country's districts. Just like several of the provincial parties had already figured out, Jim declared that his top priority as the party's leader would be to run a candidate everywhere in Canada. His determination on this was partly for the same reason as other Green leaders, namely that it's what a national party is expected to do. But there was another reason to undertake the ambitious campaign.

The Liberal government of Jean Chretien had recently passed a new set of election financing laws. In an attempt to cut down on the practice of parties relying on rich corporate and union donors to sustain themselves, the Liberals had added a per-vote subsidy. This simply meant that, after an election, any party that fielded candidates would be entitled to a certain amount of money for each vote that they received. The more votes you got, the more funding you got. It was a progressive policy used in many places around the world that released parties from having to appeal to rich donors just to keep their party organization running.

The idea was that it would free up parties to do what was right for their voters, instead of what was right for their donors.

The next election was set to be the first where parties would be entitled to this funding. Jim wanted to make sure that the Greens were getting as many votes as possible, so that the party could secure as much funding as it possibly could. This would allow the Greens to operate as a real professional organization, to hire more full-time staff and to set the party up to succeed in the future. He wanted to raise the profile of the party so that it would be considered a serious contender alongside the other big parties. So he set about recruiting candidates in parts of Canada that the Greens had never managed to penetrate. He wanted to make sure that every single district had a Green candidate to vote for. The Greens pushed the message that it was worth it to vote Green because it *would* actually have an effect to support the party even if the candidate wasn't elected.

Jim in 2004

It was a massively successful initiative. In the 2004 election, the Green Party got over five times as many votes as in the previous election. In fact, the party got twice as many votes in this single election than it had across its entire combined history. It produced a more serious and professional platform than ever more, produced with the help of the technological and business acumen that Jim had brought with him from his corporate life. Despite heavy campaigning from the Greens to allow Jim into the federal leaders debate, he was still excluded. The media gave the same reasoning that they had in the provinces: until the Greens won a seat in the legislature, they would not be invited to debate. Jim tried to argue that the Bloc Quebecois (the Quebec separatist party) was running candidates in only seventy-five districts (only in the province of Quebec) and yet was still being invited to debate, whereas the Greens were being excluded even though they were running in every district. The argument was unsuccessful in convincing the media consortium.

Despite massively raising the public profile of the Greens and delivering them their best ever election, Jim was still a controversial figure within the Greens. He didn't pass the purity test for many of the more left-leaning members and was accused of shifting the party too far to the right. After the 2004 election he even faced a leadership challenge from another member who wanted to reverse some of the changes in focus and direction from Jim's leadership. Jim won re-election as leader, but criticism of him and his efforts continued by many among the membership.

Jim Harris led the party in the next election as well. The 2004 election had returned only a minority government for Paul Martin and the Liberal party. Just two years later, the Conservatives and the NDP teamed up with the Bloc Quebecois to force a new early election. In 2006, the party once again ran a full slate of candidates, and once again Jim wasn't invited to the leaders' debate,

CHAPTER 5 – PROFESSIONALIZING CANADA'S GREEN PARTIES

despite heavy campaigning again on his part to be allowed in. The Greens increased their vote share by a slight margin, but remained in mostly the same place as after the 2004 election.

After the 2006 election, Jim stepped down as leader. The reason he stated to the media was that he had led the party through two campaigns and thought that it needed a new face to keep the momentum going. He was replaced by Elizabeth May, an environmental lawyer who had spent the last few decades as director of the Sierra Club of Canada. Despite ending his term as leader, Jim remained (and remains) active in the party, but returned to his day job as a professional speaker and author. He left the party in a far stronger state than he had inherited it, and passed a capable organization over to Elizabeth.

"I must study politics and war that my sons may have liberty to study mathematics and philosophy."

(John Adams)

GREENS IN CANADA'S REMAINING PROVINCES

Partially thanks to the work being done by the federal party, during the 2000s provincial Green parties finally popped up in some of the other Canadian provinces beyond Ontario, Quebec, and BC.

Alberta: A Difficult Place for Green Ideas

Although the Alberta Green party had been founded in 1993, they ran only a handful of candidates for their first three elections, and fared quite poorly. Like the other provincial Greens they eventually undertook a professionalization push, and in 2004 they set a goal to run a majority of candidates. That year they got 3 percent of the province's vote; however, this election featured a few individual Greens that did extraordinarily well, especially in a fossil-fuel dominated province like Alberta. The Green candidate in Drayton Valley placed second, and the Greens defeated candidates from the older Liberal and NDP parties in a number of districts.

In 2008, the Alberta Greens ran a nearly full slate of candidates and increased their vote share to 5 percent, their current record. Again, they had a couple of standout districts, such as candidate Joe Anglin's second-place finish in Lacombe–Ponoka. The party was clearly hovering on the edge of being able to elect their first member of parliament, three years before any other Canadian Green party would manage to do so.

Sadly, after the 2008 provincial election, the Green Party of Alberta completely imploded.

The party was scheduled to hold their annual general meeting in September, when suddenly a surprise early federal election was called. No one had predicted the snap 2008 election, and the Alberta Greens' annual meeting was right in the middle of the campaign period. Despite protestations from members who wanted to postpone the provincial meeting so that they could focus on the federal election, the meeting went ahead.

Alberta Green organizers began to hear rumours that Joe Anglin, the candidate who had done so well in the recent election, had signed up a large number of brand-new members that he was planning to bring to the meeting. He and the new members had introduced a number of motions to be voted on that made it look as if he was aiming to force out the current party leader and stage a takeover.

When the attendees for the meeting assembled, it was obvious that a large number of those attending were brand-new members brought by Anglin. The party's existing leadership was worried. Many of the usual members weren't present because they were hard at work on the federal campaign, and it looked like Anglin and his group were going to be able to overpower the small number of long-term members who were present. Most members had decided to skip the meeting to work on the federal campaign, because they thought nothing important would be happening at the provincial event. So, before the first meeting of the day was scheduled to begin, the executives of the party made the strange decision to gather a group of delegates in the parking lot below the hotel and to vote to adjourn the convention completely.

Technically, the convention *was* held. The party's rules required a certain percentage of members to be present for any decisions, and there was enough of them there. The meeting was opened, the attendees voted to postpone all matters until the next meeting, and the meeting was closed. It all happened within the space of a few minutes, but enough members had gathered in the parking lot that it was all legal and technically complied with the party's own rules.

However, the move understandably angered Joe Anglin and the people that he had brought. He and those attending with him stayed at the convention and convened their own meeting without any of the official party leadership. At this meeting the members voted to elect a new executive council, passed their motions, and appointed Anglin as "interim leader" of the party.

The party fell apart. Both groups claimed to be the legitimate leadership team of the Alberta Greens. Joe Anglin sent out an e-mail to the membership describing himself as "interim leader" and outlining his version of events. The previous leader (or current leader, depending on your side in the dispute) George Read claimed that Anglin's meeting and election was illegitimate. The dispute continued until April of the next year, when the dysfunctional party neglected to file its annual financial paperwork with the Alberta election authority.

CHAPTER 5 – PROFESSIONALIZING CANADA'S GREEN PARTIES

By failing to file their paperwork, the party stopped officially existing. Elections Alberta delisted the party, meaning that it would not be able to compete in the next election. Less than a year after their most successful election to-date, the party was gone.

Some of the membership of the now-defunct Green Party joined the Alberta Party, a small centrist party that had existed since the early '80s but had been almost non-existent in recent years. In 2008, it had fielded a single candidate who had placed last in her district. The migration of Greens helped revitalize the party, and the Alberta Party eventually successfully elected a sole MLA in 2015, leader Clark Gregg. Others from the Greens, such as Joe Anglin, went to join the newly formed Wildrose Party, a right-wing populist conservative party. The party had a moderate breakthrough in the 2012 election when it became the official opposition, which included Joe Anglin being elected as one of its new MLAs. He lasted two years with the party and then quit mid-term, spending the rest of his term as an independent. He wasn't subsequently re-elected. The Wildrose Party eventually merged with the Progressive Conservative Party of Alberta in 2017, forming the new United Conservative Party.

Meanwhile, the rest of the local Greens went about trying to rebuild the Alberta Green Party. Because of Alberta election laws they couldn't simply re-form the party and run in the next election. The law said that when a party was delisted it had to wait one full election before reforming and beginning again. So the Greens began again from scratch, registering a new party that called itself the Evergreen Party.

After the 2012 election, they changed their name back to the Green Party; however, they'd lost most of the momentum, knowledge, and trust that they'd built up by 2008. The party hasn't been able to run a full slate or break 1 percent of the vote since the reformation. They did make some news in 2018 when they elected Cheryle Chagnon-Greyeyes as their new leader, making her the first Indigenous woman to lead an Albertan political party.

More Prairie Greens

The other prairie Green parties haven't had as eventful or problematic a history as the Alberta Greens. Both the Saskatchewan and Manitoba Green parties formed in 1999. The federal Green party had held its annual convention in Winnipeg the previous year, and that energized Manitobans enough for a group of them to get a local provincial party up and running.

Manitoba in 1999 was governed by the centre-right Progressive Conservative Party, so the new Green Party rose out of frustration with right-wing governance in the province. Saskatchewan, on the other hand, had a dominant centre-left NDP government with the Conservatives as a distant third in voter support. The Saskatchewan Greens were formed mostly by politically involved individuals who had initially supported and been part of the Saskatchewan NDP but had become critical of the party after eight years in government. While the Liberals and Conservatives in the 1999 election were working on a plan to unite and challenge the NDP from their right wing, the new Saskatchewan Greens planned to challenge an already centre-left party from their left flank.

Saskatchewan is one of two provinces in Canada in which the NDP has been so successful that it's scared the older Liberal and Conservative parties into abandoning their partisanship and banding together instead. In both Saskatchewan and British Columbia the two parties have combined into a single party, believing that doing so was the only way they'd be able to defeat the strong provincial NDP. In doing so they collapsed the province from a strong multiparty system into a two-party us-versus-them arena. They also yielded the position of "third party" to the local Greens, although the Saskatchewan Greens haven't yet managed to capitalize on it as has been done in British Columbia.

Neither the Saskatchewan nor Manitoba Greens were very successful in their first election attempts. But both parties continued to grow afterwards and fielded more candidates in subsequent elections. Both parties cracked 1 percent of public support in 2007, and the Green party of Saskatchewan has been fielding full slates of candidates since 2011.

In Manitoba, the local Greens are still competing with the Liberal party for the position of "third party." They've actually had quite a high amount of support in pre-election polls, at least compared to Greens in other provinces. They received 5 percent of the overall vote in 2016, and placed second in four districts. David Nickarz in the district of Wolseley came within a few percentage points of the NDP incumbent. However, the party only bothered running candidates in half of the province's districts, meaning that their vote total would certainly have been higher if they'd run a full slate.

The Maritimes Pick up the Pace

Following Jim Harris' term as leader of the federal party, provincial Green parties began to form in the Maritimes, as well. The Greens had never really had much success in penetrating the political scene of Canada's three maritime provinces, but when Jim made it his mission to recruit and run candidates in every part of the country the party finally developed some organizational structure and interest in the eastern provinces.

Prince Edward Island (PEI) was the first of the Maritimes to officially found a Green party. The province of PEI is unique in Canada: it's Canada's smallest province both by area and by population. A tiny island on Canada's east coast, its population is barely 150,000. This puts it at about the size of a medium city in one of the country's other provinces. The politics of PEI have always been dominated by just two parties: the traditional Progressive Conservative Party and the Liberal Party.

The New Democrat Party has a presence on the island, but in its entire history it has only elected a single member, who only lasted a single term.

The PEI Green Party was founded by Sharon Labchuk, a local environmental activist who had been recruited as a federal candidate by Jim Harris's big organizational push. After the 2004 federal election, she built off of the momentum to officially register the provincial party. Unlike the parties in the rest of Canada that had started very small and worked their way up, the PEI Greens already had a ready-out-of-the-box organizational structure and team as soon as they were founded. They got right to work recruiting candidates for their next provincial election, intending to run a full slate right from the start.

Federally, PEI only has four districts. The average district in a Canadian election has seventy thousand voters. But when the island province became a part of the Canadian federation it was promised that it would always have at least four districts represented in parliament, so each of its four districts now contain only about thirty thousand electors. The provincial case is even more extreme: Prince Edward Island has the smallest districts of any Canadian province. The voters of PEI elect twenty-seven members to their provincial legislature, each district containing only about five thousand people.

After only having to fill four spots for the federal election, it proved to be more difficult than expected to fill all of the twenty-seven PEI provincial districts. Sharon and the PEI Green Party wound up running only eighteen candidates. This was still more than were fielded by the PEI NDP, and in it's very first election the PEI Greens actually beat the NDP in the total vote count. This was the first time in Canada that a Green party had ended an election ahead of one of the big three parties. In addition, the 2007 election for the PEI Greens was the first time that a provincial party anywhere in Canada had run a slate of candidates in which more than half were women. This particular accomplishment was a point of pride for party leader Sharon when I spoke with her. Still, the party was unsuccessful in breaking the two-party dominance on the island. They elected no one on their first attempt. They did not give up.

Sharon led the PEI Greens through another election in 2011 where the party increased their number of candidates and overall vote total, but still elected no one. She then stepped down as leader and was replaced by Peter Bevan-Baker, a multiple-time Green candidate and dentist by trade. His leadership wound up being the breakthrough for the PEI Greens when he was elected in 2015.

Nova Scotia Hit the Ground Running

The founding of the PEI Greens was followed closely by the Greens in Nova Scotia. Nova Scotia is the biggest of the Maritime provinces in both size and population, although with just under a million residents it's still much smaller than most other provinces. Unlike in PEI where the NDP had never managed to have a breakthrough, the party was strong and organized in Nova Scotia, and was currently serving as the official opposition to a Progressive Conservative government.

The Nova Scotia Greens spawned off of the organizational groundwork of Jim Harris and the federal party, just like in PEI. One of the founders, a local student named Nick Wright, became the party's first leader. Nick was an Ontario transplant, and at the time of the party's founding was in his early twenties and pursuing a law degree at Dalhousie University. As in the federal arena, Nova Scotia had just announced that they would be implementing per-vote subsidies for their elections, and Nick made a promise as leader that the newly formed Nova Scotia Green Party would run a full slate of candidates in its very first election.

Nick was surprised to receive some pushback from Green members at this promise. For him it was the obvious thing that a party should do, and he thought that it should be a clear expectation of a party leader to make sure it happened. But many among the Greens in Nova Scotia still saw the Green movement as a sort of "anti-party" and preferred the group to be more of a think tank than an actual party. Nick described to me in an interview that a lot of the early Greens in Nova Scotia came from academic circles rather than traditional political circles, and as such they were more interested in theorizing and philosophizing rather than actively trying to win elections.

Nick didn't let the criticism slow him down. After the 2004 federal election, a lot of the local Green organizers and volunteers had burnt out, so Nick ran the party as a one-man-show for the first year, working to sign up members and candidates but not having a lot of structural support from those that were onboard. Eventually, the burnt-out volunteers began drifting back, and by the time the provincial election in 2006 rolled around the base was once again active and passionate.

Nick proudly told me that the Nova Scotia Greens ran a full slate of candidates in their very first election. They even ran more candidates than the local Liberal party, who had come up one short. The Nova Scotia Greens are the only provincial Green party to run candidates in every district in their first election, and hit the ground running harder than any of the other provincial Green chapters. But, like the Greens in other provinces, despite their impressive organization efforts, the party was unable to elect anyone. The party ended with just above 2 percent of the vote, enough to secure public funding under the per-vote subsidies as Nick had hoped.

After the election Nick stepped down as leader. He needed to finish his degree, and afterwards planned to move back to Ontario. The party struggled without Nick to take care of organizational details, failing to file some critical paperwork with the Nova Scotia election authority, but new leader Ryan Watson managed to lead the party through the 2009 election with another full slate of candidates. He also stepped down after contesting an election, and the party went dormant. They fielded only sixteen candidates in 2013, but by 2017 had begun rebuilding under Thomas Trappenberg, their latest (and current) leader. They ended the 2017 election with their highest ever vote total, but still not electing any candidates.

CHAPTER 5 – PROFESSIONALIZING CANADA'S GREEN PARTIES

New Brunswick, Late to the Game but Strong

The final maritime province to get its own Green Party was New Brunswick. Unlike the other two parties who formed during Jim Harris' tenure as federal leader, the New Brunswick Greens didn't organize until 2008, after Elizabeth May had replaced Jim as leader. The forming was led by Mike Milligan, who had been a federal candidate in the 2008 election. Like in PEI and Nova Scotia, the federal Greens in New Brunswick used the organizational structures built from the federal campaign to jumpstart a provincial version of the party. And like in PEI, New Brunswick is traditionally a two-party dominated province. As with their island neighbour, the provincial NDP has had very little success, never having more than a single elected representative.

Mike Milligan didn't remain leader for long. In 2009, Jack MacDougall was acclaimed as the party's first nominated leader (Mike had been an interim leader, put down on paper when the party first registered). Jack was a veteran organizer for the provincial Liberal party, and had even run for the leadership in 2002. He came from a strong organizational background, having also been responsible for a million dollar campaign to save the local Imperial Theatre in Saint John. He didn't plan to be a long-term leader of the party, as he was unable to speak French, which was a big challenge for a politician in a bilingual province like New Brunswick. Nevertheless, Jack brought his organizational ability to the party and succeeded in recruiting a nearly full slate for the party's first election in 2010.

It was a strong first-showing for the party, but Jack stayed on as leader only until 2011 when he stepped down to return to his job as a teacher. In a leadership convention in 2012, the party elected David Coon, a long-time environmental educator, to the post. Like Peter Bevan-Baker in PEI, David would deliver the breakthrough that the New Brunswick Greens had been chasing. David became the second elected provincial Green in 2014.

On the other side of the country, in British Columbia, the 2009 election wasn't particularly interesting. With Jane Sterk as the party's new leader, the overall vote total for the Greens stayed almost the same as the previous election. Since their high-water mark in 2001, the Greens seemed to be stuck at about 9 percent of public support. They now had a solid one-in-ten British Columbian voters who could be counted on to support them, but they were spread so evenly throughout the province that they weren't succeeding at electing any individual MLA. First-past-the-post requires you to cluster your support in order to win, not to have broad but small support across the whole jurisdiction.

The closest area the Greens had to a stronghold was on Vancouver Island, particularly in the city of Victoria and its surrounding suburbs. Despite the party being first formed on the mainland in Vancouver, and much of its early history being very Vancouver-focused, the Greens were consistently having their best results in the south of the island.

Finally, the First Real Breakthrough

It was in one of these Victoria-area districts that the Greens would have their first real success: the election of Green Party of Canada leader Elizabeth May in the district of Saanich–Gulf Islands in 2011. As the first Green elected at a federal level in North America, she was soon followed by another first in British Columbia. In 2013, Andrew Weaver was elected in the nearby district of Oak Bay–Gordon Head, one of the suburbs of Victoria. He was the first Green to be elected at a provincial level anywhere in North America.

At the time of this book's writing, there are ten Greens elected at the provincial level or higher in Canada. Elizabeth is the sole federal Green. Andrew Weaver (now party leader) in British Columbia was joined by Adam Olsen and Sonia Furstenau in 2017. Peter Bevan-Baker in PEI was joined by Hannah Bell, also in 2017. In 2018, Mike Schreiner was elected as the first member from the Green Party of Ontario. Later that year, David Coon in New Brunswick was joined by Megan Mitton and Kevin Arseneau.

WHAT DOES GREEN MEAN?

Flyer for the Values Party of New Zealand from one of their early elections.

I'd like to vote for Values tomorrow, but....

Tomorrow we're not asking for your sympathy, we're asking for your vote. Our strength depends on our show of votes - so without your vote, your sympathy means NOTHING.

But if I vote for you I'll be taking a vote away from Labour/National.....

Isn't it about time you voted FOR something you believe in rather than AGAINST one or other of the main parties? It dosen't matter about taking votes away from them because every vote taken makes them realise that not all of us like what they're saying.

Issues like who is going to be Prime Minister after Saturday may seem important right now, but it's CRUCIAL in this election to vote for new goals for New Zealand.

But Values can't possibly become the Government this time, so I'm wasting my vote....

Not so! Being the Government isn't the only way of changing society. Every vote taken from National or Labour forces them to listen to what Values is saying; to take our policies. Enough votes FOR Values means that others will have to adopt our policies. Already they're talking about stabilizing population; women's rights, the environment... because WE forced them to. Remember, if you DO believe what we're saying but DON'T vote for us, then you're casting a vote of non-confidence against us.

These are your candidates:
Trevor Reeves, St.Kilda; Kathleen Dawson, Dunedin Central; Peter Sutton, Dunedin North; Gill Morgan, Oamaru; John Perkins, Otago Central; Alvin Duthie, Clutha; John Veitch, Wallace; Tom Clarkson, South Canterbury.

Sick and special votes, phone 76-482.

Pamphlet from the Values Party of New Zealand, addressing many of the criticisms that are faced by a new party trying to compete in a First-Past-The-Post system.

WHAT DOES GREEN MEAN?

Former Australian Greens leader and founder Bob Brown, during the Franklin Dam campaign.

Leader of the Australian Greens Richard di Natale (left) and former Senator and Australian Greens leader and founder Bob Brown (right).
(Permission is granted to copy, distribute and/or modify this document under the terms of the GNU Free Documentation License, Version 1.2 or any later version published by the Free Software Foundation.)

Early German Green leader Petra Kelly.

WHAT DOES GREEN MEAN?

Members of the first batch of German Greens elected to the Bundestag.

German Green Party politician Joschka Fischer being sworn in as Hesse's Minister for Environment, 1985.

WHAT DOES GREEN MEAN?

German Vice Chancellor and Leader of the Green Party Joschka Fischer meeting with Russian President Vladimir Putin in 2001.
(This image comes from the website of the President of the Russian Federation and is licensed under the Creative Commons Attribution 4.0 License.)

*Minister President of Baden-Württemberg and
leader of the Green Party of Baden-Württemberg Winfried Kretschmann.
(This image is licensed under the Creative Commons Attribution 2.0 License)*

*John Gormley; former leader of the Irish Green Party; Minister for the Environment,
Heritage, and Local Government from 2007 to 2011.
(This image is by Luis Diaz Alvarez, and is licensed under the Creative Commons Attribution 4.0 license)*

WHAT DOES GREEN MEAN?

*Dominique Voynet, French Green politician, Minister of the Environment from 1997-2001.
(This image is licensed under the Creative Commons Attribution 3.0 Unported license)*

Isabella Lövin (left), Swedish Green spokesperson and Minister for International Development, alongside her staff. (This image is made available under the Creative Commons CC0 1.0 Universal Public Domain Dedication)

BC Greens founder Adriane Carr and Paul George.

WHAT DOES GREEN MEAN?

The widespread blossoming of the irreverent Greens

ERIC DOWNTON
...a Vancouver writer on international affairs.

With a touch of idealism and zany humor they challenge the established parties

Petra Kelly, seedling in hand, led West German Greens.

SHEER CYNICISM displayed by both politicians and the electorate was a depressing element in the election campaign we recently endured.

In such an atmosphere it may be significant that the hustings battles preceding last week's vote marked the Green party's serious debut in Canadian federal politics.

In Vancouver, the Greens — environmentalists and social reformers — made some refreshingly idealistic contributions to the generally unimpressive campaign debating through such candidates as Jim Bohlen in overexposed Quadra, and Paul Watson in hectic Vancouver-Centre.

Many voters undoubtedly dismissed the Greens as a somewhat dotty fringe group. In fact they are part of an international phenomenon — politically activated groups winning a modest measure of public recognition because they demonstrate genuine concern for people, and for the condition of our planet.

Greens seem to be taking root in most Western European countries, North America, Australia, and New Zealand. They have 11 seats in the Parliament of Europe at Strasbourg — seven from West Germany, two each from Belgium and Holland.

The bellwether party for the world's Greens is in West Germany. There Die Grunen hold 27 seats in the *Bundestag*, the national parliament, and a total of 49 seats in six of the 11 *Land* or state parliaments.

Unlike Canadians, the Germans now take their Greens seriously. Polls indicate that about a quarter of West Germans under age 25 vote Green. In elections next year the Greens are confident they will win seats in three more *Land* assemblies.

Rebelling against the West German political establishment — the equivalent of our Tory-Liberal-NDP trio — the Greens emerged as a party in the early 1970s. They were carried on and up by the waves of anti-nuclear and pro-conservationist protest, by the younger generation's anger over high unemployment. (Doesn't that sound familiar in B.C.?)

To hard-eyed politics they brought a touch of idealism and cheerful zaniness. Backed by the voices of youth their challenge is making the established parties rethink some of their policies and rejustify them to the electorate.

Although there is no formal Green international organization, the European groups are in close and constant communion. Many of the policy statements made by Bohlen and Watson during their Vancouver electioneering — especially on banning the cruise missile, nuclear disarmament, social welfare and ecological concerns — are similar to the European Greens' declarations.

A Canadian-German family in the Vancouver area says German Greens, friends of theirs, were particularly interested to hear about Watson's proposal during the Canadian election campaign for a Canadian peace corps and a conservation corps — a proposal that did not receive much attention from the B.C. news media.

Watson argued that the federal government should get out of NATO and NORAD and use the money thus saved to create the peace and conservation corps.

As visualized by Watson, the peace corps would initially employ 70,000 members to help needy people in Canada and overseas. The conservation corps would put 80,000 people to work in Canada on projects such as reforestation, flood prevention and relief, and protecting wildlife.

Perhaps Watson's proposal is being discussed in parliamentary corridors — but in Bonn, not Ottawa. That would be an example of the kind of osmosis in ideas at work among the Greens on different continents.

Among the European Greens there is a wide diversity of political and ideological background. (The German party was deeply embarrassed last year to discover that its oldest member — aged 76 — in the *Bundestag* was a former Nazi official; he was compelled to resign his parliamentary seat and his party membership.) But they tend to share relative youth, upper middle class urban backgrounds, and above-average educational standards.

As professed libertarians they are deliberately informal, with an irreverent sense of humor. The jeans and T-shirts they wear around the German parliaments would never be tolerated by the Speaker of Ottawa's House of Commons.

Their leaders are constantly changing, and usually quarrelling among themselves. No conventional label fits the Greens. They contend that the terms "right" and "left" are out-of-date and misleading, that they themselves are "neither right nor left but out front."

A controversial former German Greens leader, Petra Kelly, described them as an "anti-party party" fighting the cosy self-serving closed shop practices of the establishment parties, with their slick, big-money party machinery. That is a line that obviously goes down well with Europe's disenchanted youth.

The Greens over there want a neutral, non-nuclear, demilitarized Europe. But they are vague as to how that can be achieved under the threat of the huge Russian military buildup and the growing Soviet nuclear arsenal.

Besides disarmament and environmental issues, the European Greens champion such causes as women's liberation, more aid for the Third World, and the rights of homosexuals. It is on their original chosen ground, the environmental front, as signified by the party name, that they are mainly making their mark.

The Green members of the German federal parliament demonstrate a practical commitment to good causes in a way unimaginable for Canada's salary-grasping MPs. They keep only a third of their salaries and expense allowances, and hand over the other two-thirds to a fund for supporting deserving projects administered by the party's parliamentary caucus.

Will the Greens survive and expand as a political force in Europe, and on the international scene, including Canada? Perhaps.

A Green ginger group in our House of Commons might help dispel some of the odor of cynicism tainting the Ottawa air. □

Article from the Vancouver Sun in 1984, showing the coverage the German Greens were getting in the Canadian press.

Issue #3 of the Canadian Green's newsletter, covering the convention where the federal party was established.

Canadian Green newsletter from directly after the party's first Canadian election in 1984.

WHAT DOES GREEN MEAN?

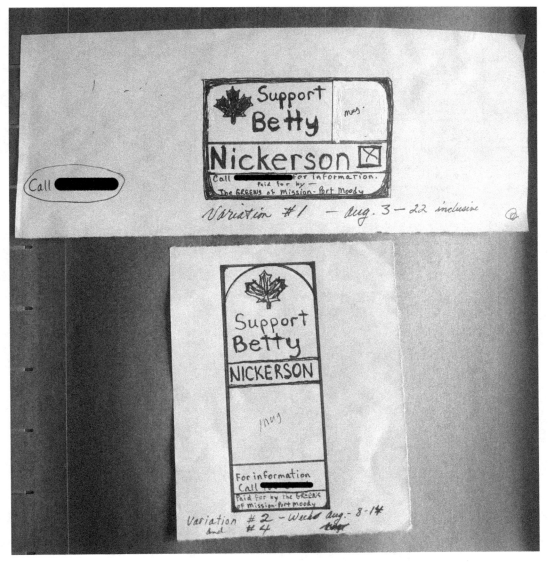

Original planning sketches for the campaign material for the Green Party of Canada's first federal candidate, Betty Nickerson.

Greetings — from the GREENS
Meet Betty Nickerson

We are honoured and proud to present to the voters of North Vancouver-Burnaby a special person with a very sensible message.

Betty Nickerson was Canada's first federal Green Party candidate (Mission-Port Moody byelection '83) and through the Green Party, she represents a fast growing group of people who feel the time has come for a new and inspiring vision for Canada and the world.

In her work and travels Betty has visited all regions of Canada and over 50 countries as a writer and commentator. Of the many places she has lived, she chose to return to the west coast, Canada's gateway to the exciting potentials of the Pacific Rim.

Betty's lifetime of involvement in teaching and demonstrating wise use of our resources and the environment is of importance in a riding which carefully guards the water supply of the Lower Mainland but overlooks the salt water foreshore of Burrard Inlet.

This riding contains mountains and sea, lumbering and fishing, shipping and refining, education and recreation and among its many ethnic groups, it contains wisdom from around the world.

For a mature, responsible voice and new and appropriate approaches to our difficulties, you will want to hear the Green message from Betty Nickerson.

Green Candidates (l-r)
Dr. Wally Thomas (Capilano)
Betty Nickerson (North Vancouver-Burnaby)
and Ted Mousseau (Vancouver-Kingsway)
share their optimism for a Green Future

Betty's Biography

Elizabeth (BETTY) Smith-Nickerson: B.A. in Geology, M.A. in Agriculture (U. of Manitoba), Ph.D. program in communications (McGill University). Betty was born in Kansas and grew up on the Oregon coast. She has lived in Winnipeg, Montreal, Ottawa, Coquitlam and she has two sons, a daughter and four grandchildren.

Her career began as a radio commentator in the 1940's and 50's; moved to her own television show and wrote two books in the 1960's. (How the World Grows its Food, Celebrate the Sun.)

Betty has organized special projects for Commonwealth House in England, Montreal's Expo 67, the UN Habitat Conference in Vancouver and the Commonwealth Games in Edmonton.

In 1972 she founded ALL ABOUT US CANADA, a national foundation to encourage the creativity of youngsters by publishing and exhibiting their work. She developed national projects for young Canadians funded by Secretary of State, Dept. of the Environment, Energy, Mines and Resources Canada, Fitness and Amateur Sport, CMHC, UNICEF and other international agencies. In 1979 Betty was selected to serve on the Canadian Commission for the International Year of the Child. She has received the Queen's Jubilee Medal in recognition of her work with young Canadians.

A member of the Writers Union of Canada. Betty has continued to write, weave, garden and is active in the cultural and political life of the local community.

Betty and the GREENS are thinking about the next generation.

Campaign material from Betty Nickerson, from the first election the Green Party of Canada contested in 1984.

WHAT DOES GREEN MEAN?

If you care about...
- your future and your children's future
- the environment
- social responsibility
- people participation in decision making
- egalitarian values/feminism
- non-violence at all levels

...welcome to the Green movement!

In many places in the industrial world people have formed Green Parties to bring these issues directly onto the political stage. The first Green Party in North America was formed in British Columbia in 1983. Similar parties have existed in Europe, Australia, and New Zealand since the 1970's and have elected representatives to local, regional, and national legislatures. Greens come from all walks of life. We are active in our communities, working on projects such as recycling, wilderness protection, and public education.

Our position in the political spectrum is neither left nor right. It is based on the realization that we must move from a system of unlimited growth — favoured by all other political parties — to one that considers the long-term consequences of our actions. The health of the planet and of the life it supports is at stake.

The Crisis of Industrial Society

The current world view of modern industrial society sees the universe as a mechanical system composed of elementary material building blocks, the human body as a machine, life as a competitive struggle, and believes in unlimited material progress. This vision has resulted in massive national debt, the wide and growing disparity between rich and poor, arms stockpiling, environmental destruction, and dwindling resources. It is leading humankind to suicide.

The Green Vision

Green Party philosophy upholds a vision of reality based on love of life, respect for nature, its life forms and natural processes, and awareness of the interdependant nature of the world. All things are connected in the web of life. We recognize that we are part of nature — not above it — and that our lifestyles and the continuation of life itself depend on our wise interaction with the biosphere. Our *political* and *economic* decisions must be made with this in mind. Green Party policies are guided by a long term view of the global future and are founded on these interconnected principles:

Ecological Wisdom

The Greens recognize that the Earth sustains all life forms. Sound ecological principles must be the basis of economic activities. In order to ensure a high quality of life and preserve nature in all its diversity, we must live within the physical limits of our planet, and practice conservation and sustainability.

Real Democracy

Greens believe in direct, participatory democracy by all citizens in formulating and implementing policies and practices at all political levels. Every person has the right to influence and participate in decisions that affect her/his life. These decisions are the political and economic ones in the local community and the areas on which these communities depend, as well as decisions at the regional, national, and international levels.

Social Responsibility

Greens believe that every person has the right to lead a self determined life of purpose and dignity. Each of us must accept responsibility for the Earth and for the rights of everything living on it. Relationships between peoples must reflect compassion, equality, mutual respect, justice, cooperation, and non-coercion. These attitudes must also guide our relations with the other living beings with whom we share the planet.

Egalitarian Values/Feminism

Traditional values of power and control over people and nature must yield to a new way of relating that is healthy and balanced, made up of qualities that both women and men share. Every person must be valued as a full, equal, participating member of society. Greens believe in empowerment of all, and in equality of rights, opportunities and responsibilities.

Non-Violence

Greens reject violence as a way of settling disputes — it is shortsighted, morally unacceptable, and ultimately self-defeating. The qualities that will ensure a sustainable society are flexibility, cooperation, respect, and fairness. We must fully support all non-violent efforts to resolve conflicts around the world and work to put an end to war forever.

Community

The local community is the fundamental organizational unit of society and participatory democracy. In our communities we can create values that are directed towards caring, personal enrichment, cultural development, and the appreciation of the natural world. Greens believe we must foster the building of communities. Greens recognize that the word community applies not only to people who live in one locality, but can also mean those people who share common interests.

Are You Green?

If you agree that we've got to change our way of thinking and our actions to preserve this planet, you are probably Green. Green Party support has come from people of every political leaning, including many who had given up on the political process as a way of creating meaningful change. The Greens are not just another political party. *Our ideas are both idealistic and realistic.*

An early brochure for the Green Party of Canada, outlining some of the party's beliefs.

Your Green Party Candidate Bill Marshall

- An independent business person who provides communications services to major non-profit organizations.
- An editor, designer and photographer.
- A director of Canadian Wheelchair Sports in B.C. and a director of the B.C. Greens.
- A co-founder of the Green Party of Canada.
- Bill is a former university administrator and a retail food store owner in Quebec.
- Bill holds a B.Sc. in Anthropology.
- A resident of Port Moody since 1983.
- Bill's wife, Kate, is a teacher (and their five-month-old son, James, has yet to choose a career).

Help our campaign —

Bill's strong communications and administrative experience make him a natural for politics and government.

Make your vote count! –

Every Green vote sends the message to Ottawa - a clean environment is our number one priority. The time to act on pollution is now. **Say it with a Green vote.**

BILL MARSHALL GREEN PARTY

IT'S TIME

- To send Ottawa a clear message about **your** concern for the environment, for action on pollution, for <u>clean air</u>, water and food — what could be more important than that?!

- For FAIR trade policies on our <u>sustainable</u> resources, products, goods and services.

- For recycling ALL 'wastes' and quickly reducing the burning of fossil fuels to save our <u>local</u> and global environment.

- For universal access to publicly funded, <u>non-profit</u> day care.

- For sustainable economic development for renewable and non-renewable resources.

- For neutrality and peace-keeping.

- For non-partisan constituency office responses to your needs.

- For frequent 'Town Hall' meetings.

It's time to vote — GREEN!

Authorized by Dave Pehota - Official Agent for Bill Marshall

Pamphlet from the campaign of the author's father, Bill Marshall, in 1988. The author is pictured as a five-month old baby.

WHAT DOES GREEN MEAN?

Green Party of Canada leader Elizabeth May.

BC Greens leader Andrew Weaver alongside former BC Green leader and founder Adriane Carr (center).

BC Greens leader Andrew Weaver with former BC Greens leader Jane Sterk.

WHAT DOES GREEN MEAN?

BC Greens leader Andrew Weaver (left) with BC NDP leader John Horgan (right), as they declare their intent to sign a Confidence and Supply Agreement.

BC Green MLA Sonia Furstenau and Canadian environmentalist David Suzuki.

BC Green MLA Adam Olsen.

New Brunswick Green leader David Coon with Green Party of Canada leader Elizabeth May.

WHAT DOES GREEN MEAN?

New Brunswick Green MLAs Kevin Arseneau (left), David Coon (Center), and Megan Mitton (left).

From left to right: PEI Green leader Peter Bevan-Baker, Green Party of Canada leader Elizabeth May, New Brunswick Green leader David Coon, Ontario Green leader Mike Schreiner, and PEI Green MLA Hannah Bell.

PEI Green leader Peter Bevan-Baker and Green Party of Canada leader Elizabeth May.

PEI Green leader Peter Bevan-Baker (third from left) and Green MLA Hannah Bell (fourth from left), alongside members of the PEI Green shadow cabinet.

WHAT DOES GREEN MEAN?

Ontario Green leader Mike Schreiner.

CHAPTER 6

ELIZABETH, ANDREW, DAVID, PETER, MIKE, ADAM, SONIA, HANNAH, MEGAN AND KEVIN

"Until now I believed that the nation that has done most to sabotage a new climate change agreement was the United States. I was wrong. The real villain is Canada. Unless we can stop it, the harm done by Canada in December 2009 will outweigh a century of good works."

(George Monbiot, British environmental writer)

ELIZABETH, ANDREW, DAVID, PETER, AND MIKE

AND ADAM, SONIA, HANNAH, MEGAN, AND KEVIN

Decades before she became Canada's first elected Green, Elizabeth May was born in Hartford, Connecticut. Her father was a classic '50s workingman, putting in long hours as an accountant in order to provide for his family. Her mother, on the other hand, was a fiery and passionate activist in the American anti-war movement. Elizabeth grew up being brought along with her mother to anti-Vietnam war protests and nuclear proliferation protests, and often found herself labelled as a "communist" by her schoolmates when they found out about her mother's activism. She grew up during the height of the fear of nuclear war, watching the devastating spraying of Agent Orange in Vietnam, and observing a series of horrific American invasions and military actions abroad.

Overwhelmed by what they saw happening in their home country, the May family immediately fell in love with Canada when they visited Cape Breton in Nova Scotia on a family holiday when Elizabeth was a teenager. Within a year of their first visit they had packed up all their belongings, sold the family home in Connecticut, and moved the whole family to a small village in the Maritimes.

Elizabeth says that she doesn't think of herself as an American, even though it's where she was born. She gained her Canadian citizenship shortly after moving to Canada, and went to school and has spent the rest of her life as a Canadian. Upon moving to Canada, she remarked how much more she liked many aspects of Canadian life than American life. In particular she saw Canadian news and political media, as well as Canada's socialized healthcare system, as light-years ahead of America's.

After working as a waitress for several years to save up enough money, she enrolled at Dalhousie University, aiming for a law degree. Having been in Canada for only a few years, she had already jumped into the activism life in the country, joining a campaign against aerial pesticide spraying over the province's forests. Elizabeth had grown up alongside her mother fighting against the use of the Agent Orange defoliant in Vietnam, and it left her deeply distrustful of the unintended side effects of any sort of mass chemical spraying. She was able to gain admittance to university through her high profile in Nova Scotia's environmental movement, as well as by including in her application a personal appeal from the governor of Arkansas, Bill Clinton. This was years before Clinton would run for president, but the Clintons were active in the anti-war protests so they personally knew Elizabeth through her and her mother's activism in the United States.

Before even graduating from law school, she found herself wrapped up in a fierce legal battle, taking a group of multinational corporations to court to prevent them from spraying the forests of Nova Scotia with the same Agent Orange compound used in Vietnam. Elizabeth missed her own graduation ceremony because she was cross-examining an expert witness in court. She'd been immediately articled to one of the other lawyers on the case as soon as her graduation papers were formalized, before she'd even gotten the chance to walk across the stage for her graduation.

Elizabeth and the other environmental lawyers fighting against the spraying lost their appeal. A judge ruled that Agent Orange was safe and that it could be used in Nova Scotia. However, the court case had lasted long enough that the manufacturer of Agent Orange itself had taken the product off the market after numerous countries had banned its use. Although it remained legal in Canada, the forestry companies could no longer find any for sale. Despite losing the case, Elizabeth and her team achieved their goal. But in doing so they wound up owing the corporations huge amounts of money in court costs. Without telling her daughter, Elizabeth's mother sold the family's plot of land in order to pay down the owed costs.

CHAPTER 6 – ELIZABETH, ANDREW, DAVID, PETER, MIKE

Working in the Mulroney Government

Even though they'd technically been successful in preventing the spraying, the court case had emotionally exhausted Elizabeth. Trying to find a less emotionally draining way to spend her energy and expertise, she moved to Canada's capital in 1986. While there, she was approached by a representative from the government of Progressive Conservative Prime Minister Brian Mulroney. Mulroney's Environment Minister, a Prince Edward Islander named Tom McMillan, wanted to get a prominent environmental activist on to his team as an expert advisor. He wanted an ambassador for the environmental movement to act as a go-between for his office and the movement.

Elizabeth was torn. She called up her friends in the environmental movement and got mixed responses. Some said that she should go for it. Others warned that she was only going to be there as window-dressing, as a way for the government to point at her and say, "See, we have an environmentalist on staff!" This was a Progressive Conservative government, not the side of the political spectrum that was traditionally environmentally focused. In the end, she decided to take the job. If it turned out that she was just being used a prop, she could always quit.

For two years, Elizabeth worked in Tom McMillan's Environmental Ministry office as a senior advisor. She can point to dozens of achievements during that time that she's immensely proud of. One of those was the establishment of a national park on the same Haida Gwaii islands that her friend Adriane Carr and husband Paul George had been campaigning for in British Columbia. During her time with McMillan, they put in place the Canadian Environmental Protection Act, negotiated the Montreal Protocol to protect the ozone layer, put in place the National Round Table on the Environment and the Economy, and more. In Elizabeth's memory, Tom McMillan and Prime Minister Mulroney truly were passionate leaders on environmental issues. They were a very different kind of conservative than Elizabeth would encounter later in her career.

However, eventually Elizabeth did resign from the job in protest. Despite many positive steps forward, this was still a Progressive Conservative government, a political ideology that she didn't align with. The last straw was a granting of dam permits in Saskatchewan without an environmental review, a plan orchestrated by the Prime Minister's chief of staff who was a former corporate executive from Imperial Oil.

The federal NDP jumped on Elizabeth's resignation as a way to attack the Prime Minister. In the leader's debate for the 1988 election, Elizabeth was brought up by name when NDP leader Ed Broadbent attacked Mulroney over "his own environmental advisor quitting in protest."

Sierra Club of Canada

Figuring that she had burned all her bridges in Ottawa and wasn't likely to work in government again, Elizabeth set out to find her next path. She received a call from a volunteer with the Sierra Club, the American-based environmental organization. They wanted to set up a Canadian affiliate of the organization and offered Elizabeth a job and a grant if she would take charge of setting it up. She accepted and became the first executive director of Sierra Club Canada, a position she then held from 1989 to 2006.

As the head of one of Canada's top environmental NGOs, Elizabeth was a part of every major environmental lobbying and organizing effort in Canada for nearly two decades. One of the key successes for her was working with the United Nations Framework Convention on Climate Change (UNFCCC) in 1992, which led eventually to the adoption of the Kyoto Protocol in 1997. The Kyoto Protocol was an agreement among almost every country on earth to reduce their greenhouse gas output to combat climate change.

Elizabeth happily worked in the environmental movement, lobbying politicians from the outside until 2005. In that year, a series of events came to pass in the political world that she considered so catastrophic that she had to enter politics herself.

In 2005, Canada was governed by the Liberal government of Prime Minister Paul Martin. It was a minority government, meaning that the Liberal party hadn't gained enough seats in the last election to hold a majority in the Canadian parliament. This meant that the government was at risk of falling if the opposition Conservative, NDP, and Bloc Quebecois parties ever decided to team up in order to vote it down.

That year, Canada was set to host a follow-up meeting to the Kyoto Protocol, in which delegates from around the world would gather in Montreal to present their plans and achievements in meeting the Kyoto targets. This was the most important thing in the world for Elizabeth and other environmentalists in Canada. This was a chance for environmentalists to pressure the Canadian government to meet its commitments, and for Canada to show the world that it could be a leader in environmental stewardship.

Partisanship and Politics Instead of Doing the Right Thing

The opposition parties in parliament had other plans. Banding together in an uneasy alliance, the three opposition parties issued an ultimatum to Prime Minister Martin. They threatened that on the very first day of the high-profile convention, with foreign attendees watching, they would bring forward a "motion of no confidence" to take down the government. Their demand was that the Prime Minister call an early election. Each party thought that they were in a position to make big gains, and wanted an election in the immediate future so that they could have their chance at winning control of government. If Prime Minister Martin refused, then they were going to force it on him, and make it painful and embarrassing by doing so during a conference that the world was watching. Elizabeth was appalled. Politicians were using an international conference intended to save the planet's ecosystems as a piece of political leverage and theatre.

Sure enough, on the same day as thousands of international attendees to the conference arrived in Canada, the opposition parties pulled the trigger and forced out the Liberal government. The delegates landing in Canada found themselves in a country that suddenly didn't have a government. Their hosts had been booted out of office, and Liberal Environment Minister Stéphane Dion announced to the conference that he was now "working on behalf the United Nations" and was determined to see the conference be successful even though his government had just fallen, and he was thus no longer the Minister for the Environment.

Somehow the conference managed to pull through. Elizabeth had recruited her old friend Bill Clinton (now a former president) to attend, and his presence managed to repair some of the damage being done by the Bush administration, which was attending and was determined to derail the Kyoto agreements. The conference ended with a deal, and the attendees went home. The 2006 Canadian election immediately followed.

The effort to bring down Paul Martin's Liberal government had been spearheaded by the leader of the newly formed Conservative Party of Canada, Stephen Harper. The election in 2000 had featured a fractured right wing of Canadian politics, with the conservative brand split between the Progressive Conservative Party and the Canadian Alliance Party. Stephen Harper, the new leader of the Canadian Alliance Party, organized a merger of Canada's right wing after the election and formed the new united Conservative Party. The newly strengthened coalition competed in the election of 2004 and had managed to knock the governing Liberal Party from a majority into a minority government. Since 2004, Harper had been looking for any excuse to force an early election and to get a second try at dislodging the Liberals. Thinking that they'd also be able to make gains on the Liberals, the NDP and Bloc Quebecois Parties were happy to cooperate with the Conservatives.

In early 2006, directly following Canada's Kyoto conference, Stephen Harper made the breakthrough he had been looking for. With about 36 percent of Canadian voters casting their ballot for the Conservatives, Harper was rewarded with a minority government of his own. He was sworn in as Canada's 22nd Prime Minister. One of the key promises that he'd made in the campaign was that his government would abandon the Kyoto Protocol promises. He immediately started to ignore Canada's commitments upon his election. In 2011 (once he had finally gotten his own majority government), Canada became the first and only country to formally withdraw from the agreement.

Had Stephen Harper not derailed the Kyoto conference and then managed to become Prime Minister, Elizabeth May might have remained out of politics. But she now was witnessing the political rise of an individual who she believed to be the most powerful and organized opponent to Canadian climate leadership. Viewing the state of Canadian politics as dysfunctional and broken, Elizabeth began considering if she could do some good by getting directly involved in politics herself.

Leader of the Green Party of Canada

Four months after the 2006 election, Elizabeth resigned from her job as executive director of the Sierra Club of Canada and put her name forward as a candidate for leader of the Green Party of Canada. Incumbent leader Jim Harris was stepping down, and Elizabeth was competing as a party outsider against long-time party insider David Chernushenko. She won on the first ballot with 65 percent of party members voting in her favour.

May's first attempt at election as leader of the Green Party was later that year, when the Liberal MP for London North Centre resigned, and a by-election was called. Despite not living in London, the Green Party parachuted their new leader in to take a crack at gaining entry into the Canadian parliament. Although she didn't win, the new leader did remarkably well, finishing a close second place. The new high-profile environmental lawyer with decades of experience was proving to be a boon for the party.

Her second attempt was for the 2008 election. In this case, she decided to run in her home district of Central Nova, in Nova Scotia. She would be running against a Conservative incumbent cabinet minister (Peter McKay), and due to her friendly relationship with Stéphane Dion, the Environment Minister who had hosted the Kyoto conference back in 2005 and who was now leader of the Liberal Party, she was able form an agreement with the Liberals. The Liberals would not run a candidate in Central Nova if the Greens agreed not to run a candidate in Dion's home district. Both parties had the goal of defeating the Conservatives, and didn't want to overly get in each other's way.

As is the usual experience for Green parties in Canada, the TV networks initially refused to let Elizabeth May participate in the leader's debate during the election. But the Greens had a trump card this time. In 2007, a Liberal MP, Blair Wilson, was kicked out of his party due to him failing to declare some of his own personal financial issues before he was elected under their banner. He remained an independent for a year, then two months before the 2008 election was called he announced that he was joining the Green Party of Canada. Since the legislature was on their summer recess, he never actually sat in the parliament as a Green, and he had of course originally been elected as a Liberal. However, when a sitting MP agreed to switch his allegiance to the Green Party, it gave the party the leverage it needed to talk its way into better recognition from the media. After much arguing and campaigning Elizabeth managed to get herself included in the election debate.

CHAPTER 6 – ELIZABETH, ANDREW, DAVID, PETER, MIKE

The 2008 election was a high point for the Green Party of Canada: it achieved nearly 7 percent of the overall vote. Unfortunately, Elizabeth was still not elected. Despite the Liberals not fielding a candidate, once again she placed second in her district. The results of the election were the same as the last election two years earlier. Stephen Harper was still Prime Minister, but it was still a minority government. Blair Wilson also failed to get re-elected, after this time running as a Green. To the Greens' great disappointment, he placed last in his own incumbent district, even after spending more money on his re-election bid than any of the other local candidates.

The result of the 2008 election for the Green Party of Canada was mixed. On one hand they had gotten their highest ever vote total: nearly a million Canadians had voted for Green candidates. On the other hand, they had still failed to elect a member of parliament. As anyone competing in a first-past-the-post system knows, the vote total doesn't matter. It only matters if you can win an individual district.

Trying a New Strategy

After 2008, the Greens had a strategic re-tooling. The party contacted a number of political strategists who had experience helping small parties win under first-past-the-post systems. So far, the strategy for the Green Party had been to invest in election races relatively evenly across the country, trying to win support everywhere. This had succeeded in getting the Greens a growing support base, but in first-past-the-post it was a losing strategy. The way to win in Canada's electoral system was to invest everything in a single stronghold, and then attempt to grow outwards regionally from that epicentre. Other political parties knew this. The big parties only bothered campaigning in places where they thought they could win, and left candidates in "losing" districts on their own to just be placeholders. If the Greens wanted to win in a Canadian election, they had to stop campaigning as if everyone's votes mattered. They had to focus on a single district, and gain a foothold.

The Greens commissioned a group of pollsters and strategists to identify which districts were most likely to elect a Green. Elizabeth's only personal demand was that she wanted to campaign against and beat a Conservative party incumbent, preferably a Conservative cabinet member. Elizabeth had gotten into politics to combat Stephen Harper's Conservative Party, and wanted her first victory to be over a powerful Conservative MP. They poured over election data, looked at the strength of on-the-ground organizers, and finally identified a district in British Columbia in the south of Vancouver Island as the best contender.

Saanich–Gulf Islands is a district composed of the north half of the Saanich Peninsula as well as islands in the Juan de Fuca Strait separating Vancouver Island from mainland British Columbia. Demographically it's the oldest district in Canada, meaning that the average age of the district's inhabitants is the highest in the country. It has a large retiree population, a large immigrant population, and a large Indigenous population.

There was a strong group of passionate Green organizers on the ground, and the Greens had always fared quite well there. The provincial BC Greens had a strong second-place finish in the area, and the federal Greens had some decent results as well. Also, in the 2008 election the New Democratic Party candidate had withdrawn at the last second due to a scandal, leading to a total collapse of the NDP organization in the district. Many of the upset NDP volunteers and campaigners had migrated over to the Greens, and the Greens were doing everything they could to keep them supporting the party and to capitalize on the collapse.

The Greens announced that for the 2011 election, the third early election in a row due to three consecutive minority governments, Elizabeth May would be moving across the country to British Columbia to run in Saanich–Gulf Islands. The Greens dumped loads of party money and effort into the campaign, focusing more than they ever had before on a single district. Less effort and money were spent on other races around the province; the party instead wanted to secure its foothold. Once again, the TV networks moved to exclude May from the leaders debates, and without the leverage of a Green floor-crosser this time, they succeeded in keeping her out.

Despite being excluded from the leaders' debate, the Greens' new strategy worked. Elizabeth May was elected as the MP for Saanich–Gulf Islands, defeating the incumbent Conservative Cabinet Minister Gary Lunn. Despite winning their first seat in parliament, the overall vote share for the Greens in Canada dropped significantly, down to just under 4 percent. But that had been expected. The Greens were now trying to play the same game as the other parties: focus on the winnable districts, not on the overall picture.

The big downside of the 2011 election for Elizabeth and the Green Party of Canada was the results for the other parties, specifically for the Conservatives. She'd gotten into politics because she didn't want to see a Stephen Harper government. But now Elizabeth was going to take her seat in parliament across the aisle from the new, first-time *majority* government of Prime Minister Stephen Harper.

"On my 70th birthday, I was asked how I felt about mankind's prospects. This is my reply: We are behaving like yeasts in a brewer's vat, multiplying mindlessly while greedily consuming the substance of a finite world. If we continue to imitate the yeasts, we will perish as they perish, having exhausted our resources and poisoned ourselves in the lethal brew of our own wastes. Unlike the yeasts, we have a choice. What will it be?"

(Farley Mowat)

BREAKING INTO PROVINCIAL POLITICS

Elizabeth May moved to Vancouver Island in 2010 to work on building her profile in the local community and preparing for her run in the next election. She had the weight of the federal party behind her, and she had a strong team of local organizers, but she was still new in town and wanting to connect with influential Saanich locals.

One of these locals turned out to be a Saanich Councillor named Adam Olsen. Adam was born and raised on Tsartlip First Nation, an Indigenous community in Brentwood Bay on the Saanich Peninsula near Victoria. He'd previously volunteered with both the federal Liberal Party and the Green Party, and while interviewing him he reminisced to me that he thought he'd probably voted for candidates from every party except the Conservatives at some point in his life.

Adam is an intense person, always bursting with energy, very outgoing and often cracking jokes. He has a way of focusing in on the person that he's talking to, coming across as almost intimidating until you realize that it's just his way of giving his full attention to who he's speaking with. He grew up on First Nations territory, and it's an important part of his life, although despite his heritage I've heard him describe himself as being able to "pass for white," so he's aware that his lived experience isn't the same as for many other First Nations people. He keeps his head shaved and often sports a goatee, and alternates between being all smiles and jokes or sporting a frustrated scowl, depending on the environment.

In 2008, he was elected as a councillor for the city of Saanich, and when he heard that the leader of the federal Green Party had moved into his hometown and was planning on running there he picked up the phone and gave her a call to introduce himself. Elizabeth jumped at the opportunity.

> Elizabeth May moved into Saanich–Gulf Islands to run federally, and I was intrigued by this move and by her. So I reached out to her, and within like forty-eight hours I was sitting in a meeting with her and my sister (who was on Tsartlip First Nation council at the time). And she was really interested in getting to know us because we were local First Nation governance, and she didn't know anybody here. So she came and met with us right away and her story really intrigued us.
>
> We were very much taken by the small party idea, you know, representing constituents first. We were taken by the values of the Greens in terms of intergenerational equity and the long-term decision-making over short-term decision-making, and that constituencies mattered, and that values and principles matter. (Adam Olsen, from an interview with the author, 2018)

Adam was a fan of independent politicians. He was an independent city councillor and was skeptical of the effects of a rigid party system and how it affected the integrity of politics. He saw the Greens as the closest thing you could get to a party of independents. If they were able to elect Elizabeth as their local MP, then it'd be pretty close to having an independent representing him, someone who'd have the ability to really champion the concerns of the district and who wasn't constrained by a restrictive party apparatus. The Greens hired Adam as a local organizer, and he got to work building Elizabeth's profile in the community.

Recruiting Star Candidates

After Elizabeth was successfully elected in 2011, the Greens held an after-party to celebrate. The party was held in a hanger at the Victoria airport (I neglected to ask why), and at the celebration Adam was approached by Jane Sterk, who was now leader of the provincial BC Green Party. Jane asked Adam if he'd be willing to run as their local candidate in the next provincial election. Adam accepted, and got to work preparing for his own campaign. As one of the core organizers for Elizabeth's successful election, he had a big head start already.

As part of her job as party leader, Jane Sterk had been crisscrossing British Columbia trying to recruit star candidates for the party. The area around the province's capital district in Victoria was the part of the province where the BC Greens had been strongest in the previous election, and so

CHAPTER 6 – ELIZABETH, ANDREW, DAVID, PETER, MIKE

they were focusing their effort there. With a sitting federal Green MP to build up the public profile of the Green brand, the party wanted to field a strong group of candidates in greater Victoria who could capitalize on the opportunity.

One of the other candidates that Jane recruited was a professor from the University of Victoria named Andrew Weaver. Andrew was born in Victoria, and although he had moved abroad to attend the prestigious University of Cambridge, he eventually returned to British Columbia and settled back into his original hometown. By the time he returned to Victoria, he had completed a BSc in mathematics and physics, a master's of Advanced Studies in Mathematics, and a PhD in Applied Mathematics. He had worked as a postdoctoral fellow at the University of New South Wales in Australia, in the Joint Institute for the Study of the Atmosphere and the Ocean at the University of Washington in Seattle, and as an assistant professor at McGill University.

Andrew Weaver's professional resume could fill up half of this book. When he was recruited by Sterk, he was at the top of his career as a public scientist. He was the Canada Research Chair in climate modelling and analysis, and he had been the president of the University of Victoria Faculty Association and was their chief negotiator during collective bargaining in 2003 and 2006. He had authored over two hundred peer-reviewed papers on the topics of climate, earth science, meteorology, education, and more.

Perhaps most notably, he had been a lead author on four of the United Nations Intergovernmental Panel on Climate Change's scientific assessments. The organization had won a Nobel Peace Prize in 2007 for its work, and as one of the core team members Andrew kept a copy of the prize on his office wall (in the form of a certificate).

Andrew's a big guy, over six feet tall and husky. He was a former rugby player in college, and had suffered through breaking his nose multiple times in athletic events. He's now in his fifties, not quite so athletic anymore, and known around the legislature for being an odd character. He's often seen wearing loud Hawaiian shirts and occasionally losing himself in phone games (Pokémon Go remains a favourite of his). He's a confident public speaker but can get a bit tongue-tied at times, and has a very slight hint of an accent on certain words that could be from his time in England, although I've also heard it described as "just the way people from Oak Bay sound." He's very personable and affable most of the time, but prone to getting worked up and passionate when confronted with hypocrisy or people that he views as making bad decisions. This last trait has been pounced upon by other politicians and parties that often try to goad him into saying something off-the-cuff that they could later use to turn on him and attack him.

He'd also already been involved politically. Andrew was a vocal supporter of former BC Liberal Premier Gordon Campbell's climate platform, and had appeared in public several times supporting the Premier:

> In 2007, the BC Government under Gordon Campbell recognized that this (climate change) was an issue that could be viewed as an opportunity as well. He announced over the coming years numerous policy measures that were designed to actually recognize the opportunity and the challenge of climate change. One of the things we did was create a climate leadership team, and I met with him and the team and the Minister of the Environment many, many times over the period of 2007 until 2009. It was an exciting time as a climate scientist in British Columbia because we'd been working as a community at large for decades. And finally there was somebody who recognized that dealing with climate change was actually an incredible opportunity. (Andrew Weaver, in an interview with the author, 2018)

Gordon Campbell had retired as BC Liberal leader in 2011, giving up the Premiership partway through his elected term. He'd been Premier for a decade, and after ten years he'd accumulated enough mistakes and issues that the electorate was signalling that it was time for him to go. The last straw was a tax increase and overhaul that Campbell had introduced a few months after the 2009 election to try to meet a campaign budget promise. The BC Liberals had made big promises on BC's finances and then discovered after the election that they wouldn't be able to keep them. Campbell tried to make up for it by combining the provincial and federal sales taxes into a single harmonized sales tax (HST) that would produce the extra revenue needed to balance the budget. The province rebelled, organized a referendum campaign on the HST, defeated the tax, and subsequently chased Campbell out of office. It's one of the more memorable political events for British Columbians in recent history.

Gordon Campbell was replaced as BC Liberal leader and Premier by Christy Clark, a former MLA who had stepped away from politics to become a radio show host, and later returned when the party leader position opened up. Upon taking up the Premier position, Clark wanted a big initiative that she could champion to try to turn around the BC Liberals' sinking poll numbers.

BC Gets Gas

After sitting through a slick sales pitch from some industry representatives from Malaysian government-owned oil and gas company Petronas and Alberta-based Progress Energy, Clark decided that her big initiative would be liquefied natural gas (LNG). LNG is a fossil fuel extracted using hydraulic fracturing, a process also commonly known as "fracking." At the time, BC had big untapped deposits of LNG in the province's north, but virtually no industry exploiting it. Clark wanted to stake everything on LNG and make it a defining promise and goal of her Premiership.

She wanted to promise British Columbians that a BC Liberal government would deliver them billions of dollars in prosperity by creating a new industry in British Columbia from scratch.

Andrew Weaver watched the progress and legacy that he'd built by supporting Gordon Campbell evaporate. The BC Liberals had gone from being led by a Premier who recognized both the challenge and opportunity of being a climate change leader, and were now led by someone who was planning on dumping millions of dollars of tax breaks into expanding BC's fossil fuel extraction infrastructure.

The BC NDP was also not a viable option for Andrew to support. In the 2009 election, the BC NDP had run on an "axe the tax" campaign where they promised, if elected, to get rid of the new carbon pollution tax that Premier Gordon Campbell had implemented. As one of the architects of the carbon tax, Weaver had no interest in supporting a party that made getting rid of the measure its main platform plank. He considered the BC NDP to be the province's climate villains.

Over the years, Jane Sterk had approached Andrew multiple times to get involved with the BC Green party. Each time, Andrew had declined. He was at the height of his career as a scientist, and had experienced a lot of success working with politicians from his position outside the political system to advance the issues that he was passionate about. But once Clark took over as leader and Andrew saw that neither of the two big parties was interested in advancing leadership on climate change, Andrew began to rethink his decision to stay out of direct political action.

BC Gets Andrew Weaver

As a professor at the University of Victoria, Andrew regularly encouraged his students to get involved politically, and at least to get out and vote. He remarked that his students often said that they didn't bother voting because the politicians seemed "all the same" to them. Andrew would counter that if none of the political candidates appealed to his students, then they should get out there and run themselves. Once Andrew started complaining that none of the political parties appealed to him anymore, his students began to call him on his bluff. He realized that if he was unhappy with the state of the candidates in the race that he might have to run himself.

On Sterk's fourth attempt at recruiting him to run as a candidate, Andrew finally relented. He agreed to run in his home district of Oak Bay–Gordon Head, where the University of Victoria was located.

Andrew Weaver and Adam Olsen joined Jane Sterk and fifty-eight other Green candidates competing in British Columbia's 2013 provincial election. Despite recruiting a number of star candidates such as Andrew and Adam, the BC Greens hadn't managed to gather a full slate of candidates. Although Vancouver and the island had candidates in every district, the party struggled to find candidates the farther they went from the province's urban core.

Andrew, in his own words, "doesn't do things half-baked." When he decided to run, he decided to run to win. At this point only one Green had ever been elected at above the municipal level in Canada, and none had been elected from a provincial Green party. Greens often say that "you don't run with the Green party if all you care about is getting elected," and going into the election Andrew admitted that he realistically didn't think he would win. But he planned to campaign as if he was going to. He recruited his long-time friend Judy Fainstein as his campaign manager. He and Judy had met and worked together in their children's school's PAC, and Judy was a non-profit organizer who had recently built up an organization from scratch. Andrew figured she'd be perfect to build him a campaign as well.

During the election, both Andrew and Adam went from considering themselves to be long-shots to believing that they stood a very good chance of actually being elected. Both candidates had massive swells of support, bolstered by the strong local teams that they had supporting them. Both candidates managed to fundraise on par with the bigger parties' candidates.

On the eve of the election, Andrew fully believed that he was going to win, and Adam knew that he stood a very good chance of winning in an extremely close race. Jane Sterk had chosen a tough district to compete in, going up against one of the BC NDP's most popular incumbents: former party leader Carole James. Although she looked to be running a strong campaign, she was still behind the BC NDP MLA in polling. Andrew was running against a BC Liberal cabinet minister, whereas Adam was running in a field of new contenders after his district's BC Liberal MLA had declined to run for re-election.

When the dust settled and the vote tallies were all added up, BC was in for a big surprise. Basically every pollster had predicted that the BC NDP was going to win the election and form government. Polls on the day before the election had the NDP several points ahead, and the party was already planning for their transition to governance. But that wasn't the case.

The First of the Provincial Greens

To everyone's surprise, including BC Liberal Leader Christy Clark's, the BC Liberals wound up with a decisive victory. Having defied all predictions and polls, the BC Liberals had actually strengthened their majority and won a few new seats. The BC NDP went down by a couple, but the election mostly just left things at the status quo. However, there would be a notable new face in the legislature. Andrew Weaver had defeated sitting BC Liberal cabinet minister Ida Chong and was elected as the new MLA for Oak Bay–Gordon Head. He was the first Green elected at the provincial level in all of Canada.

Adam Olsen, meanwhile, came devastatingly close to winning his district as well—just under four hundred votes close. The race for Saanich North and the Islands ended in an almost perfect three-way tie, with the candidates from the three parties each within a couple hundred votes of each other. The BC NDP candidate eked out a victory by less than 1 percent more of the overall vote in the district, flipping the district from its former BC Liberal hold. Jane Sterk was also unsuccessful, although she placed a strong second against the former BC NDP leader.

I spoke in an interview with Jonathan Dickie, who was a primary campaign organizer for Elizabeth May and who has been her Constituency Director since her election, as well as working on Adam Olsen's provincial campaign. He believes that one of the big reasons that the NDP failed to defeat the BC Liberals in 2013 was that they were so spooked by the Greens that they focused too much of their efforts on trying to suppress the Greens rather than competing against the BC Liberals.

The BC NDP (and the federal NDP) have long been convinced that Green voters are just an NDP splinter group that they can pull back into the party if they offer enough environmental concessions, and if they strongly focus their efforts and money on combating Green challengers. The actual data on Green voters tells a different story. Most attempts at identifying Green voters show a fairly even split between voters that, if the Green party was not an option, would vote NDP, would vote Liberal or Conservative, and who would just stay home and not vote at all. Greens appear to draw equally from all sides, as well as from the large pool of non-voters. In fact, in Elizabeth's 2011 campaign the party made a point of marketing itself towards Conservative voters—especially Conservative women voters. They needed to do so in order to flip a strong Conservative-held district.

After Elizabeth's win in 2011, the NDP invested a huge amount of resources and effort into making sure that the Greens' success on Vancouver Island didn't grow. In a 2012 by-election in Victoria, the federal Greens nearly picked up a second seat. Green candidate Donald Galloway came within a few percentage points of winning what was thought to be a safe NDP seat, surprising the local NDP organizers who hadn't thought it was going to be so close an election. When the Greens tried again to win the district in the 2015 federal election with local CBC journalist Jo-Ann Roberts as their candidate, the NDP sunk more money into defending their seat there than any other campaign in the country.

In the 2013 provincial election, the BC NDP invested heavily in their island races: traditionally NDP safe territory. They especially wanted to make sure that leader Jane Sterk didn't win her seat. In doing so, they didn't notice the strength of Andrew Weaver in a nearby district that was thought of as one of the island's few safe Liberal seats.

BREAKTHROUGHS IN CANADA'S MARITIME PROVINCES

The previous chapter mentioned in passing the selection of David Coon to head the New Brunswick Greens and Peter Bevan-Baker to head the PEI Greens. These two Maritimers would lead the next set of successes for the Greens.

David Coon was born and raised in Ontario, but he moved to New Brunswick after earning a science degree at McGill. In 1985, he was hired by the Conservation Council of New Brunswick as a policy director, and spent the next thirty years of his life as a science educator. The council is a non-profit organization headquartered out of Fredericton (the provincial capital) that advocates on environmental issues and provides educational programs and research support. As policy director, David was responsible for planning and executing all of the organization's programs, as well as doing general science education outreach.

David doesn't fit the usual mould of a politician. Most people expect politicians to be outgoing and gregarious, as it usually takes a pretty charismatic personality to get elected. David, on the other hand, is calm and quiet. He's thoughtful and doesn't have the common politician trait of talking just to hear himself talk. He's fairly unassuming in appearance: somewhat stern-faced, bald with a fringe of white hair and bright white eyebrows. For a lot of Greens, he's considered a proud example that you don't need vapid charisma to be elected. You can just be someone who's wise and hard-working.

During his time with the Conservation Council, David's work led to the province of New Brunswick adopting measures such as the Clean Water Act and petroleum handling regulations. The organization also earned recognition by the United Nations Environmental Programme, and David was honoured with an award from the Canadian Environmental Achievement Awards for his work on climate policy. He worked locally in New Brunswick to set up community agricultural co-operatives and fishery councils to manage the local resources in ways that best benefitted those that worked with them.

Despite working in the field of environmental advocacy, David was still mostly unaware of the Green party until 2006, when fellow Maritimer Elizabeth May took over as leader. The Greens had always struggled to make much headway in the Maritime provinces, and hadn't really focused on the region until Jim Harris's push to run candidates in all of Canada's districts. But as an environmental advocate and as a Maritimer, David was very familiar with Elizabeth. The two were friends, and when Elizabeth was elected as leader of the federal party, David took notice.

> My wife and I attended the first convention after she was elected, which was a thrill to see what this party was all about. You understand that here Elizabeth is regarded as a Maritimer, which she is. And so when a Maritimer did what

CHAPTER 6 – ELIZABETH, ANDREW, DAVID, PETER, MIKE

she did and got elected [as leader] to the Green Party, lots of people around the region perked up their ears and said, "Well, what's this party about? There must be something here if Elizabeth decided she wanted to be the leader of it." So that led many to start looking at the Green party. (David Coon, in an interview with the author, 2018)

David got involved supporting Elizabeth and the federal Greens, and then the New Brunswick Greens when the party was founded shortly after Elizabeth's election as federal leader. When New Brunswick Green leader Jack MacDougall stepped down in 2011, David Coon left his job at the Conservation Council and was selected as the party's new leader.

Got It on the First Try

The next provincial election was scheduled for the September of 2014, which gave David nearly two years to prepare the party and himself to compete for the Greens' first seat in the Maritimes. The party was in fairly good shape. They had run nearly a full slate in their first election and were benefitting from the organizational structures set up by the federal party. The Maritimes' incarnations of the Greens mostly managed to avoid a lot of the problems that the early Greens in other provinces faced. They were only formed after the other provincial wings had already learned their lessons and were able to provide support and advice.

David was already well known in the community and in the province. His thirty years of advocacy had left him with connections in the media, to businesses, to community groups, and to Fredericton locals. He also benefited from having a demographically very young district: about a third of the district's population was under thirty. Since Greens consistently do better with younger voters, he was able to marshal a passionate group of young New Brunswickers to support his campaign. The federal Greens had started running workshops and seminars deconstructing their wins in British Columbia and teaching other Greens around the province what was needed for a Green to run a successful campaign. David listened and learned and built a solid team and campaign. He campaigned continuously for the two years up until the election, making sure that everyone knew who he was and what he was standing for.

The race was still very close. The district of Fredericton South itself was new, having been created when Elections New Brunswick redrew the province's district boundaries, as they do every few years due to changes in population and demographics. However, the district was made up of parts of two old districts that traditionally elected conservatives. There was also a strong desire for change in the area. The New Brunswick NDP traditionally was stronger there than their average, although still not strong enough to elect any of their candidates. David needed to appeal to voters that traditionally supported all three other established parties in order to pull out a win. When the votes were tallied up on September 22nd, 2014, David was declared the winner of a close four-way race. He won the district with just barely 30 percent of the vote, becoming the third elected Green in Canada, and the first outside British Columbia.

David got into politics because he saw that the priorities of Canada's politicians were getting farther and farther away from the priorities of the people they were elected to represent. As he says on his own website,

It didn't seem to me that we were being well served by any of the old-line parties in New Brunswick. Retaining or gaining political power has taken precedence over bettering the lives of the people of our province. Governments are no longer engaging with their citizens to advance the common good; rather, they have become obsessed with manipulating public opinion to hold onto power. The priorities of governments today are far removed from the priorities of New Brunswickers and their communities. (Coon, n.d.)

As I've said before, people who run with Green parties don't do so because they want to grab onto power. Running with a Green Party is probably the most difficult and inefficient way to get into a position of power. David's message resonated with the voters in Fredericton, and he was seen as someone who could be trusted to spend his time working on their behalf rather than just playing at politics.

Hot on David's heels were a pair of Greens in nearby Prince Edward Island, starting with PEI Green leader Peter Bevan-Baker.

Great-Grandson of Confederation

Unlike David Coon who won on his very first attempt at elected politics, Peter had been in the game for a long time. His win in 2015 was his tenth attempt, having run multiple times for both the federal Greens and the provincial Greens in Ontario and PEI. He first joined the Greens in 1992, founding a local chapter in his Ontario hometown, and it took him over twenty years to finally win an election.

Peter was born in Scotland, in the small town of Fortrose in the country's far north. A town of only about a thousand people, it would be a familiar-feeling place for someone from small Prince Edward Island, where Peter eventually settled down. He moved to Canada in 1985 when an opportunity came up for him to run his own dentistry practice. He hadn't planned to stay forever, but he fell in love both with Canada and with a local woman named Ann, so he wound up sticking around. These days his Scottish accent is very light—not nearly the strong brogue that you'd expect of someone from rural Scotland.

CHAPTER 6 – ELIZABETH, ANDREW, DAVID, PETER, MIKE

Peter didn't know it when he first moved to Canada, but his family actually had a particularly impressive Canadian history of its own. He only learned about it while talking to his father during a trip back to Scotland for Christmas. Peter's great-great-grandfather had lived in Canada, and had happened to help found the country.

George Brown, considered one of the Canadian Fathers of Confederation, was born in Scotland but, like Peter, immigrated to Canada, which at the time was a British colony. He was elected to the Legislative Assembly of the Province of Canada in 1851. For a period of four days in 1858, he was even the de facto Premier of Canada, when his political rival John A. Macdonald's government lost a non-confidence vote. The complicated workings of the parliament led Brown to be considered Premier for a couple of days while he tried to put together a government and cabinet before he was also voted down.

Brown participated in the Quebec Conference and subsequent discussions that led to the creation of modern Canada through the British North America Act. He continued to be politically active after Canada was officially formed, although he didn't manage to win an elected seat. He was, however, appointed as a senator in 1873. He died in 1880 after being shot in the leg by a disgruntled employee from the *Globe and Mail*, the newspaper that he'd started. Brown's wife and two daughters then returned to Scotland, where they settled down and raised a family, eventually leading to Brown's great-great-grandson, Peter Bevan-Baker.

Despite his famous ancestor, Peter's connection to Canadian confederation wasn't what inspired him to get into politics. Instead, it was the birth of his children. Knowing that they would outlive him, he wanted to leave a better world for them to inherit. So he founded a local Green group and was talked into running as a candidate soon after. He continued to run nearly a dozen times.

When Sharon Labchuk resigned as leader of the Green Party of PEI, Peter took over the party. He had already run in two provincial elections in PEI, both in the same district against the same Liberal incumbent. When the 2015 provincial election rolled around, he signed on to run the same race for the third time, but this time as the party leader.

Got It on the Tenth Try

As was mentioned in the last chapter, Prince Edward Island has a strange, unique political situation. The island is very small, both in size and in population. British Columbia has a population of almost five million, meaning that each of its eighty-seven elected parliamentarians represents a district of about fifty thousand people. In massive Ontario, each member represents over one hundred thousand people. In tiny PEI, each elected member only represents about five thousand.

The intimacy of the election means that someone running for office is expected to personally meet each and every potential voter. In Peter's own words,

> If you don't show up at some people's doors during the (election) period, they won't even consider you as being worthy of their vote. (From an interview with the author, 2018)

It's commonly expected in PEI that just about everyone knows their representative personally, or at worst knows them as a friend of a friend. This means that there's a massive advantage for the incumbent, and that voters think carefully before replacing them with someone new.

In Peter's case, running his third election race against the same incumbent in the same district, the big difference was that he was now the party leader. Since the districts are so small many of them don't bother having formal debates with the local candidates, as usually happens during races in other provinces. Instead, most people pay close attention to the televised debate of the party leaders. As the new leader of the Green Party, Peter was now invited to this debate, even though his party had not yet elected a member to parliament. The Liberals and Progressive Conservatives likely didn't consider him a threat, or anticipate what a huge threat to their monopoly he would eventually become.

Peter credits the added spotlight of being the party leader as being the main factor that led to his win in 2015. He also ran a campaign that was more professional and well funded than any of the previous races. In his previous attempts, he'd done his campaigning on evenings and weekends since he couldn't afford to take the time off work to compete in a race that he was pretty certain he wouldn't win. But this time was different, so Peter suspended his dental practice to campaign full time.

The difference in support between his attempt in 2011 and in 2015 was massive. In 2011, he'd placed a distant third with only about 9 percent of the vote. In 2015, once voters had really gotten to know him, he rocketed up to 54 percent. He became the first Green elected in PEI, and the first Green in Canada to win an election with over half of the voters supporting him.

On a Roll

Halfway through Peter's first term in the PEI parliament, Liberal MLA Doug Currie resigned his seat. A by-election was called to replace the member from Charlottetown–Parkdale. Peter's time in the legislature had impressed islanders, and at the time the PEI Greens were polling at a much higher popularity rating than they'd achieved in the election, nipping at the heels of the second-placed Progressive Conservatives. Peter himself was consistently being polled as the most popular politician in the province. The Greens knew that they stood a very good chance of being able to pick up a by-election win.

CHAPTER 6 – ELIZABETH, ANDREW, DAVID, PETER, MIKE

They recruited Hannah Bell, the executive director of the PEI Business Women's Association to run as their candidate. The by-election was held, and Hannah was able to pick up a second seat for the PEI Greens, setting a couple of records for the Greens by doing so. Her win was the first for the Canadian Greens in a by-election, and was also the first time in PEI that a third party had managed to elect more than a single politician. The Greens in PEI had now achieved a better result than the provincial NDP had in their entire history.

"The party that won the last election wasn't the BC Liberals, it was the non-voter."

(BC Greens Leader Andrew Weaver, during the 2017 election debate on CBC)

BUILDING A CAUCUS

Peter's win made him the fourth elected Green in Canada, and Hannah's win made her the seventh. In between those two races was a much bigger election in a much bigger province. The 2017 election in British Columbia was the highest-profile and most successful election that the Greens in Canada had ever run.

The 2017 election was when I entered the story of Canada's Greens as a direct participant. I'd always been engaged and attentive to politics, but hadn't felt the need to get actively involved until around the time of the 2015 federal election. I'd gotten involved, pressuring the major parties to have an element of electoral reform in their platforms, as I was frustrated and tired of being told that my vote was a "throw-away" and that I had to "strategically vote" for a candidate that I didn't really like. The federal Greens and NDP were already on board to move Canada to a proportional representation system, and when Liberal leader Justin Trudeau made his promise that "2015 will be the last election conducted under first-past-the-post," I believed that it would be an almost sure thing.

I participated enthusiastically in the commission that Trudeau struck after the election to investigate changes to Canada's election system. I went to the touring meetings. I volunteered with local groups to do advocacy work and to educate Canadians on what the changes would mean for them. And I was absolutely crushed when, in 2016, Trudeau completely abandoned the promise. I had honestly taken him at his word and believed that he was serious when he made his promise. When he proved the worst cynics right by refusing to give up a system that had gotten himself elected, I felt even more disenfranchised with electoral politics than I had been when going into the process.

I got involved directly with politics because I was frustrated that the politicians that we were electing couldn't be trusted to keep a promise that they'd made to me, and to others like me. My thought process was essentially: *Well, I guess I have to do this myself.* Since the next federal election wasn't for three years, I refocused onto provincial politics and showed up at the BC Green Party's 2016 annual convention. I made some friends, built some connections, and when the 2017 election began to loom on the horizon I applied to run as a candidate. I was selected to run in the district of Vancouver–West End, a dense residential part of downtown Vancouver.

BC Green Leadership

Andrew Weaver was now leading the BC Green Party after being elected as leader in 2015. When he was elected to parliament in 2013, he was just a regular candidate, and party leader Jane Sterk had failed get elected in her own district. Jane retired and Andrew was asked, as the party's sole MLA, if we wanted the job. He didn't. He wanted to be able to focus entirely on the job of MLA, one that he'd been thrown into without any allies in the legislature to support him, and representing a party that had never had the experience of supporting an elected MLA.

Andrew asked fellow candidate Adam Olsen if he'd consider taking over the leadership spot and acting as the party's leader from outside the legislature. Adam accepted.

> I provided a space for [Andrew] to be able to come in and learn how to be an MLA, and for his team to be able do MLA work. To learn, to be successful, to make mistakes. To do all the things that you need to do in order to lay the groundwork for the three of us [Andrew, Adam, and Sonia] to be here. I was doing the conference calls with the provincial council, I was helping recruit new provincial councillors, I was going through the substantially frustrating financial woes that the party had at that time and just day-to-day issues. (Adam Olsen, from an interview with the author after the 2017 election)

For the first few years of Andrew's term as MLA, Adam ran the party operations, leaving Andrew to focus on everything happening in the provincial legislature. In addition to not wanting to do two brand-new jobs at the same time, Andrew also wanted to build Adam up for his next kick at the can in 2017.

CHAPTER 6 – ELIZABETH, ANDREW, DAVID, PETER, MIKE

> There's one thing about [the time] from 2013–2017 which I think is really quite important and says a lot about Andrew as a person. He understands his limitations and he understands that this [politics] is not a career for him. This is one step in a long career [inside and outside politics]. And ever since I've known him, he's been nurturing and fostering my leadership. (Adam Olsen, from an interview with the author, 2018)

Some party leaders want to be an executive at the top of power pyramid, where they're able to make all the decisions and then just delegate the execution down to their underlings. Andrew didn't want that. He didn't particularly want to be leader of the party, just as he hadn't particularly wanted to even run for elected office in the first place. He was doing it because other people had repeatedly told him that he'd be good at it, and he'd eventually relented.

By the two-year mark in Andrew's term, he'd figured out how to do the job that he was elected to do. He'd established a working relationship with the governing BC Liberal party even though he'd gotten into politics primarily because of frustration with how Premier Christy Clark was leading the party and province. But his philosophy was that he would have to work with the government if he wanted to get anything done at all. Simply being an opposing force that refused to engage with the BC Liberals wasn't going to let him achieve any of his goals.

In 2015, he relented and took over as leader of the party, and Adam stepped down and took the role of Deputy Leader. As the sole Green MLA Andrew had the highest public profile, and Adam had succeeded in getting most of the party's internal affairs in order, meaning the job of leader wouldn't be so difficult on Andrew. The party wanted to have its elected MLA lead them into the next election, and Andrew was finally up to the job.

BC had long been considered the "wild west" of money in Canadian politics. Leading up to the 2017 election, the American newspaper *The New York Times* even published a piece calling out the province as being the worst example of toxic money in politics. The province had virtually no rules on who could donate to political parties, or how much they could donate. An individual person, union, or corporation could donate an unlimited amount of money. Nor did the donor have to be British Columbian or even Canadian. Money was flowing into BC political parties from every avenue, and from far outside the province.

Both the BC NDP and the BC Greens had been pushing to change BC's laws to ban big money from corporations and unions, and to put donation limits on individuals, but the governing BC Liberal party was completely uninterested in changing the laws that were benefiting them. Despite advocating for changing the laws, the BC NDP were still bringing in huge amounts of money from many of the same sources as the Liberals. They kept saying that they had to "play within the rules of the game" if they wanted to be able to beat the Liberals in the next election. In 2016, the Greens decided to try a different tactic. They publicly announced that they would no longer be accepting any money from corporations or unions, and would only accept donations from individuals.

The Greens had never taken in a huge amount of money from non-individuals anyway, yet it was still a substantial part of the party's already very small donation base. But the strategy paid off. British Columbians frustrated with the corrupting influence of big money in BC started pouring their individual donations into the Greens. Donations to the Green increased by several fold, and by the end of 2016 the Greens were sitting on the biggest election war chest that they'd ever had available. In the 2017 campaign, they'd actually have enough money to run a campaign that could seriously challenge the big two parties.

2017 in British Columbia

The election began in April of 2017, and the Greens were immediately hit with challenges that they hadn't experienced before. In the 2013 election, the BC NDP had fully expected to win, and the loss had hit them hard. In a post-mortem review conducted after the election failure, they'd concluded that the reason they'd lost was because of party leader Adrian Dix's decision to run a "positive campaign" instead of a negative one.

It's a sad reality of politics that attack ads and negative campaigning against your opponent often work better than positive campaigning. This is especially magnified in a first-past-the-post system, because it's a much more effective message to frame a vote as being *against* the party that the voter is most afraid of rather than *for* your own party. Simply put: fear-based messaging works. First-past-the-post also encourages parties to attack their closest natural allies most viciously of all, since the more that two parties have in common the more that they share the same pool of potential voters.

The BC NDP came at the Greens hard and fast, and threw a lot of us off guard. They wanted to frame the election as a showdown between the governing BC Liberals and the BC NDP as the only party that could beat them. Having a third party thrown into the mix was ruining their messaging strategy, and they viewed the Greens as getting in the way of their big moment. The BC NDP was terrified that Greens were going to pull voters away from them and hand the election to the BC Liberals through "vote-splitting." As was mentioned earlier, the statistics didn't back that up, but the BC NDP nonetheless organized a campaign trying to convince Green supporters to strategically back the BC NDP instead of voting for Green candidates.

The campaign worked so well that some BC NDP supporters got worked up into outright hostility. While campaigning on street corners I had several passers-by spit on me, saying things like "You're ruining *everything*" and "you're *giving* this election to the Liberals." Meanwhile, Green candidates on doorsteps talking to voters were noting a fairly even distribution of supporters being both disaffected Liberals and NDPers, as well as a large number of new voters that had never felt like they had a party worth supporting.

The BC Liberals largely left the Green Party alone, instead focusing all of their efforts on discrediting the BC NDP. They were hoping that the BC NDP's worst fears would come true and that the Greens would spoil the election for them. They probably didn't realize how many of their own unhappy former supporters were peeling off to support the Greens instead.

Green candidates also hadn't anticipated the level of personal attacks and hostility that they were going to experience as candidates in an election in which the Greens were actual contenders. Overzealous partisan voters (and some paid campaign staff) began trying to attack and discredit Green candidates on a personal level, harassing them online and in the media. The Green campaign team had to scramble especially to support female candidates and those from minorities that were having to deal with sexist, racist, homophobic, and transphobic attacks. The whole experience was shocking for those of us who had never put our names forward for election before, and who hadn't experienced first-hand the toxic tactics that Canadian political parties use during elections.

One particularly sour moment for the Greens had to do with British Columbian teachers. While the party was drafting its platform for the election, Andrew had insisted that one of our main platform planks be education. He wanted us to outdo both of the other parties in our commitment to education funding and support, and hoped it would get picked up by the media and magnified to voters. As an educator and scientist himself, he considered the funding of the public education system the most important thing a government could do for its province.

An article began circling during the election describing an interaction Andrew had had with a couple of teachers who had come to talk to him in his constituency office. The authors described Andrew as rude and hostile towards them, and towards teachers in general. It somehow got lost in most of the reporting that the article and account had been penned by the campaign manager for Andrew's BC NDP rival in his home district. Andrew himself remembered the interaction very differently.

Nonetheless, it went viral among BC's teachers, a group that the BC NDP had invested heavily in courting and didn't want to lose to the Greens. BC teachers became some of the most ardent anti-Green campaigners. It was probably the lowest moment in the campaign for Andrew personally, as he'd staked so much of the platform on supporting BC education. It also taught the Greens the hard lesson that the platform itself doesn't matter if your political opponent can beat you in the messaging game.

Running a Serious Election

The BC Greens had recruited a number of star candidates for the election, hoping to repeat Andrew's success in having high-profile, organized, and experienced individuals managing to win districts through their own personal ability. A number of sitting city councillors and school board trustees were running as candidates. Adam Olsen was running again in the same district where he had nearly won in the previous election, having spent the four years since the last election building his public profile. While the BC Liberals were usually considered to be the party of businesses, and the BC NDP were considered to be the party of labour unions and blue-collar workers, Andrew wanted the BC Greens to be the party of educators, artists, scientists, and tech workers. He was particularly proud that the party managed to recruit a half-dozen candidates with PhDs in various fields.

Of the biggest star candidates for the Greens was Sonia Furstenau, running in a mostly rural district in central Vancouver Island called Cowichan Valley. Sonia's a small woman, thin, short-haired, and usually soft spoken. She's one of those people who's often described as "small but mighty" and has a personal strength that doesn't require her to be loud or bombastic. When she speaks her words are calm, measured, and well-thought-out beforehand. She can capture the attention of a room without once raising her voice. She had a history in grassroots advocacy work and prior to the election was serving as an Area Director for Cowichan Valley (similar to a city councillor, but for a rural area.)

Andrew met Sonia due to her work advocating for water issues in her home community. Sonia was engaged in a lengthy fight with a local quarry company that was dumping contaminated soil from the quarry near Cowichan Valley's main water supply. Sonia believed that the quarry soil risked contaminating the area's drinking water supply and was pressuring the provincial government to re-evaluate and rescind its permits. She had run into a brick wall and was getting nowhere with the BC Liberal government, nor was she managing to convince her local BC NDP MLA to champion the issue.

Hearing about her fight, Andrew stepped in. His own home district was near enough to Sonia's, so he hopped into a car (electric, of course) and drove up to meet her at the watershed site. A trained scientist by trade, Andrew brought along a set of sample gathering equipment, and started scooping up samples of Shawnigan Lake and the surrounding sites. He brought them back to his old lab at the University of Victoria and was able to provide Sonia with the proof she needed for her campaign.

For Sonia, the act of an MLA from a different district personally showing up and taking action on her issue surprised her. She was impressed by Andrew, and he was equally impressed with her. It took multiple attempts to convince her, but by the time the 2017 election was on the horizon, Andrew had signed Sonia up to run as a candidate. She came at the campaign laser-focused on the

BC Liberal government that had ignored her. Their dismissal of her issues would later be a huge factor in the fall of Premier Christy Clark and her government.

> Shawnigan (the contaminated lake) is not just a situation that is isolated or is exceptional. Shawnigan is a symptom of a system that was implemented by the government, and that the government now stands by in the face of what a terrible mess this has created… I realized I wanted to run (for election) because I wanted to address the root causes of this situation because I didn't want other communities to go through it. It was traumatizing. (Sonia, from an interview with the author, 2018)

Andrew and the BC Green team hoped that 2017 would be a huge breakthrough for them. With the party trending upwards in the polls, Andrew was hoping to have a situation like what had happened in Alberta in 2015, where the third-place party suddenly rocketed up from four seats to a majority due to voters getting sick of the bigger two parties. The BC Greens started their campaign fully believing that a Green government was a real possibility. One poll came out that showed the Greens leading on Vancouver Island, giving the Greens hope that their support was growing.

The BC NDP quickly refocused their own campaign to try to stamp down the surging Greens, recalling leader John Horgan from touring BC's interior and bringing him back to the island. In the last couple weeks of the campaign reality set in, as polls showed the upwards trend for the Greens had evened out, and they were unlikely to eclipse the BC NDP or Liberals. The Greens refocused to heavily support the few areas where it looked like they stood a serious chance of electing their candidates.

And Yet, Success

The night of May 9th, after the polls had closed, was a nail-biter. Polls had shown the BC NDP and BC Liberals virtually tied for support, with the Greens polling at their highest ever level but still trailing the bigger two parties. Polling analysts couldn't predict whether the election would result in a majority for the BC NDP, a majority for the BC Liberals, or a minority government with the Greens holding just enough seats in the middle to spoil the majority for the big two parties.

At the end of the night, the result was 43-41-3. The BC Liberals had lost their majority, ending one seat short. The BC NDP were very close behind. The two parties were closer in total vote count than they'd ever been: 796,000 for the Liberals, and 795,000 for the NDP. The Greens had posted their strongest ever results, earning 330,000 votes, about half what each of the other parties earned.

Andrew was re-elected to his seat in Oak Bay–Gordon Head. In a rematch in Saanich North and the Islands against the exact same BC Liberal and BC NDP candidates from the previous election, Adam Olsen seized victory. And Sonia Furstenau had picked up her district in the Cowichan Valley. Many other candidates had put up strong second-place finishes in areas all over the province. The result was the first time in Canada that a legislature would contain more than one elected Green. It was also among the best results worldwide for Greens operating in a first-past-the-post system.

The Balance of Responsibility

And even more importantly, it was a minority government situation. With neither the BC NDP nor the BC Liberals earning enough seats to form a majority, they would have to find a willing partner in order to form a stable government. Although the two old parties could have chosen to work together *without* the Greens, it was obvious to everyone that they would never consider that as an option. Instead, the Greens were being described as "holding the balance of power" and as "kingmakers." The Greens preferred to refer to situation as holding the "balance of *responsibility*," since both the BC Liberals and the BC NDP were expected to approach the small Green caucus and petition for their support to form government. It was a massive amount of responsibility and pressure put onto the small, three-person caucus.

Both Andrew and Sonia had gotten into politics because of frustration with the actions of Christy Clark and her BC Liberal government. But none of the three MLAs were fans of the BC NDP either, having just suffered through a campaign where the party attacked the Greens with tactics and a viciousness that had been shocking to the Greens, whose core message was one of civility and cooperation. Now the tables had turned, and both parties needed the Greens. It was going to make for an interesting set of negotiations.

"If I could go back to a point in history to try to get things to come out differently, I would go back and tell Moses to go up the mountain again and get the other tablet. Because the Ten Commandments just tell us what we are supposed to do with one another, not a word about our relationship to the earth. Genesis starts with these commands: multiply, replenish the earth, and subdue it. We have multiplied very well, we have replenished our populations very well, we have subdued it all too well, and we don't have any other instruction."

(David Brower, American environmentalist)

QUEENS PARK, AND ANOTHER MINORITY

Like fellow Green leaders Elizabeth May and Peter Bevan-Baker, Green Party of Ontario leader Mike Schreiner is an immigrant who came to Canada and loved it too much to leave. He was born and raised on a farm in Kansas, and moved to Ontario in 1994 when his wife accepted a job at the University of Toronto. Growing up on a farm in the countryside meant that eating local produce had been the natural way of life for Mike. When he arrived in Toronto and suddenly found himself living in Canada's biggest city, he turned back to his farm roots and started a food delivery business connecting people to local food producers.

For the first decade of his Canadian life, Mike didn't get involved in politics. In 2005, once it was very clear that he'd be staying in Canada and becoming a Canadian, he began to volunteer with the Ontario Green party. In 2007, he served as the party's critic for agriculture, along with helping draft agriculture-related parts of the party's platform. That was the last election for leader Frank de Jong because in 2009, just two years after becoming an official Canadian citizen, Mike took over as leader of the party.

Mike's first attempt at winning a Canadian election (and even getting to vote in one) was in March of 2009, just a few months before he won the party's leadership. John Tory, leader of the provincial Progressive Conservative Party, had lost his seat during the 2007 election. That was the same election in which the Ontario Green Party had posted its best ever results.

This failure was particularly embarrassing for Tory since as the leader of the second biggest party at Queen's Park (the nickname for the Ontario legislature) he was the official Leader of the Opposition and was expected to be in parliament holding the governing Liberals to account. By 2009, he'd been leading the party from outside the legislature for two years, and was facing criticism for being a weak leader. Rumour had it that he couldn't convince any of the sitting Progressive Conservative MPPs to resign so that he could take their spot.

In March of 2009, one of them finally did, and a by-election was called in the district of Haliburton–Kawartha Lakes–Brock to replace her. John Tory stepped up to run, confident that he would win. The Liberal and New Democrat parties selected their candidates to take him on, and the Green Party of Ontario picked Mike Schreiner as theirs.

Mike didn't win in 2009, although he did finish ahead of the NDP candidate, which was a small victory. But the big news out of the by-election wasn't the third-place result for the newly Canadian food delivery entrepreneur. John Tory actually lost the election to the Liberal candidate, leaving him stuck outside the legislature and handing the Liberals a win in what was considered a "safe" Conservative district. His leadership didn't last long. He resigned the next day.

Leader of the Ontario Greens

In 2011, Mike took his first crack at a full provincial election, now as the leader of the Green Party of Ontario. He ran in his home district of Simcoe–Grey, a group of towns and suburbs north of Toronto. Again he was unsuccessful, placing a distant fourth. Mike had chosen to run in the district where he lived, which was a noble move but a terrible strategy. The district was a solid Conservative stronghold, and was not going to be a likely place to flip to Green. The overall provincial Green vote collapsed from its high point in 2007, reduced to a third of their previous vote total. The election itself set a record in Ontario for the lowest overall voter turnout: 48.2 percent. The governing Liberals remained in power after the election, but lost their majority and instead wound up with a minority government. The Progressive Conservatives and the NDP both increased their seats, but were still behind the Liberals. The election was essentially considered a failure for every party.

2011 was also the year that Elizabeth May was elected to the parliament of Canada after moving to the opposite side of the country to find a district that was willing to take a chance on a Green MP. The federal party had done an extensive search of districts across the province to determine where would be a viable place for a Green to make a breakthrough, and they were happy to share some insights with the Ontario Green team after their own loss.

One of the top spots considered by Elizabeth's team was the Ontario city of Guelph. Elizabeth had nearly wound up moving there to try to pick up Canada's first Green seat, but had decided against it because the district was held by a Liberal and Elizabeth wanted her win to be at the

CHAPTER 6 – ELIZABETH, ANDREW, DAVID, PETER, MIKE

expense of a sitting Conservative. The district itself had been the closest result in the country for the Green Party of Canada in 2008. And since Ontario elections use the same district boundaries as federal elections, the Ontario provincial district of Guelph was identical to the federal one.

Mike had been doing business in Guelph for many years already and knew the city well. It was only about an hour's drive from his current home, and he felt that he already had a deep local connection to the area through his business history. And he jumped at the idea of being able to run in the province's most likely Green district.

Mike's first attempt in Guelph in the 2014 provincial election didn't go as planned, although he did post his best result yet. He finished a very close third, with nearly 20 percent of the vote. But the district remained strongly held by the incumbent Liberal.

Between 2014 and 2018, Mike didn't hold a seat in the Ontario legislature. But he could have fooled the press corps at Queen's Park. During the four years until the next election, Mike made a point of regularly attending proceedings of the legislature, even though he wasn't an elected member. He was stuck sitting upstairs in the gallery, and unlike the MPPs on the floor, he wasn't allowed to bring in his phone or laptop, which made communication and note-taking much more difficult. But when the day's business was over he'd be standing around the halls, making himself available to the press just like the leaders and MPPs from the other parties. The Greens wanted to prove that they were serious.

Voting Against, not Voting For

In 2018, the Green Party of Ontario took another shot. They were in the best position that they had ever been when going into an election. After the 2014 election, the Liberals had passed new political finance laws, banning corporate and union donations to political parties and adding a per-vote taxpayer subsidy to political parties as was already done in other parts of the country. Donations from individuals to the Ontario Green Party were also up, and so the GPO was sitting on the largest election war chest that it had ever had to work with.

The GPO went into the election with the realistic hope of electing a small Green caucus for the first time. British Columbia had just managed to elect a group of Greens, and the Ontario party was hoping to do the same. The party decided to invest heavily in a few key districts that they thought were winnable, dumping as much money and support as possible into the areas that had posted good Green results in the previous election. Mike Schreiner's district in particular was the biggest focus. Polling was showing that the district was a close four-way race among all of the major parties.

The 2018 election in Ontario was the definition of a "change election." The vast majority of voters wanted something different than the Liberal government that had been in power for over a decade. The voters just weren't in agreement on what kind of different they wanted. Both the Progressive Conservatives led by Doug Ford and the NDP led by Andrea Horwath surged ahead of the Liberals in the polls, with the two parties jockeying for first position throughout the campaign.

The "strategic vote" message from the NDP was brought out against the Greens in full force, claiming that a vote for the Green Party would "enable a Doug Ford government," something that they assumed most Greens would be afraid of. In polling after the election nearly half of all voters surveyed admitted that they had cast their vote specifically to try to block a party that they didn't like, rather than to support the party that they did like.

Greens suffer whenever an election becomes defined by fear. Voters using the first-past-the-post system get scared that they'll "waste" their vote and wind up being governed by their last choice, and so aren't willing to take a chance on a party or candidate that isn't considered a "sure thing." The Greens watched as the support that they were hoping to gain in their targeted districts didn't appear. Only Mike's district appeared to be polling well for them.

There was also a massive amount of frustration when it was announced that Mike was being excluded from the party leaders' debates. The Greens made the case that there were four parties in Ontario that had gotten enough votes in 2014 to qualify for tax-payer funding, and that Ontarians deserved to hear from all four of those parties. The Greens ran a campaign (entitled #MikeAtTheMic) to try to get Mike into the debates, including fielding protesters with green tape over their mouths. The media wouldn't budge.

By the end of the campaign, the party decided to gather all hands on deck for Mike's campaign. They put everything they had into campaigning in Guelph, pulling in supporters from surrounding districts to canvas the leader's district rather than working in their own. Polling still showed a close race in Guelph and it looked to be the only possible breakthrough area for the party.

On election night, the Greens were in for a surprise. When the polls opened they were cautiously optimistic that Mike was going to win, but knew that nothing was a certainty. When the polls closed it was revealed that Mike had overwhelmingly beaten the other candidates in the district. His final vote total was double the result of the second place candidate.

The party had been hoping for a minority government situation where Mike would be able to exert some influence and work with the other parties, but the result of the election was a disappointing majority government for Doug Ford's Progressive Conservatives. But the single win for the GPO in Guelph was still a cause for celebration for the Greens. A few weeks later, Mike Schreiner was sworn in as the first Green MPP in Ontario history, which marked the first time in six decades that a fourth party had won a seat in Queen's Park.

CHAPTER 6 – ELIZABETH, ANDREW, DAVID, PETER, MIKE

The Third Caucus

When the writ was dropped for the New Brunswick provincial election in October of 2018, Greens were serving in the legislatures of four of Canada's provinces. In two of those provinces, BC and PEI, there were multiple elected Greens. In the other two, Ontario and New Brunswick, the Greens were represented solely by the party leader. The goal of David Coon in the New Brunswick election was to grow his caucus, to join BC and PEI and become the third province to have a group of Greens in the parliament.

Early polling didn't suggest that the Greens were going to make any breakthroughs. Political pollsters were predicting that David would hold on to his own seat, but didn't think it was likely that the Greens would pick up any extra seats. The overall percentage of voters supporting the Greens was up in the polls from the 2014 election, but unless that added support could be concentrated into a few specific districts it wouldn't mean anything for the party.

The other big unknown in the election was the insurgent People's Alliance Party (PA), a breakaway party from the local Progressive Conservatives. They'd been formed in 2010 and ran in the 2014 election but failed to elect anyone. The PA is a conservative party based on rural populism, and is seen as being pro-English language and anti-bilingualism, notable because New Brunswick is Canada's only official bilingual province, with about a quarter of the population being native French speakers. This time around, pollsters were predicting that the People's Alliance's popular leader, Kris Austin, would likely win his own seat and that there was a possibility that they'd pick up one or two more.

Polls showed that the trio of smaller parties were severely eating into the vote share of the two big dominant parties. Both the Greens and the PA were likely to elect at least one member. The NDP wasn't predicted to elect anyone but was nonetheless occupying between 5 and 10 percent of the vote. The narrative of the campaign became that there were two races going on: the contest between the Liberals and the Conservatives for the top spot, and the three-way race among the trailing parties to turn their support into elected members.

The Greens were focusing on a couple of districts that they thought were winnable. Megan Mitton had placed a relatively strong third in the district of *Memramcook–Tantramar* in 2014, and was returning in this election for a second try. The district of *Kent North* was one of the second place finishes in 2014, and although a new candidate (Kevin Arseneau) was running, they still had a solid base to work from.

A Very Weird Result

Right up until voting day, most pollsters were still predicting that the Greens would only re-elect David. Trying to predict an election under first-past-the-post when there are five parties is a big challenge for pollsters, since the election is so dependent on the results of individual districts rather than the overall popular vote.

The elections results wound up being one of the most bizarre in Canadian history, and likely the most pronounced example of the strangeness of the first-past-the-post system in the history of the country.

The New Brunswick Liberal Party was the leader in the popular vote by a mile. They finished with just under 38 percent across the province. Justin Trudeau's Liberal Party in 2015 was rewarded with a strong majority government for finishing with 39 percent support across the country, and in first-past-the-post a result of 38 percent is often enough for a party to win a majority of seats, depending on how the other parties split the remainder of the vote.

The New Brunswick Liberals did not get a majority government, nor did they even get the most seats. They elected twenty-one members, which was four shy of a majority. Meanwhile, the Progressive Conservatives elected twenty-*two* members, also below a majority. The big story was that the Conservatives only got 32 percent of the popular vote across the province. They'd managed to win more districts than the Liberals despite having significantly less support among New Brunswick's voters. This spread of 6 percent is the biggest difference in Canadian history when it comes to a party with fewer votes winning more seats. It happens fairly regularly under first-past-the-post, but the spread is usually within a couple percentage points, not a full 6 percent.

Results of the 2018 New Brunswick election
49 seats to be elected for the House of Representatives
25 seats needed for a majority

	LIBERAL	**PROGRESSIVE CONSERVATIVE**	**PEOPLE'S ALLIANCE**	**GREEN**	**NDP**
Vote %	**37.8%**	31.9%	12.6%	11.9%	5%
Seats	21	**22**	3	3	0

CHAPTER 6 – ELIZABETH, ANDREW, DAVID, PETER, MIKE

Gerry and the Salamander

The reason why the Progressive Conservatives managed to eclipse the Liberals is because they barely squeaked out a win in most of the districts that they won. They won those local races against Liberals by a very small margin, usually with less than 40 percent of the vote. Meanwhile, when the Liberals won a district, they tended to do so in an absolute blowout, with majorities of 60 or 70 percent. The "extra" votes in these blowouts didn't accomplish anything extra for the Liberal Party. All they needed to do was to get more votes than the other candidates.

Whether you win a local race with 30 percent of the vote or 90 percent of the vote doesn't matter—it only matters if you get the most. When all these excess votes were added into the total, it meant that far more individual voters supported the Liberals, but the Conservatives had still won more of the individual districts. Pollsters refer to this as how "efficient" a party's votes are under first-past-the-post. A party with low vote efficiency might get a lot of votes but elect few people. One with high efficiency can elect more people even with fewer votes.

This phenomenon is often abused in countries using first-past-the-post. It's most famous in the context of the United States, where it's earned the name "gerrymandering." It's named after a former Governor of Massachusetts named Elbridge Gerry, who specifically designed the state's districts in a way that would benefit his own party. Operating on a neighbourhood-by-neighbourhood basis, he drew a couple districts that were overwhelming full of voters for the opposing party, thus stuffing his opponents into a few districts to reduce their voter efficiency. Then he carefully distributed the few remaining opposition voters into the remaining districts, ensuring that his party had a majority in many more of them. One of the districts was remarked to be so strangely shaped and distorted that it looked like a salamander on the map. Thus, the gerrymander.

Those who claim that first-past-the-post produces simple results are obviously ignoring elections such as New Brunswick in 2018, plus the entirety of the American political system.

In the New Brunswick election, both the Greens and the People's Alliance surprised the pollsters by each electing three members. The Greens doubled their vote share from the last election, settling in at just under 12 percent. The People's Alliance experienced massive growth, going from 2 percent in 2014 to just over 12 percent in 2018. A similar result for both parties in a proportional representation election would have awarded them each six seats. Like the Liberals, their vote shares were wildly different from their actual results.

Everyone Wins?

The election produced no clear winner. Liberal leader Brian Gallant and Progressive Conservative Blaine Higgs both immediately declared victory and began referring to themselves as the "Premier-elect," a term that has no official meaning in Canada and grossly misunderstands the way our parliament works. Gallant claimed the win because his party had clearly received the most votes, while Higgs claimed the victory because his party had clearly received the most seats. Voters were mostly left confused at how this result had happened and who their next government was going to be.

Meanwhile, David Coon and two newly elected Green colleagues were in a position remarkably similar to the Green caucus in British Columbia after the 2017 election. People's Alliance leader Kris Austin and his two new colleagues felt the same. The two competing bigger parties were likely going to appeal to the two smaller parties for support rather than choose to work with each other.

David's new caucus members were Megan Mitton and Kevin Arseneau, each achieving narrow wins in their districts. With Kevin's win in Kent North, he became the first francophone elected as a Green. David himself had been easily re-elected, going from a very close win in 2014 to a blowout majority in 2018. His win continued a pattern seen with Greens in Canada: so far every Green that has run for re-election has won with a greatly increased majority. It seemed that when people tried having a Green representative, they realized that they liked it.

Megan Mitton's district was the closest race in the province. The initial count showed that she had won the seat by only eleven votes. A mandatory recount confirmed the number a week later.

Let no one ever say that a single vote doesn't count.

CHAPTER 7

THE GREEN GOVERNMENTS OF GERMANY

"This papal endorsement finally elevates Germany's Greens to the status of a party that is incapable of horrifying or provoking anyone. It has served its time as a party of protest."

(German newspaper Der Spiegel, 2011, after the Pope's visit to Germany in which he praised the German Green Party)

THE GREEN GOVERNMENTS OF GERMANY

In 1998, voters in the Federal Republic of Germany went to the polls to vote for their nation's highest offices. They delivered a rebuke to the conservative-led government of the past two decades. For the first time, voters put the Green Party of Germany in a position where it could be part of the country's government.

The Greens in the government of Germany from 1998–2005 give us the clearest and most high-profile view of what a Green party in government looks like. When Canadians look at our Green Party of Canada and think, *I don't know what a Green party government would do in office*, they are likely unaware that the Foreign Minister of Germany for seven years was a Green politician. This is Germany's top diplomatic post, responsible for the German government's coordination and diplomacy with the rest of the world.

This was a period of recent world history that included events such as the civil war and breakup of Yugoslavia, the 9/11 attacks, and the American invasions of Afghanistan and Iraq. It was a period in which Germany reasserted itself as a major player in world politics and diplomacy. During all of these major events, the head of Germany's foreign affairs department was a Green.

Canadians likely don't know that Germany's Minister for Environment in these years was likewise a Green, and that Germany's modern-day leadership role in clean-tech and alternative energy sources was largely because of initiatives developed during the Greens' participation in government.

Parties in Coalition

As of the spring of 2019, when I submitted the final version of this book for print, we have yet to see any Canadian Greens in government. The closest that we've come is the aftermath of the 2017 provincial election in British Columbia, in which no single party elected enough individuals to make up a majority of the legislature. Faced with such a result, the small BC Green caucus of three members opted to support the BC NDP to form government. Despite the media and other politicians repeatedly mis-naming the agreement, this was in fact *not* a coalition, and thus the BC Greens in no way are a part of the government in British Columbia.

The distinction is a bit of a confusing one at first. Many people like to use the word *coalition* in a casual sense, just to mean when two groups agree to cooperate. However, in elections and governments, the word "coalition" has a specific meaning: it means when two parties formally join into a single governing team and share the powers and responsibilities of government. In such a situation, all the parties involved would share government ministries and positions. The larger partner would gain the Prime Minister (or equivalent) title, and a number of important portfolios. Junior partners would be given a number of titles and responsibilities reflecting their party's size within the coalition.

Confidence and Supply

This is not what happened in British Columbia. There is no "Andrew Weaver, Minister of the Environment" or "Adam Olsen, Minister for Fisheries." Instead, the deal made in BC was one that's known as a "confidence-and-supply agreement." The agreement, referred to by BC politicians using the acronym CASA, is a formally written up set of rules and expectations for all parties involved. It states that the government will be a BC NDP government in its entirety, with no government positions for the BC Greens. However, the Greens agree to support this government in certain specified cases such as budget votes.

In return, the BC NDP has a set of Green expectations that it promises to follow. As long as the government follows the word and spirit of the document, the Greens pledge to support the government in "confidence motions." This means simply that the Greens won't allow the government to fall and to thus trigger a fresh election. The Greens remain an entirely independent party and the governing BC NDP must seek their votes on all individual issues beyond the ones agreed to in the document.

These two forms of cooperation, the coalition and the CASA, are common in democratic systems whenever a single party fails to achieve a majority. In Canada, we've never seen Greens in a true coalition, and the PEI Greens are just beginning to write the history of Canada's first Green government. Since Elizabeth May's election in 2011 we've had examples of single Greens or small caucuses in opposition, but no examples of Green governments for Canadians to observe and understand.

Green Governments in the Rest of the World

We're in luck, though, because if we look outside of Canada and to the rest of the world there are many examples of governing Greens. Although Canadian Greens and their overseas cousins are unique and different in many ways, they likely share more in common than they have differences. And the best place to observe how Canadian Greens might act in government is in a country whose political system shares many similarities with ours, and whose local Green movement has influenced the Canadian Greens more than any other. I'm referring to Die Grüne, the Green Party of Germany.

The next three chapters of this book will cover the experience of Green parties serving in government in Germany, Ireland, and Sweden. The idea is to inform readers of what Canadian Green governments might look like based on examples from elsewhere in the world where it's happened. It's not a perfect comparison, but I hope that it will give readers an idea of what we might be able to expect from a Canadian Green government. I hope it will inform Green supporters of what types of things they should look out for if the Greens in Canada continue to grow in popularity. And provide some wisdom and caution for the Greens in government now in PEI.

Readers who would prefer to just learn about Canadian-specific Green history can continue on to Chapter 10, where I resume covering the Green experience in Canada.

A Very Short History of Post-War German Politics

In order to compare the Green experience in Canada to that in Germany, we need to be able to compare the political environment in both countries. That means covering a quick history of post-war Germany's politics.

When the Nazi regime fell and Hitler's Germany was defeated, the country was split in two. The western half was given over to American guidance while the eastern half was ceded to the

Soviets. In the west, the first political force to establish itself was the Christian Democratic Union (CDU) led by its founder Konrad Adenauer. He was West Germany's first Chancellor after the war and stayed in the position for fourteen years, ushering West Germany through the reconstruction of its economy and its re-entry into the global community. This solidified the CDU as the "natural governing party" for many Germans.

In terms of ideology, the party is socially and fiscally conservative, draws heavily from the Christian history and the culture of Germany for its ideological positions, and from the start was powerfully pro-American and pro-market economy. Adenauer wanted to bring Germany back into the global community and economy by adhering enthusiastically to America's demands and desires for what they wanted in a new, reconstituted Germany.

Countering the CDU was a party that existed since pre-Nazi times, but had been banned by the Nazi regime. The Democratic Socialist Party (SPD, from its German acronym) began out of labour rights movements, and was unabashedly socialist and skeptical of both the American-led western bloc and free market capitalism in general. For years the SPD attempted to unseat the CDU, to convince Germans that socialism and state-guided industry would be better for them than the free market conservatism of the CDU.

Eventually, the SPD realized that if they ever wanted to lead a government then they were going to have to compromise on some of their more "extreme" beliefs, and after moving towards the political centre they were elected to lead their first federal government in 1969. They remain the most established and largest left-wing progressive force in German politics.

The third of Germany's major parties is the Free Democratic Party (FDP), a classical liberal party that formed in the first years after the fall of the Nazi regime. The FDP has always had less voter support and therefore fewer seats in the legislature than the other two big parties. As such, its position in German politics is that it is very often chosen as the junior coalition partner by one of the two bigger parties when they finish an election without enough support to form a majority on their own.

Thus, the FDP has been in government more years in total than either of the big parties, but has never led a German government either at the federal level or the state level. Although the FDP calls itself "classical liberal" its positions often lead critics to call it a Libertarian party. It is sometimes described as a party only for the rich, since it takes relatively little interest in policies designed to help the underprivileged. It instead expects people to help themselves and the party's mission is to keep the government out of their lives and pockets.

Throughout modern German political history, other parties have popped up and then faded away after a few elections. These parties tend to form when disgruntled members of the three big parties feel that their party is trending too far away from their previous ideological position and break off to form a new party apparatus, or to bolster a small party that had been languishing without support for some time.

CHAPTER 7 – THE GREEN GOVERNMENTS OF GERMANY

German / Canadian Comparisons

Comparing the German political parties to Canadian ones is possible, but not perfect. The SPD is the party that most easily matches with a Canadian political group. Both the SPD and Canada's New Democratic Party (NDP) belong to the international organization Progressive Alliance. Both were spawned out of organized labour movements and consider blue-collar unionized workers to be their base of support and biggest driving force. Both positioned themselves as progressive forces in the social sphere, and both have made environmental concerns a part of their platforms, although not the main concern.

Canada's Conservatives are a little harder to match with a German equivalent. Both the Conservative Party of Canada and the Christian Democratic Union are members of the International Democrat Union, the international organization of conservative parties that also includes the US Republican Party. But there are a number of policy and ideological differences between Canada and Germany's biggest conservative movements.

In Germany, there are two conservative parties: one that's considered centre-right (the CDU) and a much newer one that's often labelled as far-right (the Alternative for Germany, AfD). Similarly, in Canada we have the Conservative Party and the recently formed People's Party of Canada. The Conservative Party and the People's Party each share various ideological and policy similarities with the two major German conservative parties.

Finally, the Liberal Party of Canada and the Free Democratic Party really can't be directly compared, even though they both belong to Liberal International, the same international organization. Both parties do share some policies in common, such as championing the free-market and liberal values, but their different positions within the political environment set them apart.

The Liberal Party of Canada works very hard to straddle the middle of the political spectrum, considering itself a broad coalition of centrists and technocrats who find the right-wing and left-wing parties too ideologically rigid. The Liberal Party considers itself to be Canada's "natural governing party": a status that the CDU in Germany covets rather than the FDP. The FDP instead seems content to be a small party that can act as a trusted coalition partner to larger parties—that is, a natural and cooperative ally that can extract some concessions on key issues from their senior partners in exchange for their support.

THE POLITICAL ORGANIZATION OF GERMANY

Like Canada, Germany is a federation of states. This means that it is a country that has a central government, but that the country is made up of a number of self-governing states or provinces that operate under the overarching federal government. Since Canada has a Queen, it's known as a "federal monarchy," whereas the royalty-less Germany is a "federal republic." However, since Canada's royal family takes a hands-off approach to governance, the distinction is pretty minimal.

Canada has ten provinces of varying size and population, as well as three territories that function in many ways the same as a province. Germany has sixteen states, three of which are "city-states" that are geographically much smaller than the remaining thirteen states. The least populous state, the city-state of Bremen, has about the same population as the Canadian province of Newfoundland. The most populous state, North Rhine-Westphalia, has about eighteen million inhabitants, which makes it a bit more populated than Canada's largest province, Ontario, with its fourteen million.

In the north, states such as Mecklenburg-Vorpommern are coastal and sparsely populated, with economies that rely heavily on tourism from their unspoilt environment and healthy coasts. In the south, states such as Bavaria are heavily populated and wealthy, their economies relying on manufacturing and technology. Others, such as the geographically small Saarland, have long relied on extractive energy industries such as coal for their prosperity.

The parallels can be seen with the Canadian provinces. In Canada, we also have our tourism-focused coastal states with large swaths of pristine environment. We have our central resource-industry-dependent provinces. We have our large manufacturing-dependent provinces, with populations that dwarf several of the other provinces. We have our rural agricultural-based provinces.

Like Canada, Germany has a number of political parties, the biggest of which were covered earlier. While Canada currently has five political parties that have been elected at the federal level, Germany currently has six. As in Canada, each of these political parties has state-specific versions that contest each of the states' local elections. These state elections and governments are a great place for those who are curious about Green governments to look to see how Greens act when in government.

Greens in Government

Since Germany uses a proportional system of elections, majority governments are rather rare. Bavaria was the last state to have a single party majority government, prior to their most recent election in late 2018. Each of the other fifteen states is governed in a coalition with two or three parties working together. These state government are often seen as test-beds for the different possible

CHAPTER 7 – THE GREEN GOVERNMENTS OF GERMANY

coalitions between Germany's multiple parties, before a similar coalition arrangement is tried at the federal level. Many different combinations of parties, either as a duo or a trio, have been attempted and then studied by German political scientists to see what worked well, and what was challenging.

As of 2019, the German Greens are currently in a coalition in nine of the sixteen state governments. In eight of these governments they are the junior partner, as their co-governing party received more votes and seats during the last election. Only in the southern alpine state of Baden-Württemberg did the Greens themselves get the most votes, and hence they lead the coalition government. The leader of the Greens of Baden-Württemberg, Winfried Kretschmann, is the current Minister President for the state, and is the first Green to serve in the office.

German state coalitions involving the Green Party

GERMAN STATE	COALITION	NOTES
Baden-Württemberg	Green - CDU	Relatively new coalition type, and between parties that are usually opposed. Known as a black–green or green–black coalition due to the party's colours.
Hessen	CDU - Green	
Hamburg	SPD - Green	The usual, traditional coalition of choice for the two parties. Known as a red–green coalition.
Bremen		
Niedersachsen		
Nordrhein-Westfalen		
Thuringia	Left - SPD - Green	New combination of parties, and the only government led by the Left Party.
Schleswig-Holstein	SPD - Green - FDP	Known as a traffic light coalition due to the traditional colours of the three parties being red, yellow, and green.
Rhineland-Palatinate		
Saxony-Anhalt	CDU - SPD - Green	Involving both of the usually dominant centre-left and centre-right parties, as well as the Greens. Known as a Kenya Coalition due to the parties' colours matching those on the Kenyan flag.

As is shown in the figure above, numerous combinations of parties can be found in the German states, and each combination can give us an idea of how a Canadian Green coalition might function.

A red–green coalition refers to an agreement between the Greens and the SPD, the traditional left-wing labour party of German Politics. A Black-Green coalition is a cooperation between the Greens and the CDU, the traditional conservative party. In some cases, a third partner is needed to form a majority, such as the centrist FDP or the Left Party. In one state the CDU, the SPD, and the Greens are all in a coalition together.

These many examples of political cooperation give us an idea of how a possible future Canadian coalition involving the Greens could operate. In addition to showing us how Greens are able to build common ground with parties on the left and right of the political spectrum, the examples of these state governments also show us how competent (or not) Greens can be when actually given an avenue to advance their policy ideas.

The First Attempts at Green Coalition-Building

Germany's so-called red–green coalitions between the Greens and the dominant left-wing party are the most common pairing for the Greens in the country. The Greens first won election to a state legislature in the 1979 election in the city-state of Bremen. Election to several other states followed quickly, including the state of Hesse in 1982.

Hesse is a landlocked state in central Germany, surrounded on all sides by other German states. It boasts a population of about six million, and is about the same size in total area as the US state of New Jersey. Its largest city is Frankfurt, one of Germany's (and the world's) busiest and most economically important cities.

The 1982 election in the state was a shock to the established party order. For the past several elections there had only been three parties that had won elected office: the centre-left SPD, the centre-right CDU, and the centrist liberal FDP. Before that there had been other fourth parties that were present for an election or two before fading away, but the trio of the SPD, CDU, and FDP was a constant.

A Crisis of Government

In 1982, the Greens (who had unsuccessfully contested the previous election as just a disorganized list of individuals) surged ahead of the FDP, gaining entry into the Hessian parliament for the first time. Even more shockingly the FDP failed for the first time to reach the 5 percent threshold of voter support, meaning that they were unable to elect anyone. This was a crisis for both the SPD

CHAPTER 7 – THE GREEN GOVERNMENTS OF GERMANY

and the CDU, who had counted on having the FDP around to support either of them in a coalition in order to form government.

This was the first entry into parliament for the Greens in Hesse, and was still a year before the federal Greens entered the federal Bundestag. The Greens at this point were at their highest level of "anti-party" status and were completely uninterested in joining a coalition with any of the large parties that they had entered politics to try to oppose. Petra Kelly, the closest thing the Green movement at the time had to a leader, was adamantly against any cooperation with the other parties.

> When the Social Democrats shut down all the nuclear power plants, quit the arms race and start building ambulances instead of tanks, then we can talk. The day the Greens start sending Ministers to Bonn (the capital of West Germany) then it's not the Greens I wanted. (Hockenos, 2008, page 159)

The Hessian Greens themselves had arrived at the first sitting of the legislature all dressed in WWII-era gas masks and long white doctors coats and carrying a handwritten sign that read, "Green Anti-Catastrophe Service: Parliamentary and Extra-Parliamentary." Unsurprisingly, none of the large parties had any interest in the Greens as a coalition partner either. They all considered them a temporary addition to German politics that would go away if they waited long enough and ignored them. Holger Börner, the SPD Minister President of Hesse at the time, caused a stir by remarking that, "I regret that my high state office forbids me from hitting those guys in the face" and that "down on the construction site" guys like the Greens would be disciplined by a whack to the head from a two-by-four.

The SPD and the CDU could have formed a grand coalition with each other, but neither wanted this arrangement. They were far too used to opposing each other rather than collaborating. Instead the SPD operated as a minority government for a year before calling a new election, hoping for a different result. A new election was scheduled for 1983, with Holger Börner urging Hessians to return a majority SPD government. He stated that he steadfastly refused to work with the Greens, and that, "For me the Greens are outside any calculation. I exclude not only a coalition, but any cooperation with them."

In the 1983 election, the FDP returned to the Hessian parliament, but the SPD still had a problem. The FDP had decided that they were not, under any circumstances, going to support another SPD government. They were instead looking to support a CDU government, but that pairing didn't have enough elected members to make up a majority. The parliament was stuck in the same quagmire, with the parties refusing to work together. The Greens were proving to be just enough of a spoiler that the traditional parties were unable to form majority governments in the composition that they desired.

For another two years, Börner led a minority SPD government, tolerated by the other parties, but the goal was still that he would be able to build a majority coalition. Within the Hessian Green party, debate was fierce between the *fundi* (radical) and *realo* (pragmatist) camps over whether they could actually bring themselves to form a coalition with another party. *Realos* believed that participating in governance was the best way for the party to achieve its goals. The *fundis* detested the entire system of German politics and wanted to be present in the legislature only as an opposition force and to protest the system. Internally, the SPD was also struggling with the possibility of inviting the Greens into a coalition.

The First Green Coalition - Perhaps Far Too Early

The stalemate was broken in 1985 when the SPD and the Greens finally agreed to attempt an official coalition, the first red–green cooperation agreement in German history. The Greens received a single cabinet post, which was assigned to party spokesperson Joschka Fischer, who was an ardent *realo* and one of the main forces urging the Greens to consider the coalition. He became the Minister for Environment in Hesse, the first position in state or higher-level government for the German Greens.

This first attempt at a coalition with the Greens was a struggle for all parties involved, and didn't last long. The ministry that the Greens were given was created specifically for them and was mostly toothless. Their SPD partners wanted the Greens as weak as possible in government and fought to keep them that way. And in the rest of Germany, both the federal Greens and the federal SPD were still adamantly against cooperation between the two parties and wanted the arrangement being attempted by their Hessian counterparts to fail.

And then, a year into the coalition, the Chernobyl nuclear power plant in Soviet Ukraine experienced a meltdown.

One of the largest groups in the formation of the Greens had been the anti-nuclear movement, and this was their moment to say, "I told you so." But the Greens in Hesse had made what many anti-nuclear activists considered a deal with the devil. As part of the coalition agreement, the Greens had compromised with the SPD, who were still very much in favour of nuclear power. The Greens agreed to suspend their demand for a dismantling of Hesse's nuclear facilities, and the SPD agreed that they wouldn't build any new facilities. They'd meet in the middle, and both settle for the status quo.

When the Chernobyl meltdown occurred, it was inevitable that the Hessian Greens had to take another look at the compromise it had made. The Greens told the SPD that, in light of new circumstances, they were demanding that the deal be changed. The Hessian SPD refused.

Taking things even further, the SPD First Minister was forging ahead with plans to upgrade one of the state's nuclear reactors, which the Greens wanted shut down entirely. The Greens had had enough. After fourteen months in the coalition they pulled their support and left. Hesse called a new snap election, in which the CDU and FDP together were able to gain enough seats to replace the SPD, ending the first experiment of Greens in government.

The Second Coalition - More Successful, but Just as Short

The city-state of Berlin, then divided between the West German and East German halves, was the next to experiment with a red–green coalition. The coalition that governed the West German side formed after the elections in 1989, and lasted for a single year until German unification when a new election for a unified Berlin was called. This red–green coalition was in place when the Berlin Wall fell, with the Greens serving as Berlin's Ministers for Education, Urban Development and Environment, and Women's Issues. The last office was used by Minister Anne Klein, who was openly gay, to create the novel new Department for Same-Sex lifestyles, a first in Germany.

After the unification of the eastern and western parts of Berlin, the two cities' councils attempted to govern as partners, but this only lasted for about a year before they decided to formally merge the cities' governments, thus requiring a new election. After this subsequent election, a coalition was formed by other parties that didn't include the Greens. This experiment in red–green governance was relatively successful, at least compared to the first attempt in Hesse.

As was mentioned in Chapter 3, the unification of West and East Germany shocked the Greens into a number of reform measures. The '80s were a period of radicalism for the German Greens, whereas the '90s were the beginning of the reforming of the party into a more traditional political entity, although still radical as compared to the decades old established parties. After their merger with the East German Greens and the party reforms of 1990 the Greens became much more acceptable as a coalition partner. By that time the *fundi* wing of the party had been defeated and the *realos* were firmly in charge.

Red–green coalition governments formed in the states of North Rhine-Westphalia (Germany's most populous state) and Schleswig-Holstein, both of which were remarkably stable and lasted an entire decade. They joined slightly shorter coalitions in Saxony-Anhalt and Hamburg that lasted a single term, but were still stable and mostly successful. They even made a second attempt in the state of Hesse in 1991, this time lasting an entire eight years until the coalition was defeated by a CDU/FDP alliance in the 1999 election.

Ready for a Federal Coalition

The states of Germany often serve as a test bed for coalition arrangements that are considered on the federal scale. After serving as a coalition partner in seven different German states the SPD believed by 1998 that the Federal Republic of Germany might be ready for a red–green coalition at the top level of government.

The pragmatist wing of the Greens had largely won out; they'd worked out a lot of the kinks in how to work with other parties, and they had years of examples of how the Greens and the Social Democrats could cooperate and find common ground policies on which to govern. They'd found conflict-resolution mechanisms for the two parties to use internally. They'd conducted public research to find if a red–green coalition would be acceptable to a majority of Germans. The two parties understood how such an arrangement would work and what could be expected of both parties.

In the 1998 federal election Germany elected something very different, something that it had never before attempted at its highest level of government. The coalition between the Christian Democrats and the Free Democratic Party, which had governed for sixteen years, since before German unification, was ousted and was replaced by a coalition of the Social Democrats and Greens. As part of the coalition, the Greens were awarded three ministries.

Predictably, they received the office of Minister of the Environment, as well as the Minister for Health. SPD leader Gerhard Schröder became the new Chancellor of Germany, but the second-in-command Vice-Chancellorship and the prestigious Foreign Affairs Ministry was granted to the Greens' Joschka Fischer, who had served as the first state-level Green minister in Hesse thirteen years prior. Thus, a Green revolutionary took over as the person responsible for the foreign policy of Europe's largest economy and most populous country.

"We can change. We are not desperate idiots of history, unable to take their destiny in their own hands. It has been told us for centuries. Many historical signs indicate that history is not an eternal circle where only the negative must triumph. Why should we renounce to this historical possibility and say: we give up, we cannot make it, sometimes this world will come to an end.
Exactly the opposite. We can construct a world as humanity has never seen before; a world that will distinguish itself for the absence of war and hunger. And this on the whole globe. This is our historical possibility, and we should let it go? I'm not a professional politician, but we are men who do not want the world to follow this way, and for this reason we will fight, we already started to fight . . ."

(Rudi Dutschke)

JOSCHKA FISCHER: THE REVOLUTIONARY

Joschka Fischer is probably the world's highest-profile Green. As Vice-Chancellor and Foreign Minister of Germany, he's undoubtedly the highest-achieving Green politician in global history. His own story is incredibly interesting, and I think it serves to show the character arc of a revolutionary youth finding their way into the highest annals of power, and what changes a person undergoes along that journey. This is particularly poignant for Greens, since so many of the individuals on the ground fighting for the party come from a similar background, frustrated with society and wanting to radically change it.

As such an important figure within the Green movement, I felt I couldn't get away without telling Joschka's story, long though it may be. If you'd like, feel free to skip ahead to "Greens in the Government of Germany" later in this chapter if you'd prefer to get right to the experiences of the Greens in Germany's government.

Born into a Broken Nation

Joschka Fischer was born in the German-speaking region of Baden-Württemberg in 1948. But he wasn't born in Germany, because at the time Germany didn't exist as a country. In the years after the fall of Nazi Germany, the territory that had been Germany was split up under the administration of the various Allied powers. The Federal Republic of Germany wouldn't be officially created out of the so-called "Allied Zones of Occupation" until Joschka was one year old. Nor was Joschka's family even German—at least not by nationality.

Prior to the war, ethnic Germans had been spread all across Europe, living in places like Hungary, Poland, and Czechoslovakia. Hitler's Nazi regime used the presence of these ethnic Germans as part of the justification for invading these countries, claiming that Germany was just protecting the interests of ethnic Germans abroad. As a response, when the Nazis were defeated, other European countries began expelling their German populations. This happened despite the local ethnic Germans often having nothing to do with Hitler's Germany, and having lived abroad for generations.

Joschka's family came to Germany after the war as refugees from Hungary. They had been forcibly removed from their homes and all of their land and most of their possessions had been confiscated from them. They arrived destitute in Germany, a territory in which the economy was in shambles after the war and which was relying on the Allied powers to just keep running. They went from being a middle-class family in Hungary, in which Joschka's father ran a successful butcher shop, to being the poorest of the poor in a country that was foreign to them.

The family tried to raise Joschka and his two sisters with the sensibilities of the middle class that they had left behind in Hungary. They enrolled him in good schools and encouraged him to focus on his studies and to succeed in his education. German secondary school education is divided into three tiers, and Joschka was enrolled in *gymnasium*, the most advanced tier. If someone growing up in Germany ever wanted a white-collar job after graduation it was a necessity that they would graduate from a *gymnasium*.

Although Joschka was a good student as a child, he became jaded as a teenager and stopped trying to succeed in his education. He dropped out of high school and took up an apprenticeship in photography, which he also quickly quit. He then became a vagabond, hitchhiking around Europe and the Middle East, making it all the way to Kuwait before his family managed to contact him to tell him that his older sister was sick and that he needed to return.

He returned to Germany just in time to witness both his sister succumb to sickness and his father to die suddenly from a heart attack while at work in a factory. His father was just fifty-six years old at his death. He had literally worked himself to death trying to support the family and reclaim the life that the war had taken from the Fischers.

Rattled by the seeming unfairness of the post-war existence in Germany, Fischer got involved in the radical left-wing student movements of the 1960s. He began attending lectures at local universities, although he never formally enrolled. During this time he met Edeltraud, another student revolutionary, and the two teenagers eloped to Scotland where they'd be able to marry without their parents' permission. They returned to Germany and lived together as *Gammler*, part of a

CHAPTER 7 – THE GREEN GOVERNMENTS OF GERMANY

counterculture movement that rejected capitalism and societal norms. The two alternated between street homelessness and squatting, and survived by shoplifting for food and through Joschka stealing counterculture philosophy books and reselling them to other poor radical students. Detlev Claussen, one of Joschka's fellow student revolutionaries who later in life went on to Chair the University of Hanover's Sociology department, recounted,

> I thought, this guy isn't really educated or well read but he has excellent taste in books, and was excellent at stealing them as well—a real professional. (Hockenos, 2008, page 73)

The '68er Generation

There's a particular generation in Germany known as the '68ers. These were all people who had been born just after the war and reached adulthood during the 1960s. Like the student movements in the United States and in France during this era, the students were critical of authoritarianism in their governments, critical of imperialism and wars abroad such as the one currently waging in Vietnam, and critical of many of the conservative traditions and expectations of society as a whole.

The '68ers were a hodgepodge of pacifists, anti-imperialists, communists, and any other counterculture groups that you could think of. Students in Germany also witnessed that many of the older generation who were active in government and education during the Nazi years were still around and active in modern Germany. The students saw themselves as being blamed for the crimes of their parents' generation, while meanwhile the perpetrators of those crimes were still participating in and leading German society.

The selection of the year 1968 as the basis of the name of the student movement comes from the events of that year, which was when the movement reached its boiling point. The previous year, in 1967, a student protest had culminated in the death of Benno Ohnesorg, a student protestor who was shot in the back of the head by West German police during the confusion of a protest. His death provided the movement with a martyr, and by 1968 the movement was at its biggest and most angry.

A student activist named Rudi Dutschke had become one of the central figures of the movement, giving lectures in universities to radical students and acting as a uniting figure among the various groups in the movement. In April of 1968 during an anti-Vietnam war summit in West Berlin organized by the students, Rudi was shot point-blank in the face by a lone shooter who had travelled to Berlin specifically to assassinate the student leader.

Rudi initially survived the attempted assassination, but suffered severe brain damage as a result. He had to learn to speak again, and died a few years later from complications from the injury. The man who shot Rudi Dutschke, an anti-communist who reportedly called Rudi a "dirty communist pig" right before shooting him, had been turned into an assassin by reading coverage of the student protests in Germany's right-wing print media. The conservative German media had been calling for "someone to stop Rudi Dutschke!" for the good of the republic. The student movement held the media responsible for his death far more than they held the individual assassin responsible.

Joschka's Radicalization

Joschka Fischer wasn't present in West Berlin at the summit where Rudi was shot, but he immediately joined the protests that resulted from the shooting. He was living in Stuttgart at the time and participated in a blockade of one of the conservative-media's biggest printing houses, physically blocking the building along with other protestors so that the newspaper couldn't be printed.

During the years after Rudi's shooting, Joschka became a core figure in the student movement. First he moved from sleepy Stuttgart up to Frankfurt, where the counterculture movement was particularly active. He befriended Daniel Cohn-Bendit (the future leader of the French Greens), who was a French student leader who had become stranded in Germany after being banned from returning to France due to his activism. Joschka often worked behind the scenes while Cohn-Bendit became the figure in the spotlight.

In 1971 they, along with other student radicals, engaged in an ambitious project to infiltrate a German car manufacturing facility in order to radicalize the labourers for the coming communist revolution. The students went undercover and got themselves hired as assembly line workers, where they began spreading literature and trying to whip the labourers into a revolutionist frenzy. They did eventually manage to start a riot, but when they tried to pass control to the regular labourers it fizzled out. Their mission failed, and the students were honestly happy when they were discovered and fired from their gruelling factory jobs. They were relieved to be able return to their lives as anti-conforming unemployed intellectuals. As a 1973 *Revolutionary Struggle* release recounted,

> Now we've been at Opel (the auto manufacturer) for so long, doing factory work and busting our asses. And? Why—for what—where to—to accomplish what? It's simply bull-headed to rail on against the number of hours worked when most workers would gladly take on even more . . . those workers who absolutely must have a color TV, a new car or bedroom, simply will not take a stand against overtime. (Hockenos, 2008, page 102)

In the early 1970s, the student protest movement took a sharp, violent turn. Rudi Dutschke had been a powerful pacifist voice within the movement, his imperative being "violence against things: yes. Violence against people: no." With him incapacitated and the movement further radicalized by the attempted assassination, groups began to turn to violence as a means for furthering their political goals. One of most notorious groups gained the name "The Red Army Faction," and began employing pipe bombs and Molotov cocktails, and later on kidnappings and assassinations. Their embrace of violence spilled over into the rest of the radical-left movement. Squatters began to defend themselves when police arrived to try to clear them out of their hippie co-op living situations. While police had been using clubs and violence on protesters for years, the protesters had never answered with violence of their own. In the early 1970s, they began to fight back, clubbing the police in return and pelting them with rocks, bottles, and eventually Molotovs.

Joschka wasn't involved with the most violent elements of the radical-left, but he skirted the line closely. He was known as a go-between for the violent radicals and the more regular counterculture groups. He also was involved in several of the brawls with police as they tried to clear out the squats. One of these events was caught on film, and the picture of a young Joschka Fischer beating a downed police officer with a club would resurface much later in his life when he became Foreign Minister of Germany.

In 1976, Joschka was arrested. This was the first time since he was a teenager that he'd been caught and imprisoned. During a protest that turned violent, a group of protesters had thrown a Molotov into a police car and nearly killed the officer within. The police rounded up a big group of unrelated protesters, including Joschka, knowing that they probably didn't have the culprits but wanting to put some fear into the revolutionaries. Joschka was released only a day later when the police admitted that he had nothing to do with the Molotov, but the attempt to scare them straight had worked on Joschka. We don't know what exactly spurred his epiphany, but he came out of his one-day jail stint with a new, radically different message.

Changing Course

The very next day after his release, Joschka gave a speech to ten thousand assembled revolutionaries in Frankfurt in which he denounced violence and implored the revolutionaries to give up the violent struggle and return to attempts for peaceful change. He was able to capture the attention of thousands of radical left-wing activists because he had such high street credibility within the militant left that they were willing to listen. Richard Herding, a fellow student revolutionary, described the feelings of those listening,

> Only someone like Fischer, with his street credentials, could have made a speech like that and be listened to by the spectrum of the Frankfurt left. It wasn't like

some pacifist was telling us we should be peaceful. No one would have listened. But it was Fischer. (Hockenos, 2008, page 122)

Many radicals listened to Joschka. He succeeded in pulling back a large contingent of the revolutionary left from the brink. And he did it just in time. Later that year, one of the worst events of the "Red Decade" came to pass. Two West Germans from the *Revolutionary Cell* group teamed up with a group from the Palestinian Liberation Organization and hijacked an Israeli airliner. They threatened the passengers with death unless the Israeli government would release a group of their imprisoned German and Palestinian comrades. The airliner was stormed by Israeli commandos and the hijackers were all killed in the operation. German society was shocked.

Joschka had already began pulling his comrades away from their support of the militant left, but the event still shook him and the entire radical left-wing of German society. Joschka withdrew himself from the public and from politics and revolution. He got a job as a taxi driver and kept a low profile for the next few years, trying to come to terms with the last whirlwind decade of his life.

Connecting with the Greens

At the same time as the Revolutionary Struggle (as Joschka's student revolution group was known) was active and gaining in notoriety, other grassroots civic groups around Germany were forming. The 1970s featured an explosion of local activist groups of all sorts. Anti-nuclear protest groups, feminist advocacy groups, environmentalist groups, anti-war pacifists: thousands of them sprung up across the country. These myriad groups would eventually come together at the end of the 1970s and form the German Green party as a way to bring their concerns into the legislature itself instead of just fighting against politicians from the outside.

Joschka wasn't involved in the founding of the Greens, but some of his friends from the Revolutionary Struggle days had joined up early on. He watched the movement grow and contest its first few elections, but was skeptical of whether it was worth supporting. During his years out of the spotlight as a taxi driver he occasionally would write opinion columns in left-wing newspapers. In one column he tore into the Greens, stating that they were nothing like the groups that he had been a part of, and that his contemporaries shouldn't be bothering with them. But he also admitted that he didn't have any better ideas of how to achieve the goals that they had sought together.

In 1981, he broke out of his funk, and also changed his mind and decided that the Green project was worth supporting. He joined up as a member and threw himself enthusiastically into the new party. He rose through the ranks very quickly due to his high profile and his organizational skills. His friend and co-revolutionary Dany Cohn-Bendit had been involved with the Greens from the beginning, but didn't want to actually do the work of an elected official, so he convinced

CHAPTER 7 – THE GREEN GOVERNMENTS OF GERMANY

Joschka to put his name forward instead. Fischer was elected as part of the very first group of Greens into the federal Bundestag in 1983.

From the very beginning of his time with the Greens, Joschka wanted the Greens to be a party that joined the other, big parties in coalitions. He was a leader of the *realo* wing within the party, wanting the Greens to be a competent political force that worked towards societal and economic change piece-by-piece. His attempted revolution in the '60s and '70s had shown him that you couldn't force a societal overhaul onto people who weren't ready for it.

His years as a taxi driver had also shown him how much of a bubble he'd been living in, and how different the lives and opinions of other Germans were from his own. He'd learned his lessons the hard way, and was now a passionate advocate for trying something different than just protest and revolution. This put him at odds with fellow Greens like Petra Kelly, who wanted the Greens to be an anti-party of fundamental opposition.

In 1985, he finished his first stint in the Bundestag. The early Greens were so insistent that power inevitably would corrupt politicians that they went even farther than imposing term limits on themselves. The earliest Greens wouldn't even let their parliamentarians *finish* a single term. They insisted that halfway through a term, all of the elected Greens had to rotate out for a replacement group that were waiting in the wings. So Joschka only spent two years in the federal legislature before his time was up.

In the state of Hesse, where Joschka was based, the local Greens had just formalized an agreement with the SPD to form the first red–green coalition (as covered earlier). Fischer was selected as their choice to be the world's first Green minister. He was a controversial choice to some, because he was set to become Minister of the Environment, but he didn't come from the environmental wing of the party, nor did he know much about environmental issues. He was picked because he was an ardent coalition-builder and had the leadership skills and organizational ability to do the job.

Even the event of his swearing-in as a government minister caused waves. Fischer showed up to the ceremony in white Nike sneakers, blue jeans, and a thrift store jacket. No German minister had ever been sworn-in in anything less than a full suit and tie. Industry in Frankfurt and Hesse was terrified of the incoming Green minister. Many of the existing laws on pollution were already loosely enforced, and Greens were sure to change that and to introduce even stricter regulations. Large industrial companies mused about relocating out of the state, and conservative newspapers printed (untrue) stories claiming that companies were already fleeing.

When the Chernobyl nuclear power plant melted down during the middle of Joschka's term as minister he was thrown even further into the German media spotlight. "What did Germany's only Green Minister have to say about this?" asked the media. The Hessian Greens pulled out of the governing coalition shortly thereafter in protest.

As covered in Chapter 3, the German Greens fell apart during German unification. As the party put itself back together early '90s, Joschka Fischer was one of the leading voices pushing the Greens in a new, less oppositional direction. The *fundi/realo* split was largely resolved during these years, with the *realos* declaring victory. The Greens reformed and became a party that could be trusted to work constructively with other parties (although at this point they were only seriously considering coalitions with the SPD). Joschka pushed the Greens to set their sights on the highest of political goals: a coalition in the federal government.

Abandoning many of their efforts to be a "leader-less" party that avoided cults of personality, the Greens accepted in the '90s that Joschka Fischer's personal popularity and recognition among German voters was their best chance at gaining a spot in government. From the early '90s until they joined government in 1998, Joschka was presented as a "Minister-in-waiting," and by the time he was made Minister for Foreign Affairs he was one of the most well known and most popular politicians in all of the country.

When Joschka was sworn in for his federal ministership, he was no longer the long-haired, jeans-wearing youth that had been sworn in as Hessian minister almost fifteen years prior. Nor were the Greens themselves the brand-new counterculture party of the radical opposition. Both were aged and matured. Joschka was now a middle-aged man with glasses and greying hair, looking nothing like the rough-and-tumble athletic hippie youth that he used to be. He took his federal oaths in a suit and tie, spectacles on his nose, sneakers nowhere to be seen.

"In order to change society you have to change yourself, and in order to change yourself you have to change society."

(Fritz Teufel, co-founder of Kommune I)

THE RED-GREEN COALITION

The SPD and the Greens had let the German voters know before the election that they intended to form a coalition government after the election if possible. However, as is usual in German politics, the two parties didn't engage in any formal coalition talks until after the vote. Neither party knew what the voters would opt for in the election. The SPD could have wound up with a majority on its own, or the two parties might have needed a third party in the coalition to reach a majority.

The results of the election informed the parties of what level of power each coalition partner could expect. The SPD had achieved a dominant 41 percent of the vote, whereas the Greens had finished with just under 7 percent. The Greens knew that they were the junior partner, and that they were the junior by far. With a fraction of the voter support of their larger partner they wouldn't be able to push for any of their more radical and transformative ideas. They were going to have to fight within their partnership for each of their policy proposals, and they would have to compromise and accept defeat often.

But the opportunity of being in government was extremely important for the party. For the first time on the federal stage they could demonstrate to Germans that Greens could be trusted to govern competently. They could demonstrate that their policy ideas could actually work, and that they would be good for the country. Then, at a later date, maybe they would be able to push some of their bigger ideas into reality.

There are some definite concrete wins that the German Greens can point to from their terms in government. The Greens had been given the Environment Ministry (predictably) and their renewable energies legislation was fantastically successful. The government began offering tax breaks, incentives, and investments in all forms of renewable energy. It had an immediate impact, and Germany's use of renewables grew quickly. Other countries have since adopted the same policies that the German Greens introduced, and replicated their success.

Also, the measures proved successful in ways that the Greens hadn't even fully anticipated. By 2005, *Friends of the Earth Germany* estimated that the renewable energy sector investments had generated over 130,000 new jobs. In the 1998 election that brought the Greens and SPD to power, job-creation was the absolute top-of-mind issue for voters, with a staggering 90 percent of voters in polls marking it as their top concern. The Greens had planned to leave the job-creation goal to their SPD partners, but their renewable energy investments wound up being a very helpful contributor.

The Greens also managed to enact a carbon tax on the nation's polluters, another campaign promise. This proved to be a major fight for the party, as their SPD partners were not initially in favour of the added tax on polluting industries, and obviously the industry was also not in favour. Environment Minister Jürgen Trittin fought long and hard and finally built the support for the tax, which was immediately successful in reducing carbon emissions. The Greens had wanted the revenue from the tax to go into renewable energy research, but the SPD wrangled it away from them and instead agreed to the proposal only as long as the revenue went into the country's social security system. They'd made big promises on pensions, and the carbon tax revenue was a convenient way to pay for it.

The one environmental fight that the Greens didn't succeed wildly at was the country's nuclear program. As the party was born out of the anti-nuclear movement, they had long promised that their goal was a total dismantling of Germany's nuclear program. But they were still alone as a party on this goal, and their much larger partner wasn't giving any ground. In the end they managed to negotiate a plan in which Germany would build no more nuclear facilities, but that current facilities would be allowed to serve out the rest of their "natural lifetimes," which gave the denuclearization of Germany an end-date of 2030.

This fight was mostly lost by the Greens because cancelling nuclear contracts early would have meant the government would have had to pay massive reparation damages to the energy companies because of the lost revenue on their investments. The cost of cancelling the contracts would have been staggering. Still, the anti-nuclear contingent of the Greens' grassroots was furious at their party for capitulating to the industry. Many supporters walked away from the party over the perceived surrender.

CHAPTER 7 – THE GREEN GOVERNMENTS OF GERMANY

One of the proudest moments for the Greens was the passage of a Green-led law to legalize same-sex partnerships. The Greens had wanted to give LGBT Germans full legal marriage-equality, but had to settle for a "domestic partnership" law as has been seen in most countries as a predecessor to full legal equality. Support wasn't present among the other parties for full equality, at least not yet. Germany wouldn't fully legalize same-sex marriage until 2017, but the measures enacted by the Greens in 2001 were the first step.

A Green goal that experienced partial success was a reforming of Germany's citizenship laws. Prior to the Greens' time in government, German citizenship was directly tied to German ethnicity. Refugees from other countries with German heritage were able to sail through obtaining their citizenship, but non-ethnic Germans who were born in Germany still had an extremely difficult time obtaining full citizenship rights.

Germany had been a multi-ethnic country since after the war when scores of "guest workers" had been invited into the country, and for a long time the Greens had wanted to liberalize Germany's immigration and citizenship laws to grant full status to people who came to Germany and lived their entire lives there. The Greens managed to push through a number of measures to relax the extreme requirements for citizenship, although the laws didn't go as far as the Greens had wanted. It was a compromise, and a partial win for Green policy goals.

In government, the Greens also experienced their share of challenging, transformative experiences. There was one event, beginning merely days after the election, that challenged the Greens like no other.

A Crisis of Ideology

For most of the '90s, the European country of Yugoslavia had been embroiled in a civil war. In 1995, units of the Bosnian Serb Army marched into the city of Srebrenica and massacred over eight thousand Bosnian Muslims in a clear case of ethnic cleansing. The massacre was labelled as a genocide. In Germany, the Greens were watching, and were appalled. The Greens were a pacifist movement in post-Nazi Germany, and their rallying cry was "never again war, never again Auschwitz." These two statements defined the Greens' worldview. Never again would they sanction Germany engaging in war, and never again would they allow a genocide as had been perpetrated in World War Two.

But the massacre in Srebrenica, on Germany's doorstep, shocked many Greens into realizing that they couldn't hold both ideals simultaneously. Germany and the other countries of Europe had the ability to step in and prevent further massacres in Yugoslavia. But in doing so they would violate their directive of "never again war." Though if they refused, and Germany sat and watched, then they would violate "never again Auschwitz."

The debate within the Greens became a firestorm. Pacifist hardliners argued that Germany should never, under any circumstances, march their military into a foreign country. Others argued that they had a responsibility to come to the aid of neighbours who were being slaughtered, if they were able. They argued that Yugoslavia was an exceptional case.

Joschka Fischer was one of the main leaders of the pro-interventionist wing of the Greens during the mid '90s. He published opinion pieces to the party's members urging them to support an intervention for peacekeeping reasons. In a vote by party members in late 1995, 60 percent of Green delegates voted against Germany joining the NATO-led (North Atlantic Treaty Organization) peacekeeping force in Bosnia. Despite this overall failure for the pro-interventionists, they still saw it as a partial victory. In the past, even 40 percent supporting military action would have been unheard of. Green member opinion was moving, albeit slowly.

Only days after the 1998 election, another crisis appeared. The SPD and the Greens were still deep in their coalition negotiations, and Helmut Kohl of the CDU remained acting Chancellor of Germany until the new government was agreed upon and sworn in. But the civil war in Yugoslavia wasn't going to wait for the new government to finish its inter-party negotiations. Led by President Bill Clinton in Washington, NATO wanted to begin aerial bombardment of Yugoslav President Slobodan Milosevic's army in Kosovo before another Srebrenica massacre occurred. Germany's NATO allies, especially the United States, wanted Germany's support.

The problem was that Yugoslavia was not a NATO country, nor was it engaged in war with a NATO country. NATO was not defending itself. It instead would be launching an attack on a sovereign country. International law required the alliance to go to the United Nations in order to get an authorization from the international community for military action. However, the alliance couldn't do this, as both Russia and China sat on the permanent UN Security Council, and would veto any attempt by NATO to get a mandate for action. They did not want NATO in Yugoslavia. Therefore, what NATO was proposing was an illegal, unilateral military action. The moral argument was that it was doing so in order to avoid a humanitarian catastrophe, but it was still a non-UN approved illegal invasion.

The German Greens were already opposed to the existence of NATO. Their position was that Germany should withdraw from NATO entirely. Many of them saw the organization, and America, as an imperial power that was imposing itself unwanted on other countries and trying to act as a worldwide police force. The German Greens believed deeply in the legitimacy of the UN as a body for diplomacy but barely felt comfortable with military action *with* a UN mandate, let alone *without*. But now Germany was being asked to ignore the UN and to join NATO in an illegal military strike.

Chancellor Kohl immediately recalled the old Bundestag's members for a special session, in which a majority voted for German participation in the NATO action. A majority of the elected

CHAPTER 7 – THE GREEN GOVERNMENTS OF GERMANY

Greens even voted in favour. But in Kosovo, Milosevic backed down at the last minute, and the military action by NATO and Germany was postponed temporarily. The threat worked.

Many among the Greens' grassroots were furious at their leadership. Fischer took up the job as Foreign Minister days later, and immediately had to deal with a party base that was in an uproar over an issue that his ministry was responsible for. For the next year, debate raged within the party over what the Green position should be. Meanwhile, Fischer ran around doing the job of Foreign Minister, flying to Belgrade in Yugoslavia to negotiate directly with Milosevic to try to diffuse the situation. Fischer alternated between trying to halt a war in Europe with trying to keep his own party together over the issue.

In 1999, at a special meeting of the Greens called to discuss and vote on the military question, Fischer was in attendance along with the rest of the Green leadership team. Despite the presence of heavy security meant to protect the politicians, the meeting began with a group of anarchist peace protesters breaking through the security cordon. One protestor threw a paint-filled balloon on stage, hitting Fischer directly in the face and covering him with red paint. Fischer's doctor later identified that the balloon had caused him to burst an eardrum, but Fischer ignored the pain in order to give a speech to the gathered delegates, urging them to support him and his policies. At the end of the day, he was successful. The delegates voted with a majority in favour of supporting NATO military action to avoid catastrophe in Kosovo.

It was thus under the direction of a Green Foreign Minister, backed by the membership of the pacifist Die Grüne, that Germany engaged in its first military action abroad since the end of World War Two. For the first time in fifty years, Germany sent troops abroad in a military capacity, directly engaging in combat.

The country only sent a handful of planes, mostly as a show of solidarity with the United States, who provided the bulk of the airstrike capacity. Joschka Fischer then led the creation of a plan to de-escalate the conflict by allowing the United Nations to take over administration of Kosovo from Yugoslavia until the conflict died down. As the United Nations effort would include Milosevic's ally Russia, he agreed. Greater humanitarian catastrophe was avoided. The incident brought Germany into the international arena as a foreign policy power, a country that could be counted on as a mediator and a source of diplomatic strength. It was a complete realignment of Germany's role in Europe, and in the world.

9/11 – An Even Greater Challenge

Fischer himself became the most popular politician in the German Republic, even more so than the Chancellor. With his heightened popularity came increased attacks from his political opponents. It was during the later years of his first term in government that the opposition managed to dig up a series of photographs from Fischer's squatting years in which he can be clearly seen in a brawl with a riot-gear clad police officer. Fischer is visible standing over the downed officer, gloved fist raised and ready to hit the officer.

Fischer weathered the storm. Part of Fischer's appeal to the German public was that he was not a born-and-raised politician. He came from a different background. He wasn't from high society; he wasn't a stodgy old member of the political class. His rough background had served him well, and he acknowledged it when responding to the photographs,

> Yes, I was a militant. That's my biography. That's me, Joschka Fischer. Without my biography today I'd be someone else and I wouldn't like that . . . We squatted houses, and when the police raided them we defended ourselves. We threw stones. We got beat up by the cops but we dished it out too. I've never covered that up. (Hockenos, 2008, page 287)

In 2001, an even greater crisis than Kosovo befell the red–green alliance. On September 11th, 2001, Joschka Fischer watched on television the coverage of the attack on the World Trade Center towers in New York City. Besides the obvious humanitarian tragedy, Fischer knew that this would become a dire political situation for the coalition. The NATO alliance was built on the understanding that if one of its members was attacked then all of the members were expected to come to that country's aid. America had just been attacked and would be expecting Germany to jump to its side. That evening, Chancellor Schröder stood before news cameras with Fischer at his side, and declared that Germany would "stand shoulder to shoulder with the US and show unlimited solidarity."

What "unlimited solidarity" meant immediately reignited the controversy within the Greens, and within German society. The Greens had narrowly approved military action in Yugoslavia to prevent a humanitarian crisis. Now they were likely going to be asked to support a US led war against an enemy that had directly attacked a NATO ally.

Sure enough, the US requested the support of Germany in its October 2001 invasion of Afghanistan. Germany's army is deployed only with the approval of the Bundestag, meaning that Schröder and Fischer couldn't send in the military without the approval of the members of the legislature. The great worry was that not enough of the Green parliamentarians would vote to support the invasion. Schröder could easily count on the MPs from the CDU and FDP to support the move and could thus expect a clear majority in favour. But if his own partner in government wasn't in support then it would mean an end to the red–green coalition. The government couldn't survive a disagreement on such a critical matter.

In order to force a decision from the Greens, Schröder undertook an incredible measure. He combined the vote on military action with a vote of confidence on his own government as a whole. The CDU and FDP, always eager for a new election in which they could hope to defeat their rivals and gain control of government, were set to vote against the measure even though they approved of the military action section. So if the Greens wanted to continue the red–green coalition they would have to approve the deployment of the German army to Afghanistan. Schröder declared that the government participation and the military invasion were a package deal.

The vote passed by a single vote. Several of the Green MPs voted against the resolution, but just barely enough approved that the government held. Germany joined the US in its invasion of Afghanistan.

The German Greens and the American Republicans

Germany's relationship with the US during the years of the Bush government were difficult, especially for the Green-controlled Foreign Ministry.

From 1998–2000, Joschka Fischer's counterpart in the Clinton government was Secretary of State Madeleine Albright, who he reportedly got along well with. Bill Clinton had been active in the Vietnam War protests, just as Joschka had been, so the two men had a shared history and a good relationship as well. The relationship wasn't nearly as warm with George W. Bush and his Secretary of State Colin Powell. Whereas the Clinton government had been tepidly supportive of climate-change action, the Bush government was outright hostile. Bush himself even denied the reality of man-made climate change, a position that couldn't have been farther from the Greens'.

And the interventionist war-hawk attitude of the Bush Republicans was the exact worldview that the Greens had been created to oppose. The Socialist-Green government of Germany did not have much in common with the new Republican administration of the United States, who they were now cooperating closer with than ever due to the state of war after the September 11th attacks.

Between the attack on America in 2001 and the next German federal election in 2002, the United States was speculating wildly about what form its new "war on terror" would take. European foreign policy departments were trying to guess which of the many countries on the US's new "axis of evil" they would be asked by the United States to help invade next. The United States mused about military action against targets such as Iraq, Iran, Pakistan, and North Korea. The suggestion that Germany would be expected to join the US on these endeavours was deeply unpopular in Germany, and the governing red–green alliance was struggling in the pre-election polls as voters were unsure of where the government stood.

There was also zero chance that the Greens would vote to support military action in these countries, none of which had been directly involved in the attack on America in September of 2001. The vote to support military action in Afghanistan had passed by only the slimmest margins. Foreign policy and the looming wars were major campaign issues during Germany's 2002 election, and when Chancellor Schröder came out confidently to declare that a red–green coalition would not be supporting a hypothetical US invasion of Iraq their lagging poll numbers turned around.

In the 2002 German election, the red–green coalition was re-elected to a second term in government. The SPD actually lost two percentage points in the popular vote, but their Green colleagues gained a nearly equal amount. The CDU increased its share of the vote, nearly matching the SPD's results (the totals were within a few thousand of each other). But the strength of the Greens as the third biggest party in the Bundestag provided just enough votes for the coalition to retain its majority. A major German newspaper ran a political cartoon after the election showing Joschka Fischer running across a finish line, holding a relaxing Gerhard Schröder in his arms.

The Second Governing Term, and the Collapse of the SPD

During the second term of the red–green coalition, the two parties continued to pursue their goals much as they had in the first. But now Joschka Fischer was much busier managing the relationship with an angry and frustrated United States. The coalition had won its re-election by promising to keep Germany out of further American wars, and George W. Bush knew it and was not pleased with his German partners.

Although the Greens continued to chalk up wins in their ministries during their second term, their SPD partners were floundering. The SPD had made a declaration in 1998 that if they don't turn unemployment around during their term that voters should not re-elect them, and unfortunately they were failing in their own challenge. Unemployment, especially in the states of the former East Germany, was getting worse. The SPD was pushing through reform packages on welfare and social assistance in order to balance budgets that were not popular among SPD supporters.

Germany has a bicameral parliament, meaning that there's an upper house and a lower house, similar to in Canada, the United States, and many other countries. Only the lower house, the Bundestag, is directly elected in Germany. The upper house, the Bundesrat, is made up of delegates from each of Germany's sixteen states as chosen by those states' governments. Any legislation passed by the lower house has to be approved by the upper house, so if the governing party in the Bundestag starts losing control of the state legislatures it can make their job in government much more difficult.

By 2005, this is what had happened for the SPD. While the Greens were consistently improving their own results in the state elections, the SPD was losing control to the CDU. In 2005, a year before the next election was scheduled, Chancellor Schröder made a decision.

CHAPTER 7 – THE GREEN GOVERNMENTS OF GERMANY

The Chancellor called for an early election by introducing a motion of non-confidence in his own government. He wanted an early election to try to revitalize the SPD brand, rather than suffer through another year of paralyzed government.

Joschka Fischer was still one of the most popular politicians in Germany at the time. But his second term had put him through the ringer. Fischer's foreign policy department staff didn't actually like him very much; it turns out that he wasn't a very enjoyable boss to work for. Many accused him of becoming full of himself, and full of hubris.

He'd also been knocked around by a controversy known as "the visa affair," in which a Green-led loosening of tourist visa requirements had inadvertently been abused by criminals to engage in human trafficking of sex workers into the country. The department had been slow to catch on to what was happening, and the Greens were blamed for overlooking the abuses, and for introducing the legislation that led to it in the first place.

Nonetheless, Joschka and the Greens hit the campaign trail in 2005 with the same enthusiasm that they had in previous elections, toting all the successes of the Greens during their time in government. Voters delivered the Greens virtually the same result as in 2002, with only a mild drop of half a percent in the vote. However their coalition partners were thoroughly routed. Both the SPD and the CDU took hits to their vote share, although the SPD's hit was much more significant. Voters fled the traditional large parties in favour of the few smaller parties. But even with their losses the CDU came out of the election as the overall vote winner.

Lose Some, Win Some

Despite the Greens staying static in the vote share they were nonetheless bumped from their position of third party, landing in the fifth party spot. Both the smaller FDP and Die Linke chalked up big wins at the expense of the usually dominant parties. Voters hadn't abandoned the Greens, but neither had the party managed to attract any of the voters that were abandoning the big two parties.

The electoral math after the election meant that the red–green coalition was no more. They didn't have the numbers to continue as a majority. As the leader of the biggest party, Angela Merkel of the CDU was given the Chancellorship and charged with building a new coalition. The CDU and the SPD wound up creating a grand coalition of their own, with the SPD demoted from its place as government leader and thus becoming the junior partner of the CDU. The Greens were booted out, and left in opposition alongside the other two smaller parties.

Fischer retired from politics after the coalition ended, and took a job as a professor at Princeton University. Jürgen Trittin and Renate Künast, Fischer's Green cabinet colleagues, remained involved and took up leadership positions as the Greens moved back into opposition.

But the Greens had now shown that they were competent in government at the highest level in German politics. After their stint in the federal government the Greens went on to join other governing coalitions at the state level, and in 2011 they were even elected for the first time to *lead* a state government coalition. In late 2018, polls began to show that the Greens would likely eclipse the SPD and become the second biggest party in the next federal election (scheduled for 2021). It's currently considered likely that the German Greens will once again participate in a governing coalition following that election.

CHAPTER 8

THE CONSERVATIVE GREENS

"The earth, the kind and equal mother of all ought not to be monopolized to foster the pride and luxury of any men."

(Edmund Burke, widely considered the philosophical founder of modern conservatism, from Reflections on the Revolution in France, *1792)*

THE CONSERVATIVE GREENS

2011 marked the beginning of a new chapter in German politics. For the first time the Green Party became the second biggest party after a state election. This was a big deal.

Since the end of the war, the SPD (Social Democratic Party) and the CDU (Christian Democratic Union or Christian Social Union in Bavaria) had simply alternated the position of biggest and second biggest party between themselves in state elections. The only exceptions were in the states of former East Germany, in which the Left Party (the successor to East Germany's communist party) did very well. But 2011 was the first time in western Germany that one of the big two parties had lost their spot on top. A quarter of voters in the southwest state of Baden-Württemberg cast their votes for the Greens—a higher number than had been seen in any state or federal election thus far. The Greens could no longer be called a minor-party; they were now very much a major party.

In addition, the governing CDU had been knocked out of its dominant place in a state considered to be one of Germany's most conservative, and most CDU-safe. With a combined majority of elected members, the Greens and the SPD were going to be able to form a coalition of their own to supplant the conservative government. But this wouldn't be yet another red–green coalition. For the first time a German state would be attempting a *green-red* coalition.

The Landtag of Baden-Württemberg was about to select long-time Green Winfried Kretschmann as its new Minister President, the first Green in such a post in German history. By 2016 he would lead the Greens to a re-election in which they became the *biggest* party in the state, this time governing in a green–black coalition. And Kretschmann himself would become the most popular Minister President in the entirety of Germany.

The experience of leading a coalition government is very difficult than being the junior partner in a coalition. Despite having been in government many times, this meant that the German Greens were once again going to have to learn some new lessons, possibly the hard way. But no party was as ready and prepared for the job as the Baden-Württemberg Greens.

Winfried Kretschmann: The Statesman

The environment that both Joschka Fischer and Winfried Kretschmann were born into was remarkably similar. Both men were born in 1948, both in the region of Baden-Württemberg, and both as the children of recently arrived ethnic German refugees from other parts of Europe. While Fischer's family came from foreign Hungary, Kretschmann's family came from a region of former Prussia called Warmia. The territory had been absorbed by Germany after World War One, and in the aftermath of World War Two it was ceded to Poland. Like in Hungary, the ethnic Germans in the area were expelled back to the core German territories.

Winfried Kretschmann's family were deeply Catholic, and while Fischer was sent to an elite *gymnasium*, Kretschmann was sent to a Catholic boarding school. There he suffered under the violent teaching techniques of Catholic schools in Germany in the 1940s, where beatings of students were a regular occurrence. The experience there caused him to develop a deep skepticism of authority and a disgust for any forms of power based on fear and violence.

Unlike Joschka Fischer who dropped out to school to become a homeless intellectual, Kretschmann stuck with his studies. He eventually escaped from Catholic school and qualified for university. West Germany at the time had compulsory military service for young men (something that Joschka had dodged), and Kretschmann completed it without complaint before moving on to study biology, chemistry, and ethics at the University of Hohenheim in Stuttgart.

During his time as a student Kretschmann became interested in the same radical student movement as Fischer, as did many of the Germans growing up as part of the '68 generation. He became involved in the Communist League of West Germany, reading and following the works of Mao Zedong.

But it didn't stick. Kretschmann was looking for something different than the status quo of Germany, and communist and left-wing radical thinking was the most obvious "something else" on offer. But it wasn't what he wanted. He only remained involved in the movement for a few years in the mid-1970s before moving on with his search, and later in his career he would describe his time there as "political misapprehension" and as a "fundamental political error." It was a youthful flirtation with the radical left before he was drawn back to his conservative roots.

His first job after post-secondary school was as a teacher, but he only remained in the job for a few years. He was still looking for something different in German politics, and in 1979 he was part of the founding group of the Greens in the state of Baden-Württemberg.

Conservatives in the Green Movement

When the Greens were first founded in Germany, they were intended to be a group that was neither left-wing nor right-wing, and were instead something beyond the traditional political spectrum. They welcomed members who came from either the traditionally understood political left or right, and the organizers made a point of trying to keep the Greens from trending too far to one side. Greens still feel this way about themselves and often describe themselves as centrist or as transcending the left/right dichotomy, but the reality of politics is that a party is defined by the people who join and build it. In the early 1980s, the new Green party attracted far more members from the political left than from the right, and it quickly swung farther to the left than many had wanted.

Herbert Gruhl was one the highest-profile conservative-Greens involved in the founding of the party. From 1969 until the party's founding, he was an elected member of the Bundestag from the CDU, but he had always been somewhat at odds with the rest of the party over his focus on environmental issues. He served as the party's environmental spokesperson until 1975, when he published a book entitled *"Ein Planet wird geplündert – Die Schreckensbilanz unserer Politik (A Planet is Plundered - A Record of our Policies)"* in which he put forward many of the arguments that would become the founding ideologies of the Greens. The CDU leadership remained mute on the book, and afterwards began to remove him from party positions and take him out of the spotlight.

Gruhl resigned from the party in 1978 and went on to be one of the founders of the Greens, alongside Kretschmann and many other conservative-minded members. In the first few years of the Greens' existence Gruhl struggled with the direction of the party, as it was flooded with members who wanted to pull the group towards the traditional left. He only lasted until 1982, when he resigned and formed yet another party called the *Ökologisch-Demokratische Partei (ÖDP)*, the Ecological Democratic Party, so that conservative ecologists could have a home away from the increasingly left-dominated Greens. To this day, the party still exists but has never had anywhere near the level of success as the German Greens. They currently have no members elected to any of the state or federal governments in Germany, and their only elected member is a single MEP in the European Parliament.

While Gruhl and many other traditionally conservative thought-leaders left the Greens early on, others like Winfried Kretschmann remained. In 1983, Kretschmann and a group of leading Greens from the conservative side of the party gathered and formed a group called the *Ökolibertäre*, the EcoLiberals. They began publishing their ideas, which were centred around German philosophies of conservative stewardship and protection of the land, ecological humanism, and the religious ideal of preservation of God's creation. Their publications were densely philosophical and had little effect on the public, but they allowed conservative leaders within the Greens to sort out and work through the philosophical underpinnings of their beliefs.

The EcoLiberals only met and worked together as an organized group for a few years before they disbanded and melded into other groups within the Greens. In particular, they became driving forces within the *realo* wing of the party that wanted the Greens to offer practical governance solutions rather than just exist as a protest party. Kretschmann remained the most determined and long-lasting Green member from the group.

Kretschmann was an elected member of the Landtag of Baden-Württemberg from 1980–1982, and then a city councillor in the Stuttgart suburb of Esslingen from 1982-1984. When Joschka Fischer became the first Green Minister in Hesse, Kretschmann moved up north to become a spokesperson for Fischer's short-lived environment ministry. In 1988, he was re-elected back into the Landtag in Baden-Württemberg, where he has remained ever since. In 1996 he became the chairman of the Committee on the Environment in the parliament and in 2002 he took over as leader of the state party.

The Green Party of Baden-Württemberg has always been a bastion of the *realo* wing of the party. Whereas local Greens in other parts of the country (and the world) have been content with remaining as an opposition party that pushes the government on issues they care about, the Baden-Württemberg branch of the party instead always aspired to be a governing party. They've put great care into making sure that any policy proposals that they make and campaign on are realistic, practical, and achievable.

When you're an opposition party you can demand anything, but when you're in government your hands are often tied as to what's actually possible to implement. The Baden-Württemberg Greens wanted to make sure that they would actually be able to implement every promise that they made. This rankles some Green supporters who want the party to be more aggressive and urgent, but appeals to others who appreciate practical and workable solutions over idealism.

Kretschmann led the party in the election of 2006, in which the Greens made solid gains in popular support and moved from being the fourth biggest party into the third-party spot. But it wasn't until 2011 when Winfried Kretschmann, then sixty-three years old, was finally acknowledged by German voters and became the first Green Minister President in German history.

CHAPTER 8 – THE CONSERVATIVE GREENS

Becoming Government Leaders

I wanted to have a firsthand look at the kind of place that would elect a Green party into office as its biggest party, and to understand what kind of changes the Greens there would have had to undergo to reach such a broad level of support. So, in the summer of 2018 I travelled to Stuttgart, the capital of the state of Baden-Württemberg. This was a city with a Green Party Mayor, the biggest city in a state with a Green Party state government. This level of Green political dominance is still very rare.

Stuttgart itself is home to over six hundred thousand people, while the metropolitan area surrounding the city is made up of over five million. The metropolitan area is the fourth largest in Germany and consistently makes it into the top twenty-five in lists ranking cities worldwide by quality-of-life. The state of Baden-Württemberg, in the southwest of the country, is both Germany's third largest state by area and third largest by population. Nearly eleven million people live in an area a bit bigger than Vancouver Island.

Upon arriving in Stuttgart by bus I noted that it's not at all what you might expect from a city with the distinction of having both a Green Mayor and Green state government. It looks much like any other German capital city: a mixture of old and new, with modern high-tech buildings alongside old stone pre-war structures and facades; tight small streets interspersed with attempts to introduce new high-capacity roads; lots of people from many walks of life busily making their way about.

You might expect a Green governed city to be flush with green spaces, trees and parks on every corner. Unlike my home city of Vancouver, this was definitely not the case in Stuttgart. The city is dominated by concrete and stone, with even the parks having little in the way of trees and grass. It struck me not as a city that obviously *had* a Green government, but rather as one that obviously *needed* a Green government.

Nor was the state of Baden-Württemberg a perfect green paradise. I'd taken the bus from Luxembourg and as we passed into the state one of the first things that I noticed were the unmistakable smokestacks of a coal power plant just outside the city of Heilbronn. Later I visited the nearby town of Esslingen, home to one of the state's only remaining medieval town squares, and found a beautiful town with cobblestone roads, a river running through the middle, and surrounded by vineyards on the hills. But when I climbed up the walls of the old castle to look out across the town, I could see yet another coal power plant on the edge of town. They were everywhere I looked.

Folks in Stuttgart chuckled when I said I had come there to see an example of a Green city, and told me that I should have gone to Freiburg instead. In the far southwest of the state, buried behind the famous Black Forest, is the state's true green city—or so I was told. When Kretschmann took over as state party leader in 2002, it was because the previous leader had been elected Mayor of Freiburg (the first Green mayor of a major German city), and the city has now had a Green government for as long as most people can remember. The city has won numerous awards over the years for its efforts to become an "eco-city."

But turning a tourism-focused, sleepy, medium-sized city of two hundred thousand people green is a far easier task than transforming a bustling metropolitan industrial region of almost six million.

Stuttgart itself isn't much of a tourist city—at least not for those visiting Germany from abroad. It doesn't cater to tourists with the same enthusiasm as Munich or Berlin, or other German towns that make a point of trying to attract foreign tourism. The main tourist draws in the city itself are the Porsche and Mercedes museums, which betray what makes the state's economy tick. Baden-Württemberg, and Stuttgart in particular, is the industrial manufacturing powerhouse of Germany, and the auto industry dominates the state's economy.

This makes the state a bizarre choice for the country's first Green-led government. How could the Greens, who normally preach the values of post-materialism, sustainability, connection to the natural world, and responsibility for the planet succeed in a place defined by its reliance on polluting industry and gas-belching automobiles?

How to Elect Greens in Car Country

Up until 2011, the Greens in the state had been no more popular than in most other German states. They scored between 5 and 12 percent of the vote in the various elections since the party's founding. Then in 2011, a combination of events came together and propelled the Greens and their leader Winfried Kretschmann over the edge and into power.

As I stepped off the bus at the main train station in Stuttgart, I immediately spotted a ramshackle little structure in front of the station: a tent covering a group of tables, themselves covered in literature and signs. A tired-looking German couple were seated inside, waiting to talk to anyone who came by. The tent was plastered with signs: the words "Stuttgart 21" with a big red slash through them.

"Stuttgart 21" is the name of a project to replace the main aboveground train station in downtown Stuttgart with a new underground transit hub. After having been in the planning stages for many years, the project was approved and financed in 2006, with the Greens in parliament being the only party to vote against the proposal. The "21" in the name was the planned completion-date of 2021. Upon approval, the plan was immediately hit with fierce protests.

The size of the protests against Stuttgart 21 strike me as a quintessentially German phenomenon. I went to speak to the retired German man at the protest booth outside the train station, and he attempted in limited English to explain to me the opposition to the project. Much of the

CHAPTER 8 – THE CONSERVATIVE GREENS

reasoning was very detailed criticism of the engineering of the station itself. In Canada, you'd be hard-pressed to find a protest surrounding such a detailed and complex engineering issue. But to the Germans I spoke to it seemed perfectly natural.

The man in the tent criticized railway junction bottlenecks, issues with track inclination and safety since the station was going to be below-ground, contamination of water deposits below the city, difficulty of access and added energy costs from being underground, instability due to the mineral composition of the ground below the city, as well as overrun costs and the lack of civic engagement around the project. The project was also causing a massive disruption to the historic city centre of Stuttgart, and the huge amounts of money being poured into it meant other infrastructure projects in the state were left in limbo.

All in all, "Stuttgart 21" was a perfect example of man fighting against nature, trying to force through a massive engineering project in an area where the very ground itself wouldn't allow for it. The project's opponents wanted the government to admit that not every proposed project is just an engineering problem waiting to be solved by human determination and tons of cash, and that sometimes you should accept when nature just won't allow it. The gentleman in the tent said that he'd been manning this booth for eight years, since the height of the protests in 2010, still fighting the good fight.

Upon approving the project back in 2006, the governing CDU/FDP alliance had massively underestimated the opposition. The government was inundated with petitions, and demonstrations became a weekly occurrence. On September 30th, 2010, the protests came to a head when over a thousand protesters descended on the Castle Garden in Stuttgart and began blocking roads and climbing up into trees. Police were called in, who used batons, water cannons, and pepper spray to attempt to disperse the protesters. Hundreds of people were injured, some very seriously. One protester, an elderly engineer named Dietrich Wagner, was hit in the eyes with a water cannon, which almost permanently blinded him. The photos of the bloody-eyed protester that appeared in the next day's newspapers became a symbol for the protesters, who started wearing red paint under their eyes as a show of support for Wagner. The whole event gained the ominous name "Black Thursday."

The next day, over fifty thousand people appeared at a follow-up protest. The protest against the rail station had now also become one against police brutality and government refusal to respect and engage with those that opposed their plans. This would sound familiar to the protesters who formed the United Tasmania Group back in 1972.

When the next state election arrived in 2011, the governing CDU-FDP coalition was not in good shape. The protests and the reaction by the government had mobilized support against the alliance, and voters who had previously supported the parties were abandoning them. Both parties suffered the worst election results in their histories.

However, the other "natural governing party" of German politics, the SPD, was not likely to pick up any of the voters fleeing the centre-right coalition. The CDU had long been massively popular in Baden-Württemberg, as the state is known as one of Germany's most conservative. Conservative German voters looking elsewhere than the CDU and FDP didn't want to move their votes over to the socialists. As well, the SPD was still in favour of the Stuttgart 21 project, as it had been when it voted for the legislation to approve it. The only party left for voters who both disapproved of the project and didn't want an SPD-led government was the Greens.

An additional (but depressing) boost for the Greens was the accident at the Fukushima nuclear power plant in Japan a week before the election. Greens tend to get a noticeable bump in their voter support whenever an ecological disaster happens before an election. People tend to forget about ecological issues when they're not immediately confronted with them, and will be jolted back into taking them seriously when a disaster occurs abroad.

Results of the 2011 Baden-Württemberg State Election
138 seats to be elected for the Landtag
70 seats needed for a majority

	CDU	GREEN PARTY	SPD	FDP
Vote %	39%	24.1%	23.1%	5.3%
Seats	**60**	36	35	7
Change since 2006	-5.2%	**+12.4%**	-2.1%	-5.4%

The First Green-Led Government

In the 2011 election, the Greens doubled their share of the vote at the expense of every other party. Despite everything surrounding the Stuttgart 21 project and the protests, the CDU was still by far the most popular party in the state, but the haemorrhaging of votes from the party and its alliance partner meant that they no longer had the numbers to form a majority government. Meanwhile the Greens, now the second biggest party, and the SPD had enough seats in the parliament to form a coalition government of their own, if they wanted to.

CHAPTER 8 – THE CONSERVATIVE GREENS

Although the SPD was in favour of Stuttgart 21, they had stated that they'd be open to a popular referendum to settle the debate on the project. A government led by the Greens in partnership with the SPD, with a guaranteed referendum on Stuttgart 21, was as good as the project's opponents were going to get. Even with the boost to Green votes the anti-project parliamentarians were still outnumbered by the pro-project members.

The Greens had only edged out the SPD by an extremely narrow margin. The Greens held thirty-six of the seats in the new parliament, while the SPD held thirty-five. As the bigger party the Greens would be the senior partner and their candidate for Minister President (Winfried Kretschmann) would get the spot; however, their partnership would be an extremely even one due to the closeness in numbers. The parties sat down to hammer out a coalition agreement, and on the twelfth of May 2011, Green Party founder Winfried Kretschmann became Minister President to eleven million people in one of Germany's biggest industrial states, guiding an economy the size of Sweden's.

"Should the emancipation and secularization of the modern age, which began with a turning-away, not necessarily from God, but from a god who was the Father of men in heaven, end with an even more fateful repudiation of an Earth who was the mother of all living creatures under the sky?
The Earth is the very quintessence of the human condition, and earthly nature, for all we know, may be unique in the universe in providing human beings with a habitat in which they can move and breathe without effort and without artifice."

(Hannah Arendt, The Human Condition)

GREENS AS GOVERNMENT LEADERS

The first challenge for the Baden-Württemberg Greens was coming to an agreement on governance with their new SPD coalition partners. Greens in Germany have been in coalitions with the SPD dozens of times, but it had always been as a much smaller junior partner to the social democrats. That was the way the SPD liked it. The fact that they now had to be the junior partner to the Greens was difficult for the SPD to accept. It wasn't the natural order of things.

The Greens placated their partners by offering for them to have more total Ministries than the Greens, although the Greens held the office of Minister President and enough junior ministries to have a majority vote in the cabinet itself. This made the coalition a bit more palatable to the SPD, who still felt that they should be in charge because of their history and experience.

Although the Greens had served in governments and held Ministries many times before, the reality of leading a government was still very different. They'd never held the office of Minister President before, and it came with responsibilities that were new for the Greens. They were expected to manage the entirety of the coalition, which meant managing the relationship with their junior partner rather than being the ones managed. They were also expected to staff a number of departments that the Greens hadn't ever been responsible for, which meant finding qualified and capable bureaucrats.

Staffing is always a worry for Greens (or any party) entering government for the first time. When you inherit a department, it means you have to fill it with people who can carry out the tasks. If the party hasn't done the work beforehand to cultivate and recruit capable experts, then they may find themselves floundering without the expertise and manpower to do the things that they want to do. In the case of the Baden-Württemberg Greens, they had planned for this. Since they'd long been a party that aspired to governance, they'd made sure to develop a strong group of capable government staffers through the various city councils throughout the state that the Greens served on. Even still, the process wasn't without challenges and learning experiences for those Greens who found themselves newly responsible for government departments.

The Greens were also surprised to find allies already waiting within the civil service. The CDU had governed the state for an uninterrupted fifty-seven years and the Greens expected to find a bureaucracy that was CDU dominated from top to bottom. But within the staff of the various government departments were a number of people who had been patiently waiting for the chance to have a more progressive, more environmentalist government to work for, and they jumped at the chance when the Green-SPD coalition took over. Rather than the slash and burn that you sometimes see in the civil service when a new government takes over, the Greens made a point of developing a relationship with the existing bureaucracy. They knew that they'd need their expertise, since the Greens hadn't had the opportunity to develop it themselves.

Stuttgart 21

The next challenge for the Greens was what to do about the Stuttgart 21 project. They opposed it, but their coalition partners as well as the rest of the Landtag were still in support. As a party that valued practical, realistic solutions, the party had been very careful not to make an election promise that they would fully halt the project. They instead promised specifically that they would do everything that they could to stop it. They promised their effort—not their guaranteed success.

This is a lesson in the management of supporter expectations for any party looking to go into government. If you make an absolute promise to voters, then they will hold you to account if you fail. And they'd be right to, since it was a promise that you made. If instead you promise only your best effort, then it provides a way to explain yourself to voters if you fail.

The best that the Greens could do was to organize a referendum on the project. With the support of the SPD, a referendum was planned for later that year. The question was: "Do you approve of the government's decision to cancel the funding for Stuttgart 21?" A "yes" meant that the project would be cancelled. A "no" meant that it would go ahead as planned. The SPD agreed that the referendum would be binding. If a majority voted to stop the project, then they would accept the will of the people and change their position to match that of the Greens. The Greens agreed that if a majority voted to continue the project, that they would respect the decision and the matter would be closed.

The referendum was a clear victory for the "no" side, and thus the supporters of the project. Nearly 59 percent of the state voted for the project to continue as planned. In only a handful of jurisdictions did the majority vote to scrap the project (including Freiburg, the green city in the southwest). Even in Stuttgart itself, a majority voted to continue the construction, although it was a less strong majority than elsewhere.

This could have been disastrous for a government if they had staked their reputation on it as a clear campaign promise. When UK Prime Minister David Cameron allowed a referendum on the United Kingdom leaving the European Union, and then subsequently lost that referendum for the side he supported, he resigned in disgrace. But the Greens had been very careful in what they had promised. They had never promised success; they had only promised their best effort. It was now clear that the project was going to happen no matter how much of a fuss was put up by the Greens and by the project's opponents. Kretschmann made the case that the battle was lost, the case was closed, and it was time to move on.

Not everyone was happy to accept the result. To this day, there are still weekly protests in front of the train station, although they're now quite small. As far as the Green Party is aware, they didn't lose too many voters over their lack of success in cancelling the project. Some abandoned them, but many remained, in agreement that the party had done everything that it realistically could.

Some Stuttgart 21 opponents I talked to even had a specific piece of praise for the Green government: since they were opposed to the project, they were playing extreme hardball with the construction contractors. They are absolutely refusing to pay more for the construction than what was initially quoted and then allocated. And the contractors know that they won't be able to milk any more money out of the government since the Greens didn't want the project approved in the first place, unlike the CDU. If the contractors mess up and try to charge the government any more than was agreed upon, then the Greens are only too happy to pull the plug on the whole thing.

The Stuttgart 21 referendum could have turned the Green government into a flash in the pan, like the collapse of Bob Rae's NDP government in Ontario in 1995. Instead, the Greens had managed expectations well enough to avoid catastrophe over the issue. Rather than lose support in the next election, they'd actually increase their number of voters when 2016 arrived.

Other Challenges as Government Leaders

One area in which the Greens realized they needed to do better with voter expectations was in the public perception of the Green–Social Democrat coalition. Many voters in Canada consider the Canadian Greens and the NDP to be the most similar parties—a view cultivated by the NDP because they want to attract Green-leaning voters. Likewise, in Germany, most voters (especially Green voters) believed that the Greens and SPD were relatively similar, and would have no problem working together and getting things done. When the Greens took over leading government, they realized that this was nowhere near as true as the public believed.

The Greens repeatedly hit walls when trying to find agreement with their Social Democrat partners. Through hard work, they managed to find compromises and ways through their differences, but this didn't change the fact that the public *thought* that things would be moving *fast*. When change didn't happen quickly enough, some in the environmental movement began blaming the Greens, since they were the political face of environmental politics. Winfried Kretschmann was the Minister President now—why couldn't he just make things happen?

The BC Greens have experienced this too, in which groups that should be supporting the Greens instead turn on them when their elected members don't produce immediate results. The Greens in Baden-Württemberg needed the non-governmental organizations to be pressuring the SPD, as they were the ones blocking the progress on issues that the Greens already wholeheartedly supported. Instead, they faced backlash both from organizations and voters who wrongly expected that the coalition would be united on these issues, and thus blamed the Green government leaders for just dragging their heels.

The Green Transition

Many of the changes that the Greens wanted to make in Baden-Württemberg were massive structural problems that had been baked into the systems of the state through decades of CDU control. The whole post-war economy of the region was built around automobiles and coal and nuclear power, and these weren't things that could be just switched off at will. The Greens dove into the work, drafting legislation and regulations to transform the economy of the state into one that was sustainable and environmentally positive. But many transformations were going to take years, if not decades.

Streets in the cities had never been built in a way that allowed for increased bicycle or public transit infrastructure. Electric grids weren't powerful enough to deliver enough electricity to someone's house to allow them to transition to an electric car. The CDU had locked the state into energy contracts with dirty emitters, and renewable energy infrastructure didn't yet exist to replace them. A sustainable technology sector needed to be developed so that people transitioning away from emission-heavy manufacturing jobs had somewhere to go, instead of just the unemployment office.

In addition to these huge complicated problems, the Greens also found that there were plenty of small things that could be changed by a single directive from the government office, and that could have profound impact on people's lives.

CHAPTER 8 – THE CONSERVATIVE GREENS

One of the Green staffers at the *Landtag* (the state legislature) told me that before the Greens became the government, same-sex couples were able to enter a civil union (marriage equality was a federal issue that wouldn't be legalized until 2017), but that they couldn't go to the courthouse and get their license in the same way as a heterosexual couple. Instead, they had to visit the same office where people went to register their car. This was a fairly direct message to same-sex couples that their civil union was *not* the same as an actual marriage.

As soon as the Greens realized that they now had the power to change this with a quick stroke of a pen, they did so. Same-sex couples could immediately get their license or conduct a non-religious courthouse service in the same way as heterosexual couples, at the same office in the same place (although the underlying inequality of marriage vs. civil union still existed). The Greens kept looking for easy wins that they could achieve now that they had control of the bureaucracy.

The Road to Re-Election

As 2016 approached and the Baden-Württemberg Greens' first term as government leaders was ending, the party began to plan for their re-election campaign. They were proud of what they had achieved, but obviously needed many more years to finish what they had started. As they looked back at their record, and looked at polls of public opinion, they came to realize something. By far the most popular aspect of the Greens' time in government was the performance of Minister President Winfried Kretschmann himself.

The Green Minister President had become one of the most popular and respected politicians in all of Germany, both within his state and without. Kretschmann, a grandfatherly and statesman-like figure who enjoyed gardening, woodworking, and quoting the works of German philosopher Hannah Arendt, was the exact type of leader that the conservative German southwest traditionally liked. Not only did polls show that he had earned the approval of a majority of citizens of the state, but he was even more popular among CDU voters than *their own* candidate for Minister President, Guido Wolf.

But for Winfried Kretschmann to remain as the Minister President of Baden-Württemberg, the Greens would have continue as government leaders. Like Canada, the top government post goes to the leader of the party that forms government, and is not directly elected by voters. So, the Greens took a difficult and very un-Green decision in how they were going to frame their party's re-election campaign.

Many Greens that I spoke to in the state expressed their discomfort with the decision, including many that were in quite high-up positions in the party. The Greens decided to frame their campaign almost exclusively on the character and personality of their leader himself. This goes against the core identity of a lot of Greens, who in the 1980s were so opposed to the concept of individual power that they refused to let their MPs even finish a term, and specifically avoided having a leader at all. The Greens that I spoke to were mostly frustrated by the fact that focusing their campaign solely on Kretschmann actually *worked*. In fact, it worked extremely well—which is both a blessing and a frustration for Greens. Although they're happy that things worked out for them, they don't like that they were politically rewarded for going against one of their core ideals.

The slogan for the campaign in 2016 was "Vote Green for Kretschmann," and the message was "if you like the Minister President, then vote for Green candidates to keep him in his post." Billboards went up across the state featuring the smiling face of Kretschmann alongside the slogan. An extremely well-received television ad was produced featuring the leader. It began with a series of artfully done shots of Kretschmann in his workshop working by hand on a carpentry project. The Minister President's narration describes his vision for the state in calming and reassuring tones. He steps back to admire the piece of furniture he was working on, then puts down his tools and steps outside. Instantly he's out of his work clothes and in a professional suit. He confidently looks into the camera and states, "I am Winfried Kretschmann, your Minister President," and then steps into the back of a luxury Baden-Württemberg produced automobile, which drives off.

It's not at all what you would expect from a Green Party campaign ad, but it nicely illustrates the difference between the Greens in the southwest German state and Greens in many other parts of the world. The Baden-Württemberg Greens are most certainly not a protest party, not an anti-party, and not radicals. Instead, they're a party that frames their identity as stability and wisdom, sustainability and calm rationality—and as a merging of old traditions and artistry, and modern technology and forward-thinking industry.

The campaign worked. When the votes were counted in March of 2016, the Greens had eclipsed the CDU and become Baden-Württemberg's most popular party. No one had thought it possible for the partly rural, partly industrial, automobile capital of Germany to be the first to go Green dominant, but that was now the case.

However, the Greens now had a new challenge because their coalition partners (the SPD) had suffered a magnificent collapse in the election. The Greens had stated before the vote that they'd like to continue their green-red coalition for another four years, but the terrible result of their partner meant that that was no longer a possibility. This meant that they would either have to expand their coalition to include a third partner or drop the SPD altogether in favour of a coalition with the formerly dominant conservative CDU.

The Conservative Greens

For many Canadians, the idea of a coalition between Greens and conservatives sounds unthinkable. Our conservative movement in Canada is outwardly hostile to many of the values that motivate Greens. It's difficult to imagine the two parties finding common ground when many of their signature campaign promises are directly contradictory. But the situation is quite different in Germany.

The conservative movements of Canada and Germany have taken a very different path over the past forty years. Back when the Progressive Conservatives of Canada were the party of Brian Mulroney there was considerably more in common, but since the rise of the Reform Party of Canada and the Stephen Harper-led uniting of the Canadian conservative movements, the two countries have grown in different directions. While Canadian conservatism has largely embraced neo-liberalism and libertarianism, the German conservatives instead stuck with the old European ideas of Christian Democracy.

Different Types of Conservatism

The Christian Democratic Union (CDU) in Germany in particular has always had an interesting connection to environmental issues from a religious standpoint. American (and to an extent Canadian) religious conservatism often takes the stance that man could never truly destroy the environment because God would protect us from any action on our part that would imperil us. God put resources in the ground because He wanted us to use them, and therefore how could the actions of mere humans change the fundamental composition of the Creation that God left for us? This had led to religious conservatives in North America denying the reality of man-made climate change, since God would never allow it to be real.

On the other hand, many Christians in Germany see the natural world as something that God entrusted to humans to care for, and that there's a religious duty to protect the environment because it is God's Creation.

This difference in views over environmental issues is why Greens in Germany and Europe are often able to find ways to constructively work with conservative parties in coalitions—although this honestly surprises even some Greens. I spoke with a number of Greens in Germany, young millennials who weren't particularly religious. They admitted that they were surprised by how receptive conservatives can be to Green ideas if the messaging is just changed to put it into a religious stewardship-of-Creation frame. They would never have thought to frame it that way, since it wouldn't have resonated with them personally.

This is where Winfried Kretschmann excelled as a public figure. He wasn't a young radical (at least not anymore). Instead, he was an elder statesman, a pious Catholic, a respectable and traditional German grandfather. He resonated with young people because he talked about the environmental and social issues that they cared about, but he also resonated with Germany's older, conservative, and religious voters because he spoke to them in their own language. The Greens found that with Kretschmann they were able to grow their party to include a large number of conservative voters that didn't usually align themselves with the Green movement.

It also helped the Greens pick up conservative votes when Kretschmann came out publicly as a supporter of federal CDU leader, Chancellor Angela Merkel. Going somewhat against the stance of his federal Green cousins, he admitted that he "prays every day" for Merkel's health because he believed she was doing an admirable job holding the country together. In particular, he praised her handling of the refugee crisis, a contentious issue in German politics.

A Green-Black Coalition

Kretschmann's popularity among conservative was fortunate for the party, because when the votes were tallied up in 2016 it looked like the Greens were going to have to a form a coalition with the conservative CDU. They first approached the small FDP (the centrist free-market party) and asked them if they were interested in joining with the Greens and the SPD in a three-party coalition, but the FDP declined. This left the only viable option as the CDU.

In 2016, for the first time, the new Alternative for Germany party (AfD) had received enough votes to elect a small number of MPs in the state and all of the other parties wanted to stay as far away as possible from the party that they considered to be radical far-right neo-Nazis. A coalition between the conservative CDU and the AfD was unthinkable, even though both parties are considered "right-wing" and it would have allowed the CDU to be government leaders. Instead, both the Greens and the CDU knew that the best option for the state would be for them to choose to work together, and to exclude the AfD from any chance at power.

There were a few examples of black–green coalitions in German history, although they were much rarer than the red-green option. The idea of cooperation between Greens and conservatives went as far back as 1995, when a group of younger federal MPs from both parties began to meet to exchange ideas. The first meeting was at an Italian restaurant in Bonn, which led to the meeting being given the moniker of "the Pizza Connection," named after a famous Sicilian mafia drug ring in the United States. The name was given to the group by the Secretary-General of the CDU, who didn't like the idea of younger CDU members fraternizing with the Greens, and who threatened to keep a close eye on them.

The Greens and the CDU had worked together on city councils starting in the 1990s, but the first black–green coalition at the state level wasn't until 2008 in Hamburg. It was followed by

CHAPTER 8 – THE CONSERVATIVE GREENS

another in Hesse in 2013. There were only two examples, compared to the dozens of times that the Greens and the SPD had formed red–green coalitions.

Nevertheless, the Baden-Württemberg Greens and the CDU sat down and hammered out a policy book stating the goals of their new coalition government, which they then released to signal the start of the Greens' second term as government leaders. The Greens kept most of the same Ministry positions that they had held in their previous coalition, although now that they were a considerably bigger party than their partner they were able to flex their muscle a bit more and kept a few extra Ministries for themselves. In particular, they held onto the State Ministry, which was responsible for coordinating the affairs of the state with the federal government. In 2011, the Greens had left this portfolio to their SPD partners, an oversight that became frustrating and difficult to manage because of the mixed messages the federal government was getting from the Green government leaders and the SPD Minister.

The coalition with the conservatives produced a couple of key differences from the coalition with the Social Democrats. One interesting difference was in the expectations from the public. When the Greens were in a coalition with the SPD they encountered a misinformed public perception that the partnership would be an easy one, and that they should be moving forward on Green goals quickly and easily. Now that they were in a coalition with the conservatives that public perception was reversed.

Green voters believed that it would be a hard slog for the Greens to come to any agreements with their partner, and thus expectations were much lower and voters were much more forgiving. In reality, the Greens didn't find negotiating with the CDU much more difficult than negotiating with the SPD, but the difference in public perception gave them some much-appreciated breathing room.

The Greens also looked forward to working with the CDU because it meant that any legislation and government decisions that they crafted together would have real sticking power. Up until 2011, the state had an uninterrupted CDU-led government for its whole existence, and it would be foolish to assume that eventually the CDU wouldn't return to power as government leaders. When the Greens and the SPD were serving as government there was always a worry that anything that they achieved would just be undone by the CDU at a later date when they took over again. But by working alongside the CDU now the Greens were insulating their achievements from being undone by their partners in a later government. It would be unlikely for a future CDU government to claim that they were wrong in the past and to repeal their own work.

The Greens have had to compromise some of their positions now that they're working alongside the CDU. One particularly difficult concession for the Greens was to move closer to the CDU's position on refugees when trying to find a middle ground. The CDU in Germany has lost a large number of votes to the AfD in recent years, and they've been trying to earn them back by being stricter on immigration and refugee policy, the main policy area that motivates AfD voters. The push and pull between the Greens and CDU has landed the Baden-Württemberg Greens in a position that's considerably stricter than most of the other state and federal Green parties in the country, which has earned them some scorn from their Green colleagues.

As of this book's writing, the second term of the Greens as government leaders is at its halfway mark. Kretschmann and the party are still popular. Opinion polls have the Greens holding steady since the election, but neck-and-neck with their CDU partners. Interestingly, the far-left party Die Linke is up by a large amount in the polls. I spoke to a couple people in the state at an environmental issues street party who said that they were now supporting Die Linke because they felt the Greens had been pulled too far away from their radical routes due to their government position and collaboration with the conservatives. Die Linke is likely trying to pick away at the Greens' left-flank to draw away frustrated voters who still feel the Greens haven't been moving fast enough, or been progressive enough.

Kretschmann himself is now seventy years old, although he appears to be in great health. Those who know him personally describe him as having a remarkably relaxed attitude for someone in such a high position of power and in such a likely stressful job. Rumours are occasionally bandied about that he would make a great President of Germany although he hasn't publicly shown any interest in the job. For now he and the Greens have another two years of work leading the government of Baden-Württemberg and are hoping that they've set the Greens up to be a new political dynasty in the state. They aspire to be the new *volkspartie*: the natural governing party for all people.

CHAPTER 9

GREEN GOVERNANCE CHALLENGES AND MISTAKES

"The dilemma for policy makers is that the scope of change required for managing without growth is so great that no democratically elected government could implement the requisite policies without the broad-based consent of the electorate. Even talking about them could make a politician unelectable."

(Peter Victor, Canadian Ecological Economist; from Managing without Growth: Slower by Design, Not Disaster)

GREEN GOVERNANCE CHALLENGES AND MISTAKES

The Republic of Ireland and Sweden are two recent examples of when a Green Party underestimates how difficult the job will be. Looking back, most involved with the parties don't consider the decision to join government to be a mistake. However, most would also acknowledge that mistakes were made in the process. Their stories can serve as an example to Canadian Green supporters and politicians of what they need to be careful of if the opportunity arises for the Canadian Greens.

Germany is without a doubt the country where Greens have had the most success. But they've been at it for a long time, with plenty of mistakes along the way. In many other countries, the experience of Greens in governments is still new. The low-stakes first attempt for the German Greens in the state of Hesse did not go well. It took a couple tries before the German Greens and the other parties learned how to work together and how to have a constructive and positive relationship.

Germany's federal system also meant that there were smaller province-level governments in which the Greens could learn the art of governance with smaller stakes than being in a national government. Not every country has a federal system with state or province level governments though. In many cases, the Greens have made the large and difficult jump from a long-term opposition party to one with the responsibility of national government on their shoulders.

Every one of these Green parties can point to a number of positive contributions that they made during their time in government. Many initiatives wouldn't exist without them having had the power to push them through. But in many cases the Green voters weren't used to backing a party that was in a situation where it had to compromise on issues with other parties. Green voters haven't always been forgiving of their party when they see it fail to stick hard to its values.

The life of a party as a junior coalition partner is difficult. They have comparatively little leverage and are usually forced to compromise a lot more often than they fully get their way. That makes sense, of course. They're the junior partner because fewer people voted for them. It's fair to expect that they'd get less of what they want than their more popularly supported partner. But it still stings. And it's always a difficult learning process both for the party's elected politicians and for the party's supporters.

"How can we have infinite growth on a finite planet? It is a total illogicality. And we're the only party. Think about this. We're the only party that asks that question. Just at the time when our message is more relevant than ever we suffered our worst electoral defeat."

(John Gormley, former Leader of the Green Party of Ireland)

THE IRISH GREENS

The most infamous example of a Green party being punished by their voters after their term as a junior coalition partner is surely the example of Ireland. The Irish Greens made the extremely difficult decision to join a coalition with the dominant Fianna Fáil party in 2007. That year they had achieved their best-ever result in an election. In 2011, after four years as the junior partner in a governing coalition, they were completely wiped out, losing every one of their elected MPs.

The Dáil and the Taoiseach

Politics in the Republic of Ireland may seem confusing for those outside the country, although part of this is because the country uses a mix of English and the Irish language for their political terms. As well, since green is such an iconic colour for Ireland, three major parties all use the same colour as their official party colour (although they do at least use different shades).

For a long time, Ireland was one of many countries that is described as having a "two-and-a-half-party system," meaning that there were two large dominant parties and one smaller party. That era also ended in 2011, when both the Green Party and their senior coalition partner went down in flames and a number of previously small parties rose dramatically in popularity.

The two traditionally dominant parties in Ireland are the similar-sounding Fine Gael (meaning "Tribe of the Irish") and Fianna Fáil (meaning "Warriors of Destiny"). Both parties spun out of factions formed during Ireland's war for independence from Britain. Fine Gael began as the group supporting an agreement called the Anglo-Irish Treaty, whereas Fianna Fáil opposed the treaty. Both parties are described as being on the centre-right of the political spectrum, and both share a remarkable number of ideological and policy positions.

Despite looking somewhat indistinguishable to those viewing Irish politics from the outside, the parties remain at each other's throats even decades after Ireland's successful independence, largely due to long-lasting tribal loyalties. Jackie Healy-Ray, a politician associated with Fianna Fáil, famously said, "Them that know don't need to ask and them that ask will never know" when asked to describe the difference between the two parties. John Gormley, one of the Irish Greens, likes to tell a story in which he asked a couple of Fine Gael campaigners, "Can you tell me what the policy differences are between Fine Gael and Fianna Fáil?" To which he got the response, "I suppose there aren't any, but I think you'll find that in Fine Gael you find a better class of person."

The two parties dominate the right side of the political spectrum in Ireland. On the left there are a fractured group of parties, all of which are usually smaller than the ever-warring Fine Gael and Fianna Fáil. The Labour party is a classic social-democrat labour interest party, and is the "half" party that has often served as a coalition partner to one of the big two. There's also Sinn Fein, which is a left wing-party that campaigns for a united Ireland.

Various other left-wing parties occasionally pop up and then disappear or are merged into other parties after a few election cycles. And of course, there's the Green Party of Ireland.

Ireland also uses its own set of terms for the institutions and positions of the legislature, although they function similarly to other legislatures. The lower house of the legislature itself is called the Dáil Éireann (Dáil for short), and the position of Prime Minister is the Taoiseach (pronounced *tee-shukh*, where "kh" is the sound at the back of the throat in words such as the Scottish *loch*). Ireland also has a President, although the position is mostly ceremonial and holds very little power on its own. The Irish Senate likewise has little power, and is appointed similarly to the Senate in Canada.

Irish Greens Join the Government

In 2007, Fianna Fáil was seeking a fourth term as the government leader, following three successful elections. They succeeded, easily remaining the largest party in the Dáil after the election. However, they were still a few seats short of a majority, and so set about putting together a coalition. The Greens were surprised when incumbent Taoiseach Bertie Ahern approached the party with the offer of joining the government for the first time. Interestingly, Fianna Fáil didn't strictly need the Greens to build a majority. They had already recruited a bunch of independent TDs (Teachta Dála,

CHAPTER 9 – GREEN GOVERNANCE CHALLENGES AND MISTAKES

the Irish term for a member of the legislature) as well as the two members of the tiny Progressive Democrat party (which, despite what the name implies, are a free-market conservative party). It appeared that the Greens were being brought in to bolster the majority in case of defections from the Independents. Coalition negotiations began.

Results of the 2007 Irish Election
165 seats to be elected for the Dáil Éireann
84 seats needed for a majority

	FIANNA FÁIL	FINE GAEL	LABOUR PARTY	GREEN PARTY	SINN FEIN	PROGRESSIVE DEMOCRATS	INDEPENDENTS
Vote %	41.6%	27.3%	10.1%	4.7%	6.9%	2.7%	n/a
Seats	77	51	20	6	4	2	5

Prior to the election, the Greens had been very critical of the Fianna Fáil government, and the party's hope for the election was that Fianna Fáil would get the boot from voters and that the Greens could join into a coalition with one of the other parties. When the election returned Fianna Fáil as the strongest party by far, the Greens had to back off on their previous reluctance to consider a coalition with them. The voters had spoken, and if the Greens wanted a shot at government then this was the only viable option. Still, their comments before the election were brought up to criticize them, including a "Planet Bertie" speech by Green TD John Gormley at a pre-election event:

> On Planet Bertie [Ahern, the Taoiseach] you can sign blank cheques, because everyone does it apparently. On Planet Bertie you can spend the average industrial wage on make-up. On Planet Bertie you can save €50,000 without a bank account. And on Planet Bertie climate change doesn't exist... It is so strange and so alien to our sensibilities that it's a planet that we Greens would like to avoid. For let there be no doubt, we want Fianna Fáil and the PDs [Progressive Democrats] out of government. (Minihan, 2015, 21)

The Greens knew that they were walking a very fine line when they were considering accepting the offer from Fianna Fáil. Although their overall vote percentage in the election was their highest ever result, they'd still only elected six members, same as in the previous election.

Ireland uses a form of proportional representation called "single transferable vote," in which voters rank their preferences and elect three to five TDs per district. The Greens had barely held on to the six seats that they went into the election with, and were disappointed since pre-election polls had suggested they would do considerably better. The Greens also were in close contact with other Green parties around the world who had served as junior coalition partners in governments and who had been punished brutally by their voters for it. And on top of all that, Fianna Fáil's coalition partner from the previous election (the Progressive Democrats) had been almost eradicated after their term in government, which was of course why Fianna Fáil was searching for a new partner.

But the allure of actually being in government, of actually being able to enact some of their policies, was powerful. There's a saying in political circles, that "the worst day in government is better than the best day in opposition." Even if it's difficult being in government, you can at least say that you're accomplishing something. As an opposition party all you can do is loudly complain. Ciarán Cuffe, one of the Green TDs, posted online shortly after the election,

> Let's be clear. A deal with Fianna Fáil would be a deal with the devil. We would be spat out after five years, and decimated as a party. But… would it be worth it? Power is a many-faceted thing. (Minihan, 2015, page 32)

The Greens had never served in a government in Ireland before. One of the benefits of this for the party was that they'd never had to fully commit to a preference for Fianna Fáil or Fine Gael when it came to coalition building (the "Planet Bertie" speech was more about kicking out a long-term incumbent government). The party benefited from being able to draw its voters from those Irish who would otherwise have supported either of the big parties. By agreeing to a coalition with Fianna Fáil they'd be angering those of their supporters who wanted Fianna Fáil out of government at all costs.

Eventually the Greens did agree to join Fianna Fáil in a coalition. As a result of the negotiations, a policy book was created that outlined the goals and plans of the new coalition government, drawn from platform promises of each party. The Greens had to give up quite a few treasured policies, but had a number of their goals agreed to by their coalition partner. The energy policy of the new government mostly came out of the Green's election manifesto, as did a number of measures in the justice section. The Greens were actually fairly happy with Fianna Fáil's environmental promises, but were skeptical that the party would actually follow through on them once elected. Little was changed in the environmental program in the negotiations, and the Greens planned to just make sure that everything that was promised was actually implemented. Taxation and public health were probably the sections that the Greens were least happy with, but they felt they could live with the results.

CHAPTER 9 – GREEN GOVERNANCE CHALLENGES AND MISTAKES

In a meeting of Green party members to approve or reject the proposal the members voted an overwhelming 86 percent in favour of the Greens joining the government. Trevor Sargent, the leader of the Greens, did, however, resign his leadership. He had pledged before the election that he did not want to lead the Greens into a coalition with Fianna Fáil, although he accepted the will of the party when it decided that it wanted to do so. He remained a supportive party member and TD, but stepped aside so that a leader who was more enthusiastic about the coalition could take over. Fellow TD John Gormley was chosen as the new leader.

Learning the Ropes of Government

The Greens signed the coalition agreement and took their places alongside their new partners on the government benches in the Dáil. They'd also negotiated themselves two government ministries. John Gormley was going to be the Minister for the Environment, Heritage, and Local Government. Eamon Ryan would be the Minister for Communications, Energy, and Natural Resources. The environment ministry had been an obvious choice that Fianna Fáil gave up without a fight. The Greens went into the negotiations wanting the Ministry of Transportation, but Fianna Fáil wasn't willing to give it up. Surprisingly, they were offered the Ministry for Energy and Natural Resources instead, which the Greens were happy to accept. The two new Green Ministers set about learning the ropes of their new government jobs.

The first big challenge for the Greens in government had to do with Taoiseach Bertie Ahern himself. Ahern had served in the government's top role for eleven years, but got in trouble prior to the last election due to accusations that he'd taken money for political favours. An official investigation tribunal was underway, but the Greens had been critical of the Taoiseach and the weakness of the tribunal when they were an opposition party. Once in government alongside Ahern they had to tread carefully, and shifted their message to being supportive of the tribunal doing its work to discover the truth. The opposition parties accused the Greens of hypocrisy and having thrown away their morals for power.

Although the tribunal couldn't definitely link Ahern to favour payments, they also couldn't rule it out. Bertie Ahern resigned as Taoiseach one year into the government's mandate, and was replaced by Brian Cowen. Green leader John Gormley stood alongside Ahern when he made the public announcement that he was resigning, which was not a good look for the usually morally impeccable Greens. The wishy-washy handling of the episode by the Greens wasn't popular among the Irish public. Fine Gael leader Enda Kenny, criticized the Green TDs personally in the legislature,

> Last year Deputy Sargent, a man of impeccable standards and principles, sat on this side of the House as an admirable man who week after week rose to his feet to excoriate Fianna Fáil and the Taoiseach, in particular, for the lack of standards manifest in his taking of money. He now sits behind the Taoiseach, his mind utterly changed having been seduced by the attraction of power. (Minihan, 2015, page 46)

Despite their poor handling of the Taoiseach turnover, the Greens chalked up some wins in the first year of the Cowen government. In their own ministerial portfolios, the Green Ministers introduced plans to move Ireland further onto renewable energy, as well as introducing emissions-based motor taxes. The Green base was also pleased by an episode in which the Chinese Ambassador to Ireland stormed out of the Greens' annual convention over party criticism of Chinese human rights abuses in Tibet—although this caused more of a headache for Fianna Fáil, who held the Foreign Affairs ministry.

The Greens also began work on the Civil Partnership bill that they had fought hard for in the coalition negotiations. Like in Germany, the Irish Greens were in favour of full marriage equality for same-sex couples, but had to settle for a watered-down civil partnerships bill since both Fianna Fáil and Fine Gael were opposed to the full measure. The Greens settled for the weaker measure, knowing that it was at least was a step in the right direction, and that it later could be expanded. Their Green bill legalizing Civil Partnerships was passed in 2010.

After the Greens and Fianna Fáil were booted out of government in 2011 the next government took up the issue again. A popular referendum was announced and passed with 62 percent support. In 2015, the new government finished the job that the Irish Greens had started, and Ireland achieved full marriage equality for same-sex couples. The Greens still consider it proudly as one of their greatest achievements in government, and worth the pain that they went through.

Near the end of their first year in government, the Greens were doing well. They were polling at nearly double the support they had received in the previous election. But the honeymoon period would soon be over.

And Then It All Went Wrong

A financial crisis had been brewing in Ireland for some time, and not long into the Greens' first-ever government term it finally struck. This was late 2008, and the world was working its way through the financial repercussions set off by the subprime mortgage crisis in the United States. The Great Recession and the European Debt Crisis were looming on the horizon, and Irish banks were about to face a crisis of their own.

CHAPTER 9 – GREEN GOVERNANCE CHALLENGES AND MISTAKES

Since the early 1990s, Ireland had been in a period of massive economic growth. The trend was so significant that Ireland was referred to as the "Celtic tiger," named after the "four tigers," a group of Asian countries (Hong Kong, Singapore, South Korea, and Taiwan) that have been undergoing massive growth since they began rapidly industrializing in the 1960s. Ireland's growth put it on par with the rapidly growing countries of the developing world, which was an oddity for a western European country.

The causes of this growth are complex. A significant factor was Ireland's embrace of extremely low corporate tax rates and high investment subsidies, combined with the country's low wages and easy connection to Europe. The result was an influx of foreign companies moving their operations to Ireland, which in turn increased reliance on foreign energy and markets. That inflated the construction sector and property markets, increased wealth inequality, triggered a migration from rural areas to urban areas, increased immigration to Ireland, and sent Irish banks into a borrowing frenzy. The government used the added revenue to massively increase government spending in a number of sectors. Overall, it was a rapid and substantial altering of the Irish way of life.

Many good things came out of the period of rapid growth. Unemployment dropped, disposable income grew, infrastructure was modernized. But when times are good, people tend to think they're just going to continue on being good. Our growth-dependent economic system and cultural worship of growth means that when growth decreases, we panic. Rapid growth like Ireland had been experiencing couldn't last forever, let alone continue to increase. Many of the methods that we use to trigger a period of high growth contribute to an eventual crash, or a bursting of the bubble. It's known as a boom and bust cycle and is an accepted aspect of today's capitalist economies. By late 2008, the time for Ireland's bubble to burst had come.

For Greens, what was unfolding in Ireland was a classic "I told you so" situation. Greens remain critical of a growth-dependent economic system for precisely the reasons that Ireland was about to experience. An economy that requires growth to survive will inevitably try to chase as much growth as possible, and when that constant craving for more leads to an economic collapse, people's livelihoods can be ruined.

> As Greens, we question the value of what is presented as economic growth, and we reject the constant goal of achieving economic growth as being the keystone economic policy. For Greens, how growth is defined is flawed as any economic activity, no matter how negative, is seen as contributing to economic growth.
>
> For political reasons, we chose not to emphasise this in the 2007 election. It was a silence brought about by a fear of being misrepresented. Or economic proposals promoting positive activities would create short-term economic growth. In the longer term, our commitment to sustainability meant that the constant utilising of depleting resources was not possible and shouldn't be the cornerstone

of economic policy. For those whose support we sought, we believed it was understood where the Greens stood on such issues. (Boyle, 2012, page 26)

Greens had been criticizing the system for years. Since this was their first time in government, they had had no part in implementing the policies that had led to the collapse. But they *were* in government now, alongside the party that *was* responsible. This meant that they were about to share the blame, and they were going to be expected to fix things. As Green TD Eamon Ryan explains,

> We went into the Irish Bankers Federation as much as anything else because we realized we may be going into Government and they wanted to talk to us and we wanted to talk to them. We went in saying we thought that mortgage lending was completely out of hand and the lending was gone awry. We were told we didn't understand the markets, we didn't see the fundamentals. (Minihan, 2015, page 65)

None of the small caucus of six Green TDs were economists by training. They were educated and intelligent individuals, but their degrees were in fields such as urban planning, education, computer science, and business commerce. Stewardship of Ireland's national economy and the powerful Ministry of Finance were firmly in the hands of their senior coalition partner, Fianna Fáil. In fact, the new Taoiseach Brian Cowen had been the Minister of Finance in the Bertie Ahern government before moving into his new role. The new Minister of Finance was Brian Lenihan, a long-time Fianna Fáil stalwart who came from a political dynasty family (his father, brother, aunt, and grandfather had all been TDs.) Lenihan was a lawyer who had previously been the Minister for Justice, but he didn't have much in the way of economics training. No one doubted his intelligence and work ethic, but he went into the job without a strong background in the field.

Cowen, Lenihan, and the rest of Fianna Fáil quickly scrambled to try to address the imminent crash of Ireland's economy. Irish banks had been borrowing far more than they were ever going to be able to repay and were on the verge of failing, just like in the United States. Individual Irish citizens were terrified that their savings were going to be wiped out if the banks failed. Fianna Fáil began throwing together plans to bail out the banks using public funds.

How Banks Work, and How They Don't

The popular understanding of the banking system is simple. People store their hard-earned money in banks, keeping their money in the bank's accounts. The banks then use this money to lend out to others who are in need of loans. Those loans are repaid eventually with interest, part of which is kept by the bank and part of which is given to the individuals who've stored their money in the bank and allowed the banks to use their money to finance the loans. This is how we're told banks work, and it's how most people assume they work. But it's really *not* how it works at all.

In reality, banks are lending out magnitudes more money than they actually have stored in the bank at any time. This is known as "fractional-reserve banking," and what it means is that when you store money in a bank they are not actually required to keep that money available for you to withdraw at any given time. When you deposit money in a bank it's not as if it's sitting in a vault somewhere, waiting for you to retrieve it.

In fact, when you deposit money into a bank you don't legally own that money anymore. Instead what you own is a "promise" from the bank that it will give you real money on demand. In other words, by depositing your money in the bank you're actually giving the bank a loan. Some deposits can be "guaranteed" (insured) but earn much less. Regulators require banks to keep "some" cash reserves but mostly for day-to-day transactions. In a crunch, if you want to take "your" money out, somebody else has it, not the bank.

If everyone who had stored money in a bank decided to withdraw their savings simultaneously, the bank would not be able to accommodate them. This is known as a "bank run." And if the people and companies that the bank was loaning money out to fail to repay their loans then the bank is out of luck. So are any people who had stored their money in that bank, and now just own a "promise" that the bank can't fulfill. So, in our economic system, banks can't be allowed to fail, because the repercussions would be catastrophic for the people who'd trusted them to hold their money. That's what we mean when banks are called "too big to fail."

The Green goal of a steady-state economy doesn't include fractional-reserve banking. The book "Modernizing Money" by Andrew Jackson (the British economist, not the American President) and Ben Dyson outlines a broad series of banking reforms that would eliminate the problem of banks being "too big to fail," as well as the ability of banks to "create money" through lending. These ideas are often incorporated into steady-state economy models, which are popular among Greens. Organizations such as Positive Money and the International Movement for Monetary Reform work with countries to try to promote these ideas. A proposal in Switzerland even made it into a national referendum in 2018, called the "Swiss sovereign-money initiative." It was defeated, with 75 percent voting against it. Still, a quarter of the country was ready to embrace a complete re-ordering of the entire basis of the nation's economy, which is promising news for those that are trying to build support for such reforms.

In Ireland in 2008, the Greens didn't have the option of going back in time and moving Ireland onto a non-growth focused banking system that would be immune to the problems it now faced. Instead, they had a problem to fix that was looming right in front of them. As much as it went against their core ideology, the Greens knew that if they didn't support bailing out the banks that it was going to hit regular Irish citizens the hardest. The Greens looked long and hard at what Fianna Fáil was suggesting and in the end found that they had to agree. They didn't like it, but they saw no other choice.

Facing the Blame Anyway

They were immediately leapt upon both by the opposition parties in the Dáil and by their own party members. In the past, the Greens would have fought a plan to give away public money to huge banks that had screwed up. They would have seen it as rewarding the banks for bad behaviour. It was extremely frustrating for the Green TDs, as was remarked on by Paul Gogarty:

This is what really pisses me off about the Shinners [Sinn Fein] and the Socialist Workers [party]. If you did what they were saying you wouldn't have the rich paying for it, because the rich would have departed the country, you'd have the ordinary people paying for it. I mean it's a false argument. If they don't know that they're delusional. But then again, to be fair, we might have been saying the same thing and it's only from being in Government that you actually face reality and make a decision based on what's true rather than what you'd like it to be. (Minihan, 2015, page 70)

To make things even worse, Fianna Fáil's plan also involved cutting public spending in a number of sectors. Government spending was out of control, because in the midst of a growth boom the government had assumed that money was going to just keep rolling in, and so kept spending more and more. When it dried up they'd backed themselves into a corner, because any public spending that they cut was going to be massively unpopular.

The Greens accepted that spending needed to be reined in, but dug in their heels and negotiated on which sectors would be spared from the cuts. They threatened to walk away from government immediately if any cuts were leveraged on students, deciding that protecting the education system was going to be their top priority. Fianna Fáil agreed not to cut any of the student spending, but did go about cutting pay and benefits for teachers instead.

The Greens were facing calls from all sides to walk away from their governing coalition. Members of the party in city council elected positions, as well as one Senator, quit the party in protest. In local city council elections and European Union elections partway through the term the Greens were nearly wiped out. Opposition parties harangued the Greens in the Dail to take down the government, appealing to their sense of morals and responsibility. In one particular exchange, Green TD Paul Gogarty was being heckled during a Dáil debate, with attacks from the opposition directed at him personally for propping up the government. Addressing Labour Party Chief Whip Emmet Stagg, he snapped,

> With all due respect, in the most unparliamentary language, fuck you Deputy Stagg. Fuck you. (Minihan, 2015, page 90)

Without missing a breath, Gogarty immediately began apologizing and retracting his statement. He'd been caught in a moment of frustration, and immediately regretted his outburst. Nevertheless, the video of the moment went viral online within the day, and was deeply embarrassing for the

CHAPTER 9 – GREEN GOVERNANCE CHALLENGES AND MISTAKES

Greens, who had always presented themselves as champions of parliamentary respect and decency. They were barely a year into their first term in government, had been thrown into Ireland's worst economic crisis since the republic was founded, and were exhausted and fraying.

Despite the calls from party members and the opposition to drop their support of the government, the Green TDs held out. They believed that even though opposition parties were speaking out against their economic decisions now, that if those parties were in government they'd be supporting the exact same decisions. Loudly criticising the government was political theatre for the angry voting public. These measures were going to be passed no matter what, and it would be better for the Greens to remain involved rather than willingly take themselves out of the decision-making process.

While the economic crisis dominated most of the government's agenda, the Greens were still trying to advance their legislative agenda at the same time. To the Greens' surprise, one of these agenda items that the Greens considered relatively small became one of their biggest political headaches.

The Rural / Urban Divide

Animal welfare had long been part of the Green policy book. The party had a long list of issues that it wanted addressed during its government term. One of the issues that the Greens saw as low-hanging fruit was ending Ireland's stag hunt. The practice was an old tradition, and involved domestically bred deer being purposefully released and then chased down by hunters driving a pack of starved dogs. When the terrified deer was caught, it was bundled back into a truck and returned to its pasture to await the next hunt. The Greens saw the practice as barbaric and needlessly cruel. They weren't opposed to hunting for food, but this wasn't in any way a sustenance hunt. They saw it as pure animal cruelty.

The Green TDs pursued a legislative agenda to ban the stag hunt, as well as reforms around dog breeding of hunting dogs. Advocates for the traditional hunt rose up in revolt, with a passion that took the Greens by surprise. Five out of the six Green TDs were from urban districts, four of them in Dublin alone. They hadn't realized the extent to which they were seen as an "urban party" that was out of touch with rural Ireland. Angry rural protesters showed up at Green meetings and derided leader John Gormley as "a fella on a bicycle in Dublin telling you how to run a farm" while trying to pelt Green TDs with eggs.

Meanwhile, the Green party base considered the legislation being proposed by the TDs as the bare minimum of what they had hoped would be much broader reforms of Ireland's animal welfare laws. The rural protesters saw the stag hunt ban and dog breeding rules as the thin end of a wedge that would lead to more changes by the government to their way of life. Green TDs tried to deny this, but the protesters were right. This was supposed to be an easy, no-brainer start to the Greens' animal welfare agenda.

The Greens had support for their bills among the leadership of Fianna Fáil, but the issue soon began pitting rural and urban TDs against each other. Angry Fianna Fáil rural TDs opposed the goal of the bills in party meetings as they were being drafted, and introduced resolutions to attempt a "compromise," but that essentially made the bills worthless.

What was supposed to be a relatively minor piece of legislation exploded into a fight that rattled the already shaky coalition. The leadership of Fianna Fáil expended considerable effort trying to whip the votes of the rural backbenchers who didn't want to support the legislation, and who were publicly speaking out and opposing it. The government barely managed to pass its own bill, with multiple disgruntled rural TDs reluctantly voting in favour and only one outright refusing. Mattie McGrath, the sole defector, criticized the Greens,

> Green people want to close the zoo, want to stop horseracing, they want to stop the pussycat going after the mouse. (Minihan, 2015, page 163)

Green Senator Dan Boyle conspiratorially believed that the revolt from Fianna Fáil backbenchers was partially manufactured theatre by the party, in an attempt to weaken their own coalition partners. It was in Fianna Fáil's interest to keep the Greens from demanding too much of their senior partner, and he thinks the backbencher rebellion was encouraged (or at least tolerated) by the leadership because it put the Greens on the ropes.

Either way, the amount of attention on the issue overshadowed most of the Greens' other legislative efforts. Green opponents tried to present the issue as the only thing that Greens cared about, and the party as one that was seeking to dismantle Irish rural life. It became a continuing struggle for the party. Gogarty said,

> I think there's this narrative out there that the Greens are about taxing people and we care more about animals than people. It's not true and it's totally unfair… We are perplexed at how to communicate we are more interested in people than animals, and not in trying to tax people for the fun of it. (Minihan, 2015, page 170)

Meanwhile, the economic crisis was in full swing. In November of 2010, the Irish government formally applied to the European Union and the International Monetary Fund for a bailout package. In order to get the bailout money, they'd have to agree to a suite of brutal austerity measures. In doing so they would be giving over control of Ireland's economy to the EU and the IMF, and surrendering it from the hands of the politicians that the people of Ireland had elected.

The IMF is not known for making politically popular decisions when it comes in to manage an economic crisis, since they don't have to worry about electoral outcomes. Ireland was the second country to ask for the EU and IMF's help, after Greece had requested a similar bailout earlier that year. The austerity package that the EU and IMF had demanded be passed in Greece led to violent street protests during which three people were killed.

The Government's Collapse

On the morning of November 22nd, 2010, the Green Party of Ireland announced to the press that they would be leaving the government, and that they believed a new election should be scheduled for early next year. The Green TDs had been going back and forth on the decision for months, and the IMF bailout plan was the nail in the coalition's coffin. By surrendering the nation's economy to the international organization, the Irish government was clearly admitting that it had failed in its job. Green Leader John Gormley announced that the Greens would stay with the coalition long enough to present a four-year budget and secure the IMF funding, but then they believed Irish voters should be owed an election to decide the next steps for the country.

The decision to announce that they were leaving the government but still planning to remain for a budget vote confused and angered Irish voters. The Greens thought they were doing the responsible thing: letting voters know in advance of their intentions, but not immediately pulling out of government and causing a sudden political collapse. They wanted to ensure as much stability as possible in the transition. They hoped they would be thanked for their honesty and responsibility, but miscalculated how it would play with the public.

Unfortunately, the Greens didn't even manage to stick it through to the budget as they had planned. After they announced their departure, Fianna Fáil began to disintegrate. Brian Cowen attempted a cabinet reshuffle to revitalize Fianna Fáil before the election, but the public relations stunt was botched and he soon faced a rebellion from members of his own caucus and cabinet. Seeing that the government had become entirely dysfunctional, the Greens announced that they were withdrawing from government early. They joined with the opposition in order to negotiate a quick compromise budget between all the parties in the Dáil. The budget passed and an election was called immediately after.

Bad for the Party, Good for the Country

The Greens had known for a while that they were likely to be wiped out in the next election. At some point they had just accepted that it was probably inevitable, and had instead focused on trying to make the best decisions that they could for the country, rather than paying any mind to retaining their seats in the next election. Their goal was to get as much good legislation passed as they could manage, and to do as much with their individual ministries as possible before an election in which they expected that most of them would not be re-elected. John Gormley, leader of the Greens, released a statement that the party would be leaving overnment,

It has been a rare privilege to serve in government. It would of course have been preferable if our time in government had not coincided with the worst economic downturn in our nation's history. It has meant having to take the most difficult decisions that any party could have faced.

We did so it because it was the right thing to do.

I am proud of our many achievements in the areas of planning, renewable energy, energy standards of buildings, water conservation and other environmental areas. I'm proud that we gave rights to gay couples through civil partnership, and that we persisted in our belief that education and the arts should be protected. These two areas are absolutely vital for our economic recovery…

Our record is one of responsibility, reform, steadfastness, and creativity.

And these are the very characteristics that will enable this country to get back on a path of sustainable recovery, underpinned by a very different set of values. (Boyle, 2012, page 258)

Despite suspecting that they were in for an electoral wipeout, the party still campaigned vigorously in the ensuing election. They hoped that they might be able to barely hold on to two of their stronger seats, those held by Eamon Ryan and Trevor Sargent. But when the results came in they had lost all six.

Meanwhile, Fianna Fáil suffered the worst defeat of any Irish governing party in the history of the country. In 2007, they had won seventy-seven seats. In 2011, they were reduced to twenty. They were bumped from their position as largest party in the Dáil down to the third largest. Astoundingly, this was the first time since 1927 that they were not the legislature's largest party. The total collapse of the government had broken their eighty-four year run as Ireland's most popular party.

It's hard to say how much of the Greens' electoral wipeout was due to their own performance, and how much was due to Fianna Fáil taking the Greens down with them. It's possible that any other party that would have hitched itself to Fianna Fáil would have gone down in flames as well. The Greens had signed on to govern alongside the popular and well-tested Taoiseach Bertie Ahern, but had then found themselves part of the new Brian Cowen government soon after. Brian Cowen himself was described in the media leading up the election after the government's collapse as "the worst Taoiseach in the history of the state," and it's hard to see how any other party could have

CHAPTER 9 – GREEN GOVERNANCE CHALLENGES AND MISTAKES

survived serving alongside him. It's also possible that *any* governing party that found itself trying to navigate the post-2008 Irish economic crisis would have been doomed to failure.

At an event after the election as the Irish Greens began rebuilding, the guest speaker was a Swedish Green politician. She was there to talk through how the Swedish Greens rebuilt after an electoral wipeout. The experience isn't new for Greens, nor is it new for any party that's experienced being a junior coalition partner. Parties rarely come out of such a situation unscathed, and Greens in particular.

The Labour Party of Ireland, who became the junior partner to Fine Gael in the Irish government following the 2011 election experienced this as well. Just like the Greens had, they lost nearly all of their seats in the 2016 election after their term as junior coalition partner. In that election, the Greens rejoined the Dáil, winning two seats—the first step in their rebuilding. Eamon Ryan was the only one of the six government TDs who returned to office, along with newcomer Catherine Martin. Both seats were won in Dublin.

John Gormley, who had resigned as leader and was replaced by Eamon Ryan, gave a speech at the event in 2011, providing a post-mortem of their time in government and suggestions for the party going forward. During his speech he addressed the ironic result of the election: that the party that was most critical of the economic system that led to the banking crisis had the bad luck to join government just as the whole system imploded. And that they were thrown out of office while trying to fix a system that they had been claiming for decades was broken.

"You only talk about moving forward with the same bad ideas that got us into this mess, even when the only sensible thing to do is pull the emergency brake. You are not mature enough to tell it like it is. Even that burden you leave to us children…"

(Greta Thunberg, Swedish High School student, organizer of the School Strike for Climate)

THE SWEDISH GREENS

The Green Party of Baden-Württemberg in Germany is an example of a Green party that's done just about everything right during their time in government, and were rewarded by voters for it. The Green Party of Ireland surely had a few mistakes, but their downfall was more due to events and circumstances that were unavoidable for the party. Maybe they could have handled them better, or saved their own skin by backing out of government as soon as things got tough. They made their decisions based on what they thought was best for Ireland, even if it wasn't what was best for the party.

In Sweden, on the other hand, the Greens' struggle in government was mostly of their own making. In terms of policy achievements, they were actually quite successful, but they massively failed to manage the expectations of their voters (something that the Baden-Württemberg Greens excelled at). They lost control of the narrative of their time in government and had to spend the second half of their government term just trying to repair their relationship and trust with their voters.

The Swedish Scene

The Swedish political landscape is fairly easy to understand, although it may seem daunting at first. The Swedish parliament is called the Riksdag and it currently is made up of elected members from eight parties. However, those parties have grouped themselves into three separate alliances, meaning that someone looking to understand Swedish politics can easily divide their politics into three clear camps.

Following the 2014 election, Sweden was governed by the centre-left alliance. Prime Minister Stefan Löfven led the largest party in the bloc, the Social Democratic Party. In a coalition with the Social Democrats was the smaller Swedish Green Party, serving their first term in government. The third partner in the bloc, the Left Party, signed a confidence-and-supply agreement to support the government from the outside. They would receive no government Ministers, but could be counted on to vote alongside the alliance.

The centre-right opposition alliance to the Löfven government was led by the Moderate Party, alongside three smaller parties: the Christian Democrats, the Liberal Party, and the Centre Party.

Despite the uninspiring name, the Centre Party is quite interesting for those interested in Green politics. The party was founded in the early 1900s as The Farmer's League, and is an agrarian, liberal, and environmentalist party. The Swedish Greens are the "official" Green party of Sweden, as they're members of the Global Greens and are closely associated with other Greens around Europe and the world. However, the Centre party shares quite a few Green ideals, especially in terms of the environment, decentralization, equality, and immigration. In a way, Sweden has two "green" parties: one that's unabashedly left wing, and one that comes from the more eco-capitalist side of environmental politics. Both parties even use different shades of green as their official colour.

Then, finally, there are the Sweden Democrats (SD), who stand alone with no allies. The SD is by far the newest party in the Riksdag and is a nationalist and populist right-wing party in a similar vein as other nationalist movements in Europe such as the AfD in Germany, UKIP in the United Kingdom, and the Front National in France. Their roots come from the neo-Nazi movement, although the party has been working over the past years to moderate their image and distance themselves from their past. For instance, they've recently joined the same "Europarty" as the British Conservative Party when competing in European Union elections.

Nonetheless, in 2014, both the Swedish centre-left and centre-right alliances refused any form of political cooperation with the SD. They were to be purposefully kept isolated in the parliament.

CHAPTER 9 – GREEN GOVERNANCE CHALLENGES AND MISTAKES

Results of the 2014 Swedish Election
349 seats to be elected for the Riksdag
175 seats needed for a majority

	SOCIAL DEMOCRATIC (CENTRE-LEFT ALLIANCE)	MODERATE (CENTRE-RIGHT ALLIANCE)	SWEDEN DEMOCRATS	GREEN PARTY (CENTRE-LEFT ALLIANCE)	CENTRE (CENTRE-RIGHT ALLIANCE)	LEFT (CENTRE-LEFT ALLIANCE)	LIBERAL (CENTRE-RIGHT ALLIANCE)	CHRISTIAN DEMOCRATS (CENTRE-RIGHT ALLIANCE)
Vote %	31%	23.3%	12.9%	6.9%	6.6%	5.7%	5.4%	4.6%
Seats	113	84	49	25	22	21	19	16

A Series of Avoidable Mistakes

When the Baden-Württemberg Greens entered government, they did so as a party that had been preparing for it from their beginning. They had always existed as a party whose goal was to form a government and their platform and organization reflected it. They went to great effort to make sure everything that they promised was achievable and realistic and not just an ideological wish. They made sure that they had an army of capable bureaucrats waiting in the wings to staff up their departments. They managed the expectations of their members and supporters so that they didn't expect more of them than was going to be possible.

The mistake of the Swedish Greens is that they didn't prepare for their time in government like the Greens of Baden-Württemberg. The party had been around for just as long as their German cousins and had first entered the Swedish Parliament at the same time in the early 1980s. But they'd always been far more of a protest party, agitating and petitioning the government from the outside. Over the years, factions within the party pushed to reform the party into one that aspired to govern. By 2014, enough of the party had moved into this camp that they decided to give it a shot. They told the Social Democrats that they were interested in a coalition if the two parties had the numbers to form a government after an election.

The Swedish Greens had one of their best results in 2014, electing twenty-five MPs to the 349-seat Riksdag. Their coalition partner, the Social Democrats, elected 113, meaning that the Green MPs made up about 20 percent of the governing alliance. Correspondingly, they were given one-fifth of the government Ministries to manage, which added up to six portfolios. I spoke with one of the Green MPs elected in 2014, and he admitted that this was the party's first mistake.

The Greens in Sweden had never really moved past being seen as a one-issue party, because they'd been happy to stay as the small environmental protest party. In Germany and Canada and other places, the local Greens have struggled to break out of being seen as a one-issue party, but in Sweden that push had never been as strong.

Additional to the Ministry for Climate and the Environment, the Greens also took the Ministries for Housing, Culture and Democracy, Education, Consumer Affairs, and International Development. Democracy and International Development are a natural fit for most Green parties, but the Housing, Education, and Consumer Affairs ministries were new territory for the party. Swedish voters didn't think of the Greens when they thought about these issues. The party hadn't built the trust among voters that they'd be capable on these files. As well, they hadn't built up the staff pool to fill their new ministries with capable, experienced people.

By taking on six Ministries, the Swedish Greens spread themselves too thin. Had they focused only on a few of their core competencies they might have been able to impress the public more, and to win the battle of public perception. On the other hand, by taking on Ministries that weren't their usual focus, the Swedish Greens have now done a lot of the work that they should have focused on before the election: they've developed an internal group of experienced staff. Had they not taken on the extra ministries, they wouldn't have learned a lot of the lessons that they now have learned. They threw themselves in the deep end and learned the hard way.

Communicating their achievements outwards to the public was a big struggle for the party. News media tends to report when things go wrong; not when things go right. There was a lot of work done in their portfolios that the Greens are very proud of, especially in the education file. But since the public perception was that the Greens were inexperienced in these files, the mistakes were magnified and the successes glossed over. More than anything else, the time in government for the Greens was a learning experience in how to manage their relationship with the media and the public.

The Greens also learned the massive importance of making realistic promises before entering government. They also learned to be very careful about promises that are highly symbolic, and promises that have a hard "pass" or hard "fail" result and that don't have any middle ground. One MP that I spoke with estimated that the party had delivered on probably about 85 percent of the goals that they had laid out in their pre-election manifesto, which should have been considered a great result for a party that was serving as a junior coalition partner and didn't have the ability to ram through every one of its goals. However the remaining 15 percent of promises that went unfulfilled were highly symbolic to the membership, and held in far higher profile than the successes.

Voters Don't Like Complicated

In September of 2018, I was seated at a cafe in Brussels, speaking with Jakop Dalunde. He was elected in 2014 with the Swedish Greens, although in 2016 he swapped his seat in the Swedish Parliament for one in the European Parliament since he was more passionate about working on

CHAPTER 9 – GREEN GOVERNANCE CHALLENGES AND MISTAKES

pan-European issues. Tall, blonde, and clean cut, Jakop is only a couple years older than I am and we began our cafe meeting with a chat about my day job as a video game developer before moving on to politics. He's one of the passionate young Greens who've been trying to push his colleagues towards being a party of governance instead of a protest party. He got involved with politics after touring Palestinian refugee camps in the Middle East and seeing how different the lives of people in Sweden and other parts of the world are.

Jakop arrived at the meeting in good spirits, but got visibly frustrated and more stressed as we dug into the challenges that the Swedish Greens had faced. He recounted one issue in particular that was symbolic of their failure to recognize the difficulties of governing. It was obvious that this had been the source of endless headaches for many of the Greens working in the government.

Sweden has a national energy company called Vattenfall, owned by the state, that buys up energy projects and administers them on behalf of the Swedish people. Profits from these projects go into government coffers. Before the Greens were elected into the government, Vattenfall, on behalf of the previous government, had bought up a number of coal plants in Germany. Naturally, the Greens didn't want the government of Sweden to be in the business of operating coal plants since they believed that the dangers of climate change meant that society needed to divest itself from fossil fuels. And coal is, of course, one of the dirtiest of all fossil fuels.

The specific promise that the Greens made before the election was that they would halt the expansion of coal plants, and that they would stop the government from investing any more money in coal infrastructure. Sure enough, when they entered government, they made sure that the government's energy company was instructed not to invest in any more coal infrastructure.

But environmental groups and the Greens' voting base wanted more. They continued to pressure the Greens to shut down and dismantle the coal plants entirely. Environmental groups declared that anything but a total dismantling of the plants would be considered a failure.

The problem for the Greens was that it was actually impossible for them to mandate a dismantling of the government-owned coal plants. To begin with, they were just the junior partner to a larger party that didn't share all of the Green goals. Furthermore, Vattenfall was operating under a framework that stated that it had to treat all of its investments as commercial assets, and they were legally required to operate them for profit and to then return that profit to the Swedish people. Even if the Greens had a majority of MPs to vote to do so, they were unable to instruct the company to dismantle the coal plants. Doing so would amount to the destruction of publicly held assets, and was against the operating procedures of the government-owned company. In order to do so they'd have to open up the legislation that created the company in the first place, and change the entire way it was meant to operate.

Explaining this to voters and environmental groups was not an easy task. It's an issue of complicated government bureaucracy. To many it sounded like they were admitting failure.

Through great effort the Greens eventually managed to negotiate a compromise with their governing partners and the other parties in the legislature. They instructed Vattenfall to divest from the coal plants: to sell them off. The Greens in government considered this a big success, since it went beyond what they had originally promised and took a large amount of effort and deal-making on behalf of the party. But to many environmental groups and the supporters that they communicated their message to, it was even worse. Now the coal plants were out of the government's hands, and would *never* be dismantled by their new owners.

The whole issue spiralled out of control because of a lack of clarity from the Greens as to what was within their power to achieve. There was also a lack of understanding from environmental groups who were pressuring the party for things that it was never going to be able to deliver on. The Swedish Greens faced the same difficulty as the Greens in Canada and Germany and everywhere else, in which groups that *should* have been their allies instead became their greatest critics.

The lack of understanding of what the Greens were able to achieve in government was a running theme throughout their term. I haven't even mentioned yet that the coalition government of the centre-left alliance was in fact a *minority* government, making things even more difficult.

Requiring the Support of the Right

In 2014, the far-right Sweden Democrats elected forty-nine members to the Riksdag. This chunk of MPs meant that neither of the two other alliances had quite enough elected members to form a majority government. However, the Swedish parliament has a history of being considerably more collaborative than many other parliaments. Successful minority governments were common. Since the centre-left alliance was considerably bigger than the centre-right alliance, the centre-right alliance stepped back and allowed Stefan Löfven to become Prime Minister and to form government. The Sweden Democrats were the only party to vote against Löfven, breaking with the Swedish tradition of deferring to the largest alliance in order to allow for stable government.

Within the first year, the Sweden Democrats found another way to use their votes to throw the legislature into chaos, this time over the government's budget. It's not important to go into detail about what exactly happened, since it's a convoluted matter of legislative procedure and traditions. Simply put, it was another case of the new populist party breaking with tradition in order to try to gain recognition and influence for themselves. It forced the two mainstream alliances to work together even closer in order to prevent the Sweden Democrats from having any power in the legislature.

The end result was that the minority government could continue, the centre-right alliance could maintain their independence, and the ability of the Sweden Democrats to affect policy and

CHAPTER 9 – GREEN GOVERNANCE CHALLENGES AND MISTAKES

throw the system into chaos was curtailed. In return, the government had to agree to a number of compromises with the centre-right on a variety of issues.

For the Green Party, this complicated series of negotiations and deals meant that not only were they the smaller party in a coalition government, but they were also part of a minority government that required the support of the centre-right parties in the parliament in order to operate. It was an ultimate government of compromise, built in such a way to avoid the influence of the extremist elements of society.

Such a thing is only really possible under a system of proportional representation, in which an "extreme" party might elect members to parliament, but can then be kept isolated by the more moderate parties if their views are considered too radical. In a first-past-the-post system, the multiple parties would have collapsed down to a couple of "big-tent" parties, and the individual Sweden Democrat voters and activists would likely have instead joined one of these big tents and pushed it in their chosen direction, and possibly achieved a seat at the government table from inside the party. That's what we see both in Canada and to a greater extent in the United States.

Communicating to environmental groups and to their members that the Greens had limited ability to enact change was very difficult for the party. Anything they wanted to do could be stopped by the centre-right alliance if they considered it too radical. The solutions and proposals from the Greens had to be developed in such a way that they'd get approval across the broad majority of the political spectrum. For environmental groups and voters who wanted strong action immediately, this was a very hard sell.

A Matter of Optics

One of the lowest points for the Greens was the controversy and resignation of Mehmet Kaplan, one of the Green ministers. Kaplan was of Turkish origin, but his family immigrated to Sweden when he was eight years old. He'd been active within the Swedish Greens for decades, serving as an executive board member as far back as 2003, and was first elected with the Greens in 2006. In addition to his political activity with the Greens, he'd also been part of various Swedish Muslim organizations, including Swedish Muslims for Peace and Justice, which he helped found in 2008. The Greens have long considered him one of their strongest links to Sweden's Muslim population, helping to spread the Green message and values to the community. When he became the Minister for Housing in 2014, he was the first Muslim to serve as a Swedish government minister.

Muslims in Sweden have been growing as a demographic group since the late twentieth century. The growth has increased in recent years as Sweden has opened its borders to an unprecedented number of refugees from Syria and other Middle Eastern countries embroiled in civil wars. Sweden's refugee admittance policy is extremely liberal by comparison to other countries, and they welcome far more refugees as compared to their population than most other European countries.

The policy is controversial, and it's the primary motivating issue for the Sweden Democrats. As such, the Greens were proud that the first Muslim Minister came from their party. They hoped that Kaplan could both improve the perception of Muslim immigrants among Swedes, as well as help integrate the immigrants into Swedish society. He could be a shining example of a Muslim immigrant becoming intimately part of Swedish culture and politics. Instead, Kaplan may have accidentally achieved the opposite.

As part of his lifelong work with Sweden's Muslim community, Kaplan had always been willing to meet with anyone who wanted to speak with him. This included groups within the Muslim community that are considered "radical." As a founding member of Swedish Muslims for Peace and Justice, his goal was to preach his pacifist message to the whole of the community, and the ones who most needed to hear it were the ones closest to the brink of violence.

Kaplan's big mistake was in continuing with this philosophy once he became an MP and then a government minister. A firestorm of controversy was set off when media published photographs of Kaplan present at a Ramadan dinner with members in the leadership of various Turkish and Muslim radical organizations. These included members of the Turkish ultra-nationalist group the Grey Wolves, and a European Islamic organization called Millî Görüş. Investigations then revealed a number of meetings Kaplan had had over the years with these and other similar groups.

As a private citizen, Kaplan could claim that he was he was serving as an ambassador to groups that were on the fringes of Swedish society, working to reintegrate them into the moderate mainstream. His presence was nothing more than a fellow Turk and Muslim petitioning his fellows to give up their "extreme" views. But as an MP and government minister, he was sending a very different message. By agreeing to meet with these groups, he was legitimizing them and their beliefs. He was giving them the attention from the government that they desired, and might be accidentally encouraging them far more than he was succeeding in pulling them back into society. When the President of the United States agreed to meet with North Korean dictator Kim Jong-un in 2018, many warned that he was inadvertently doing the same thing.

Kaplan resigned both his ministerial post and his seat in the Riksdag in April of 2016. The Greens were deeply embarrassed by the debacle. They continued to defend Kaplan's character and motivations, but admitted the mistake in his conduct. Prime Minister Stefan Löfven, upon accepting Kaplan's resignation, commented, "I've come to know Mehmet Kaplan as a man of humanistic and democratic values, but a minister should be able to represent Sweden in an unquestionable way."

CHAPTER 9 – GREEN GOVERNANCE CHALLENGES AND MISTAKES

Picking Themselves Back Up

The repeated failure of the Swedish Greens to manage public expectations and the reporting of their successes and challenges hammered down the party's support in the polls. After Kaplan's resignation, the polled support for the Greens began to dip below 4 percent, a significant number because Sweden's threshold for representation in an election is set at 4 percent. If the Greens didn't reach that threshold in the next election, then they would lose all of their electoral members and be kicked out of the Riksdag entirely.

The next two years of government for the Greens were a tough slog to drag their support numbers back into comfortable territory. It was a constant worry that they were going to end their first term in government in the same way as the Irish Greens: with a total wipeout. It wasn't until a couple months before the election that their polling numbers began to creep up to a more comfortable 5 to 6 percent. It was still below their result in 2014, but at least barely enough to keep a few of them in the legislature.

The Swedish Greens survived their first term in government, although it cost them dearly. In the 2018 election, they finished with 4.4 percent, which plunged them from their spot as the fourth biggest party in 2014 down to being the smallest party to qualify for representation. Their campaign in 2018 brought them back to their basics. They campaigned heavily on environmental issues, almost to the exclusion of anything else. Their message was "you need to elect Greens if you care about the environment. Only we can make sure it's treated with the importance it deserves." They rarely brought up their record in government, knowing that the Löfven government was unlikely to be re-elected, and that even if it was that they'd have a reduced role in it.

The 2018 election itself produced a bizarre result. Both of the traditional alliances virtually tied in voter support. The governing alliance that included the Greens wound up with only one more seat than the centre-right alliance. Meanwhile, the Sweden Democrats increased their vote share very slightly, although they still remained much smaller than either of the traditional alliances.

Technically, the Greens were re-elected into government, since their alliance remained the biggest grouping in the Riksdag. But it was still an acknowledged failure. Ulf Kristersson, the leader of the centre-right alliance, promised to bring down the government and claimed that he had received a mandate to lead, even though his alliance was smaller by one member, and was still far below a majority of support.

This time two member parties of the centre-right alliance acknowledged that they'd be willing to work with the Sweden Democrats if it meant kicking the Social Democrats and Greens out of office and taking control with their own alliance. However, the other two members of the alliance steadfastly refused to entertain the idea.

After lengthy negotiations, the Centre Party (the right-wing "greenish" party) and Liberals switched sides and agreed to abstain on the Prime Ministerial vote. This meant that Prime Minister Stefan Löfven and his Green Party allies had enough votes to continue governing.

The Swedish Green Party is set to have a second term in office, lasting until the next election in 2022. It's still a minority government, meaning they have to heavily compromise with parties from other parts of the political spectrum. It is in fact a reduced minority, meaning they will likely have to compromise even more than they did in their first term.

We'll have to wait and see if they get better at managing their supporter's expectations, and if they're able to deliver results that their voters can be proud of.

Conclusions

The examples of Ireland and Sweden show two parties that struggled to make the move from opposition party to government for the first time. Both examples show us a number of mistakes that Green parties can make and provide a cautionary tale of what to avoid. But in both cases, the parties can point to a number of achievements that wouldn't have happened if they hadn't taken the plunge and entered government. They both learned lessons that they wouldn't have otherwise learned, and will likely emerge more powerful and wise once they finish their retrospection and recovery.

Elsewhere in the world, there are other Green parties serving their first terms as part of government. For instance, the New Zealand Greens are only halfway through their first governing term alongside two other parties, and are likely beginning to see many of the same issues that confronted the Swedish and Irish Greens. Whether they'll fall completely out of office like the Irish Greens, struggle and recover like the Swedish Greens, or thrive like the German Greens remains to be seen.

Outside of Prince Edward Island, our local Greens are nipping at the heels of government in many places. Minority governments in both British Columbia and New Brunswick have given the Greens a rare opportunity to participate in governing decisions from the outside. Moves towards proportional representation in Quebec mean that the opportunity for Greens to serve as part of government coalitions is growing. As the Canadian Greens across the country prepare for their first chance at governing, the final chapter of this book will look back at what they've achieved in opposition so far.

CHAPTER 10

OUR CANADIAN GREEN PARLIAMENTARIANS

"First-past-the-post can't stop us. We can stop it."

(Elizabeth May, Bi-annual Green Party Convention, 2018)

OUR CANADIAN GREEN PARLIAMENTARIANS

We've now covered some of the Greens in other parts of the world, in countries where Greens regularly serve as a part of government. But the state of Greens in Canada is very different. As of this book's writing, Greens have never served as a part of government in Canada. The total number of elected Greens at the federal and provincial level is fewer than two dozen. The number of elected individuals from the Liberal, Conservative, and New Democrat parties each number in the hundreds (both federal and provincial) and we have numerous examples of governments led by each party. Canadians instinctively know what happens when we elect members from these larger parties, because we've seen their governments in action. We have so many examples to pick from.

The experiences of Greens in Europe can give us an idea of where Greens in Canada are going. It can inform us of some of the challenges that Canadian Greens can expect to face if they continue to elect more and more members to Canadian parliaments. But it is not a perfect analogue. Canada is not Europe. Although we have many similarities, we have just as many differences.

We do have a small but growing group of elected Greens in Canada to look at as examples of where Canadians Greens could be going and to look at what issues and goals drive the Canadian Green movement. We have real Canadian examples and concrete successes that Greens have already been able to achieve and can see where they continue to struggle. We're beginning to develop a set of individuals who can show Canadians by example what it means when they elect Greens.

In an earlier chapter, I covered the personal histories of the Green personalities in Canada, as well as their path towards eventual elected office. In this final chapter, I'll cover the achievements and goals of Canada's Green parliamentarians. Although none (outside of PEI) have yet served in a government role, each of the Greens have still managed to have an effect on their province (or on Canada as a whole). Even if it seems under the radar compared to the big governing parties.

The First Green in Parliament

Elizabeth May had been hoping that the 2011 federal election would result in yet another minority government situation, just like the previous three elections. As she was campaigning, and as it was looking more likely that she was actually going to be elected, she was thinking about what she'd able to do as a single Green member of parliament when faced with a minority government. She'd harboured the goal of being able to broker a coalition government between the non-Conservatives parties, or at least be able to push them in that direction. The election of Stephen Harper's Conservative Party to lead a majority government was deeply disappointing. It forced Elizabeth to rethink what effect she could have in the legislature as a sole MP facing down a government that was her polar opposite.

When a new member is elected federally or provincially, one of their first tasks is to sit through a series of training meetings with parliament staff to teach them the ins and outs of the job. In addition to the training sessions, they're handed several giant tomes outlining parliamentary procedure. Landing on Elizabeth's desk was a thousand-plus page beast of a book entitled *"House of Commons Procedure and Practice, Second Edition"* by Audrey O'Brien and Marc Bosc. The book contained such exciting chapters as "The Process of Debate," "Private Members' Business," and "Rules of Order and Decorum."

Elizabeth devoured the book, trying to find each and every procedural rule and precedent that she could use to maximize her presence in the House. Since she was the only member of her party elected, she wasn't even going to be recognized as officially representing a party. Canadian parliamentary rules require a party to elect a minimum of twelve members before they're officially recognized. Official recognition is important because it comes with extra funding, extra staff, dedicated time for party MPs to ask questions in the House, and guaranteed seats on committees. Our democratic system isn't well prepared for parties that consist of only a handful of MPs, or for independent members.

That's what Elizabeth was considered: an Independent MP. The Bloc Quebecois had only elected four members, which meant she at least had some company as "independent" members, but the status severely curtailed her ability to be heard and to have any influence in the parliament's business.

CHAPTER 10 – OUR CANADIAN GREEN PARLIAMENTARIANS

Parliamentarian of the Year — Hardest Working MP — Best Orator

Elizabeth's studious obsession with parliamentary procedure paid off. Every year, *Maclean's* magazine organizes a poll of all three-hundred-plus MPs, asking them who they think should be recognized for a number of awards such as "Most Knowledgeable MP," "Best Orator," and "Rising Star." In 2012, one year after she was elected, Elizabeth was recognized with the award for "Parliamentarian of the Year." Despite all belonging to other parties, her colleagues had recognized the monumental amount of effort she was putting into the job. They don't tend to award the highest honour to the same MP two years in a row, but in 2013 Elizabeth was instead voted as "Hardest Working MP." In 2014, she was awarded "Best Orator."

The parliament has an official seating plan, and Elizabeth was relegated to "seat 309"—literally the very last possible seat. She was wedged into a corner of the hall, back against two walls. From that spot, she proved herself to be an outsized presence, taking every possible opportunity that she could to speak and be heard. She barely ever left her seat. Other MPs would come and go during the day, figuring that with dozens of party colleagues present they probably weren't actually needed. Since Elizabeth had no one to relieve her of duty, she remained. In one all-night debate of one of Stephen Harper's omnibus bills, she was one of only five MPs to be present for every one of the 157 votes on the gigantic bill. It was a twenty-three hour marathon session, and she received a standing ovation from opposition MPs when she cast the final vote against the mega-bill.

The work of an MP also consists of being part of a number of committees. Committee work is where a lot of decisions are made and worked out before they're brought to the actual chamber for a vote (and for the associated theatrics). Normally, a party can split their members between the many committees that are scheduled throughout the day. A particular MP may be on a couple of committees, but they rarely conflict with each other and there are always fellow party MPs on the committee if a member happens to have two scheduled at the same time.

For Elizabeth, once again there was no one else to offload the work to. She signed up for every committee that she was able to be on, and would frequently find herself sprinting through the halls trying to be present for a vote at one committee before running off to the next one for yet another vote. On occasion, a friendly MP would try to delay the vote if Elizabeth wasn't there, knowing that she was probably halfway across the building hustling at full speed on her way over.

In December of 2013, one of the NDP MPs, Bruce Hyer, defected from his party and joined the Greens. He'd been sidelined by the NDP for daring to vote against the party line on hunting rifle legislation, and stripped of all his of his party perks. He stated he was joining the Green Party caucus because he believed in their leader and platform, and because it was the only party that allowed MPs to vote with their conscience and constituency, instead of just the party line. His defection gave the Elizabeth some much-needed backup in the House. She at least wouldn't have to be on *every* committee anymore.

Elizabeth's biggest and most lasting contribution is probably that she was able to display to journalists and parliamentarians what to expect from a Green MP, and where the Greens stood on issues that they hadn't been consulted on previously. Before Elizabeth's election, the Greens were seen as even more of a one-issue party than they are now. After two terms of her presence in Parliament, the party had staked out its position on hundreds of issues that it hadn't been questioned on before. Her work in the House pushed the Greens toward building policies in areas that had gone unexamined in the party.

Demonstrable Achievements

Her hard work actually produced some concrete results, as well. In 2012, she tabled a Private Member's Bill (Bill C-442) to create a national framework to tackle Lyme disease. The bill was approved and enacted: an extreme rarity among Private Members' Bills from opposition parties. It was even passed with unanimous consent by all members of both the House of Commons and the Senate. The motivation for the bill was a report by the Intergovernmental Panel on Climate Change linking the rise of Lyme disease cases to climate change, since the changing environment has led to the number of Lyme-carrying ticks increasing. She also managed to have two amendments to Bill C-46, the Pipelines Safety Act, adopted. Her Lyme disease bill was the first Green legislation enacted in Canadian history, and her two amendments were the first Green amendments accepted. She was also the first MP to publicly oppose the infamous Bill C-51, the Anti-Terrorism Act. She proposed sixty amendments to the bill, none of which were accepted by the Harper government.

Working in the Local Constituency

Only half of the work of an MP is what is done in the House of Commons. Since each MP is elected to represent an electoral district, the other half of the work is done in the district itself. On this front, Elizabeth wanted to make sure that she was the best local representative that Saanich–Gulf Islands had ever had. Their previous MP, Conservative Gary Lunn, had represented the district for fourteen years, and for the last five had been a government minister. By nature of their high position in government, ministers tend to have a diminished ability to be present in their local district.

For instance, Prime Minister Justin Trudeau was elected to represent a district in Montreal, Quebec. However, in 2018, he admitted that he had voted in the Ontario provincial election in the district in Ottawa where he resides with his family, rather than in the Quebec provincial election in what is supposed to be his "home" district. Mr. Trudeau received a large amount of criticism from the media, public, and fellow MPs over this admission. It's dubious how much of a representative for the voters of Papineau Mr. Trudeau is able to be, while living and even voting so far from his home district.

Elizabeth didn't want her role as both leader of the Green party and as the sole Green in parliament to overshadow her job as the representative of Saanich–Gulf Islands. It's a piece of advice that she's passed on to other elected Greens, as well. Newly elected Green MPP for Guelph Mike Schreiner admitted at the 2018 biannual Green Party Convention that the first advice he got after his election was that he needed to be the "best damn MPP Guelph has ever had."

Some Green staff have told me about a disturbing observation. They believed that they'd seen opposition party MPs and staff purposefully drag their heels on issues in their districts, so that the party could use those festering issues as motivators during the next election when they were petitioning to be elected into government. People are motivated to vote more when something is going wrong and they want change, rather than when everything is going well. Leaving issues unaddressed meant they could be used for political purposes later.

It's not really possible to fact check an accusation like this, or to tell how common it is, but it displays how people working for Elizabeth saw the difference between her and other MPs. Leaving solvable issues unsolved for political reasons was unthinkable to the Greens, and that's how they were determined to be different.

The 2015 Disappointment

2015 was supposed to be the big breakthrough for Elizabeth and the Greens. They'd wedged open the door with Elizabeth's election in 2011 and had proven to Canadians that it *was* in fact possible to elect Greens if only Canadians would make the choice to vote for them.

The Greens recruited a number of star candidates to run in districts across the country for the 2015 general election. In 2012, the Greens managed to secure a strong third place finish in a by-election in Calgary, with local journalist Chris Turner earning 25 percent. If 25 percent was possible in the heart of fossil-fuel-obsessed Alberta, then it should have been possible to pick up at least a few seats in more Green-friendly parts of the country.

The Green hopes in 2015 didn't materialize. The party started the campaign with a goal of achieving "official party status," which meant that they'd have to elect at least twelve members. They thought that this was a realistic possibility, an achievable goal. What they didn't count on was how brutal and overwhelming the "vote split" narrative would become, and how it would dominate much of the campaign.

The Strategic Vote

For many Canadians, 2015 was an "ABC" election, meaning "anything-but-Conservative." The narrative of the campaign was, "How do we remove Stephen Harper and the Conservatives from power?" Thus, the strategy for both the Liberal Party and the NDP became trying to convince voters to vote for them instead of for the Greens (and instead of for each other), because they stood the best chance of defeating the Conservative candidates. Environmental groups such as Leadnow even ran campaigns to convince voters *not* to vote for Green candidates, despite the Green platform aligning with the environmental groups' goals far more than any of the other party platforms.

Jo-Ann Roberts, who ran in the district of Victoria, remarked that "people were coming up to us on the day of the election saying, 'We love everything you're doing and we believe in your whole platform but we voted for the New Democrats. We had to vote strategically, we'll vote for you next time.'" There was no chance that the Conservatives were going to win in Victoria. It was a two-way race between Jo-Ann and the NDP candidate. But still, that's how afraid voters were. Greens across the country heard the same story on the doorstep. The sheer volume of people promising to vote Green "next time" could have meant multiple Greens being elected had they instead voted Green *"this* time."

The 2015 election was the most well-funded, professional, and serious election that the Greens had ever run. They spent over $4.5 million dollars over the course of the campaign. They'd identified fourteen new districts (eight in British Columbia, two in Ontario, three in Quebec, and one in New Brunswick) that they thought were winnable and poured $100,000 from the central campaign fund into each one of those districts, as well as providing them with experienced campaign staff.

Elizabeth handily won her district, but she was the only Green to do so. Bruce Hyer, who had switched to the Green party, was defeated in his re-election bid, leaving Elizabeth alone in the House once again. The result was crushing for the party. Many campaign staff didn't know what they could have done better. The vote-splitting narrative, and the desire of Canadians to kick Stephen Harper out of office at all costs, overwhelmed anything the Greens could have done.

Elizabeth called Justin Trudeau, the leader of the incoming majority Liberal government, on election night to congratulate him on the win. The silver lining of the election was that the Conservatives were out of government, and Elizabeth had always had a soft spot for the Liberals. She figured that she'd at least have an easier time working with them than she had with the Conservatives. The relationship even started off on a strong footing: the Liberal party invited Elizabeth to accompany them at the United Nations Climate Change Conference in Paris that year. During the Harper government years, Elizabeth had only been able to attend the conference by getting herself attached to the delegation from Afghanistan as a volunteer advisor.

The Green Party leader went into the Liberal's government term with high hopes. She chose to believe Justin Trudeau's promises on electoral reform, on climate leadership, and on Indigenous reconciliation. She has mostly been disappointed, although she's said on several occasions that she still remains tentatively hopeful and truly wants him to succeed. She's tended to be far more critical of the people that the Prime Minister surrounds himself with: those in the bureaucracy and his cabinet members.

Halfway through the Liberal's term, the Green Party released a report card on the government, reviewing its performance on various files. Some areas were mostly positive. Immigration, Public Safety, Health, and Fisheries all received Bs. Its handling of Environmental Law and Agriculture both received Ds, while Indigenous Peoples was given an "incomplete." Transportation and Democracy were the two Fs. Elizabeth threw herself enthusiastically into the commission struck by the Prime Minister to examine changing Canada's election system after he promised that "2015 would be the last election under first-past-the-post." His cynical abandonment of the promise was probably his biggest betrayal for Elizabeth and the Greens.

Andrew Weaver and the BC Greens

When Andrew was first elected in 2013, he was the very first Green elected to a Canadian provincial legislature. There wasn't much of a roadmap for him to follow as a sole Green. He had only Elizabeth May, who fortunately was representing a district very near to where Andrew was elected and was eager to help.

But Elizabeth and Andrew are very different people with different outlooks and histories. What might work for Elizabeth wouldn't necessarily work for Andrew. As well, the political reality of the federal legislature and the BC legislature were quite different. Although the federal parliament of Canada is considered quite toxic and partisan, it pales in comparison to some of the provincial legislatures, BC being one of the worst.

Who to Work With

Andrew had previously had a relationship with the BC Liberals, who were the surprise winners of the provincial election in 2013. All of the pollsters had predicted an NDP win, and as it looked more and more likely that Andrew was going to win his single seat he and his team were expecting that he would have to try to work with an NDP government. When Christy Clark and her BC Liberal party pulled out a surprise win, it may actually have been a boon for Andrew on a personal political level. The BC NDP had absolutely no interest in working with the Greens in any capacity. They didn't want the Greens to exist, and if they had been the government then it's possible that they would have gone out of their way to ignore and diminish any attempts by the Greens to assert themselves and to get any "wins."

But with a BC Liberal win, Andrew stood a chance at being able to actually work with the government. The BC Liberals wanted a Green party nipping at the heels of the BC NDP, throwing them off their game and peeling away just enough votes to throw elections over to the Liberals. So the strategic move was to build Andrew up, to nurture the "vote split" that dominates the narrative of elections under first-past-the-post voting systems.

It remains dubious that Green parties spoil elections for the NDP anyway. Andrew himself won his seat away from a BC Liberal MLA. Adam Olsen likewise contributed to flipping a traditionally BC-Liberal-held district. Polling consistently shows that Green voters come as much from the Liberal and Conservative sides of the political spectrum as they do from the left. Nevertheless, the narrative has persisted.

Despite getting into politics because he was upset with the direction that Christy Clark was taking the BC Liberals, Andrew found himself faced with a Premier and governing party that was surprisingly friendly towards him. But if the BC Liberals were hoping that they could use Andrew as a useful pawn, then they were severely underestimating the effort that he was prepared to put in to hold the government to account.

Private Member Bills

In a Westminster Parliamentary system (named after Westminster in the United Kingdom where the system originated), it's technically possible for parties that aren't part of government to submit proposed legislation for the parliament to consider. This is what Elizabeth May did when she got her Private Member's Bill passed. But the unfortunate reality for opposition parties is that their proposals very rarely reach the floor of the chamber and get called for debate.

The governing party controls the schedule of what gets debated and when it happens, and usually has no interest in debating any bills that they didn't introduce themselves. In fact, at the time of Andrew's election, in the history of British Columbia, a Private Member's Bill from an opposition party member had *never* been passed by the legislature. In addition, the government has an army of lawyers that they are able to task with writing up the legislation itself, and which aren't available to opposition members. This means that Private Members' Bills often have legal issues that would require them to be mostly rewritten in order to be legally sound.

In spite of this, Andrew decided that his strategy in the legislature would be to flood the governing BC Liberals with his own Private Members' Bills. He knew that probably none of them would be picked up by the governing party, or even brought to debate. But he wanted to accomplish two goals. First, he wanted the tiny one-person Green party to be able to outdo the BC NDP. He saw the BC NDP as a party that didn't have any constructive ideas. They were a party that existed only to oppose the BC Liberals, and not to offer solutions or to do anything with their opposition role other than attack the government. He wanted to be able to point to the record of the Greens and to be able to say, "Look, with only one of us we managed to introduce more legislation than the entire BC NDP caucus of several dozen members."

Second, although the government almost never allows debate and a vote on Private Members' Bills, they do occasionally read over them and then take the ideas and re-introduce them as government bills. These bills then swiftly pass through debate and are voted on and passed by the government caucus. The media picks them up and reports the bill as being a new action by the government, despite the idea originating in a Private Member's Bill from another party.

One of the factors that causes Green politicians to struggle politically is that they don't particularly care if someone else gets the credit for their actions. They care more about seeing things get done than being able to seize the credit. This is what Andrew was hoping would happen. He hoped that the government would pick up one of his bills and that it would get turned into a government bill and passed. He wouldn't get the credit, but at least he'd have actually done something. It's a messaging conundrum that continues to plague Green parties.

Andrew succeeded in his goal of outdoing the BC NDP in sheer volume of proposed legislation. He was a prolific submitter of private bills. At the end of his first term, in the run-up to the 2017 election, he dropped a heavy stack of nineteen bills onto the legislative calendar. In a single week, this outdid the eighteen bills that the BC NDP had submitted over the past four years. It was meant to demonstrate exactly the types of things that a Green government would do if voters elected them in the upcoming election. Each bill was an example of what voters could expect from a Green government.

Medical Service Plan Premiums, and Other Green Initiatives

None of Andrew's bills were passed (as was expected). But a few of them did re-emerge as government bills. One of his earliest attempts was a targeted attack on BC's Medical Service Plan premiums (MSP premiums). Unique among the provinces, British Columbia charges every resident a flat monthly rate in healthcare costs. The rest of Canada rolls healthcare taxation into general income tax and other taxes. Income taxes are progressive, meaning that someone who is low-income pays a smaller portion of their income as taxes than does someone who has a very high income. The MSP premiums were a flat tax, meaning that everyone pays exactly the same amount regardless of their financial situation.

Andrew targeted the MSPs as a "regressive tax" that was unfair to low-income British Columbians. He rode the issue hard and tackled it before either of the other parties had it on their radar. When the 2017 election arrived, he had turned it into an election issue. All three parties made promises to get rid of the MSP. The Greens proposed rolling it into the progressive income tax, the BC Liberals promised to cut it in half if re-elected, and the BC NDP promised to get rid of it but didn't specify a way to make up the lost government revenue. As of 2018, the BC NDP government is on its way to getting rid of those premiums and will likely be rolling them into the income tax, as was the Green plan.

Another of Andrew's big legislative pushes was for a bill to address sexualized violence on college campuses. Before his election, Andrew had worked as a professor at the University of Victoria and there were many aspects of British Columbia's university system that he wanted re-examined. His first attempt at submitting legislation that was meant to reduce sexual assault cases on university campuses was rejected, but the BC Liberal government eventually re-introduced their own bill using a number of Andrew's suggestions and proposals. Andrew and the Greens never got much credit in the media for his push on MSP premiums, but they started to get at least some mention when the government proposed its sexualized violence legislation. Journalists working in Victoria began to notice the origin of some of the government's bills.

Who Has to Wear Heels?

Another big moment came from one of the proposals in Andrew's mighty stack of nineteen bills, all submitted at once before the 2017 election. One of the bills was a simple one: it banned restaurants from requiring their female servers to wear high-heeled shoes. The rationale was simple. High-heeled shoes are uncomfortable and painful and could cause injuries to the wearers. There was no such requirement that male servers wear damaging shoes, and therefore it was unfair that women should be expected to.

The proposal went viral. It got picked up in news outlets not only in British Columbia but internationally as well. It was appearing in newspapers as far afield as Brazil, being reported that a Canadian politician was proposing ending forced heel-wearing on the job. It proved enormously popular. Unfortunately, the farther it got from the origin, the less likely it was that Andrew and the BC Greens got mentioned as the originator of the idea.

Christy Clark's government let the bill die by ignoring it, but Clark noticed the popularity of the idea and pounced on it herself. She announced to the media that although they weren't going to support Andrew's bill, the government would move to regulate the proposed changes through a simple decree from the Ministry of Labour. The headlines shifted over to Christy Clark, giving her the initial credit for the move. "Premier Christy Clark Promises to End Mandatory High Heels for

CHAPTER 10 – OUR CANADIAN GREEN PARLIAMENTARIANS

Women in the Workplace" exclaimed one headline. The following quotation appeared as the first sentence at the beginning of another CBC article announcing the change: "The BC government has banned workplace requirements that force women to wear high heels. A mandatory high-heel dress code 'is a workplace health and safety issue,' says the release put out by Premier Christy Clark and Labour Minister Shirley Bond." Further down in both articles, Andrew is mentioned and credited as introducing the original idea, but he had lost the battle for the headline. Nevertheless, the change was made. It was a victory even if the credit wasn't there.

"I want to trust the BC Liberals, but it will take more than words to make that happen. It will take action. I have a lot of experience with the words of this government, words that did not match the reality that I and my community were experiencing. I know this from personal experience in my community of Shawnigan.

We spent years fighting this government simply for the right to protect our water. My community has lost not only millions of dollars drained from the pockets of the people in Shawnigan and all through the Cowichan Valley. More importantly, we lost our trust in government. We lost our faith that government institutions were there to protect us as citizens…

It is with my community first and foremost in my mind as I support this amendment."

(Sonia Furstenau, from her first speech in the BC Legislature, in which she supported a BC NDP amendment to declare No Confidence in the BC Liberal government)

A MINORITY GOVERNMENT IN BRITISH COLUMBIA

Andrew had initially hoped that the 2017 election would produce a Green wave that would sweep the Greens from their single seat and into a majority government. This was, to say the least, overly optimistic. As the election moved along, the BC Greens realized that the best that they could realistically hope for was a small but influential caucus. When the votes were counted up, Andrew was joined by Adam Olsen and Sonia Furstenau, two powerhouses of local organizing skill and momentum.

Despite constituting only three of the eighty-seven members of the BC legislature, the trio of Greens are a powerful group. Both the BC NDP and the BC Liberals have a number of "safe seats." These are districts where everyone knows the party that's going to win there. The often-told joke is that the party could run a potted plant and it would still get elected. This often means that the party doesn't need to run a candidate who's fiercely determined and energetic. If the party wants to, they can run a "safe" candidate in a "safe" seat. Estimates on how many seats are "safe" vary, although it's often suggested that at least 60 percent of British Columbia's districts are considered safe for one of the big two parties. There's virtually no chance that they'll change hands in an election.

There's no such thing as a Green safe seat. Any Green who gets elected in Canada has to claw their way through a system designed specifically to exclude a smaller party like them. Every Green elected in Canada got there through having several times the energy, the effort, the ideas, and the enthusiasm than many of the elected members they share the legislature with. The BC Liberals were surprised by the energy and dedication that Andrew brought to the job. The MLAs elected in 2017 were likewise surprised by the enthusiasm brought by Adam and Sonia when they joined the legislature.

> I think part of what makes us unique in this place is that we took the least direct, most difficult route to get here. So when I see people here interacting with us they're really quite taken aback by it. Because we didn't get elected by a big party machine, or by an undercurrent of the tides turning like we're seeing right now with the Ontario NDP (this interview was in the midst of the Ontario election, when the Ontario NDP were surging) . . . We got elected because something else was going on. (Adam Olsen, from an interview with the author, 2018)

The job for a small party like the Greens has difficulties that larger parties don't experience. A provincial government has over a dozen individual ministries as well as numerous committees at any given time. With their caucus of forty-three members, the official opposition BC Liberal party is able to assign several MLAs to shadow each of the government ministers and to criticize and cover the work of each ministry. With only three MLAs, the Green members each have to cover a half-dozen ministries on their own.

Each MLA also gets funding for a couple of staff members to support them in their work, and to do research and preparatory work for the MLA. The BC Liberals have nearly a hundred full-time staffers with them in the legislature, whereas the Greens have only a handful doing the same job. Each of the Green MLAs has mentioned to me that they frequently hear from their MLA colleagues in other parties that they're jealous of the Green staff, and wish that their own staff had the energy and dedication that the Green staffers do. The Green staff doesn't have a choice. The workload is the same as the bigger parties, but there's a fraction of the people on staff to do it.

The three Greens in British Columbia have each settled into their realms of strength and have focused in on issues that they're passionate about. The three of them are quite similar in outlook if you're considering their overall philosophy and work ethic, but they've each honed in on a different aspect of what they see as wrong with the direction of the province.

CHAPTER 10 – OUR CANADIAN GREEN PARLIAMENTARIANS

There for Policy

Andrew is a climate scientist. His frustration with the government is on their disregard for science and for evidence, and how they often (or usually) choose politics over actual settled science. He makes liberal use of the term "evidence-based policy," which has been picked up by other parties such as Justin Trudeau's Liberal Party, but is not always used with a full dedication to the spirit of the term. Andrew's focus is often on the concrete issues. He's a policy wonk, and someone who's convinced that problems can be fixed through clever targeted legislation. He makes a point of proposing concrete steps that the government could use to tackle a problem and prides himself on proposing tangible solutions when he sees problems with government plans, rather than just criticising.

> We're there for policy. We're driven by policy and we're not driven by power. And I know it sounds weird but there was one MLA where someone asked him, "How did you get into politics?" And he responded, "Somebody asked me and I said yes." Well, wow! For many of us it's a passion and a desire for public policy, and it is not a career path! But it's the policy that drives us. And even now we desperately want to work with the BC Liberals, but it's virtually impossible because for them it's all a game. (Andrew Weaver, from an interview in 2018 with the author)

Sonia's views of governance take things up a level in terms of abstraction. Andrew got into politics because he had helped the previous government under Gordon Campbell to craft science-based policy that he then saw getting ignored by Christy Clark. Sonia got into politics not because she saw a specific policy being ignored for political reasons, but because she saw an entire system that was built on corrupt practices.

Policing Themselves

The target in Sonia's crosshairs is a practice called "professional reliance," introduced by the BC Liberals in the mid 2000s. The practice is a cost-saving measure for government, as well as a way for the government to simplify things and to generally get the answer that they want instead of one that might be problematic for them.

Instead of keeping a staff of government employed impartial experts, the government of British Columbia has long relied on the industry itself providing the experts for any sort of consultation process. Simply put, when an industry petitions the government for something, the government will then engage in a consultation process to see if it's a good idea. But the experts for the consultation are hired and selected by the industry that's petitioning the government. It's fast, and it's cheap. But it definitely can't be claimed to be robust, independent, or free from conflicts of interest.

Sonia found out about the professional reliance model while trying to get the government to pay attention to the issue of the contaminated landfill near Shawnigan Lake near her home. Her goal since her election has been to dismantle the professional reliance model and replace it with capable government scientists and experts.

Sonia's mistreatment by Christy Clark and her government came back to bite them after the 2017 election when Sonia became one of the three elected Greens who were asked by both larger parties to break the virtual tie between them for government control. Both Andrew and Adam went into the negotiations with the two parties wanting to give each of them a fair hearing. Sonia went into the negotiations with a solid grudge. The BC Liberals were acutely aware of how Sonia felt about them, and about Christy Clark in particular as the face of the party.

It was reported in the media multiple times that Christy Clark was not personally attending the negotiation meetings between the two parties, whereas BC NDP leader John Horgan was a central participant. It seemed haughty and disrespectful at the time—as if Clark wasn't even considering the meetings important enough for her to be physically present. It was later revealed by Victoria journalists Richard Zussman and Rob Shaw in their book *"Matter of Confidence"* that the reasoning behind her absence was that they didn't want to anger Sonia with Clark's mere presence. The BC Liberals felt that if Sonia was seated across from Clark, then they were surely doomed, but if she was kept at arm's length that they might have a chance in winning her over.

Like Andrew, when Sonia joined the legislature, she was flabbergasted at the way that the elected MLAs comported themselves. She immediately saw that the rot in the system went much further than just the professional reliance model. One of the things that bothered Sonia most was the blind loyalty that MLAs show to their party, even on things that they may not agree with. One of the files that Sonia was in charge of was the plan for British Columbia to conduct a public referendum on reforming its electoral system to a proportional representation system. Because it was a process initiated by the Greens and the BC NDP, the BC Liberals were utterly and completely opposed to the entire idea. One particular exchange during the debate over the legislation struck Sonia:

> There was a moment when we were at, like, thirty-seven out of forty-one speeches (by the BC Liberal members) against the enabling legislation for a referendum on electoral reform. And I could literally mute the TV screen and parrot exactly what was being said. And I don't think that all of them think that electoral reform is bad. I think that some of them actually believe that electoral reform is good. And so I realized that the thing that really sets us apart is that I'm not here in allegiance to the party. I ran with the Greens and I'm proud to be in the Green

Party because the principles and the values of the party very much reflect my own. But when I'm standing up in the House speaking out, I'm not filtering that through "does it serve the party?" I'm not here for the party. And so I think this is a huge break from what we see in the political landscape, which is people having to stand up and serve the party even when they don't agree. (Sonia Furstenau, from an interview with the author, 2018)

Sonia recounted to me a particular anecdote about another MLA in the BC legislature. She often tells the story at conventions and public talks when trying to get people to understand how sad our politics has become. This MLA stopped her in the hallway after he had given a particularly fractious speech on the legislature floor. The MLA told her that he keeps a picture in his office of himself when he was a much younger man, because sometimes when he comes away from a combative exchange in the legislature he needs to remind himself who he used to be. Because the person that he becomes when he's deep in political theatre isn't the person who he thinks he really is inside. He says things that he doesn't believe, because it's what he was instructed to do by the party.

The exchange stuck with her. I've heard her recount it multiple times. Sonia very clearly does not want to be a different person when she's in front of the legislature cameras than she is behind closed doors.

Even the Room Itself Is Designed Wrong

While Sonia has put her focus on reforming the institutions that control how government interacts with the private sector, one of Adam Olsen's focuses has been on how the government and the legislature interacts within itself. Both Adam and Sonia are passionately committed to electoral reform. Time and again the BC Liberals and many within the BC media have accused the Greens of supporting electoral reform because it's likely to result in them picking up more seats in the legislature. Although it's true that the Greens are vastly underrepresented from their share of the vote, the main motivating factor for the Greens' support of electoral reform is that they honestly believe that it will reform the brutal toxicity of the legislature itself.

First-past-the-post eventually collapses a political system down to two parties that exist only to oppose each other. Each party is fighting for a majority government that will give them the power to completely ignore their rivals, and to control the operations of the government as they see fit.

This isn't the philosophy that drives the Greens. The three Greens in the legislature like minority governments specifically because it forces the governing party to work with other parties to find common ground. Adam will go out of his way to say that he wouldn't want the Greens to lead a majority government because he thinks that when a party is granted a majority it makes them unaccountable.

Adam has remarked on a couple occasions that he wants to be Premier of British Columbia. He wants the job because it would allow him to radically shakeup the way the government and the legislature functions. He doesn't want the job because he wants the power to be a dictator. In fact, it's the exact opposite:

> I've always said that if I became Premier of this province that my cabinet would be all parties. All parties would be represented. If you have a person of incredible expertise sitting on the other side (of the aisle) . . . then how does it benefit the people (of the province) not to use them? Or at the very least we could go and say "can this person be the critic for this file?" Because we would listen to them. We *want* their expertise, and their voice on this file. (Adam Olsen, from an interview with the author, 2018)

Adam's proposal is virtually unheard of in parliamentary politics. Even in systems that are considered extremely consensus-based, such as Switzerland's government system, the governing coalition doesn't contain all the parties. The only times that governments have been formed that feature real, tangible inclusion of all parties have been emergency wartime governments, when the parties agree to put aside their partisan weapons and stand together against a great outside threat. Adam's goal of leading a government that relies on every party working with goodwill to contribute to the best of their abilities seems like a pipe dream to many, especially to those who have spent a long time in politics. But it's the way he sees an ideal system as functioning: all hands on deck.

Adam's ideas around reforming the toxicity of the legislature go beyond the organizational structure of the cabinet, all the way down to the physical structure of the legislature building itself.

If you go and visit a Canadian legislature you can get a tour of the building, including the legislature chamber where debates between the elected members occur. The chamber is a regal room, always featuring a richly coloured carpet and elaborately decorated walls and ceilings. At the head of the room is a single elevated desk for the Speaker: the one member whose job it is to lead the business of the legislature. In front of the Speaker's desk are several rows of desks, arranged on each side of the room directly facing each other. The governing party sits on one side, while the opposition parties sit on the other side.

Your tour guide might tell you a fun piece of trivia. Supposedly the rows of government and opposition desks are spaced exactly two sword-lengths apart, a holdover from the early days when debates could get so heated that a member might draw his weapon and leap across the aisle to stab an opposing member. The very room in which decisions are made in our government system is designed for elected members who disagree so violently that they need to be separated or they might kill each other. Or so the legend goes.

This is a unique feature of Westminster style parliaments used in Canada and other former British colonies. Legislatures in Europe don't use the same layout. Instead, they're arranged in semicircles, with each party taking a wedge of the circle. The parties still sit together, but they're not facing down the "opposing" parties. They're beside them, facing a speaker in the front. In some parts of the world, the legislature is instead a big circle, with everyone facing inwards.

This circular configuration is Adam's favourite. If he had his way, the two swords-length corridor between MLAs would be removed, and everyone would be moved into a big circle, the members from different parties all interspersed with each other. Furthermore, the desks would be removed, and every member would just be given a simple chair or bench to sit on. These days the only thing the desks are used for is for the members to bang loudly on while hollering whenever a party colleague says something that they like, or an opposing member says something that they don't like.

> I'd like to see us fully exposed on benches like they have in Great Britain. Completely exposed. So we can't hide behind the desk and we can't lean on them. We would be completely wide open, and tactically off guard. So for me, I think there are things we can talk about like needing proportional representation to improve our democracy. Sure, I agree with that totally. But I think that we could be improving our democracy by things like using committees more, and by tinkering with the way that we lay out the legislature. (Adam Olsen, from an interview with the author, 2018)

Wanting to Take Down the Government?

The three Greens elected in British Columbia see their job as an opposition party very differently from how their BC Liberal colleagues see their same role. To each of the Greens during an interview, I recounted a particular quote.

Alison Smith was the leader of the Wildrose Party in Alberta from 2009 until 2014. In 2012, the Wildrose party became the second biggest party in the Alberta legislature, and Smith became the Leader of Opposition. During this time, she was quoted as saying, "If you're going to be the official opposition, then you really need to want to take down the government."

I read this quote out to all three Greens, and all three of them buried their heads in their hands and let out a pained sigh as soon as I did. The trio all see the job as an opposition party fundamentally differently from Danielle Smith and others like her. They do not want to take down the government. They want the government to succeed on behalf all of the people that it governs.

They of course think that their party and their ideas would make the best government. But when given the role of opposition party by the voters, they don't consider their job to be taking down the government at any cost. They see their job as proposing solutions to problems. They see their job as bringing up ideas that the government may not have thought of, and making that government the best that it can be. If they see an action by the government that they disagree with, they try to propose a way to fix it. And then, when the next election rolls around, they try once again to convince voters that they should elect Greens. But they have no desire to sabotage the government, or to force an early election, or to contribute to a government failing.

After Christy Clark's BC Liberal party was defeated in 2017, she stepped down as leader. A leadership election for the BC Liberals followed, and the eventual winner was Andrew Wilkinson. The leadership election wrapped up late in the evening on February the 3rd of 2018. I was actually with Green leader Andrew Weaver at the moment when the results were announced, sitting next to him at a junior hockey game in the interior BC city of West Kelowna. A by-election was being held there to replace Christy Clark, and so the party leader and a number of volunteers (such as myself) had made the trip up to help out the local Green candidate.

As soon as Andrew Wilkinson was confirmed as the new BC Liberal leader, the Green communications team sent out a prepared press release congratulating Wilkinson on his new role on behalf of Andrew Weaver and the BC Green Party. The release stated that Andrew and the team were looking forward to working with the new BC Liberal leader to ensure the best government for all British Columbians.

Within minutes of the press release going out, Wilkinson was in front of a camera giving his victory speech. Thronged by cheering BC Liberals, Wilkinson stated that his goal as leader was going to be "to hold the NDP to account with smart, incisive questions that will make their skin crawl." He went on to declare that "our job is to drive a wedge between the Greens and the NDP and make sure they are more and more uncomfortable with each other."

I leaned over to Andrew and showed him the quote in a tweet from a journalist covering the speech. In his very first speech, the new BC Liberal leader was making a pledge to drive his colleagues apart, and to put an end to any goodwill and cooperation. Andrew just shrugged and shook his head. Despite a cheery press release expressing hope that the opposition Greens and BC Liberals might be able to work together constructively under their new leader, I doubt Andrew had expected anything less from the BC Liberals' new party leader.

CHAPTER 10 – OUR CANADIAN GREEN PARLIAMENTARIANS

The CASA

The results of the 2017 election in British Columbia left the province in a situation that tends to be uncomfortable in Canadian politics. No single party had won enough seats to form a majority government on its own. Traditionally in Canada, this means that the biggest party would stumble along for a year or two as a minority government until the other parties all decided that it would be in their own interest to vote down the government and force an early election. In an adversarial system like first-past-the-post, it's expected that opposition parties exist mostly to make the government miserable and that they'll jump at any chance to force a new election in the hope that they could win their own majority instead.

Journalists and the public in British Columbia weren't aware of the political philosophy of the Greens. For the most part, they still aren't. The Greens had said over and over that their goal if they wound up in a minority situation would be to do their best to provide long-lasting stable government for the province, not to try to win political points or to gain power for themselves. But there's never been a party elected in BC (or in the rest of Canada) that actually held to a commitment like that when they actually found themselves in this situation. So the media remained skeptical. They assumed that the Greens would do what the other parties had a track record of doing: try to exploit a minority government situation to empower themselves at the expense of the government.

Negotiations

The BC Liberals and the BC NDP had completely ruled out the possibility of working together. This left the Greens in the middle, with both larger parties appealing to the three-person caucus for their votes to form government (or just to stay in government, in the case of the BC Liberals).

Media dubbed the Greens (and Andrew Weaver in particular) as the "kingmakers" and declared that they had the "balance of power." The Green caucus themselves weren't comfortable with the term. They've attempted since to rebrand the position of the party as one with the "balance of responsibility." With the two big parties deadlocked, the Greens were responsible for choosing which party should be entrusted with governing the province. Andrew Weaver, in an interview with reporters after the 2017 election, stated,

> We are humbled by the responsibility that British Columbians have bestowed upon us. The BC Greens take this very seriously, we take this responsibility very seriously. We are committed to bring stability to this province. And we are committed to ensuring that the decisions we make over the next few days make government work in British Columbia.

Most minority governments in Canada last under two years. This was the absolute last thing that Andrew Weaver wanted to see happen. Andrew is (small-C) conservative in quite a few ways. One of those ways is that he cares deeply about providing stability to businesses in the province. He didn't want British Columbian businesses stressing over whether the government was going to be stable or fall any second. He wanted businesses to confidently know that the deal that the Greens signed would provide for a stable, predictable four years of governance. And he wanted the Greens to be seen as a party that could be relied on for stability, not for the chaos that so many doomsayers in BC political circles were predicting.

The Greens formed working groups with each of the other parties after the election. They'd meet for hours to try to hammer out a deal that would work for both sides. Andrew and the Greens went to great lengths to claim that they were treating both options evenly and that they were trying to go into the negotiations without a favoured partner. For both Andrew and Adam, this was mostly true. But for Sonia, the idea of working alongside the BC Liberals was admittedly distasteful. She held a deep grudge against Clark and the party, and didn't trust that they'd be willing to fix the problems that they had created.

Different people who have followed what happened in the negotiation meetings will point to different issues or decisions that led to the Greens choosing to support the BC NDP. There was a powerful campaign from public interest groups to pressure the Greens into supporting the BC NDP, spearheaded by groups like Leadnow. The difficulties between Sonia and Christy Clark were substantial. It's impossible to point to one moment or issue that sealed the deal for the Greens. The best that I can do in this book is to explain the reasoning that the Green caucus gave to its own party membership at its annual convention later that year.

Who Really Gets It?

Speaking to members of the party gathered in Sidney on Vancouver Island, the caucus spoke about the very different approaches that the BC Liberals and the BC NDP had brought to the meetings. When meeting with the BC Liberals, the overwhelming feeling that they got was that they were being asked how much it would take to buy them off. The BC Liberals came at the Greens with offers and concessions to gain their support, but the experience was like a business transaction. The Greens were being asked for the price of their votes.

On the other hand, when the BC NDP sat down with the Greens they opened up both the BC NDP and BC Green platform booklets and began pointing out places where the two parties aligned. They identified spots where the parties agreed, and dug into areas where they disagreed on specifics of the solution but still agreed on the problem itself. They attempted to find a compromise between Green and BC NDP ideas and goals.

CHAPTER 10 – OUR CANADIAN GREEN PARLIAMENTARIANS

The core of the Green philosophy of governance is cooperative, consensus decision-making. The BC NDP weren't completely nailing the Green way of doing things, but the effort was at least there. The Greens could see that there was a possibility that they could get the BC NDP to work with them in the constructive way that they wanted. They struggled to see the same potential in the BC Liberals. It just wasn't the way the party did things.

Andrew and the Greens eventually decided to support the BC NDP in forming the provincial government. On May 29th, 2017, Andrew and BC NDP leader John Horgan went before the press to announce that they had reached an agreement to work together. On June 29th, the BC Liberal government of Christy Clark (which had become a minority after the election) was defeated in a confidence vote by the combined votes of the BC NDP and the Greens.

Christy Clark went to the office of the Lieutenant Governor of British Columbia and asked for a new election to be called, expressing her belief that the deal between the Greens and the BC NDP was untenable and wouldn't be able to provide governance. The Lieutenant Governor refused, and instead called John Horgan to her office and offered him the Premiership.

Since then, the special relationship between the BC Greens and the BC NDP has been both challenging and a great opportunity for both parties. The confidence-and-supply agreement (CASA) document written up between the two parties specifies a number of shared goals, as well as a number of areas in which the parties have agreed to disagree. In a press release issued by the BC Greens, they identified a number of specific goals that were outlined in the confidence-and-supply agreement:

- Reforming our electoral system, getting the influence of big money out of politics, and reforming lobbying rules
- Recognizing that education is about lifelong learning and fast-tracking enhancement to K–12 education funding
- Protecting and promoting public healthcare, creating a proposal for an essential drugs program, and giving families the security of quality, affordable child care
- Getting people moving with better transit
- Giving the opioid crisis the attention it deserves
- Establishing an Emerging Economy Task Force and an Innovation Commission
- Eliminating Medical Services Premiums
- Implementing a basic income pilot project
- Fighting climate change while creating good jobs and introducing rebate cheques that will mean most people pay less while increasing the carbon tax beginning in 2018
- Sending the Site C project immediately to an independent review
- Opposing the Kinder Morgan pipeline expansion project

In amongst these plans were a few policy items that originated in the BC Greens election platform. The "Emerging Economy Task Force" and "Innovation Commission" were plans by the Greens to push British Columbia towards a new economy and to move the province away from resource industry dependence. The basic income pilot project was also a BC Green initiative.

The Greens had promised unequivocally to halt construction on the Site C project and to move British Columbia over to new electoral system. On both of these fronts they were unable to convince the BC NDP to go as far as the Greens had promised. Instead, there was to be a planned referendum on electoral reform that both parties pledged to support (unlike the previous referendums in which the BC NDP had opposed the proposal), and the Site C project was to be sent to an independent review.

Still Going

As of this book's writing, the BC NDP government has passed the two-year mark and is still going strong. A number of the commitments from the CASA have already been implemented. The relationship with the Greens remains strong, although there have been clear areas of strong and public disagreement between the parties.

The BC NDP did indeed send Site C to an independent review, but when that review came back to them they made the decision to continue with the project's construction. This wasn't what the Greens wanted to happen. They made their disappointment known loudly in the press. The media speculated whether the Greens might pull their support and take down the government. They did not. The CASA promised that the project would go to review, not that it would be stopped. So the CASA had not been broken, and the Greens were not about to be the first ones to break it. Andrew was determined to stick to the deal and keep a stable government for BC. He didn't want the Greens to be the first to blink.

The moment of greatest tension between the parties came in May of 2018, just a few weeks after the Greens had voted in favour of the yearly government budget (which would have been the time to take down the government, had they wanted to). John Horgan announced that the government would be offering a number of subsidies to the LNG (liquefied natural gas) industry to try to attract business. This was the same industry that Christy Clark had promised to create from scratch in 2013, and that had won her the election. Andrew had also gotten into politics specifically to oppose Christy's plans to build a new polluting extractive industry in the province.

Andrew was livid. He raged against Horgan and the BC NDP, even taking some of his staff and colleagues by surprise. He accused the BC NDP of coming dangerously close to violating the CASA. The agreement stipulated that the BC NDP needed to put forth a climate a plan that ensured that British Columbia would meet its carbon emission targets. Green support was contingent on the BC NDP government introducing and meeting this plan. But the details of the plan itself were to be left to the government. It'd be the BC NDP plan, not the Green plan.

The problem was that several studies had shown that it would be physically impossible for the province to meet its climate targets if it pursued an LNG industry. That was the main reason why the Greens opposed the industry. So if the BC NDP was now courting LNG investors, it must mean that they were giving up on meeting their climate targets, said Andrew.

In the end, he backed off. The BC NDP assured the Greens that they had a way to have both an LNG industry *and* a viable climate plan. The Greens stepped back, and basically said, "Prove it."

Some Progress on a Low-Carbon Economy

In late 2018, the BC NDP government introduced their climate plan, entitled Clean BC. Andrew Weaver and the rest of the Greens had been working alongside the government for months, advising them on whether the BC NDP's plan would meet the Greens' criteria for support. When the new plan was introduced to the media, Weaver joined Premier Horgan and Environment Minister George Heyman in presenting it. Many in the media remarked that it was "just as much Weavers' plan as it was Horgan's."

The plan included a massive suite of programs designed to transition BC to a low-carbon economy. It included funding and support of building retrofits, electricity grid and infrastructure improvements, a carbon tax increase, support for zero-emission vehicles, and more. Much of it was tailored towards reducing the carbon impact of individual people, although it also included many incentives to encourage industry to transition to low-carbon technologies.

The plan was estimated to get British Columbia 75 percent of the way to its climate goals. The remaining 25 percent was promised to be coming over the next couple years. And it still included the plan to add a massive amount of liquefied natural gas fracking to the province's economy and emissions.

It isn't the plan that the Green Party would have put forward. It was a BC NDP plan through and through. But it was a BC NDP plan that the Greens had their hands in throughout the whole process. It was a BC NDP plan that needed the Greens to support it in order for it to be enacted. So it was a plan that couldn't be full of holes, couldn't be all smoke and mirrors, and had to actually achieve what it claimed it was trying to achieve. It wouldn't have existed without the Greens breathing down the BC NDP's neck. The existence of the plan alone was a huge example of the value that having Greens in the legislature could bring.

The Referendum Disappointment

A referendum was held in October 2018 in British Columbia to decide on if the province should switch to a form of proportional representation. In an extremely disappointing result, it was a brutal failure for those advocating for a newer, fairer system. The existing first-past-the-post system was selected by 61 percent of voters.

The results were varied throughout the province. My home area of Vancouver had the strongest support for the change. My neighbouring district voted by nearly 75 percent in favour of change. Greater Victoria was also majority in favour. If nothing else, the referendum showed the deep difference of opinion in how we want our politics to work in different parts of the province. It showed the deep dissatisfaction in the urban cores with the status quo. It also showed a deep reluctance for change in the more rural areas.

It'll take a full post-mortem to understand why the referendum failed. Some of the reasons are obvious. The questions put on the referendum were widely considered to be too confusing, and there was massively inadequate public education on what it meant. Also, many of the details were left to be decided after the results came in, which gave the proposal an unfinished air. Many people weren't comfortable voting for something when all the details weren't already set.

The groups in the province that already had entrenched power came out with full force to try to oppose the referendum as well. The BC Liberals ran a fear-based campaign against the change, as did the official "No" group, which was headed by a BC NDP strategist and lobbyist. Some conspiratorially minded individuals also believed that both the governing BC NDP and the official "Yes" side were purposefully running a bad campaign in order to try to torpedo the referendum, as well.

This was also the third referendum in thirteen years, which meant many people were checked out and tired of being asked. Remember that in 2005 the province overwhelmingly approved changing the system. In that year, 58 percent of voters and seventy-seven out of seventy-nine districts voted in favour. But the governing BC Liberals had demanded a 60 percent result in order to enact the change.

Had the BC NDP government decided to just run the process exactly as it had been in 2005, complete with an independent arms-length Citizens' Assembly to decide on the best system and to work out the details, we may have had a very different result. As it is, we may never know if that strategy would have worked instead. The fact that the BC NDP didn't just decide to replicate the path to success from 2005 definitely adds to the conspiracy that they wanted it to fail.

The setback in British Columbia was a major one for such a core Green principle. But there were still chances in other provinces. The governing party of Quebec (after the 2018 election) has been promising that the province will move to a system of proportional representation without a necessary referendum. The public will also appears to exist in PEI, and in other places around

CHAPTER 10 – OUR CANADIAN GREEN PARLIAMENTARIANS

Canada. But still, it was a crushing disappointment for the thousands and thousands of grassroots volunteers in British Columbia who poured their hearts into a campaign meant only to help people realize their democratic voice.

"We have an opportunity here that New Brunswickers have given us by electing three Green MLAs, three Alliance MLAs, and pretty much a saw-off between the Liberals and Conservatives; to actually create a legislative assembly where it's collaborative, where MLAs are liberated from party discipline so that they can be freer to participate with the agency that their voters have given them. That's the kind of legislative assembly that I want to see."

(David Coon, from a CBC interview on September 28, 2018)

GOVERNMENTS IN THE MARITIMES

As the sole Green elected to the New Brunswick parliament in 2014, David had to follow the playbook that was being written by Elizabeth and Andrew. New Brunswick is a traditionally two-party dominated province, and people weren't used to having a third party (or a single "independent" member) involved. Since the official opposition Progressive Conservatives were spending most of their time opposing everything that the governing Liberals did, David was able to create a place for himself as a single opposition member who was willing to work with the government to suggest productive solutions.

Over the course of his first term, David regularly introduced amendments and Private Members' Bills whenever he could. He found some success with his introduced bills on education and his motion to create an official code of conduct for New Brunswick MLAs.

He stumbled into a big win after introducing a bill in 2016 to ban political donations from corporations and trade unions. The bill was ignored by the governing Liberals, but later in the term they introduced their own electoral financing bill, intended just to reduce maximum personal donations to political parties. Seemingly on a whim, the Progressive Conservative Party introduced an amendment parroting David's bill: to ban corporate and union donations. And then, seemingly on another whim, the Liberal party MPs voted to accept the amendment. David Coon remarked that it looked like the Progressive Conservatives introduced the amendment not thinking that it would be accepted.

> It kind of felt like an accident, but I'm still trying to process what happened, and I think the Official Opposition may be in the same position. (David Coon, CBC news interview in March of 2017)

However sudden and roundabout it happened, David and the New Brunswick Greens were thrilled that the government had picked up on their initial proposal. As usual, when the newspapers were printed, most of the credit went to the governing Liberals and the opposition Progressive Conservatives. "Gallant Government Agrees to Ban Corporate, Union Political Donations" was the headline on *CBC*. Part way down the article it explained that opposition leader Higgs had introduced the amendments. David Coon is quoted in the article as saying that it was great news, but nowhere does it mention that the proposal had originated with the Greens the previous year.

After the 2018 election, David was joined by new fellow Green MPs Megan Mitton and Kevin Arseneau. Like in British Columbia in 2017, the election resulted in a minority government, meaning that things were about to get interesting right away for the newly elected Greens.

Another CASA? Or Maybe Not

There was a key difference between the results of the British Columbia and New Brunswick elections, however. In BC there were three parties elected, meaning that it would only take two parties to work together to enable a working majority in the parliament. But in New Brunswick, there were four parties elected. With twenty-two seats, the Progressive Conservative party needed to only win over one of the two smaller three-seat parties (the Greens and the People's Alliance) in order to have a bare majority of votes. But with twenty-one seats the incumbent Liberal party needed four more votes to make a majority. So they would either need both small parties, or some defectors.

After the election, incumbent Premier Brian Gallant reached out to both the Green Party and the Progressive Conservative Party. The Liberals made a point of not looking for a deal with the People's Alliance. The anti-bilingualism aspect of the People's Alliance platform meant that the Liberals were discounting them as a partner. Gallant was adamant that it wasn't worth staying in power if it meant working with groups that he fundamentally disagreed with.

> I think it is more honourable to say, "Look I'm not going to work with just anybody to form a government and to stay in power." I have a duty and a responsibility, in my opinion, to see if I can gain the confidence of the house by also ensuring we're respecting our fundamental values. (New Brunswick Premier Brian Gallant, CBC news interview, October 1st 2018)

CHAPTER 10 – OUR CANADIAN GREEN PARLIAMENTARIANS

Blaine Higgs, leader of the Progressive Conservative Party, stated in absolutely certain terms that he would refuse to work with the Liberals, and that he was instructing his caucus to do the same. Some commentators, such as former Progressive Conservative MLA and MP and Fredericton Mayor Bud Bird, encouraged the two parties to form a grand coalition, excluding both the Greens and People's Alliance. But the bad blood between the parties was too great for Blaine Higgs. The Progressive Conservative leader was repeatedly referring to himself as the rightful Premier and making comments to the media showing a misunderstanding (either wilful or ignorant) of how Canadian parliamentary procedure works.

In Canadian governance, the Premier (and the government) is the group that can command a majority of votes in the parliament. That doesn't simply mean that it's whatever party is the biggest. We saw this in British Columbia, and Higgs must have known this. Likely he was trying to win the battle for public perception, by repeating something enough times that people began to accept it.

The Greens were thus put in a difficult spot. Their ideal election result would of course have been a Green government. But since that was now an impossibility, they were being asked if they were going to support either the Liberals or the Progressive Conservatives. If they supported the Liberals, it would likely be for naught. Most New Brunswick political watchers suspected that the People's Alliance was going to throw their weight behind Blaine Higgs, and vote down the Liberal government.

In an interview on *CBC*, David Coon outlined his vision of how an ideal legislature would work, given the circumstances:

> I've been hearing from constituents, saying, "David, why can't all parties cooperate to govern the province? Why does someone have to win? It's a minority situation, why can't everyone collaborate?"
>
> What's going on in the legislature, what's going on in government these days; it has become all about seizing power, not providing good governance. And so the discussion became about who should have the power to rule, rather than about how we could provide good governance to New Brunswickers. (David Coon, from an interview on *Information Morning* on October 11, 2018)

On November 1st, Liberal Premier Brian Gallant presented the government's throne speech. Blaine Higgs informed the media that he had instructed his caucus to vote against it. People's Party leader Kris Austin did likewise. David Coon informed the media that the three Greens would each independently be making up their own mind on whether to support the speech. There would be no formal deal like there had been in British Columbia. Instead, the Greens would be supporting government legislation piece-by-piece, if they felt it was worth supporting.

Before the speech, David, Megan, and Kevin produced a document entitled "Declaration of Intent," which they all signed. It stated:

Whereas the results of the recent provincial election are unprecedented in New Brunswick's history;

> ***Whereas*** the seat distribution challenges all elected representatives to find a way to work together in the best interest of all citizens;
>
> ***Whereas*** high rates of poverty, climate change, reconciliation with First Nations, and growing fiscal and ecological debts represent critical challenges for New Brunswick;
>
> ***Whereas*** Members of the Legislative Assembly must be committed to finding common ground that reflects the foundational principles upon which our society is built, including:
> - The recognition and affirmation of aboriginal and treaty rights of the indigenous peoples of New Brunswick;
> - The equality of the English and French linguistic communities both in principle and in practice, including the right be served in English or French by government, and the right to distinct educational and cultural institutions;
> - The right to a healthy and safe environment;
> - Respect for the autonomy and authority of the Legislative Assembly, to ensure good and accountable governance.
>
> ***Be it resolved that*** we, the undersigned, commit to working collaboratively with all Members of the Legislative Assembly who share these goals.

The three Greens invited all the other members of the legislature to also sign the document. The hope was that since the results of the election were so muddled, that the best path for the legislature was for all of the elected MLAs to choose to work together for the best interests of New Brunswickers, rather than to form into partisan teams and compete against each other for power. Forty-six of the forty-nine Members of the Legislative Assembly took them up on their offer and signed the declaration.

On November 1st, all three Greens voted in favour of the Liberal government's throne speech. Faced with the forced binary option of either a Liberal government or a Progressive Conservative government, they felt that the Liberals had included enough in their throne speech that they were worth supporting. Nevertheless, David Coon had harsh words for the incumbent government:

> The political meddling in the work of the legislature, the neglect of our health, child protection and senior care systems, and of the poor, the firing of our chief medical officer of health and the dismantling of her office, the handing over of

extramural to Medavie, the inaction on renewable energy and climate change, and the degradation of our forests have all left our province worse off. (Coon, Global News piece, November 1st 2018)

The entire caucuses of the Progressive Conservatives and the People's Alliance voted against the Liberal throne speech. The Conservatives and People's Alliance mustered one more vote than the Liberals and Greens. Under Canadian parliamentary procedure, this meant that the government had lost the confidence of the house, and thus must end. Defeated Premier Brian Gallant went to the Lieutenant Governor's house, and asked her to allow Blaine Higgs to have an attempt to form a government and test the parliament to see if he had the majority's support.

Blaine Higgs was sworn in as Premier of New Brunswick on November 9th, 2018, heading a Progressive Conservative minority government. One of his first promises was to fight against the federal Carbon Tax being implemented by Justin Trudeau and the federal Liberal Party. In doing so, he was clearly signalling that he had little intention of working with the New Brunswick Green Party, and was instead going to be counting on the support of the People's Alliance Party.

It remains to be seen what kind of effect the Greens will have in New Brunswick. They're in a minority government situation, which means that they could have a great deal of influence. But it'll depend on whether or not the People's Alliance Party falls completely in line with the Progressive Conservatives, or if they stay separate enough that Premier Blaine Higgs needs to approach the Greens for support at some point.

The vast majority of the legislature signed the Greens' declaration of intent, and thus promised to all work together collaboratively in the greater interest of the province. In time we'll see if their pledge was genuine.

A Government in Waiting: Peter Bevan-Baker and the PEI Greens

In May of 2017, the PEI edition of the *Guardian* published an article titled "Green's Bevan-Baker Now More Popular than PEI Premier." They were citing a recent poll that found for the first time that Peter Bevan-Baker, leader of the PEI Greens, was voters' top choice for Premier. It would be an understatement to say that this was a first for Greens in Canada. Never before had a Green leader beaten any of the leaders from the other parties in a preferred-Premier poll, let alone came out on top. When I spoke to Peter over the phone for an interview, he described the feeling as equal parts exciting and terrifying.

Later that year, the supposed popularity of the PEI Greens was tested. Hannah Bell was elected in a by-election, replacing a retiring Liberal. The district that she won in, Charlottetown-Parkdale, had been the second best result for the Greens in the election that had elected Baker, and they translated that strong showing into a win for Hannah. In doing so, they became the first new party to break the stranglehold that the Liberals and Progressive Conservatives had on PEI politics. No third party in PEI history had managed to elect multiple members to the legislature.

Immediately after the by-election, the PEI Greens began rocketing up in the polls. A voting intentions poll before the by-election had the Greens at 7 percent, whereas the first poll released after the election had them at 22 percent. They continued climbing, until in January of 2018 the first poll showing the Greens with a narrow lead among all parties appeared.

I spoke with Hannah Bell over the phone on a sunny Vancouver day, a few months after her election win. Hannah is remarkably friendly and warm, something that I noticed was the case for all of the Prince Edward Islanders I interviewed. The small scale of PEI politics means that their elected representatives seem much more relaxed and personable than in other parts of Canada. PEI MLAs are able to know each and every one of their constituents on a personal level, something that wouldn't be possible in a province like Ontario where each Member of Parliament is representing over a hundred thousand people.

Hannah wasn't particularly interested in politics for most of her life, mainly because she didn't like the nastiness and partisanship in political discourse. She describes herself as a "do-er," and didn't want to be involved in navigating political fights. She wanted to get things done. Her work was with Aboriginal communities, at-risk children, and other marginalized groups. She didn't have time to mess around with anything that wasn't directly helping people.

She let herself be talked into working with the PEI Greens because she was extremely impressed by Peter Bevan-Baker. His message of bringing civility and respect back to politics and cutting through partisan fights to instead work on helping people struck a chord with her. Peter and the Greens were thrilled to have her on board because her business and economics knowledge were a huge help for the party. She helped work on the party's election platform, then served as their finance critic, and finally agreed to run in the by-election that she subsequently won.

Running to Win

I spoke with Hannah in late 2018, as she was busy preparing for the next provincial election.

Hannah remarked at how different it was to write a platform for a party that was currently polling to form the next government, rather than for a party looking to elect its first member. This is the same lesson that the Swedish Greens learned the hard way, and that the Baden-Württemberg Greens appreciated and respected before their election. In particular, Hannah remarked that a lot of their earlier promises relied on getting support and cooperation from the federal government, something that was by no means guaranteed. They were being careful to craft their new policies

CHAPTER 10 – OUR CANADIAN GREEN PARLIAMENTARIANS

and promises in a way that wasn't reliant on the federal government to succeed or fail. They also were paying close attention to timeframes, making sure not to promise anything for their first term that wasn't possible in just the four years.

The selection and vetting of candidates was also much more important this time around. When the Greens had zero people elected, it wasn't much of a worry if they picked an imperfect candidate for a district they knew they weren't going win. Some candidates were there only as placeholders, so that Green supporters in the area had someone to vote for. No one realistically expected them to win. But with the party polling high enough to elect a majority of its candidates, they had to make sure that each and every one of them was an intelligent, quality candidate, with no potential scandals in their history. Also, as government, they were going to have to pick government Ministers. They had to be sure that they had a broad range of expertise in their candidate pool, so that they'd have competent people to put into the roles.

When I spoke with Peter (who's equally as friendly and warm as Hannah), he remarked that his big fear is that he'll be a flash-in-the-pan Premier like Bob Rae in Ontario or Dave Barrett in British Columbia. In both of those cases, the province voted in a brand-new government from an untested party, which only lasted a single term before voters snapped back to the old status quo. If Peter becomes the first Green Premier, he'd be seen as an ambassador for Green politics in Canada.

If his government failed, it'd telegraph to other parts of the country that a Green government was a risky option. On the other hand, if he and his government excelled, then it'd be a huge boost for the rest of Canada's Greens. So Peter and the party are doing everything they can to set themselves up to succeed in a way that both Prince Edward Islanders and Greens in the rest of Canada can be proud of. There's a lot of pressure being put on his shoulders by the Green movement in the rest of Canada, and an outsized amount of responsibility for someone from Canada's smallest province.

Peter believes that the burgeoning popularity of the Greens in PEI is a response to fatigue with being offered the same political options over and over. And that it's part of a global turning point, where all over the word people are embracing alternatives to the political status quo. Voters in France elected Emmanuel Macron and his brand new party *En Marche!* in 2017, rejecting the existing political establishment. In Italy's 2018 election, the anti-establishment *Five Star Movement* became the largest political party in their Chamber of Deputies by far. And of course, the American election of 2016 resulted in a new President who had never before held public office, and whose ideas and actions have completely realigned their political order.

In a radio interview with *Maritime Noon* on March 12th, 2019, Peter was asked to explain the newfound popularity of the Green Party of PEI:

I'm hearing a disillusionment with the attitude and the behaviour of conventional politicians and of unimaginative politicians. And I'm hearing people who tell me in all kinds of different ways that they're ready for change.

Of course change here, historically and traditionally, on PEI has been to revert back to what you had a few elections ago and [that] you just forgot [that] you got so fed up with it. And that was the nature of change—you flipped between the red party and the blue party.

And for the first time, on PEI anyway, we have a third party that is strong enough and in a position to offer something that isn't a reversion to something you had before. It's something new and something fresh.

People are really keen to latch on to that.

I think it's a local expression of a global phenomenon... you mentioned it in your introduction with Mr. Trump and Mr. Ford and various other ways that people have gone beyond what you might consider conventional politics to look for alternatives in the hope that they will improve their community. And I think on PEI the Green Party is strong enough now, and we've managed to establish ourselves over the last four years as a credible and comfortable alternative for islanders.

And they seem to be flocking to that.

The First Official Opposition

On April 23rd of 2019, one day after Earth Day, voters in Prince Edward Island went to the polls.

The campaign was quiet for the most part, even for an election on the small and sleepy island. There were no scandals, no bombastic rhetoric from any of the party leaders, no bozo-eruptions from improperly vetted candidates, no predictions of apocalypse if such-and-such were to be elected. Instead, the parties just put in the hard work of talking to islanders and asking them for their support.

Tragedy did strike at the tail end of the election period, just a few days before voters were set to cast their ballots. Josh Underhay, the Green candidate for *Charlottetown-Hillsborough Park*, and his young son were found dead, the result of a canoeing accident. The Greens, Liberals, NDP, and Progressive Conservatives all suspended their campaign activity for the weekend as the island's political class came together over the loss.

Josh was a teacher at Birchwood Intermediate School, and a community-minded cyclist and advocate for active transportation. The few polling projections that had been made for the island's election indicated that he was likely to win in his district and become the new local MLA. Following PEI election law, the local election for his district was cancelled and a by-election was scheduled for three months after the general election.

Green leader Peter Bevan-Baker stated, "The past two days have been among the most difficult of my political life, torn between my private grief at the death of candidate and friend, Josh Underhay, and my obligations as Green Party leader. What has made this time bearable is the unconditional support that has been offered so spontaneously... In politics, it is often tempting to

CHAPTER 10 – OUR CANADIAN GREEN PARLIAMENTARIANS

remember the negative and forget the positive, but this weekend I am reminded how blessed we are to have politicians and a political culture that can be counted on to put people and community ahead of partisan differences."

The election platform that the PEI Greens drafted was built around being realistic and achievable. Although the individual Greens may have had ambitious and transformative goals, they knew that they would be a single provincial government working alongside a federal government that was likely going to be formed by a different party. Provincial programs often require buy-in from the federal government, and the Greens didn't want to promise anything that was going to be beyond their ability to deliver.

The platform made numerous references to the fact that the "strong" economy that the PEI Liberals claimed to have built was not resulting in a better quality of life for islanders. They laid out the different steps that they would take in solving the island's problems, and the different ways in which they'd measure whether the government was successfully caring for the island's people. An emphasis was put on revitalizing local communities and businesses, shifting government support towards locally developed services and producers, and taking a more whole-systems approach to the island's health and wellbeing. The following are some excerpts from the platform that I felt best outlined the PEI Green's different approach,

> The role of government should be to acknowledge and address the truly difficult problems like inequality, climate change, and maintaining the social fabric that holds our communities together. These challenges cannot be resolved in four-year increments. So throughout the platform our first mandate commitments have been linked to ten-year goals and our twenty-five year vision. This is a roadmap for a much longer journey. It is my hope that long after I (leader Peter Bevan-Baker) have stepped down from politics, other Islanders—and maybe even other political parties—will share this vision, adapt it, expand it, and continue the journey...

> We need to value individuals for who they are rather than solely for the work they do to contribute to the gross domestic product (GDP)...

> Our growing economy is not translating into growing financial stability and well-being for Islanders. People are having trouble making ends meet and there is a disconnect between our lives and the glowing words around PEI's economic performance...

We are concerned not just about the number of jobs, but the quality of jobs that are available. We must support small businesses and entrepreneurs and recognize and value the non- profit sector. The current sector-based approach should be assessed to ensure that it is meeting both employment and social needs....

At the heart of our education system is our children. In no other sector do we have such an occasion to impact the future. Children deserve the best possible space, tools, and experiences to reach their full potential...

We believe our province should strive for economic independence and greater prosperity for all Islanders by focusing on development that does not depend on unlimited growth or federal government transfers...

We believe that a health care system must do more than respond to illness, it must also promote wellness at every stage of life. All departments have a role to play in nurturing the well-being of individuals and in building healthy communities...

A Green Government would enhance support for independent offices, such as the Auditor General and the Conflict of Interest Commissioner, and create new offices to hold government to account. We would encourage MLAs to put the needs of their constituents first and reduce the control the Premier's Office has on the functioning of the Legislative Assembly and its committees...

One of our highest priorities will be laying the groundwork for a clean energy economy. We agree with the overwhelming expert opinion that climate change is an imminent crisis and that the fairest and most efficient way to encourage businesses and individuals to reduce their carbon emissions is through a revenue neutral carbon tax.

(excerpts from the Green Party of Prince Edward Island's 2019 election platform)

Roughly 31% of Island voters cast for their vote for Green Party candidates, and the Greens elected eight of their candidates to the province's twenty-seven member legislature. The Progressive Conservatives received 36%, and edged out the Greens by electing twelve members. The Liberals, who had formed the government prior to the election, were reduced to only six members. The outgoing Liberal Premier even lost his seat

CHAPTER 10 – OUR CANADIAN GREEN PARLIAMENTARIANS

The Greens re-elected Peter Bevan-Baker in *New Haven-Rocky Point* and Hannah Bell in *Charlottetown-Belvedere*. They added six new faces to their caucus: Michele Beaton, a businesswoman from *Mermaid-Stratford;* Karla Bernard, a teacher and counsellor from *Charlottetown-Victoria Park;* Ole Hammarlund, an architect from *Charlottetown-Brighton;* Lynne Lund, a community activist and former business owner from *Summerside-Wilmot;* Steve Howard, a renewable energy company owner from *Summerside-South Drive;* and Trish Altass, a researcher from *Tyne Valley-Sherbrooke*. These wins set another record in Canada: it was the first time that a Canadian province would have an officially recognized party with a majority of women as representatives.

No individual party elected a majority of their candidates. Like in British Columbia and New Brunswick, this meant that whichever party formed goverment would have to secure the support of enough MLAs from across the aisle to pass their budget and legislation. The media immediately began reporting that the Progressive Conservatives had won a minority government, since they won the greatest number of seats. As I was watching the coverage of the election, this struck me as strange.

In both the British Columbia and New Brunswick elections, the media jumped upon the narrative that the Greens would be "king-makers" and that they would hold the "balance of power" between the inevitable Liberal or Conservative governments. They described the political atmosphere after the election as being "full of uncertainty".

But after the Prince Edward Island election, for the first time, the Liberals were the ones holding the balance of power. Either the Progressive Conservatives or the Greens could form a minority government if they were able to secure the support of the Liberals. This was new territory for Canada, and new territory for the Canadian media and pundit class to grapple with.

We may still see a Green government in Prince Edward Island. As the party with the most seats, the Progressive Conservatives will likely be given the first attempt to form a government and to propose a budget and legislation. But they serve at the pleasure of the Greens and the Liberals. Unlike with majority governments, a minority means that the government can be held to account, and that it has to work constructively with the other parties to find common ground. As Peter stated after the election, "I'm a strong believer in the capacity of minority government to create a collaborative environment where competing parties can put the interests of constituents and Islanders first." Should the Progressive Conservative fail to create this collaborative environment, they may face a defeat in a vote of confidence. And we may see the Greens be given a chance to try.

The next few years in Prince Edward Island will be interesting. In at least one Canadian province, the Greens have finally shown that they should be taken seriously.

But more than anything else, the Greens in PEI have shown that it is absolutely possible to elect Green politicians. And that it's absolutely possible to elect a Green Party government, if people would just decide to do so.

FINAL THOUGHTS

The way that we've built our society, our economics, and our way of life is based on the ideas of men that lived in the 1800s and the 1900s. When these men were putting words to paper the planet was large, and much of it was still untouched by Western civilization. Their ideas were based on the notion that the planet was empty and waiting to be conquered.

In 1966, economist Kenneth Boulding began to realize how badly served we were by this worldview, and wrote an essay entitled "*The Economics of the Coming Spaceship Earth*." Boulding described the economics of the past as the "cowboy economy." The economic thought of economists of the nineteenth century was based on the romantic idea of the American cowboy. If the cowboy ran out of space for his cows to graze, he could always drive them over the next hill into fresh, untouched land. There was always room to grow, always room to expand.

By the end of the twentieth century, we started to realize that there was no more untouched land to expand into. When early Western economists developed an economic system based on limitless extraction, consumption, and growth, they hadn't accounted for what would happen when we ran out of things to extract, consume, and grow into. In reality, we aren't a bunch of cowboys living on the American frontier.

In reality, we are passengers aboard a single spaceship. The only truly limitless resource we have is the energy of the sun shining on us. Everything else has limits, and can't be extracted and consumed forever. Thus, the Spaceship Earth.

This is the core of what Green parties believe, and the reality that they are operating within. Greens in politics are trying to find ways to change our economy and our whole civilization so that we can survive on a spaceship that is rapidly running out of resources. We've grown too big for our single spaceship, and we've lost the ability to respect and understand the limits that it places upon us.

But in many cases our political system itself is built to suppress the ideas of Greens, and to keep them from succeeding. In many cases our system is built to keep those in power who already hold it, and to prevent the introduction of any new people and new ideas.

In some parts of the world the Greens have fought their way through. In Germany, Die Grüne is currently polling at their highest ever levels. In America, the Green Party of the United States has been kept suppressed by one of the planet's most rigidly dominant two-party systems, but even there Green ideas have broken through in the form of proposals like the Green New Deal. And in Canada we're starting to see Greens finally fight their way through first-past-the-post to gain entry into provincial legislatures.

In 2018, my home city of Vancouver had an election for City Council, School Board, and Park Board. That year, the Green Party of Vancouver swept the election. The top two vote-getters on Council, and the top three on School Board and Park Board, were Green candidates. Out of the ten Green candidates that the party ran for election, nine were successfully elected.

The difference in this case was the way that Vancouver (and the rest of British Columbia) runs its elections. Instead of a single vote like in provincial and federal elections, voters each got ten votes for the ten council positions. This meant that a vote for a Green candidate was unlikely to be "wasted" or "thrown away." When people were given the opportunity for their vote for a Green candidate to truly count, they were eager and willing to include Greens in their government. They believed that the contributions and ideas of Greens would enhance their city and their lives.

If Greens are going to break through in Canada at the federal and provincial levels, one of two things must happen.

One possibility is that we need to fix our electoral system so that people don't feel like their vote is wasted. They need to feel confident that they can vote for who they want, not just against who they fear.

Or, as in Prince Edward Island, people need to just get fed up enough with the traditional parties that they're willing to vote for the Greens. They need to accept that maybe their vote will be for a candidate who loses. But maybe, just maybe, if enough of them all agree that a change is needed, then their vote can actually produce that change.

It's up to Canadians to decide if they're ready to take the leap.

BIBLIOGRAPHY

Chapter 1

- Southwell, Les. *The Mountains of Paradise: the Wilderness of South-West Tasmania*. Camberwell: Selbstverl., 1983.
- Dann, Christine R. "From Earth's Last Islands: The Global Origins of Green Politics." PhD diss., Lincoln University, 1999.
- Walker, Pamela. "The United Tasmania Group." Honours thesis, University of Tasmania, 1986.
- Brown, Bob. *Optimism: Reflections on a Life of Action*. South Yarra: Hardie Grant, 2015.
- Goldsmith, Edward. *A Blueprint for Survival*. Harmondsworth: Penguin Books, 1972.
- Lowe, Philip, and Jane Goyder. *Environmental Groups in Politics*. London: Allen & Unwin, 1983.
- Green Party of Canada. "History." Accessed [2019]. https://www.greenparty.ca/en/party/history
- The New Ethic, UTG Manifesto, 1972

Chapter 2

- Camcastle, Cara. "The Green Party of Canada in Political Space and the New Middle Class Thesis." *Environmental Politics* 16, no. 4 (2007): 625–42.
- Cato, Molly Scott, and Miriam Kennett. *Green Economics: Beyond Supply and Demand to Meeting People's Needs*. Aberystwyth: Green Audit Books, 1999.

- Dietz, Rob, and Daniel W. O'Neill. *Enough Is Enough: Building a Sustainable Economy in a World of Finite Resources*. Routledge, 2013.
- Dobson, Andrew. *Green Political Thought*. London: Routledge, 2008.
- Dobson, Andrew. *The Green Reader*. London, Deutsch, 1991.
- Gaffney, Mason, and Fred Harrison. *The Corruption of Economics*. London: Shepheard-Walwyn, 2006.
- Gahrton, Per. *Green Parties, Green Future: From Local Groups to the International Stage*. London: Pluto Press, 2015.
- Haute, Emilie van. *Green Parties in Europe*. London: Ashgate, 2016.
- Jackson, Tim. *Prosperity without Growth: Foundations for the Economy of Tomorrow*. London: Taylor & Francis Group, 2017.
- Richardson, Dick, and Chris Rootes. *The Green Challenge: The Development of Green Parties in Europe*. London: Routledge, 1996.
- Barry, John. "Green Political Theory: Nature, Virtue and Progress." PhD thesis, University of Glasgow, 1996.
- Rommel, Ferdinand Muller, et al. *Green Parties in National Governments*. London: Routledge, 2012.
- Clive Hamilton, *Growth Fetish*, 2004
- Alan Finlayson, *Contemporary Political Thought: A Reader and Guide*, 2003
- Tánczos, Nándor. "The Politics of Green Coalitions - Rethinking Our Strategy and Positioning." *Monkeywrenching*. Accessed [insert approximate date of access]. https://nandor.net.nz/2017/09/29/the-politics-of-green-coalitions/.

Chapter 3

- Haute, Emilie van. *Green Parties in Europe*. London: Ashgate, 2016.
- Gahrton, Per. *Green Parties, Green Future: From Local Groups to the International Stage*. London: Pluto Press, 2015.
- Jackson, Tim. *Prosperity without Growth: Foundations for the Economy of Tomorrow*. London: Taylor & Francis Group, 2017.
- Richardson, Dick, and Chris Rootes. *The Green Challenge: The Development of Green Parties in Europe*. London: Routledge, 1996.
- Rommel, Ferdinand Muller, et al. *Green Parties in National Governments*. London: Routledge, 2012.

- Markovits, Andrei, and Joseph Klaver. *Thirty Years of Bundestag Presence: A Tally of the Greens' Impact on the Federal Republic of Germany's Political Life and Public Culture.* Washington, DC: AICGS, 2012.
- Lijphart, Arend. *Patterns of Democracy: Government Forms and Performance in Thirty-Six Countries.* Ann Arbor: Yale University Press, 2014.
- Markovits, Andrei S., and Philip S. Gorski. *The German Left: Red, Green and Beyond.* Cambridge: Polity Press, 1993.
- Meadows, Dennis L. *The Limits to Growth.* Universe Books, 1972.
- Lucardie, Paul. *Green Parties in Transition: The End of Grass-Roots Democracy?* London: Routledge, 2008.
- Wall, Derek. "Green Party hist ch1, pt 2." *Another Green World* (blog). October 17, 2006. http://another-green-world.blogspot.com/2006/10/green-party-hist-ch1-pt-2.html.

Chapter 4 and 5

- George, Paul. *Big Trees Not Big Stumps.* Vancouver: Western Canada Wilderness Committee, 2006.
- Pammett, Jon H., and Chris Dornan. *The Canadian General Election of 2000.* Toronto: Dundurn Press, 2001.
- Dornan, Chris, and Jon H. Pammett. *The Canadian General Election of 2004.* Toronto: Dundurn Press, 2004.

Chapter 6

- Pammett, Jon H., and Chris Dornan. *The Canadian Federal Election of 2008.* Toronto: Dundurn, 2008.
- Pammett, Jon H., and Chris Dornan. *The Canadian Federal Election of 2011.* Toronto: Dundurn Press, 2011.
- Pammett, Jon H., and Chris Dornan. *The Canadian Federal Election of 2015.* Toronto: Dundurn, 2016.
- Shaw, Rob, and Richard Zussman. *A Matter of Confidence: The Inside Story of the Political Battle for BC.* Victoria: Heritage House, 2018.
- May, Elizabeth. *Who We Are: Reflections on My Life and Canada.* Vancouver, Greystone Books, 2014.

- Weaver, Andrew, and David Skulski. *Keeping Our Cool: Canada in a Warming World.* New Westminster, BC: Post Hypnotic Press, 2013.
- Chong, Michael, et al. *Turning Parliament Inside Out: Practical Ideas for Reforming Canada's Democracy.* Vancouver: Douglas & McIntyre, 2017.

Chapter 7 and 8

- Haute, Emilie van. *Green Parties in Europe.* London: Ashgate, 2016.
- Gahrton, Per. *Green Parties, Green Future: From Local Groups to the International Stage.* London: Pluto Press, 2015.
- Richardson, Dick, and Chris Rootes. *The Green Challenge: The Development of Green Parties in Europe.* London: Routledge, 1996.
- Rommel, Ferdinand Muller, et al. *Green Parties in National Governments.* London: Routledge, 2012.
- Markovits, Andrei, and Klaver, Joseph. *Thirty Years of Bundestag Presence: A Tally of the Greens' Impact on the Federal Republic of Germany's Political Life and Public Culture.* Washington, DC: AICGS, 2012.
- Markovits, Andrei S., and Philip S. Gorski. *The German Left: Red, Green and Beyond.* Cambridge: Polity Press, 1993.
- Hockenos, Paul. *Joschka Fischer and the Making of the Berlin Republic: an Alternative History of Postwar Germany.* Oxford: Oxford Univ. Press, 2008.
- Schlauch, Rezzo, and Weber, Reinhold. *Keine Angst vor der Macht Die Grünen in Baden-Württemberg.* Köln: Emons Verlag, 2016.
- Henkel-Waidhofer, Johanna, and Henkel, Peter. *Der Vertrauensmann: Winfried Kretschmann - Das Porträt.* Freiburg: Verlag Herder, 2017.
- Jungjohann, Arne. *German Greens in Coalition Governments: A Political Analysis.* Brussels: Heinrich Böll Stiftung, 2017.
- Landtag von Baden-Württemberg. *Welcome to the State Parliament.* Stuttgart: The President of the State Parliament of Baden-Württemberg, 2017.
- Publicly released coalition government document, *Baden-Württemberg Gestalten: Verlässlich. Nachhaltig. Innovativ.* Koalitionsvertrag Zwischen Bündnis 90/Die Grünen Baden-Württemberg und der CDU Baden-Württemberg, 2016–2021.
- Publicly released coalition government document, *Der Wechsel Beginnt.* Koalitionsvertrag Zwischen Bündnis 90/Die Grünen Baden-Württemberg und der SPD Baden-Württemberg, 2011–2016.

BIBLIOGRAPHY

- Publicly released coalition government document, *Verlässlich Gestalten - Perspektiven Eröffnen.* Koalitionsvertrag Zwischen der CDU Hessen und Bündnis 90/Die Grünen Hessen für die 19. Wahkoeruide des Hessischen Landtag, 2014–2019.
- Weckenbrock, Christoph. *Schwarz Grün fur Deutschland?* Bielefeld: Transcript, 2017.

Chapter 9

- Boyle, Dan. *Without Power or Glory: the Green Party in Government in Ireland, 2007–2011.* Dublin: New Island, 2012.
- Minihan, Mary. *A Deal with the Devil: The Green Party in Government.* Dunboyne: Maverick House, 2011.

Chapter 10

- May, Elizabeth. *Who We Are: Reflections on My Life and Canada.* Vancouver: Greystone Books, 2014.